THE
SUNDA
2020

PEOPLE'S EDITION

Sundays Year A

From Palm Sunday 2020
to Christ the King 2020

Texts approved for use
in England and Wales, Scotland, and Ireland.

Catholic Truth Society
40-46 Harleyford Road, London, SE11 5AY

First Published 2019

ISBN

The CTS New Sunday Missal 2020 (RM34): 978 1 78469 611 5

Cover design, compilation and typographical design and layout
© 2020 Catholic Truth Society

Concordat cum originali: Paul Moynihan.

Imprimatur: ✠ Peter Smith, Archbishop of Southwark, 1 May 2019.

Acknowledgements:

The CTS is grateful for the help of the Association for Latin in the Liturgy in the preparation of this volume.

Extracts from scripture (excepting Psalm texts) from the Jerusalem Bible © 1966 Darton Longman and Todd and Doubleday & Company Inc.

The English translation of the Gospel Readings for the Palm Sunday Procession from the Catholic Edition of the Revised Standard Version of the Bible © 1965, 1966 by the Division of Christian Education of the National Council of the Churches of Christ in the United States of America. Used by permission. All rights reserved.

Psalm texts from the Grail Psalms © 1963 The Grail (England).

New English Translation 2010, granted recognitio by the Congregation for Divine Worship and the Discipline of the Sacraments, for the dioceses of the Bishops' Conferences of England and Wales (Prot. N. 915/06/L, 28 March 2010), and Scotland, (Prot. N. 1021/07/L, 23 June 2010), and Ireland (Prot. N. 516/05/L, 18 June 2010).

The English translation and chants of The Roman Missal © 2010, International Commission on English in the Liturgy Corporation. All rights reserved.

Latin text of Missale Romanum, Libreria Editrice Vaticana omnia sibi vindicat iura. Sine eiusdem licentia scripto data nemini liceat hunc Missale denuo imprimere aut in aliam linguam vertere © 2008, Libreria Editrice Vaticana.

Papal Magisterium used for introductions to feasts and seasons © Libreria Editrice Vaticana, Vatican City State.

Rite of Eucharistic Exposition and Benediction taken from *Holy Communion and Worship of the Eucharist Outside Mass* (The Roman Ritual) Vol. 1, Approved by the Bishops' Conference of England and Wales, Ireland and Scotland and confirmed by decree of the Sacred Congregation for the Sacraments and Divine Worship 29th May 1976.

Rosary Meditations and material for Preparation for Mass and Thanksgiving after Mass taken from *Eucharistic Adoration* D667 first published CTS, 2004.

TABLE OF CONTENTS

Preparation for Mass 5
The Order of Mass 9
Thanksgiving After Mass 152

5 April	Palm Sunday	162
	The Sacred Paschal Triduum	183
9 April	Thursday of the Lord's Supper	184
10 April	Friday of the Passion of the Lord	194
11 April	Easter Vigil	222
12 April	Easter Sunday Mass during the day	265
19 April	Second Sunday of Easter (Divine Mercy Sunday)	270
23 April	Saint George (England)	275
26 April	Third Sunday of Easter	279
3 May	Fourth Sunday of Easter	285
10 May	Fifth Sunday of Easter	289
17 May	Sixth Sunday of Easter	293
21 May	Ascension of the Lord (England, Wales & Scotland)	297
24 May	Ascension of the Lord (Ireland)	297
24 May	Seventh Sunday of Easter (England, Wales & Scotland)	306
31 May	Pentecost Sunday	310
7 June	The Most Holy Trinity	329
14 June	The Most Holy Body and Blood of Christ	334
19 June	The Most Sacred Heart of Jesus	341
21 June	Twelfth Sunday in Ordinary Time	347
24 June	Nativity of Saint John the Baptist	351
28 June	Saints Peter and Paul (England, Wales & Scotland)	360
28 June	Thirteenth Sunday in Ordinary Time (Ireland)	370
29 June	Saints Peter and Paul (Ireland)	360
5 July	Fourteenth Sunday in Ordinary Time	373
12 July	Fifteenth Sunday in Ordinary Time	376
19 July	Sixteenth Sunday in Ordinary Time	381
26 July	Seventeenth Sunday in Ordinary Time	385
2 August	Eighteenth Sunday in Ordinary Time	389
9 August	Nineteenth Sunday in Ordinary Time	392
15 August	Assumption of the Blessed Virgin Mary (Ireland)	396
16 August	Assumption of the Blessed Virgin Mary (England, Wales & Scotland)	396
16 August	Twentieth Sunday in Ordinary Time (Ireland)	404
23 August	Twenty-First Sunday in Ordinary Time	408
30 August	Twenty-Second Sunday in Ordinary Time	411

6 September   Twenty-Third Sunday in Ordinary Time...........................415
13 September   Twenty-Fourth Sunday in Ordinary Time 419
20 September   Twenty-Fifth Sunday in Ordinary Time 422
27 September   Twenty-Sixth Sunday in Ordinary Time 426
4 October   Twenty-Seventh Sunday in Ordinary Time 430
11 October   Twenty-Eighth Sunday in Ordinary Time...................... 434
18 October   Twenty-Ninth Sunday in Ordinary Time....................... 438
25 October   Thirtieth Sunday in Ordinary Time 442
1 November   All Saints... 445
2 November   Commemoration of all the Faithful Departed.................. 450
8 November   Thirty-Second Sunday in Ordinary Time....................... 458
15 November   Thirty-Third Sunday in Ordinary Time...........................461
22 November   Our Lord Jesus Christ, King of the Universe 466

Rite of Eucharistic Exposition and Benediction 471

PREPARATION FOR MASS

Prayer of Saint Ambrose

I draw near, loving Lord Jesus Christ,
to the table of your most
delightful banquet
in fear and trembling,
a sinner, presuming not
upon my own merits,
but trusting rather in your
goodness and mercy.
I have a heart and body
defiled by my many offences,
a mind and tongue
over which I have kept no good watch.
Therefore, O loving God,
O awesome Majesty,
I turn in my misery, caught in snares,
to you the fountain of mercy,
hastening to you for healing,
flying to you for protection;
and while I do not look forward
to having you as Judge,
I long to have you as Saviour.
To you, O Lord, I display my wounds,
to you I uncover my shame.
I am aware of my many and great sins,
for which I fear,
but I hope in your mercies,
which are without number.
Look upon me, then,
with eyes of mercy,
Lord Jesus Christ, eternal King,
God and Man, crucified for mankind.
Listen to me,
as I place my hope in you,
have pity on me, full of miseries
and sins,
you, who will never cease
to let the fountain of compassion flow.
Hail, O Saving Victim,

Oratio S. Ambrosii

Ad mensam dulcissimi convivii tui,
pie Domine Iesu Christe,
ego peccator de propriis meis
meritis nihil præsumens,
sed de tua confidens misericordia
et bonitate,
accedere vereor et contremisco.
Nam cor et corpus habeo multis
criminibus maculatum,
mentem et linguam non
caute custoditam.

Ergo, o pia Deitas,
o tremenda maiestas,
ego miser,
inter angustias deprehensus,
ad te fontem misericordiæ recurro,
ad te festino sanandus,
sub tuam protectionem fugio;
et, quem Iudicem sustinere nequeo,
Salvatorem habere suspiro.
Tibi, Domine, plagas meas ostendo,
tibi verecundiam meam detego.
Scio peccata mea multa
et magna, pro quibus timeo:
spero in misericordias tuas,
quarum non est numerus.
Respice ergo in me oculis
misericordiæ tuæ,
Domine Iesu Christe, Rex æterne,
Deus et homo,
crucifixus propter hominem.
Exaudi me sperantem in te:
miserere mei pleni miseriis
et peccatis,
tu qui fontem miserationis
numquam manare cessabis.
Salve, salutaris victima,

offered for me and
    for the whole human race
on the wood of the Cross.
Hail, O noble and precious Blood,
flowing from the wounds
of Jesus Christ, my crucified Lord,
and washing away the sins
    of all the world.
Remember, Lord, your creature,
whom you redeemed by your Blood.
I am repentant of my sins,
I desire to put right what I have done.
Take from me, therefore, most
    merciful Father,
all my iniquities and sins,
so that, purified in mind and body,
I may worthily taste the Holy of Holies.
And grant that this sacred foretaste
of your Body and Blood
which I, though unworthy,
    intend to receive,
may be the remission of my sins,
the perfect cleansing of my faults,
the banishment of shameful thoughts,
and the rebirth of right sentiments;
and may it encourage
a wholesome and
    effective performance
of deeds pleasing to you
and be a most firm defence
    of body and soul
against the snares of my enemies.
Amen.

pro me et omni humano genere
    in patibulo Crucis oblata.

Salve, nobilis et pretiose Sanguis,
de vulneribus crucifixi Domini mei
    Iesu Christi profluens,
et peccata totius mundi abluens.

Recordare, Domine, creaturæ tuæ,
quam tuo Sanguine redemisti.
Pænitet me peccasse,
cupio emendare quod feci.
Aufer ergo a me, clementissime Pater,
omnes iniquitates et peccata mea,
ut, purificatus mente et corpore,
digne degustare merear
    Sancta sanctorum.
Et concede, ut hæc sancta
    prælibatio Corporis
    et Sanguinis tui,
quam ego indignus
    sumere intendo,
sit peccatorum meorum remissio,
sit delictorum perfecta purgatio,
sit turpium cogitationum effugatio
ac bonorum sensuum regeneratio,
operumque tibi placentium
    salubris efficacia,
animæ quoque et corporis
contra inimicorum meorum
    insidias firmissima tuitio.
Amen.

Prayer of Saint Thomas Aquinas

Almighty eternal God,
behold, I come to the Sacrament
of your Only Begotten Son,
our Lord Jesus Christ,
as one sick to the physician of life,
as one unclean to

Oratio S. Thomæ Aquinatis

Omnipotens sempiterne Deus,
ecce accedo ad sacramentum
    Unigeniti Filii tui,
Domini nostri Iesu Christi,
accedo tamquam infirmus
    ad medicum vitæ

the fountain of mercy,
as one blind to the light
     of eternal brightness,
as one poor and needy to
     the Lord of heaven and earth.
I ask, therefore, for the abundance
     of your immense generosity,
that you may graciously cure
     my sickness,
wash away my defilement,
give light to my blindness,
enrich my poverty,
clothe my nakedness,
so that I may receive
     the bread of Angels,
the King of kings and Lord of lords,
with such reverence and humility,
such contrition and devotion,
such purity and faith,
such purpose and intention
as are conducive to the salvation of
     my soul.
Grant, I pray, that I may receive
not only the Sacrament
     of the Lord's Body and Blood,
but also the reality and power
     of that Sacrament.
O most gentle God,
grant that I may so receive
the Body of your Only Begotten
     Son our Lord Jesus Christ,
which he took from
     the Virgin Mary,
that I may be made worthy
     to be incorporated into his
     Mystical Body
and to be counted among
     its members.
O most loving Father,
grant that I may at last gaze for ever
upon the unveiled face

immundus ad
     fontem misericordiæ,
cæcus ad lumen claritatis æternæ,
pauper et egenus ad
     Dominum cæli et terræ.
Rogo ergo immensæ largitatis
     tuæ abundantiam,
quatenus meam curare
     digneris infirmitatem,
lavare fœditatem,
     illuminare cæcitatem,
ditare paupertatem,
     vestire nuditatem,
ut panem Angelorum,
     Regem regum
     et Dominum dominantium,
tanta suscipiam reverentia
     et humilitate,
tanta contritione et devotione,
     tanta puritate et fide,
tali proposito et intentione,
sicut expedit saluti animæ meæ.
Da mihi, quæso,
     dominici Corporis et Sanguinis
non solum suscipere sacramentum,
sed etiam rem
     et virtutem sacramenti.
O mitissime Deus,
da mihi Corpus Unigeniti Filii tui,
Domini nostri Iesu Christi,
quod traxit de Virgine Maria,
     sic suscipere,
ut corpori suo mystico
merear incorporari
et inter eius membra connumerari.

O amantissime Pater,
     concede mihi dilectum
     Filium tuum,

of your beloved Son,
whom I, a wayfarer,
propose to receive now veiled
    under these species:
Who lives and reigns with you
    for ever and ever.
Amen.

quem nunc velatum
    in via suscipere propono,
revelata tandem facie
    perpetuo contemplari:
Qui tecum vivit et regnat
in sæcula sæculorum.
Amen.

PRAYER BEFORE MASS

O God, to whom every heart is open, every desire known and from whom no secrets are hidden; purify the thoughts of our hearts by the inspiration of your Holy Spirit, that we may perfectly love you, and worthily praise your holy name. Amen.

Before Holy Communion

Prayer for Help

O God, help me to make a good Communion. Mary, my dearest mother, pray to Jesus for me. My dear Angel Guardian, lead me to the Altar of God.

Act of Faith

O God, because you have said it, I believe that I shall receive the Sacred Body of Jesus Christ to eat, and his Precious Blood to drink. My God, I believe this with all my heart.

Act of Humility

My God, I confess that I am a poor sinner; I am not worthy to receive the Body and Blood of Jesus, on account of my sins. Lord, I am not worthy to receive you under my roof; but only say the word, and my soul will be healed.

Act of Sorrow

My God, I detest all the sins of my life. I am sorry for them, because they have offended you, my God, you who are so good. I resolve never to commit sin any more. My good God, pity me, have mercy on me, forgive me.

Act of Adoration

O Jesus, great God, present on the Altar, I bow down before you.
I adore you.

Act of Love and Desire

Jesus, I love you. I desire with all my heart to receive you. Jesus, come into my poor soul, and give me your Flesh to eat and your Blood to drink.

Give me your whole Self, Body, Blood, Soul and Divinity, that I may live for ever with you.

THE ORDER OF MASS

ORDO MISSÆ CUM POPULO

THE INTRODUCTORY RITES

Before Mass begins, the people gather in a spirit of recollection, preparing for their participation in the Mass.

All stand during the entrance procession.

SIGN OF THE CROSS

After the Entrance Chant, the Priest and the faithful sign themselves with the Sign of the Cross:

Priest: In nómine Patris, et Fílii, et Spíritus Sancti.

A-men.

Response: **Amen.**

GREETING

The Priest greets the people, with one of the following:

1. **Pr.** Grátia Dómini nostri Iesu Christi,
   et cáritas Dei,
   et communicátio Sancti Spíritus
   sit cum ómnibus vobis.

Et cum spí-ri-tu tu-o.

   R. **Et cum spíritu tuo.**

2. **Pr.** Grátia vobis et pax a Deo Patre nostro
   et Dómino Iesu Christo.
   R. **Et cum spíritu tuo.**

3. **Pr.** Dóminus vobíscum.
   R. **Et cum spíritu tuo.**

The Priest, or a Deacon, or another minister, may very briefly introduce the faithful to the Mass of the day.

THE ORDER OF MASS WITH A CONGREGATION

THE INTRODUCTORY RITES

Before Mass begins, the people gather in a spirit of recollection, preparing for their participation in the Mass.

All stand during the entrance procession.

SIGN OF THE CROSS

After the Entrance Chant, the Priest and the faithful sign themselves with the Sign of the Cross:

Priest: In the name of the Father, and of the Son, and of the Holy Spirit.

A-men.

Response: Amen.

GREETING

The Priest greets the people, with one of the following:

1. **Pr.** The grace of our Lord Jesus Christ,
   and the love of God,
   and the communion of the Holy Spirit
   be with you all.

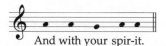

And with your spir-it.

   R. And with your spirit.

2. **Pr.** Grace to you and peace from God our Father
   and the Lord Jesus Christ.
   R. And with your spirit.

3. **Pr.** The Lord be with you.
   R. And with your spirit.

The Priest, or a Deacon, or another minister, may very briefly introduce the faithful to the Mass of the day.

PENITENTIAL ACT*

There are three forms of the Penitential Act which may be chosen from as appropriate.
Each Penitential Act begins with the invitation to the faithful by the Priest:

Pr. Fratres, agnoscámus peccáta nostra,
   ut apti simus ad sacra mystéria celebránda.

A brief pause for silence follows.

Then one of the following forms is used:

**1. Confíteor Deo omnipoténti et vobis, fratres,
quia peccávi nimis
cogitatióne, verbo, ópere et omissióne:**

(and, striking their breast, they say:)
**mea culpa, mea culpa, mea máxima culpa.
Ideo precor beátam Mariám semper Vírginem,
omnes Angelos et Sanctos,
et vos, fratres, oráre pro me
ad Dóminum Deum nostrum.**

---

2. Pr. Miserére nostri, Dómine.

Qui- a peccá- vi- mus ti- bi.

R.   Quia peccávimus tibi.

Pr. Osténde nobis, Dómine, misericórdiam tuam.

Et sa- lu- tá- re tu- um da no- bis.

R.   Et salutáre tuum da nobis.

---

* From time to time on Sundays, especially in Easter Time, instead of the customary Penitential
Act, the blessing and sprinkling of water may take place (as in pp.16-21) as a reminder of Baptism.

PENITENTIAL ACT*

There are three forms of the Penitential Act which may be chosen from as appropriate. Each Penitential Act begins with the invitation to the faithful by the Priest:

Pr. Brethren (brothers and sisters),
let us acknowledge our sins,
and so prepare ourselves to celebrate the sacred mysteries.

A brief pause for silence follows.

Then one of the following forms is used:

**1. I confess to almighty God
and to you, my brothers and sisters,
that I have greatly sinned,
in my thoughts and in my words,
in what I have done and in what I have failed to do,**

(and, striking their breast, they say:)

**through my fault, through my fault,
through my most grievous fault;
therefore I ask blessed Mary ever-Virgin,
all the Angels and Saints,
and you, my brothers and sisters,
to pray for me to the Lord our God.**

---

2. Pr. Have mercy on us, O Lord.

For we have sinned a-gainst you.

R. **For we have sinned against you.**

Pr. Show us, O Lord, your mercy.

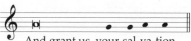

And grant us your sal-va-tion.

R. **And grant us your salvation.**

---

* From time to time on Sundays, especially in Easter Time, instead of the customary Penitential Act, the blessing and sprinkling of water may take place (as in pp.16-21) as a reminder of Baptism.

Invocations naming the gracious works of the Lord may be made, as in the example below:

3. Pr. Qui missus es sanáre contrítos corde:
     Kýrie, eléison.

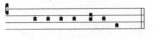

Ký- ri- e, e- lé- i- son.

R. **Kýrie, eléison.**

Pr. Qui peccatóres vocáre venísti:
     Christe, eléison.

Chri- ste, e- lé- i- son.

R. **Christe, eléison.**

Pr. Qui ad déxteram Patris sedes, ad interpellándum pro nobis:
     Kýrie, eléison.

Ký- ri- e, e- lé- i- son.

R. **Kýrie, eléison.**

The absolution by the Priest follows:

Pr. Misereátur nostri omnípotens Deus
    et, dimíssis peccátis nostris,
    perdúcat nos ad vitam ætérnam.

A-men.

R. **Amen.**

The **Kýrie, eléison** (**Lord, have mercy**) invocations follow, unless they have just occurred.

  Pr. Kýrie, eléison.

y-ri-e, e-lé- i-son.

Invocations naming the gracious works of the Lord may be made, as in the example below:

3. Pr. You were sent to heal the contrite of heart:
Lord, have mercy. Or: Kýrie, eléison.

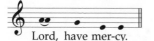

Or: repeat music/words from Latin, p.14.

Lord, have mer-cy.

R. **Lord, have mercy.**

Pr. You came to call sinners:
Christ, have mercy. Or: Christe, eléison.

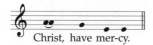

Or: repeat music/words from Latin, p.14.

Christ, have mer-cy.

R. **Christ, have mercy.**

Pr. You are seated at the right hand of the Father to intercede for us:
Lord, have mercy. Or: Kýrie, eléison.

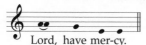

Or: repeat music/words from Latin, p.14.

Lord, have mer-cy.

R. **Lord, have mercy.**

The absolution by the Priest follows:

Pr. May almighty God have mercy on us,
forgive us our sins,
and bring us to everlasting life.

A-men.

R. **Amen.**

The Kýrie, eléison (Lord, have mercy) invocations follow, unless they have just occurred.

Pr. Lord, have mercy.

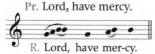

R. Lord, have mer-cy.

Pr. Christe, eléison.

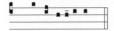

R.   Chris-te, e-lé-i-son.

Pr. Kýrie eléison.

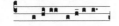 

R.   Ky-ri-e,   e-lé-i-son.   Vel: R.   Ky-ri-e,   e- lé- i-son.

RITE FOR THE BLESSING AND SPRINKLING OF WATER

If this rite is celebrated during Mass, it takes the place of the usual Penitential Act at the beginning of Mass. After the greeting, the Priest calls upon the people to pray in these or similar words:

Dominum Deum nostrum, fratres carissimi,
suppliciter deprecemur,
ut hanc creaturam aquæ benedicere dignetur,
super nos aspergendam in nostri memoriam baptismi.
Ipse autem nos adiuvare dignetur,
ut fideles Spiritui, quem accepimus, maneamus.

And after a brief pause for silence, he continues with hands joined:

Omnipotens sempiterne Deus, qui voluisti ut per aquam,
fontem vitæ ac purificationis principium,
etiam animæ mundarentur
æternæque vitæ munus exciperent,
dignare, quæsumus, hanc aquam ✠ benedicere,
qua volumus hac die tua, Domine, communiri.
Fontem vivum in nobis tuæ gratiæ renovari
et ab omni malo spiritus et corporis
per ipsam nos defendi concedas,
ut mundis tibi cordibus propinquare
tuamque digne salutem valeamus accipere.
Per Christum Dominum nostrum.
R. Amen.

Pr. Christ, have mercy.

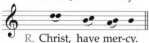

R. Christ, have mer-cy.

Pr. Lord, have mercy.

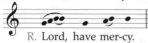

R. Lord, have mer-cy.

RITE FOR THE BLESSING AND SPRINKLING OF WATER

If this rite is celebrated during Mass, it takes the place of the usual Penitential Act at the beginning of Mass. After the greeting, the Priest calls upon the people to pray in these or similar words:

Dear brethren (brothers and sisters),
let us humbly beseech the Lord our God
to bless this water he has created,
which will be sprinkled on us
as a memorial of our Baptism.
May he help us by his grace
to remain faithful to the Spirit we have received.

And after a brief pause for silence, he continues with hands joined:

Almighty ever-living God,
who willed that through water,
the fountain of life and the source of purification,
even souls should be cleansed
and receive the gift of eternal life;
be pleased, we pray, to ✠ bless this water,
by which we seek protection on this your day, O Lord.
Renew the living spring of your grace within us
and grant that by this water we may be defended
from all ills of spirit and body,
and so approach you with hearts made clean
and worthily receive your salvation.
Through Christ our Lord.
R. Amen.

Or:

Domine Deus omnipotens,
qui es totius vitæ corporis et animæ fons et origo,
hanc aquam, te quæsumus, ✠ benedicas,
qua fidenter utimur
ad nostrorum implorandam veniam peccatorum
et adversus omnes morbos inimicique insidias
tuæ defensionem gratiæ consequendam.
Præsta, Domine, ut, misericordia tua interveniente,
aquæ vivæ semper nobis saliant in salutem,
ut mundo tibi corde appropinquare possimus,
et omnia corporis animæque pericula devitemus.
Per Christum Dominum nostrum.
R. Amen.

Or, during Easter Time:

Domine Deus omnipotens,
precibus populi tui adesto propitius;
et nobis, mirabile nostræ creationis opus,
sed et redemptionis nostræ mirabilius, memorantibus,
hanc aquam ✠ benedicere tu dignare.
Ipsam enim tu fecisti,
ut et arva fecunditate donaret,
et levamen corporibus nostris munditiamque præberet.
Aquam etiam tuæ ministram misericordiæ condidisti;
nam per ipsam solvisti tui populi servitutem,
illiusque sitim in deserto sedasti;
per ipsam novum foedus nuntiaverunt prophetæ,
quod eras cum hominibus initurus;
per ipsam denique, quam Christus in Iordane sacravit,
corruptam naturæ nostræ substantiam
in regenerationis lavacro renovasti.
Sit igitur hæc aqua nobis suscepti baptismatis memoria,
et cum fratribus nostris, qui sunt in Paschate baptizati,
gaudia nos tribuas sociare.
Per Christum Dominum nostrum.
R. Amen.

Or:

Almighty Lord and God,
who are the source and origin of all life,
whether of body or soul,
we ask you to ✠ bless this water,
which we use in confidence
to implore forgiveness for our sins
and to obtain the protection of your grace
against all illness and every snare of the enemy.
Grant, O Lord, in your mercy,
that living waters may always spring up for our salvation,
and so may we approach you with a pure heart
and avoid all danger to body and soul.
Through Christ our Lord.
R. Amen.

Or, during Easter Time:

Lord our God,
in your mercy be present to your people's prayers,
and, for us who recall the wondrous work of our creation
and the still greater work of our redemption,
graciously ✠ bless this water.
For you created water to make the fields fruitful
and to refresh and cleanse our bodies.
You also made water the instrument of your mercy:
for through water you freed your people from slavery
and quenched their thirst in the desert;
through water the Prophets proclaimed the new covenant
you were to enter upon with the human race;
and last of all,
through water, which Christ made holy in the Jordan,
you have renewed our corrupted nature
in the bath of regeneration.
Therefore, may this water be for us
a memorial of the Baptism we have received,
and grant that we may share
in the gladness of our brothers and sisters
who at Easter have received their Baptism.
Through Christ our Lord.
R. Amen.

Where the circumstances of the place or the custom of the people suggest that the mixing of salt be preserved in the blessing of water, the Priest may bless salt, saying:

Supplices te rogamus, omnipotens Deus,
ut hanc creaturam salis
benedicere ✠ tua pietate digneris,
qui per Eliseum prophetam in aquam mitti eam iussisti,
ut sanaretur sterilitas aquæ.
Præsta, Domine, quæsumus,
ut, ubicumque hæc salis et aquæ commixtio
fuerit aspersa,
omni impugnatione inimici depulsa,
præsentia Sancti tui Spiritus nos iugiter custodiat.
Per Christum Dominum nostrum.
R. Amen.

Then he pours the salt into the water, without saying anything.
Afterward, taking the aspergillum, the Priest sprinkles himself and the ministers, then the clergy and people, moving through the church, if appropriate.
Meanwhile, one of the following chants, or another appropriate chant is sung.

Outside Easter Time

Antiphon   Ps 50:9
Asperges me, Domine, hyssopo et mundabor:
lavabis me, et super nivem dealbabor.

During Easter Time

Antiphon   Cf. Ez 47:1-2,9
Vidi aquam egredientem de templo,
a latere dextro, alleluia;
et omnes, ad quos pervenit aqua ista, salvi facti sunt,
et dicent: alleluia, alleluia.

When he returns to his chair and the singing is over, the Priest stands facing the people and, with hands joined, says:

Deus omnipotens nos a peccatis purificet,
et per huius Eucharistiæ celebrationem dignos nos reddat,
qui mensæ regni sui participes efficiamur.
R. Amen.

Then, when it is prescribed, the hymn **Gloria in excelsis** (**Glory to God in the highest**) is sung or said.

Where the circumstances of the place or the custom of the people suggest that the mixing of salt be preserved in the blessing of water, the Priest may bless salt, saying:

We humbly ask you, almighty God:
be pleased in your faithful love to bless ✠ this salt
you have created,
for it was you who commanded the prophet Elisha
to cast salt into water,
that impure water might be purified.
Grant, O Lord, we pray,
that, wherever this mixture of salt and water is sprinkled,
every attack of the enemy may be repulsed
and your Holy Spirit may be present
to keep us safe at all times.
Through Christ our Lord.
R. Amen.

Then he pours the salt into the water, without saying anything.

Afterward, taking the aspergillum, the Priest sprinkles himself and the ministers, then the clergy and people, moving through the church, if appropriate.

Meanwhile, one of the following chants, or another appropriate chant is sung.

Outside Easter Time

Antiphon   Ps 50:9

Sprinkle me with hyssop, O Lord, and I shall be cleansed;
wash me and I shall be whiter than snow.

During Easter Time

Antiphon   Cf. Ez 47:1-2,9

I saw water flowing from the Temple,
from its right-hand side, alleluia:
and all to whom this water came
were saved and shall say: alleluia, alleluia.

When he returns to his chair and the singing is over, the Priest stands facing the people and, with hands joined, says:

May almighty God cleanse us of our sins,
and through the celebration of this Eucharist
make us worthy to share at the table of his Kingdom.
R. Amen.

Then, when it is prescribed, the hymn Gloria in excelsis (Glory to God in the highest) is sung or said.

THE GLORIA

On Sundays (outside Advent and Lent), Solemnities and Feast Days, this hymn is either sung or said:

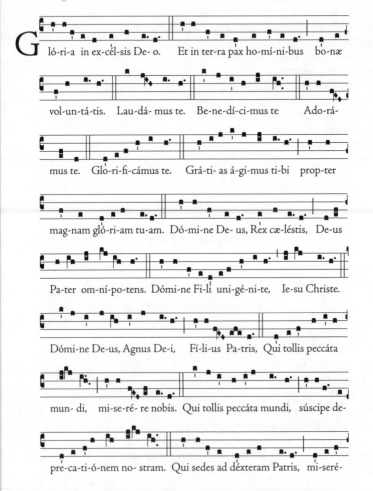

Glória in excélsis Deo. Et in terra pax homínibus bonæ voluntátis. Laudámus te. Benedícimus te Adorámus te. Glorificámus te. Grátias ágimus tibi propter magnam glóriam tuam. Dómine Deus, Rex cæléstis, Deus Pater omnípotens. Dómine Fili unigénite, Iesu Christe. Dómine Deus, Agnus Dei, Fílius Patris, Qui tollis peccáta mundi, miserére nobis. Qui tollis peccáta mundi, súscipe deprecatiónem nostram. Qui sedes ad déxteram Patris, miseré-

THE GLORIA

On Sundays (outside Advent and Lent), Solemnities and Feast Days, this hymn is either sung or said:

Glo-ry to God in the high-est,

and on earth peace to peo-ple of good will.

We praise you, we bless you, we a-dore you, we glo-ri-fy you,

we give you thanks for your great glo-ry,

Lord God, heav-en-ly King, O God, al - might-y Fa-ther.

Lord Je-sus Christ, On-ly Be-got-ten Son,

Lord God, Lamb of God, Son of the Fa-ther,

you take a-way the sins of the world, have mer-cy on us;

you take a-way the sins of the world, re-ceive our prayer;

you are seat-ed at the right hand of the Fa-ther, have mer-cy on us.

re nobis. Quóni-am tu solus Sanctus.   Tu solus Dó-mi-nus   Tu so-

lus Al-tíssimus, Ie-su Christe.   Cum Sancto Spí-ri-tu,   in gló-ri-a

De- i Pa- tris.   A-   men.

**Glória in excélsis Deo
et in terra pax homínibus bonæ voluntátis.**

**Laudámus te,
benedícimus te,
adorámus te,
glorificámus te,
grátias ágimus tibi propter magnam glóriam tuam,
Dómine Deus, Rex cæléstis,
Deus Pater omnípotens.**

**Dómine Fili Unigénite, Iesu Christe,
Dómine Deus, Agnus Dei, Fílius Patris,
qui tollis peccáta mundi, miserére nobis;
qui tollis peccáta mundi, súscipe deprecatiónem nostram.
Qui sedes ad déxteram Patris, miserére nobis.**

**Quóniam tu solus Sanctus, tu solus Dóminus, tu solus Altíssimus,
Iesu Christe, cum Sancto Spíritu: in glória Dei Patris.
Amen.**

When this hymn is concluded, the Priest, says: **Pr. Orémus.**
And all pray in silence. Then the Priest says the Collect prayer, which ends:
R. Amen.

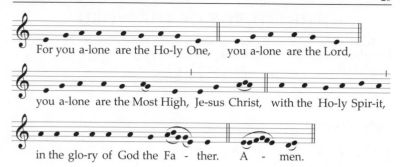

For you a-lone are the Ho-ly One, you a-lone are the Lord, you a-lone are the Most High, Je-sus Christ, with the Ho-ly Spir-it, in the glo-ry of God the Fa - ther. A - men.

Glory to God in the highest,
and on earth peace to people of good will.

We praise you,
we bless you,
we adore you,
we glorify you,
we give you thanks for your great glory,
Lord God, heavenly King,
O God, almighty Father.

Lord Jesus Christ, Only Begotten Son,
Lord God, Lamb of God, Son of the Father,
you take away the sins of the world, have mercy on us;
you take away the sins of the world, receive our prayer;
you are seated at the right hand of the Father,
have mercy on us.

For you alone are the Holy One,
you alone are the Lord,
you alone are the Most High,
Jesus Christ,
with the Holy Spirit,
in the glory of God the Father.
Amen.

When this hymn is concluded, the Priest, says: **Pr. Let us pray.**
And all pray in silence. Then the Priest says the Collect prayer, which ends:
R. Amen.

THE LITURGY OF THE WORD

By hearing the word proclaimed in worship, the faithful again enter into the unending dialogue between God and the covenant people.

FIRST READING

The reader goes to the ambo and proclaims the First Reading, while all sit and listen. The reader ends:

Verbum Dómini.

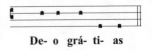

De- o grá- ti- as

R. **Deo grátias.**

It is appropriate to have a brief time of quiet between readings as those present take the word of God to heart.

PSALM

The psalmist or cantor sings or says the Psalm, with the people making the response.

SECOND READING

On Sundays and certain other days there is a second reading. The reader ends:

Verbum Dómini.

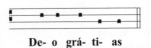

De- o grá- ti- as

R. **Deo grátias.**

GOSPEL

The assembly stands for the Gospel Acclamation. Except during Lent the Acclamation is:

R. **Allelúia!**

During Lent the following forms may be used or another similar phrase:

R. **Laus tibi, Christe, Rex ætérnæ glóriæ!** Or:

R. **Laus et honor tibi, Dómine Iesu!** Or:

R. **Glória et laus tibi, Christe!** Or:

R. **Glória tibi, Christe, Verbo Dei!**

THE LITURGY OF THE WORD

By hearing the word proclaimed in worship, the faithful again enter into the unending dialogue between God and the covenant people.

FIRST READING

The reader goes to the ambo and proclaims the First Reading, while all sit and listen. The reader ends:

The word of the Lord.

Thanks be to God.

R. **Thanks be to God.**

It is appropriate to have a brief time of quiet between readings as those present take the word of God to heart.

PSALM

The psalmist or cantor sings or says the Psalm, with the people making the response.

SECOND READING

On Sundays and certain other days there is a second reading. The reader ends:

The word of the Lord.

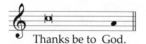

Thanks be to God.

R. **Thanks be to God.**

GOSPEL

The assembly stands for the Gospel Acclamation. Except during Lent the Acclamation is:

R. **Alleluia!**

During Lent the following forms may be used or another similar phrase:

R. **Praise to you, O Christ, king of eternal glory!** Or:

R. **Praise and honour to you, Lord Jesus!** Or:

R. **Glory and praise to you, O Christ!** Or:

R. **Glory to you, O Christ, you are the Word of God!**

At the ambo the Deacon, or the Priest says:
Pr. Dóminus vobíscum.

Et cum spíritu tuo.

R. Et cum spíritu tuo.
Pr. Léctio sancti Evangélii secúndum N.

He makes the Sign of the Cross on the book and, together with the people, on his forehead, lips, and breast.

Glória tibi Dómine.

R. Glória tibi, Dómine.

At the end of the Gospel:
Pr. Verbum Dómini.

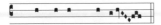

Laus ti-bi, Christe.

R. Laus tibi, Christe.

THE HOMILY
Then follows the Homily, which is preached by a Priest or Deacon on all Sundays and Holydays of Obligation. After a brief silence all stand.

THE CREED
On Sundays and Solemnities, the Profession of Faith will follow. Especially during Lent and Easter Time, the Apostles' Creed may be used.

THE NICENO-CONSTANTINOPOLITAN CREED

Credo in unum De- um, Patrem omni-poténtem factó-rem cæli et terræ, vi-sibili-um óm-nium et invi-si-bí- lium. Et in unum Dó-

At the ambo the Deacon, or the Priest says:

Pr. The Lord be with you.

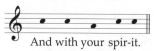

And with your spir-it.

R. **And with your spirit.**

Pr. A reading from the holy Gospel according to N.

He makes the Sign of the Cross on the book and, together with the people, on his forehead, lips, and breast.

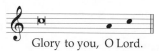

Glory to you, O Lord.

R. **Glory to you, O Lord.**

At the end of the Gospel:

Pr. The Gospel of the Lord.

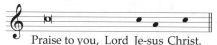

Praise to you, Lord Je-sus Christ.

R. **Praise to you, Lord Jesus Christ.**

THE HOMILY

Then follows the Homily, which is preached by a Priest or Deacon on all Sundays and Holydays of Obligation. After a brief silence all stand.

THE CREED

On Sundays and Solemnities, the Profession of Faith will follow. Especially during Lent and Easter Time, the Apostles' Creed may be used.

THE NICENO-CONSTANTINOPOLITAN CREED

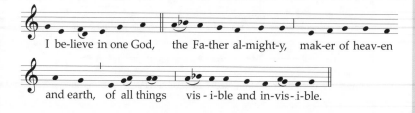

I be-lieve in one God, the Fa-ther al-might-y, mak-er of heav-en and earth, of all things vis-i-ble and in-vis-i-ble.

minum Iesum Christum, Fí-lium De-i uni-gé-ni-tum. Et ex Pa-

tre na- tum ante ómni-a sæ- cu-la. De-um de De-o, lumen de

lumine, De-um verum de De-o vero. Géni-tum, non fac-tum, con-

substanti-á-lem Patri: per quem ómni-a facta sunt. Qui propter nos

At the words

homines et propter nostram sa-lútem descéndit de cæ-lis. Et in-

that follow, up to and including **et homo factus est**, all bow.

carná-tus est de Spí-ri-tu Sancto ex Ma-rí-a Vírgi-ne, et homo

factus est. Cru-ci-fí- xus é-ti-am pro nobis sub Pónti-o Pi-lá-to,

passus et sepúl- tus est. Et resurré-xit térti-a di-e, secúndum Scrip-

turas, Et ascéndit in cæ- lum, sedet ad déxteram Patris. Et í-terum

I be-lieve in one Lord   Je-sus Christ,   the Only Be-got-ten Son

of God,   born of the Father be-fore all a-ges.   God from God,

Light from Light,   true God from true God,   be-got-ten, not made,

con-sub-stan-tial with the Fa-ther;   through him all things were

made.   For us men and for our sal-va-tion   he came down from

At the words that follow, up to and including **and became man**, all bow.

heav-en,   and by the Ho-ly Spir-it was in-car-nate   of the Vir-gin

Mar-y,   and be-came man.

For our sake he was cru-ci-fied   un-der Pon-tius Pi-late,   he

suffered death and was bur-ied,   and rose a-gain on the third day

in accordance with the Scrip-tures. He as-cend-ed in-to heav-en

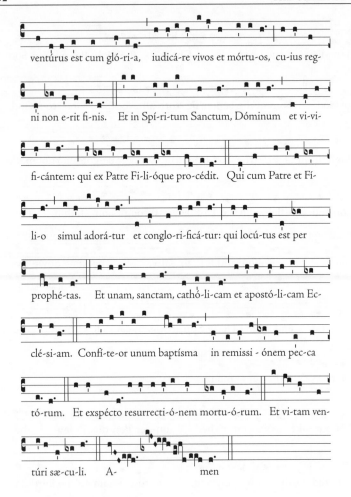

ventúrus est cum gló-ri-a, iudicá-re vivos et mórtu-os, cu-ius reg-

ni non e-rit fi-nis. Et in Spí-ri-tum Sanctum, Dóminum et vi-vi-

fi-cántem: qui ex Patre Fi-li-óque pro-cédit. Qui cum Patre et Fí-

li-o simul adorá-tur et conglo-ri-ficá-tur: qui locú-tus est per

prophé-tas. Et unam, sanctam, cathó-li-cam et apostó-li-cam Ec-

clé-si-am. Confí-te-or unum baptísma in remissi - ónem pec-ca

tó-rum. Et exspécto resurrecti-ó-nem mortu-ó-rum. Et vi-tam ven-

túri sæ-cu-li. A- men

and is seated at the right hand of the Fa-ther.   He will come a-gain

in glo-ry   to judge the living and the dead   and his kingdom will

have no end.

I be-lieve in the Ho-ly Spir-it,   the Lord, the giv-er of life,   who

pro-ceeds from the Father and the Son,   who with the Fa-ther and

the Son   is adored and glo-ri-fied,   who has spoken through the

proph-ets.   I be-lieve in one, ho-ly, ca-tho-lic   and a-pos-tol-ic

Church.   I con-fess one Bap-tism   for the for-give-ness of sins

and I look for-ward to the res-ur-rec-tion of the dead   and the life

of the world to come.   A - men.

Credo in unum Deum,
Patrem omnipoténtem,
factórem cæli et terræ,
visibílium ómnium et invisibílium.

Et in unum Dóminum Iesum Christum,
Fílium Dei Unigénitum,
et ex Patre natum ante ómnia sǽcula.
Deum de Deo, lumen de lúmine,
   Deum verum de Deo vero,
génitum, non factum, consubstantiálem Patri:
per quem ómnia facta sunt.
Qui propter nos hómines et propter nostram salútem
descéndit de cælis.

(all bow)

Et incarnátus est de Spíritu Sancto
ex María Vírgine, et homo factus est.

Crucifíxus étiam pro nobis sub Póntio Piláto;
passus et sepúltus est,
et resurréxit tértia die, secúndum Scriptúras,
et ascéndit in cælum, sedet ad déxteram Patris.

Et íterum ventúrus est cum glória,
   iudicáre vivos et mórtuos,
cuius regni non erit finis.

Et in Spíritum Sanctum, Dóminum et vivificántem:
qui ex Patre Filióque procédit.
Qui cum Patre et Fílio simul adorátur et conglorificátur:
qui locútus est per prophétas.

Et unam, sanctam, cathólicam et apostólicam Ecclésiam.
Confíteor unum baptísma in remissiónem peccatórum.
Et exspécto resurrectiónem mortuórum,
et vitam ventúri sǽculi. Amen.

I believe in one God,
the Father almighty,
maker of heaven and earth,
of all things visible and invisible.

I believe in one Lord Jesus Christ,
the Only Begotten Son of God,
born of the Father before all ages.
God from God, Light from Light,
true God from true God,
begotten, not made, consubstantial with the Father;
through him all things were made.
For us men and for our salvation
he came down from heaven,

(all bow)

and by the Holy Spirit was incarnate of the Virgin Mary,
and became man.

For our sake he was crucified under Pontius Pilate,
he suffered death and was buried,
and rose again on the third day
in accordance with the Scriptures.
He ascended into heaven
and is seated at the right hand of the Father.
He will come again in glory
to judge the living and the dead
and his kingdom will have no end.

I believe in the Holy Spirit, the Lord, the giver of life,
who proceeds from the Father and the Son,
who with the Father and the Son is adored and glorified,
who has spoken through the prophets.

I believe in one, holy, catholic and apostolic Church.
I confess one Baptism for the forgiveness of sins
and I look forward to the resurrection of the dead
and the life of the world to come. Amen.

THE APOSTLES' CREED

Credo in Deum, Patrem omnipoténtem,
Creatórem cæli et terræ,
et in Iesum Christum, Fílium eius únicum,
Dóminum nostrum,

at the words that follow up to and including **Maria Virgine**, all bow.

qui concéptus est de Spíritu Sancto,
natus ex María Vírgine,
passus sub Póntio Piláto,
crucifíxus, mórtuus, et sepúltus,
descéndit ad ínferos,
tértia die resurréxit a mórtuis,
ascéndit ad cælos,
sedet ad déxteram Dei Patris omnipoténtis,
inde ventúrus est iudicáre vivos et mórtuos.

Credo in Spíritum Sanctum,
sanctam Ecclésiam cathólicam,
Sanctórum communiónem,
remissiónem peccatórum,
carnis resurrectiónem,
vitam ætérnam. Amen.

THE PRAYER OF THE FAITHFUL (BIDDING PRAYERS)

Intentions will normally be for the Church; for the world; for those in particular
need; and for the local community. After each there is time for silent prayer,
followed by the next intention, or concluded with a sung phrase such as Christe
audi nos, or Christe exaudi nos, or by a responsory such as:

R.   **Præsta, ætérne omnípotens Deus.** Or:
R.   **Te rogámus audi nos.** Or:
R.   **Kýrie, eléison.**

The Priest concludes the Prayer with a collect.

THE APOSTLES' CREED

I believe in God,
the Father almighty
Creator of heaven and earth,
and in Jesus Christ, his only Son, our Lord,

at the words that follow up to and including the Virgin Mary, all bow.

who was conceived by the Holy Spirit,
born of the Virgin Mary,
suffered under Pontius Pilate,
was crucified, died and was buried;
he descended into hell;
on the third day he rose again from the dead;
he ascended into heaven,
and is seated at the right hand of God
the Father almighty;
from there he will come to judge the living and the dead.

I believe in the Holy Spirit,
the holy catholic Church,
the communion of saints,
the forgiveness of sins,
the resurrection of the body,
and life everlasting. Amen.

THE PRAYER OF THE FAITHFUL (BIDDING PRAYERS)

Intentions will normally be for the Church; for the world; for those in particular need; and for the local community. After each there is time for silent prayer, followed by the next intention, or concluded with a sung phrase such as Christ, hear us, or Christ graciously hear us, or by a responsory such as:

Let us pray to the Lord.

R. **Grant this, almighty God.** Or:

R. **Lord, have mercy.** Or:

R. **Kýrie, eléison.**

The Priest concludes the Prayer with a collect.

THE LITURGY OF THE EUCHARIST

For Catholics, the Eucharist is the source and summit of the whole Christian life.

After the Liturgy of the Word, the people sit and the Offertory Chant begins. The faithful express their participation by making an offering, bringing forward bread and wine for the celebration of the Eucharist and perhaps other gifts to relieve the needs of the Church and of the poor.

PREPARATORY PRAYERS

Standing at the altar, the Priest takes the paten with the bread and holds it slightly raised above the altar with both hands, saying:

Pr. Benedíctus es, Dómine, Deus univérsi,
  quia de tua largitáte accépimus panem,
  quem tibi offérimus,
  fructum terræ et óperis mánuum hóminum:
  ex quo nobis fiet panis vitæ.

R. **Benedíctus Deus in sǽcula.**

The Priest then takes the chalice and holds it slightly raised above the altar with both hands, saying:

Pr. Benedíctus es, Dómine, Deus univérsi,
  quia de tua largitáte accépimus vinum,
  quod tibi offérimus,
  fructum vitis et óperis mánuum hóminum,
  ex quo nobis fiet potus spiritális.

R. **Benedíctus Deus in sǽcula.**

The Priest completes additional personal preparatory rites, and the people rise as he says:

Pr. Oráte, fratres:
  ut meum ac vestrum sacrifícium
  acceptábile fiat apud Deum Patrem omnipoténtem.

R. **Suscípiat Dóminus sacrifícium de mánibus tuis**
  ad laudem et glóriam nóminis sui,
  ad utilitátem quoque nostram
  totiúsque Ecclésiæ suæ sanctæ.

PRAYER OVER THE OFFERINGS

The Priest says the Prayer over the Offerings, at the end of which the people acclaim:

R. **Amen.**

THE LITURGY OF THE EUCHARIST

For Catholics, the Eucharist is the source and summit of the whole Christian life.

After the Liturgy of the Word, the people sit and the Offertory Chant begins. The faithful express their participation by making an offering, bringing forward bread and wine for the celebration of the Eucharist and perhaps other gifts to relieve the needs of the Church and of the poor.

PREPARATORY PRAYERS

Standing at the altar, the Priest takes the paten with the bread and holds it slightly raised above the altar with both hands, saying:

Pr. Blessed are you, Lord God of all creation,
for through your goodness we have received
the bread we offer you:
fruit of the earth and work of human hands,
it will become for us the bread of life.

R. **Blessed be God for ever.**

The Priest then takes the chalice and holds it slightly raised above the altar with both hands, saying:

Pr. Blessed are you, Lord God of all creation,
for through your goodness we have received
the wine we offer you:
fruit of the vine and work of human hands,
it will become our spiritual drink.

R. **Blessed be God for ever.**

The Priest completes additional personal preparatory rites, and the people rise as he says:

Pr. Pray, brethren (brothers and sisters),
that my sacrifice and yours
may be acceptable to God,
the almighty Father.

R. **May the Lord accept the sacrifice at your hands**
for the praise and glory of his name,
for our good
and the good of all his holy Church.

PRAYER OVER THE OFFERINGS

The Priest says the Prayer over the Offerings, at the end of which the people acclaim:

R. **Amen.**

THE EUCHARISTIC PRAYER

Extending his hands, the Priest says:

Pr. Dóminus vobíscum.

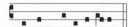

Et cum spí-ri-tu tu-o.

R. Et cum spíritu tuo.

Pr. Sursum corda.

Habémus ad Dóminum.

R. Habémus ad Dóminum.

Pr. Grátias agámus Dómino Deo nostro.

Dignum et iustum est.

R. Dignum et iustum est.

The Priest continues with the Preface appropriate to the Season or Feast at the end of which all sing or say:

S anc-tus, * Sanc-tus, Sanc-tus Dó-mi-nus De-us Sá-ba-oth. Ple-ni sunt cæ-li et ter-ra gló-ri-a tu-a. Ho-sán-na in ex-cél-sis. Be-ne-díc-tus qui ve-nit in nómine Dómini. Ho-sán-na in excél-sis.

THE EUCHARISTIC PRAYER

Extending his hands, the Priest says:

Pr. The Lord be with you.

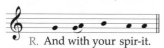

R. And with your spir-it.

R. **And with your spirit.**

Pr. Lift up your hearts.

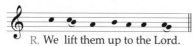

R. We lift them up to the Lord.

R. **We lift them up to the Lord.**

Pr. Let us give thanks to the Lord our God.

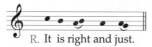

R. It is right and just.

R. **It is right and just.**

The Priest continues with the Preface appropriate to the Season or Feast at the end of which all sing or say:

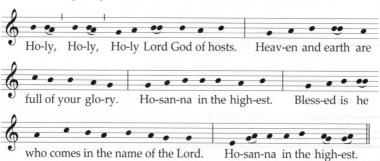

Ho-ly, Ho-ly, Ho-ly Lord God of hosts. Heav-en and earth are full of your glo-ry. Ho-san-na in the high-est. Bless-ed is he who comes in the name of the Lord. Ho-san-na in the high-est.

Sanctus, Sanctus, Sanctus Dóminus Deus Sábaoth.
Pleni sunt cæli et terra glória tua.
Hosánna in excélsis.
Benedíctus qui venit in nómine Dómini.
Hosánna in excélsis.

After the Sanctus the congregation kneels for the remainder of the Eucharistic Prayer. (Texts for the four principal Eucharistic Prayers follow: Eucharistic Prayer I at p.80, II at p.92, III at p.100, IV at p.110.)

PREFACES

ADVENT

PRÆFATIO I DE ADVENTU

De duobus adventibus Christi

In Missis de tempore a prima dominica Adventus usque ad diem 16 decembris

Vere dignum et iustum est, æquum et salutare,
nos tibi semper et ubique gratias agere:
Domine, sancte Pater, omnipotens æterne Deus:
per Christum Dominum nostrum.

Qui, primo adventu in humilitate carnis assumptæ,
dispositionis antiquæ munus implevit,
nobisque salutis perpetuæ tramitem reseravit:
ut, cum secundo venerit in suæ gloria maiestatis,
manifesto demum munere capiamus,
quod vigilantes nunc audemus exspectare promissum.

Et ideo cum Angelis et Archangelis,
cum Thronis et Dominationibus,
cumque omni militia cælestis exercitus,
hymnum gloriæ tuæ canimus,
sine fine dicentes:

Sanctus, Sanctus, Sanctus Dominus Deus Sabaoth. . .

Holy, Holy, Holy Lord God of hosts.
Heaven and earth are full of your glory.
Hosanna in the highest.
Blessed is he who comes in the name of the Lord.
Hosanna in the highest.

After the Sanctus the congregation kneels for the remainder of the Eucharistic Prayer. (Texts for the four principal Eucharistic Prayers follow: Eucharistic Prayer I at p.81, II at p.93, III at p.101, IV at p.111.)

PREFACES

ADVENT

PREFACE I OF ADVENT

The two comings of Christ

From the First Sunday of Advent until 16 December

It is truly right and just, our duty and our salvation,
always and everywhere to give you thanks,
Lord, holy Father, almighty and eternal God,
through Christ our Lord.

For he assumed at his first coming
the lowliness of human flesh,
and so fulfilled the design you formed long ago,
and opened for us the way to eternal salvation,
that, when he comes again in glory and majesty
and all is at last made manifest,
we who watch for that day
may inherit the great promise
in which now we dare to hope.

And so, with Angels and Archangels,
with Thrones and Dominions,
and with all the hosts and Powers of heaven,
we sing the hymn of your glory,
as without end we acclaim:

Holy, Holy, Holy Lord God of hosts. . .

PRÆFATIO II DE ADVENTU

De duplici exspectatione Christi

17 decembris-24 decembris

Vere dignum et iustum est, æquum et salutare,
nos tibi semper et ubique gratias agere:
Domine, sancte Pater, omnipotens æterne Deus:
per Christum Dominum nostrum.

Quem prædixerunt cunctorum præconia prophetarum,
Virgo Mater ineffabili dilectione sustinuit,
Ioannes cecinit affuturum et adesse monstravit.
Qui suæ nativitatis mysterium
tribuit nos prævenire gaudentes,
ut et in oratione pervigiles
et in suis inveniat laudibus exsultantes.

Et ideo cum Angelis et Archangelis,
cum Thronis et Dominationibus,
cumque omni militia cælestis exercitus,
hymnum gloriæ tuæ canimus,
sine fine dicentes:
Sanctus, Sanctus, Sanctus Dominus Deus Sabaoth. . .

CHRISTMAS

PRÆFATIO I DE NATIVITATE DOMINI

De Christo luce

Vere dignum et iustum est, æquum et salutare,
nos tibi semper et ubique gratias agere:
Domine, sancte Pater, omnipotens æterne Deus:

Quia per incarnati Verbi mysterium
nova mentis nostræ oculis lux tuæ claritatis infulsit:
ut, dum visibiliter Deum cognoscimus,
per hunc in invisibilium amorem rapiamur.

Et ideo cum Angelis et Archangelis,
cum Thronis et Dominationibus,
cumque omni militia cælestis exercitus,
hymnum gloriæ tuæ canimus, sine fine dicentes:
Sanctus, Sanctus, Sanctus Dominus Deus Sabaoth. . .

PREFACE II OF ADVENT

The twofold expectation of Christ

17 December-24 December

It is truly right and just, our duty and our salvation,
always and everywhere to give you thanks,
Lord, holy Father, almighty and eternal God,
through Christ our Lord.

For all the oracles of the prophets foretold him,
the Virgin Mother longed for him
with love beyond all telling,
John the Baptist sang of his coming
and proclaimed his presence when he came.

It is by his gift that already we rejoice
at the mystery of his Nativity,
so that he may find us watchful in prayer
and exultant in his praise.

And so, with Angels and Archangels,
with Thrones and Dominions,
and with all the hosts and Powers of heaven,
we sing the hymn of your glory,
as without end we acclaim:

Holy, Holy, Holy Lord God of hosts. . .

CHRISTMAS

PREFACE I OF THE NATIVITY OF THE LORD

Christ the Light

It is truly right and just, our duty and our salvation,
always and everywhere to give you thanks,
Lord, holy Father, almighty and eternal God.

For in the mystery of the Word made flesh
a new light of your glory has shone upon the eyes of our mind,
so that, as we recognise in him God made visible,
we may be caught up through him in love of things invisible.

And so, with Angels and Archangels,
with Thrones and Dominions,
and with all the hosts and Powers of heaven,
we sing the hymn of your glory,
as without end we acclaim:
Holy, Holy, Holy Lord God of hosts. . .

PRÆFATIO II DE NATIVITATE DOMINI

De restauratione universa in Incarnatione

Vere dignum et iustum est, æquum et salutare,
nos tibi semper et ubique gratias agere:
Domine, sancte Pater, omnipotens æterne Deus:
per Christum Dominum nostrum.

Qui, in huius venerandi festivitate mysterii,
invisibilis in suis, visibilis in nostris apparuit,
et ante tempora genitus esse cœpit in tempore;
ut, in se erigens cuncta deiecta,
in integrum restitueret universa,
et hominem perditum ad cælestia regna revocaret.

Unde et nos, cum omnibus Angelis te laudamus,
iucunda celebratione clamantes:

Sanctus, Sanctus, Sanctus Dominus Deus Sabaoth. . .

PRÆFATIO III DE NATIVITATE DOMINI

De commercio in Incarnatione Verbi

Vere dignum et iustum est, æquum et salutare,
nos tibi semper et ubique gratias agere:
Domine, sancte Pater, omnipotens æterne Deus:
per Christum Dominum nostrum.

Per quem hodie commercium nostræ reparationis effulsit,
quia, dum nostra fragilitas a tuo Verbo suscipitur,
humana mortalitas non solum
in perpetuum transit honorem,
sed nos quoque, mirando consortio, reddit æternos.

Et ideo, choris angelicis sociati,
te laudamus in gaudio confitentes:

Sanctus, Sanctus, Sanctus Dominus Deus Sabaoth. . .

PREFACE II OF THE NATIVITY OF THE LORD

The restoration of all things in the Incarnation

It is truly right and just, our duty and our salvation,
always and everywhere to give you thanks,
Lord, holy Father, almighty and eternal God,
through Christ our Lord.

For on the feast of this awe-filled mystery,
though invisible in his own divine nature,
he has appeared visibly in ours;
and begotten before all ages,
he has begun to exist in time;
so that, raising up in himself all that was cast down,
he might restore unity to all creation
and call straying humanity back to the heavenly Kingdom.

And so, with all the Angels, we praise you,
as in joyful celebration we acclaim:

Holy, Holy, Holy Lord God of hosts. . .

PREFACE III OF THE NATIVITY OF THE LORD

The exchange in the Incarnation of the Word

It is truly right and just, our duty and our salvation,
always and everywhere to give you thanks,
Lord, holy Father, almighty and eternal God,
through Christ our Lord.

For through him the holy exchange that restores our life
has shone forth today in splendour:
when our frailty is assumed by your Word
not only does human mortality receive unending honour
but by this wondrous union we, too, are made eternal.

And so, in company with the choirs of Angels,
we praise you, and with joy we proclaim:

Holy, Holy, Holy Lord God of hosts. . .

PRÆFATIO DE EPIPHANIA DOMINI

De Christo lumine gentium

Vere dignum et iustum est, æquum et salutare,
nos tibi semper et ubique gratias agere:
Domine, sancte Pater, omnipotens æterne Deus:

Quia ipsum in Christo salutis nostræ mysterium
hodie ad lumen gentium revelasti,
et, cum in substantia nostræ mortalitatis apparuit,
nova nos immortalitatis eius gloria reparasti.

Et ideo cum Angelis et Archangelis,
cum Thronis et Dominationibus,
cumque omni militia cælestis exercitus,
hymnum gloriæ tuæ canimus,
sine fine dicentes:

Sanctus, Sanctus, Sanctus Dominus Deus Sabaoth. . .

LENT
PRÆFATIO I DE QUADRAGESIMA

De spiritali significatione Quadregesimæ

Vere dignum et iustum est, æquum et salutare,
nos tibi semper et ubique gratias agere:
Domine, sancte Pater, omnipotens æterne Deus:
per Christum Dominum nostrum.

Quia fidelibus tuis dignanter concedis
quotannis paschalia sacramenta
in gaudio purificatis mentibus exspectare:
ut, pietatis officia et opera caritatis propensius exsequentes,
frequentatione mysteriorum, quibus renati sunt,
ad gratiæ filiorum plenitudinem perducantur.

Et ideo cum Angelis et Archangelis,
cum Thronis et Dominationibus,
cumque omni militia cælestis exercitus,
hymnum gloriæ tuæ canimus,
sine fine dicentes:

Sanctus, Sanctus, Sanctus Dominus Deus Sabaoth. . .

PREFACE OF THE EPIPHANY OF THE LORD
Christ the light of the nations

It is truly right and just, our duty and our salvation,
always and everywhere to give you thanks,
Lord, holy Father, almighty and eternal God.

For today you have revealed the mystery
of our salvation in Christ
as a light for the nations,
and, when he appeared in our mortal nature,
you made us new by the glory of his immortal nature.

And so, with Angels and Archangels,
with Thrones and Dominions,
and with all the hosts and Powers of heaven,
we sing the hymn of your glory,
as without end we acclaim:

Holy, Holy, Holy Lord God of hosts. . .

LENT
PREFACE I OF LENT
The spiritual meaning of Lent

It is truly right and just, our duty and our salvation,
always and everywhere to give you thanks,
Lord, holy Father, almighty and eternal God,
through Christ our Lord.

For by your gracious gift each year
your faithful await the sacred paschal feasts
with the joy of minds made pure,
so that, more eagerly intent on prayer
and on the works of charity,
and participating in the mysteries
by which they have been reborn,
they may be led to the fullness of grace
that you bestow on your sons and daughters.

And so, with Angels and Archangels,
with Thrones and Dominions,
and with all the hosts and Powers of heaven,
we sing the hymn of your glory,
as without end we acclaim:

Holy, Holy, Holy Lord God of hosts. . .

PRÆFATIO II DE QUADRAGESIMA

De spiritali pænitentia

Vere dignum et iustum est, æquum et salutare,
nos tibi semper et ubique gratias agere:
Domine, sancte Pater, omnipotens æterne Deus:

Qui filiis tuis ad reparandam mentium puritatem,
tempus præcipuum salubriter statuisti,
quo, mente ab inordinatis affectibus expedita,
sic incumberent transituris
ut rebus potius perpetuis inhærerent.

Et ideo, cum Sanctis et Angelis universis,
te collaudamus, sine fine dicentes:

Sanctus, Sanctus, Sanctus Dominus Deus Sabaoth. . .

PRÆFATIO III DE QUADRAGESIMA

De fructibus abstinentiæ

Vere dignum et iustum est, æquum et salutare,
nos tibi semper et ubique gratias agere:
Domine, sancte Pater, omnipotens æterne Deus:

Qui nos per abstinentiam tibi gratias referre voluisti,
ut ipsa et nos peccatores ab insolentia mitigaret,
et, egentium proficiens alimento,
imitatores tuæ benignitatis efficeret.

Et ideo, cum innumeris Angelis,
una te magnificamus laudis voce dicentes:

Sanctus, Sanctus, Sanctus Dominus Deus Sabaoth. . .

PRÆFATIO IV DE QUADRAGESIMA

De fructibus ieiunii

Vere dignum et iustum est, æquum et salutare,
nos tibi semper et ubique gratias agere:
Domine, sancte Pater, omnipotens æterne Deus:

Qui corporali ieiunio vitia comprimis, mentem elevas,
virtutem largiris et præmia:
per Christum Dominum nostrum.

PREFACE II OF LENT

Spiritual penance

It is truly right and just, our duty and our salvation,
always and everywhere to give you thanks,
Lord, holy Father, almighty and eternal God.

For you have given your children a sacred time
for the renewing and purifying of their hearts,
that, freed from disordered affections,
they may so deal with the things of this passing world
as to hold rather to the things that eternally endure.

And so, with all the Angels and Saints,
we praise you, as without end we acclaim:

Holy, Holy, Holy Lord God of hosts. . .

PREFACE III OF LENT

The fruits of abstinence

It is truly right and just, our duty and our salvation,
always and everywhere to give you thanks,
Lord, holy Father, almighty and eternal God.

For you will that our self-denial should give you thanks,
humble our sinful pride,
contribute to the feeding of the poor,
and so help us imitate you in your kindness.

And so we glorify you with countless Angels,
as with one voice of praise we acclaim:

Holy, Holy, Holy Lord God of hosts. . .

PREFACE IV OF LENT

The fruits of fasting

It is truly right and just, our duty and our salvation,
always and everywhere to give you thanks,
Lord, holy Father, almighty and eternal God.

For through bodily fasting you restrain our faults,
raise up our minds,
and bestow both virtue and its rewards,
through Christ our Lord.

Per quem maiestatem tuam laudant Angeli,
adorant Dominationes, tremunt Potestates.
Cæli cælorumque Virtutes, ac beata Seraphim,
socia exsultatione concelebrant.

Cum quibus et nostras voces ut admitti iubeas, deprecamur,
supplici confessione dicentes:

Sanctus, Sanctus, Sanctus Dominus Deus Sabaoth. . .

PRÆFATIO I DE PASSIONE DOMINI

De virtute Crucis

Vere dignum et iustum est, æquum et salutare,
nos tibi semper et ubique gratias agere:
Domine, sancte Pater, omnipotens æterne Deus:

Quia per Filii tui salutiferam passionem
sensum confitendæ tuæ maiestatis totus mundus accepit,
dum ineffabili crucis potentia
iudicium mundi et potestas emicat Crucifixi.

Unde et nos, Domine, cum Angelis et Sanctis universis,
tibi confitemur, in exsultatione dicentes:

Sanctus, Sanctus, Sanctus Dominus Deus Sabaoth. . .

EASTER

PRÆFATIO PASCHALIS I

De mysterio paschali

Vere dignum et iustum est, æquum et salutare:
Te quidem, Domine, omni tempore confiteri,
sed in hac potissimum nocte (die) gloriosius prædicare,
(sed in hoc potissimum gloriosius prædicare,)
cum Pascha nostrum immolatus est Christus.

Ipse enim verus est Agnus
qui abstulit peccata mundi.
Qui mortem nostram moriendo destruxit,
et vitam resurgendo reparavit.

Quapropter, profusis paschalibus gaudiis,
totus in orbe terrarum mundus exsultat.

Through him the Angels praise your majesty,
Dominions adore and Powers tremble before you.
Heaven and the Virtues of heaven and the blessed Seraphim
worship together with exultation.
May our voices, we pray, join with theirs
in humble praise, as we acclaim:

Holy, Holy, Holy Lord God of hosts. . .

PREFACE I OF THE PASSION OF THE LORD

The power of the Cross

It is truly right and just, our duty and our salvation,
always and everywhere to give you thanks,
Lord, holy Father, almighty and eternal God.

For through the saving Passion of your Son
the whole world has received a heart
to confess the infinite power of your majesty,
since by the wondrous power of the Cross
your judgement on the world is now revealed
and the authority of Christ crucified.

And so, Lord, with all the Angels and Saints,
we, too, give you thanks, as in exultation we acclaim:

Holy, Holy, Holy Lord God of hosts. . .

EASTER

PREFACE I OF EASTER

The Paschal Mystery

It is truly right and just, our duty and our salvation,
at all times to acclaim you, O Lord,
but (on this night / on this day / in this time) above all
to laud you yet more gloriously,
when Christ our Passover has been sacrificed.

For he is the true Lamb
who has taken away the sins of the world;
by dying he has destroyed our death,
and by rising, restored our life.

Therefore, overcome with paschal joy,
every land, every people exults in your praise

Sed et supernæ virtutes atque angelicæ potestates
hymnum gloriæ tuæ concinunt, sine fine dicentes:

Sanctus, Sanctus, Sanctus Dominus Deus Sabaoth. . .

PRÆFATIO PASCHALIS II

De vita nova in Christo

Vere dignum et iustum est, æquum et salutare:
Te quidem, Domine, omni tempore confiteri,
sed in hoc potissimum gloriosius prædicare,
cum Pascha nostrum immolatus est Christus.

Per quem in æternam vitam filii lucis oriuntur,
et regni cælestis atria fidelibus reserantur.
Quia mors nostra est eius morte redempta,
et in eius resurrectione vita omnium resurrexit.

Quapropter, profusis paschalibus gaudiis,
totus in orbe terrarum mundus exsultat.
Sed et supernæ virtutes atque angelicæ potestates
hymnum gloriæ tuæ concinunt, sine fine dicentes:

Sanctus, Sanctus, Sanctus Dominus Deus Sabaoth. . .

PRÆFATIO PASCHALIS III

De Christo vivente et semper interpellante pro nobis

Vere dignum et iustum est, æquum et salutare:
Te quidem, Domine, omni tempore confiteri,
sed in hoc potissimum gloriosius prædicare,
cum Pascha nostrum immolatus est Christus.

Qui se pro nobis offerre non desinit,
nosque apud te perenni advocatione defendit;
qui immolatus iam non moritur,
sed semper vivit occisus.

Quapropter, profusis paschalibus gaudiis,
totus in orbe terrarum mundus exsultat.
Sed et supernæ virtutes atque angelicæ potestates
hymnum gloriæ tuæ concinunt, sine fine dicentes:

Sanctus, Sanctus, Sanctus Dominus Deus Sabaoth. . .

and even the heavenly Powers, with the angelic hosts,
sing together the unending hymn of your glory,
as they acclaim:

Holy, Holy, Holy Lord God of hosts. . .

PREFACE II OF EASTER

New life in Christ

It is truly right and just, our duty and our salvation,
at all times to acclaim you, O Lord,
but in this time above all to laud you yet more gloriously,
when Christ our Passover has been sacrificed.

Through him the children of light rise to eternal life
and the halls of the heavenly Kingdom
are thrown open to the faithful;
for his Death is our ransom from death,
and in his rising the life of all has risen.

Therefore, overcome with paschal joy,
every land, every people exults in your praise
and even the heavenly Powers, with the angelic hosts,
sing together the unending hymn of your glory,
as they acclaim:

Holy, Holy, Holy Lord God of hosts. . .

PREFACE III OF EASTER

Christ living and always interceding for us

It is truly right and just, our duty and our salvation,
at all times to acclaim you, O Lord,
but in this time above all to laud you yet more gloriously,
when Christ our Passover has been sacrificed.

He never ceases to offer himself for us
but defends us and ever pleads our cause before you:
he is the sacrificial Victim who dies no more,
the Lamb, once slain, who lives for ever.

Therefore, overcome with paschal joy,
every land, every people exults in your praise
and even the heavenly Powers, with the angelic hosts,
sing together the unending hymn of your glory,
as they acclaim:

Holy, Holy, Holy Lord God of hosts. . .

PRÆFATIO PASCHALIS IV

De restauratione universi per mysterium paschale

Vere dignum et iustum est, æquum et salutare:
Te quidem, Domine, omni tempore confiteri,
sed in hoc potissimum gloriosius prædicare,
cum Pascha nostrum immolatus est Christus.

Quia, vetustate destructa, renovantur universa deiecta,
et vitæ nobis in Christo reparatur integritas.

Quapropter, profusis paschalibus gaudiis,
totus in orbe terrarum mundus exsultat.
Sed et supernæ virtutes atque angelicæ potestates
hymnum gloriæ tuæ concinunt, sine fine dicentes:

Sanctus, Sanctus, Sanctus Dominus Deus Sabaoth. . .

PRÆFATIO PASCHALIS V

De Christo sacerdote et victima

Vere dignum et iustum est, æquum et salutare:
Te quidem, Domine, omni tempore confiteri,
sed in hoc potissimum gloriosius prædicare,
cum Pascha nostrum immolatus est Christus.

Qui, oblatione corporis sui,
antiqua sacrificia in crucis veritate perfecit,
et, seipsum tibi pro nostra salute commendans,
idem sacerdos, altare et agnus exhibuit.

Quapropter, profusis paschalibus gaudiis,
totus in orbe terrarum mundus exsultat.
Sed et supernæ virtutes atque angelicæ potestates
hymnum gloriæ tuæ concinunt, sine fine dicentes:

Sanctus, Sanctus, Sanctus Dominus Deus Sabaoth. . .

PREFACE IV OF EASTER

The restoration of the universe through the Paschal Mystery

It is truly right and just, our duty and our salvation,
at all times to acclaim you, O Lord,
but in this time above all to laud you yet more gloriously,
when Christ our Passover has been sacrificed.

For, with the old order destroyed,
a universe cast down is renewed,
and integrity of life is restored to us in Christ.

Therefore, overcome with paschal joy,
every land, every people exults in your praise
and even the heavenly Powers, with the angelic hosts,
sing together the unending hymn of your glory,
as they acclaim:

Holy, Holy, Holy Lord God of hosts. . .

PREFACE V OF EASTER

Christ, Priest and Victim

It is truly right and just, our duty and our salvation,
at all times to acclaim you, O Lord,
but in this time above all to laud you yet more gloriously,
when Christ our Passover has been sacrificed.

By the oblation of his Body,
he brought the sacrifices of old to fulfilment
in the reality of the Cross
and, by commending himself to you for our salvation,
showed himself the Priest, the Altar, and the Lamb of sacrifice.

Therefore, overcome with paschal joy,
every land, every people exults in your praise
and even the heavenly Powers, with the angelic hosts,
sing together the unending hymn of your glory,
as they acclaim:

Holy, Holy, Holy Lord God of hosts. . .

PRÆFATIO I DE ASCENSIONE DOMINI

De mysterio Ascensionis

Vere dignum et iustum est, æquum et salutare,
nos tibi semper et ubique gratias agere:
Domine, sancte Pater, omnipotens æterne Deus:

Quia Dominus Iesus, Rex gloriæ,
peccati triumphator et mortis,
mirantibus Angelis, ascendit (hodie) summa cælorum,
Mediator Dei et hominum,
Iudex mundi Dominusque virtutum;
non ut a nostra humilitate discederet,
sed ut illuc confideremus, sua membra, nos subsequi
quo ipse, caput nostrum principiumque, præcessit.

Quapropter, profusis paschalibus gaudiis,
totus in orbe terrarum mundus exsultat.
Sed et supernæ virtutes atque angelicæ potestates
hymnum gloriæ tuæ concinunt, sine fine dicentes:
Sanctus, Sanctus, Sanctus Dominus Deus Sabaoth. . .

PRÆFATIO II DE ASCENSIONE DOMINI

De mysterio Ascensionis

Vere dignum et iustum est, æquum et salutare,
nos tibi semper et ubique gratias agere:
Domine, sancte Pater, omnipotens æterne Deus:
per Christum Dominum nostrum.

Qui post resurrectionem suam
omnibus discipulis suis manifestus apparuit,
et ipsis cernentibus est elevatus in cælum,
ut nos divinitatis suæ tribueret esse participes.

Quapropter, profusis paschalibus gaudiis,
totus in orbe terrarum mundus exsultat.
Sed et supernæ virtutes atque angelicæ potestates
hymnum gloriæ tuæ concinunt, sine fine dicentes:

Sanctus, Sanctus, Sanctus Dominus Deus Sabaoth. . .

PREFACE I OF THE ASCENSION OF THE LORD

The mystery of the Ascension

It is truly right and just, our duty and our salvation,
always and everywhere to give you thanks,
Lord, holy Father, almighty and eternal God.

For the Lord Jesus, the King of glory,
conqueror of sin and death,
ascended (today) to the highest heavens,
as the Angels gazed in wonder.

Mediator between God and man,
judge of the world and Lord of hosts,
he ascended, not to distance himself from our lowly state
but that we, his members, might be confident of following
where he, our Head and Founder, has gone before.

Therefore, overcome with paschal joy,
every land, every people exults in your praise
and even the heavenly Powers, with the angelic hosts,
sing together the unending hymn of your glory,
as they acclaim:

Holy, Holy, Holy Lord God of hosts. . .

PREFACE II OF THE ASCENSION OF THE LORD

The mystery of the Ascension

It is truly right and just, our duty and our salvation,
always and everywhere to give you thanks,
Lord, holy Father, almighty and eternal God,
through Christ our Lord.

For after his Resurrection
he plainly appeared to all his disciples
and was taken up to heaven in their sight,
that he might make us sharers in his divinity.

Therefore, overcome with paschal joy,
every land, every people exults in your praise
and even the heavenly Powers, with the angelic hosts,
sing together the unending hymn of your glory,
as they acclaim:

Holy, Holy, Holy Lord God of hosts. . .

PRÆFATIO I DE DOMINICIS « PER ANNUM »

De mysterio paschali et de populo Dei

Vere dignum et iustum est, æquum et salutare,
nos tibi semper et ubique gratias agere:
Domine, sancte Pater, omnipotens æterne Deus:
per Christum Dominum nostrum.

Cuius hoc mirificum fuit opus per paschale mysterium,
ut de peccato et mortis iugo ad hanc gloriam vocaremur,
qua nunc genus electum, regale sacerdotium,
gens sancta et acquisitionis populus diceremur,
et tuas annuntiaremus ubique virtutes,
qui nos de tenebris ad tuum admirabile lumen vocasti.

Et ideo cum Angelis et Archangelis,
cum Thronis et Dominationibus,
cumque omni militia cælestis exercitus,
hymnum gloriæ tuæ canimus,
sine fine dicentes:

Sanctus, Sanctus, Sanctus Dominus Deus Sabaoth. . .

PRÆFATIO II DE DOMINICIS « PER ANNUM »

De mysterio salutis

Vere dignum et iustum est, æquum et salutare,
nos tibi semper et ubique gratias agere:
Domine, sancte Pater, omnipotens æterne Deus:
per Christum Dominum nostrum.

Qui, humanis miseratus erroribus,
de Virgine nasci dignatus est.
Qui, crucem passus, a perpetua morte nos liberavit
et, a mortuis resurgens, vitam nobis donavit æternam.

Et ideo cum Angelis et Archangelis,
cum Thronis et Dominationibus,
cumque omni militia cælestis exercitus,
hymnum gloriæ tuæ canimus,
sine fine dicentes:

Sanctus, Sanctus, Sanctus Dominus Deus Sabaoth. . .

PREFACE I OF THE SUNDAYS IN ORDINARY TIME

The Paschal Mystery and the People of God

It is truly right and just, our duty and our salvation,
always and everywhere to give you thanks,
Lord, holy Father, almighty and eternal God,
through Christ our Lord.

For through his Paschal Mystery,
he accomplished the marvellous deed,
by which he has freed us from the yoke of sin and death,
summoning us to the glory of being now called
a chosen race, a royal priesthood,
a holy nation, a people for your own possession,
to proclaim everywhere your mighty works,
for you have called us out of darkness
into your own wonderful light.

And so, with Angels and Archangels,
with Thrones and Dominions,
and with all the hosts and Powers of heaven,
we sing the hymn of your glory,
as without end we acclaim:

Holy, Holy, Holy Lord God of hosts. . .

PREFACE II OF THE SUNDAYS IN ORDINARY TIME

The mystery of salvation

It is truly right and just, our duty and our salvation,
always and everywhere to give you thanks,
Lord, holy Father, almighty and eternal God,
through Christ our Lord.

For out of compassion for the waywardness that is ours,
he humbled himself and was born of the Virgin;
by the passion of the Cross he freed us from unending death,
and by rising from the dead he gave us life eternal.

And so, with Angels and Archangels,
with Thrones and Dominions,
and with all the hosts and Powers of heaven,
we sing the hymn of your glory,
as without end we acclaim:

Holy, Holy, Holy Lord God of hosts. . .

PRÆFATIO III DE DOMINICIS « PER ANNUM »

De salvatione hominis per hominem

Vere dignum et iustum est, æquum et salutare,
nos tibi semper et ubique gratias agere:
Domine, sancte Pater, omnipotens æterne Deus:

Ad cuius immensam gloriam pertinere cognoscimus
ut mortalibus tua deitate succurreres;
sed et nobis provideres de ipsa
mortalitate nostra remedium,
et perditos quosque unde perierant, inde salvares,
per Christum Dominum nostrum.

Per quem maiestatem tuam adorat exercitus Angelorum,
ante conspectum tuum in æternitate lætantium.

Cum quibus et nostras voces ut admitti iubeas, deprecamur,
socia exsultatione dicentes:

Sanctus, Sanctus, Sanctus Dominus Deus Sabaoth. . .

PRÆFATIO IV DE DOMINICIS « PER ANNUM »

De historia salutis

Vere dignum et iustum est, æquum et salutare,
nos tibi semper et ubique gratias agere:
Domine, sancte Pater, omnipotens æterne Deus:
per Christum Dominum nostrum.

Ipse enim nascendo vetustatem hominum renovavit,
patiendo delevit nostra peccata,
æternæ vitæ aditum præstitit a mortuis resurgendo,
ad te Patrem ascendendo cælestes ianuas reseravit.

Et ideo, cum Angelorum atque Sanctorum turba,
hymnum laudis tibi canimus, sine fine dicentes:
Sanctus, Sanctus, Sanctus Dominus Deus Sabaoth. . .

PREFACE III OF THE SUNDAYS IN ORDINARY TIME

The salvation of man by a man

It is truly right and just, our duty and our salvation,
always and everywhere to give you thanks,
Lord, holy Father, almighty and eternal God.

For we know it belongs to your boundless glory,
that you came to the aid of mortal beings with your divinity
and even fashioned for us a remedy out of mortality itself,
that the cause of our downfall
might become the means of our salvation,
through Christ our Lord.

Through him the host of Angels adores your majesty
and rejoices in your presence for ever.
May our voices, we pray, join with theirs
in one chorus of exultant praise, as we acclaim:

Holy, Holy, Holy Lord God of hosts. . .

PREFACE IV OF THE SUNDAYS IN ORDINARY TIME

The history of salvation

It is truly right and just, our duty and our salvation,
always and everywhere to give you thanks,
Lord, holy Father, almighty and eternal God,
through Christ our Lord.

For by his birth he brought renewal
to humanity's fallen state,
and by his suffering cancelled out our sins;
by his rising from the dead
he has opened the way to eternal life,
and by ascending to you, O Father,
he has unlocked the gates of heaven.

And so, with the company of Angels and Saints,
we sing the hymn of your praise,
as without end we acclaim:

Holy, Holy, Holy Lord God of hosts. . .

PRÆFATIO V DE DOMINICIS « PER ANNUM »

De creatione

Vere dignum et iustum est, æquum et salutare,
nos tibi semper et ubique gratias agere:
Domine, sancte Pater, omnipotens æterne Deus:

Qui omnia mundi elementa fecisti,
et vices disposuisti temporum variari;
hominem vero formasti ad imaginem tuam,
et rerum ei subiecisti universa miracula,
ut vicario munere dominaretur omnibus quæ creasti,
et in operum tuorum magnalibus iugiter te laudaret,
per Christum Dominum nostrum.

Unde et nos cum omnibus Angelis te laudamus,
iucunda celebratione clamantes:

Sanctus, Sanctus, Sanctus Dominus Deus Sabaoth. . .

PRÆFATIO VI DE DOMINICIS « PER ANNUM »

De pignore æterni Paschatis

Vere dignum et iustum est, æquum et salutare,
nos tibi semper et ubique gratias agere:
Domine, sancte Pater, omnipotens æterne Deus:

In quo vivimus, movemur et sumus,
atque in hoc corpore constituti
non solum pietatis tuæ cotidianos experimur effectus,
sed æternitatis etiam pignora iam tenemus.
Primitias enim Spiritus habentes,
per quem suscitasti Iesum a mortuis,
paschale mysterium speramus nobis esse perpetuum.

Unde et nos cum omnibus Angelis te laudamus,
iucunda celebratione clamantes:

Sanctus, Sanctus, Sanctus Dominus Deus Sabaoth. . .

PREFACE V OF THE SUNDAYS IN ORDINARY TIME

Creation

It is truly right and just, our duty and our salvation,
always and everywhere to give you thanks,
Lord, holy Father, almighty and eternal God.

For you laid the foundations of the world
and have arranged the changing of times and seasons;
you formed man in your own image
and set humanity over the whole world in all its wonder,
to rule in your name over all you have made
and for ever praise you in your mighty works,
through Christ our Lord.

And so, with all the Angels, we praise you,
as in joyful celebration we acclaim:

Holy, Holy, Holy Lord God of hosts. . .

PREFACE VI OF THE SUNDAYS IN ORDINARY TIME

The pledge of the eternal Passover

It is truly right and just, our duty and our salvation,
always and everywhere to give you thanks,
Lord, holy Father, almighty and eternal God.

For in you we live and move and have our being,
and while in this body
we not only experience the daily effects of your care,
but even now possess the pledge of life eternal.

For, having received the first fruits of the Spirit,
through whom you raised up Jesus from the dead,
we hope for an everlasting share in the Paschal Mystery.

And so, with all the Angels, we praise you,
as in joyful celebration we acclaim:

Holy, Holy, Holy Lord God of hosts. . .

PRÆFATIO VII DE DOMINICIS « PER ANNUM »

De salute per obœdientiam Christi

Vere dignum et iustum est, æquum et salutare,
nos tibi semper et ubique gratias agere:
Domine, sancte Pater, omnipotens æterne Deus:

Quia sic mundum misericorditer dilexisti,
ut ipsum nobis mitteres Redemptorem,
quem absque peccato
in nostra voluisti similitudine conversari,
ut amares in nobis quod diligebas in Filio,
cuius obœdientia sumus ad tua dona reparati,
quæ per inobœdientiam amiseramus peccando.

Unde et nos, Domine, cum Angelis et Sanctis universis
tibi confitemur, in exsultatione dicentes:

Sanctus, Sanctus, Sanctus Dominus Deus Sabaoth. . .

PRÆFATIO VIII DE DOMINICIS « PER ANNUM »

De Ecclesia adunata ex unitate Trinitatis

Vere dignum et iustum est, æquum et salutare,
nos tibi semper et ubique gratias agere:
Domine, sancte Pater, omnipotens æterne Deus:

Quia filios, quos longe peccati crimen abstulerat,
per sanguinem Filii tui Spiritusque virtute,
in unum ad te denuo congregare voluisti:
ut plebs, de unitate Trinitatis adunata,
in tuæ laudem sapientiæ multiformis
Christi corpus templumque Spiritus nosceretur Ecclesia.

Et ideo, choris angelicis sociati,
te laudamus in gaudio confitentes:

Sanctus, Sanctus, Sanctus Dominus Deus Sabaoth. . .

PREFACE VII OF THE SUNDAYS IN ORDINARY TIME

Salvation through the obedience of Christ

It is truly right and just, our duty and our salvation,
always and everywhere to give you thanks,
Lord, holy Father, almighty and eternal God.

For you so loved the world
that in your mercy you sent us the Redeemer,
to live like us in all things but sin,
so that you might love in us what you loved in your Son,
by whose obedience we have been restored to those gifts of yours
that, by sinning, we had lost in disobedience.

And so, Lord, with all the Angels and Saints,
we, too, give you thanks, as in exultation we acclaim:

Holy, Holy, Holy Lord God of hosts. . .

PREFACE VIII OF THE SUNDAYS IN ORDINARY TIME

The Church united by the unity of the Trinity

It is truly right and just, our duty and our salvation,
always and everywhere to give you thanks,
Lord, holy Father, almighty and eternal God.

For, when your children were scattered afar by sin,
through the Blood of your Son and the power of the Spirit,
you gathered them again to yourself,
that a people, formed as one by the unity of the Trinity,
made the body of Christ and the temple of the Holy Spirit,
might, to the praise of your manifold wisdom,
be manifest as the Church.

And so, in company with the choirs of Angels,
we praise you, and with joy we proclaim:

Holy, Holy, Holy Lord God of hosts. . .

PRÆFATIO I DE SS.MA EUCHARISTIA

De sacrificia ex de sacramento Christi

Vere dignum et iustum est, æquum et salutare,
nos tibi semper et ubique gratias agere:
Domine, sancte Pater, omnipotens æterne Deus:
per Christum Dominum nostrum.

Qui, verus æternusque Sacerdos,
formam sacrificii perennis instituens,
hostiam tibi se primus obtulit salutarem,
et nos, in sui memoriam, præcepit offerre.
Cuius carnem pro nobis immolatam
dum sumimus, roboramur,
et fusum pro nobis sanguinem dum potamus, abluimur.

Et ideo cum Angelis et Archangelis,
cum Thronis et Dominationibus,
cumque omni militia cælestis exercitus,
hymnum gloriæ tuæ canimus,
sine fine dicentes:

Sanctus, Sanctus, Sanctus Dominus Deus Sabaoth. . .

PRÆFATIO II DE SS.MA EUCHARISTIA

De fructibus Sanctissimæ Eucharistiæ

Vere dignum et iustum est, æquum et salutare,
nos tibi semper et ubique gratias agere:
Domine, sancte Pater, omnipotens æterne Deus:
per Christum Dominum nostrum.

Qui cum Apostolis suis in novissima cena convescens,
salutiferam crucis memoriam prosecuturus in sæcula,
Agnum sine macula se tibi obtulit,
perfectæ laudis munus acceptum.

Quo venerabili mysterio fideles tuos alendo sanctificas,
ut humanum genus, quod continet unus orbis,
una fides illuminet, caritas una coniungat.

Ad mensam igitur accedimus tam mirabilis sacramenti,
ut, gratiæ tuæ suavitate perfusi,
ad cælestis formæ imaginem transeamus.

PREFACE I OF THE MOST HOLY EUCHARIST

The Sacrifice and the Sacrament of Christ

It is truly right and just, our duty and our salvation,
always and everywhere to give you thanks,
Lord, holy Father, almighty and eternal God,
through Christ our Lord.

For he is the true and eternal Priest,
who instituted the pattern of an everlasting sacrifice,
and was the first to offer himself as the saving Victim,
commanding us to make this offering as his memorial.
As we eat his flesh that was sacrificed for us,
we are made strong,
and, as we drink his Blood that was poured out for us,
we are washed clean.

And so, with Angels and Archangels,
with Thrones and Dominions,
and with all the hosts and Powers of heaven,
we sing the hymn of your glory,
as without end we acclaim:

Holy, Holy, Holy Lord God of hosts. . .

PREFACE II OF THE MOST HOLY EUCHARIST

The fruits of the Most Holy Eucharist

It is truly right and just, our duty and our salvation,
always and everywhere to give you thanks,
Lord, holy Father, almighty and eternal God,
through Christ our Lord.

For at the Last Supper with his Apostles,
establishing for the ages to come the saving memorial of the Cross,
he offered himself to you as the unblemished Lamb,
the acceptable gift of perfect praise.

Nourishing your faithful by this sacred mystery,
you make them holy, so that the human race,
bounded by one world,
may be enlightened by one faith
and united by one bond of charity.

And so, we approach the table of this wondrous Sacrament,
so that, bathed in the sweetness of your grace,
we may pass over to the heavenly realities here foreshadowed.

Propter quod cælestia tibi atque terrestria
canticum novum concinunt adorando,
et nos cum omni exercitu Angelorum proclamamus,
sine fine dicentes:

Sanctus, Sanctus, Sanctus Dominus Deus Sabaoth. . .

PRÆFATIO I DE APOSTOLIS

De Apostolis pastoribus populi Dei

Vere dignum et iustum est, æquum et salutare,
nos tibi semper et ubique gratias agere:
Domine, sancte Pater, omnipotens æterne Deus:

Qui gregem tuum, Pastor æterne, non deseris,
sed per beatos Apostolos continua protectione custodis,
ut iisdem rectoribus gubernetur,
quos Filii tui vicarios eidem contulisti præesse pastores.

Et ideo cum Angelis et Archangelis,
cum Thronis et Dominationibus,
cumque omni militia cælestis exercitus,
hymnum gloriæ tuæ canimus,
sine fine dicentes:

Sanctus, Sanctus, Sanctus Dominus Deus Sabaoth. . .

PRÆFATIO II DE APOSTOLIS

De apostolico fundamento et testimonio

Vere dignum et iustum est, æquum et salutare,
nos tibi semper et ubique gratias agere:
Domine, sancte Pater, omnipotens æterne Deus:
per Christum Dominum nostrum.

Quoniam Ecclesiam tuam
in apostolicis tribuisti consistere fundamentis,
ut signum sanctitatis tuæ in terris maneret ipsa perpetuum,
et cælestia præberet cunctis hominibus documenta.

Quapropter nunc et usque in sæculum
cum omni militia Angelorum
devota tibi mente concinimus,
clamantes atque dicentes:

Sanctus, Sanctus, Sanctus Dominus Deus Sabaoth. . .

Therefore, all creatures of heaven and earth
sing a new song in adoration,
and we, with all the host of Angels,
cry out, and without end we acclaim:

Holy, Holy, Holy Lord God of hosts. . .

PREFACE I OF APOSTLES

The Apostles, shepherds of God's people

It is truly right and just, our duty and our salvation,
always and everywhere to give you thanks,
Lord, holy Father, almighty and eternal God.

For you, eternal Shepherd, do not desert your flock,
but through the blessed Apostles
watch over it and protect it always,
so that it may be governed
by those you have appointed shepherds
to lead it in the name of your Son.

And so, with Angels and Archangels,
with Thrones and Dominions,
and with all the hosts and Powers of heaven,
we sing the hymn of your glory,
as without end we acclaim:

Holy, Holy, Holy Lord God of hosts. . .

PREFACE II OF APOSTLES

The apostolic foundation and witness

It is truly right and just, our duty and our salvation,
always and everywhere to give you thanks,
Lord, holy Father, almighty and eternal God,
through Christ our Lord.

For you have built your Church
to stand firm on apostolic foundations,
to be a lasting sign of your holiness on earth
and offer all humanity your heavenly teaching.

Therefore, now and for ages unending,
with all the host of Angels,
we sing to you with all our hearts,
crying out as we acclaim:

Holy, Holy, Holy Lord God of hosts. . .

PRÆFATIO I DE SANCTIS MARTYRIBUS
De signo et exemplo martyrii

Vere dignum et iustum est, æquum et salutare,
nos tibi semper et ubique gratias agere:
Domine, sancte Pater, omnipotens æterne Deus:

Quoniam beati martyris N. pro confessione nominis tui,
ad imitationem Christi,
sanguis effusus tua mirabilia manifestat,
quibus perficis in fragilitate virtutem,
et vires infirmas ad testimonium roboras,
per Christum Dominum nostrum.

Et ideo, cum cælorum Virtutibus,
in terris te iugiter celebramus,
maiestati tuæ sine fine clamantes:

Sanctus, Sanctus, Sanctus Dominus Deus Sabaoth. . .

PRÆFATIO II DE SANCTIS MARTYRIBUS
De mirabilibus Dei in martyrum victoria

Vere dignum et iustum est, æquum et salutare,
nos tibi semper et ubique gratias agere:
Domine, sancte Pater, omnipotens æterne Deus:

Quoniam tu magnificaris in tuorum laude Sanctorum,
et quidquid ad eorum pertinet passionem,
tuæ sunt opera miranda potentiæ:
qui huius fidei tribuis clementer ardorem,
qui suggeris perseverantiæ firmitatem,
qui largiris in agone victoriam,
per Christum Dominum nostrum.

Propter quod cælestia tibi atque terrestria
canticum novum concinunt adorando,
et nos cum omni exercitu Angelorum
proclamamus, sine fine dicentes:
Sanctus, Sanctus, Sanctus Dominus Deus Sabaoth. . .

PREFACE I OF HOLY MARTYRS

The sign and example of martyrdom

It is truly right and just, our duty and our salvation,
always and everywhere to give you thanks,
Lord, holy Father, almighty and eternal God.

For the blood of your blessed Martyr N.,
poured out like Christ's to glorify your name,
shows forth your marvellous works,
by which in our weakness you perfect your power
and on the feeble bestow strength to bear you witness,
through Christ our Lord.

And so, with the Powers of heaven,
we worship you constantly on earth,
and before your majesty
without end we acclaim:

Holy, Holy, Holy Lord God of hosts. . .

PREFACE II OF HOLY MARTYRS

The wonders of God in the victory of the Martyrs

It is truly right and just, our duty and our salvation,
always and everywhere to give you thanks,
Lord, holy Father, almighty and eternal God.

For you are glorified when your Saints are praised;
their very sufferings are but wonders of your might:
in your mercy you give ardour to their faith,
to their endurance you grant firm resolve,
and in their struggle the victory is yours,
through Christ our Lord.

Therefore, all creatures of heaven and earth
sing a new song in adoration,
and we, with all the host of Angels,
cry out, and without end we acclaim:

Holy, Holy, Holy Lord God of hosts. . .

PRÆFATIO I DE DEFUNCTIS

De spe resurrectionis in Christo

Vere dignum et iustum est, æquum et salutare,
nos tibi semper et ubique gratias agere:
Domine, sancte Pater, omnipotens æterne Deus:
per Christum Dominum nostrum.

In quo nobis spes beatæ resurrectionis effulsit,
ut, quos contristat certa moriendi condicio,
eosdem consoletur futuræ immortalitatis promissio.
Tuis enim fidelibus, Domine, vita mutatur, non tollitur,
et, dissoluta terrestris huius incolatus domo,
æterna in cælis habitatio comparatur.

Et ideo cum Angelis et Archangelis,
cum Thronis et Dominationibus,
cumque omni militia cælestis exercitus,
hymnum gloriæ tuæ canimus,
sine fine dicentes:

Sanctus, Sanctus, Sanctus Dominus Deus Sabaoth. . .

PRÆFATIO II DE DEFUNCTIS

Christus mortuus est pro vita nostra

Vere dignum et iustum est, æquum et salutare,
nos tibi semper et ubique gratias agere:
Domine, sancte Pater, omnipotens æterne Deus:
per Christum Dominum nostrum.

Ipse enim mortem unus accepit,
ne omnes nos moreremur;
immo unus mori dignatus est,
ut omnes tibi perpetuo viveremus.

Et ideo, choris angelicis sociati,
te laudamus in gaudio confitentes:

Sanctus, Sanctus, Sanctus Dominus Deus Sabaoth. . .

PREFACE I FOR THE DEAD

The hope of resurrection in Christ

It is truly right and just, our duty and our salvation,
always and everywhere to give you thanks,
Lord, holy Father, almighty and eternal God,
through Christ our Lord.

In him the hope of blessed resurrection has dawned,
that those saddened by the certainty of dying
might be consoled by the promise of immortality to come.
Indeed for your faithful, Lord,
life is changed not ended,
and, when this earthly dwelling turns to dust,
an eternal dwelling is made ready for them in heaven.

And so, with Angels and Archangels,
with Thrones and Dominions,
and with all the hosts and Powers of heaven,
we sing the hymn of your glory,
as without end we acclaim:

Holy, Holy, Holy Lord God of hosts. . .

PREFACE II FOR THE DEAD

Christ died so that we might live

It is truly right and just, our duty and our salvation,
always and everywhere to give you thanks,
Lord, holy Father, almighty and eternal God,
through Christ our Lord.

For as one alone he accepted death,
so that we might all escape from dying;
as one man he chose to die,
so that in your sight we all might live for ever.

And so, in company with the choirs of Angels,
we praise you, and with joy we proclaim:

Holy, Holy, Holy Lord God of hosts. . .

PRÆFATIO III DE DEFUNCTIS

Christus, salus et vita

Vere dignum et iustum est, æquum et salutare,
nos tibi semper et ubique gratias agere:
Domine, sancte Pater, omnipotens æterne Deus:
per Christum Dominum nostrum:

Qui est salus mundi, vita hominum, resurrectio mortuorum.

Per quem maiestatem tuam adorat exercitus Angelorum,
ante conspectum tuum in æternitate lætantium.
Cum quibus et nostras voces ut admitti iubeas, deprecamur,
socia exsultatione dicentes:

Sanctus, Sanctus, Sanctus Dominus Deus Sabaoth. . .

PRÆFATIO IV DE DEFUNCTIS

De vita terrena ad gloriam cælestem

Vere dignum et iustum est, æquum et salutare,
nos tibi semper et ubique gratias agere:
Domine, sancte Pater, omnipotens æterne Deus:

Cuius imperio nascimur, cuius arbitrio regimur,
cuius præcepto in terra, de qua sumpti sumus,
peccati lege absolvimur.
Et, qui per mortem Filii tui redempti sumus,
ad ipsius resurrectionis gloriam
tuo nutu excitamur.

Et ideo, cum Angelorum atque Sanctorum turba,
hymnum laudis tibi canimus, sine fine dicentes:

Sanctus, Sanctus, Sanctus Dominus Deus Sabaoth. . .

PREFACE III FOR THE DEAD

Christ, the salvation and the life

It is truly right and just, our duty and our salvation,
always and everywhere to give you thanks,
Lord, holy Father, almighty and eternal God,
through Christ our Lord.

For he is the salvation of the world,
the life of the human race,
the resurrection of the dead.

Through him the host of Angels adores your majesty
and rejoices in your presence for ever.
May our voices, we pray, join with theirs
in one chorus of exultant praise, as we acclaim:

Holy, Holy, Holy Lord God of hosts. . .

PREFACE IV FOR THE DEAD

From earthly life to heavenly glory

It is truly right and just, our duty and our salvation,
always and everywhere to give you thanks,
Lord, holy Father, almighty and eternal God.

For it is at your summons that we come to birth,
by your will that we are governed,
and at your command that we return,
on account of sin,
to that earth from which we came.

And when you give the sign,
we who have been redeemed by the Death of your Son,
shall be raised up to the glory of his Resurrection.

And so, with the company of Angels and Saints,
we sing the hymn of your praise,
as without end we acclaim:

Holy, Holy, Holy Lord God of hosts. . .

PRÆFATIO V DE DEFUNCTIS

De resurrectione nostra per victoriam Christi

Vere dignum et iustum est, æquum et salutare,
nos tibi semper et ubique gratias agere:
Domine, sancte Pater, omnipotens æterne Deus:

Quia, etsi nostri est meriti quod perimus,
tuæ tamen est pietatis et gratiæ
quod, pro peccato morte consumpti,
per Christi victoriam redempti,
cum ipso revocamur ad vitam.

Et ideo, cum cælorum Virtutibus,
in terris te iugiter celebramus,
maiestati tuæ sine fine clamantes:

Sanctus, Sanctus, Sanctus Dominus Deus Sabaoth. . .

PREFACE V FOR THE DEAD

Our resurrection through the victory of Christ

It is truly right and just, our duty and our salvation,
always and everywhere to give you thanks,
Lord, holy Father, almighty and eternal God.

For even though by our own fault we perish,
yet by your compassion and your grace,
when seized by death according to our sins,
we are redeemed through Christ's great victory,
and with him called back into life.

And so, with the Powers of heaven,
we worship you constantly on earth,
and before your majesty
without end we acclaim:

Holy, Holy, Holy Lord God of hosts. . .

EUCHARISTIC PRAYER I
(THE ROMAN CANON)

Pr. Te ígitur, clementíssime Pater,
per Iesum Christum, Fílium tuum,
Dóminum nostrum,
súpplices rogámus ac pétimus,
uti accépta hábeas
et benedícas ✠ hæc dona, hæc múnera,
hæc sancta sacrifícia illibáta,
in primis, quæ tibi offérimus
pro Ecclésia tua sancta cathólica:
quam pacificáre, custodíre, adunáre
et régere dignéris toto orbe terrárum:
una cum fámulo tuo Papa nostro N.
et Antístite nostro N.*
et ómnibus orthodóxis atque cathólicæ
et apostólicæ fídei cultóribus.

Commemoration of the Living.

Meménto, Dómine,
famulórum famularúmque tuárum N. et N.
et ómnium circumstántium,
quorum tibi fides cógnita est et nota devótio,
pro quibus tibi offérimus:
vel qui tibi ófferunt hoc sacrifícium laudis,
pro se suísque ómnibus:
pro redemptióne animárum suárum,
pro spe salútis et incolumitátis suæ:
tibíque reddunt vota sua
ætérno Deo, vivo et vero.

Within the Action

Communicántes,
et memóriam venerántes,
in primis gloriósæ semper Vírginis Maríæ,
Genetrícis Dei et Dómini nostri Iesu Christi:
† sed et béati Ioseph, eiúsdem Vírginis Sponsi,
et beatórum Apostolórum ac Mártyrum tuórum,
Petri et Pauli, Andréæ,
(Iacóbi, Ioánnis,
Thomæ, Iacóbi, Philíppi,

---

* Mention may be made here of the Coadjutor Bishop or Auxiliary Bishops.

EUCHARISTIC PRAYER I
(THE ROMAN CANON)

Pr. To you, therefore, most merciful Father,
we make humble prayer and petition
through Jesus Christ, your Son, our Lord:
that you accept
and bless ✠ these gifts, these offerings,
these holy and unblemished sacrifices,
which we offer you firstly
for your holy catholic Church.
Be pleased to grant her peace,
to guard, unite and govern her
throughout the whole world,
together with your servant N. our Pope
and N. our Bishop,*
and all those who, holding to the truth,
hand on the catholic and apostolic faith.

Commemoration of the Living.
Remember, Lord, your servants N. and N.
and all gathered here,
whose faith and devotion are known to you.
For them, we offer you this sacrifice of praise
or they offer it for themselves
and all who are dear to them:
for the redemption of their souls,
in hope of health and well-being,
and paying their homage to you,
the eternal God, living and true.

Within the Action
In communion with those whose memory we venerate,
especially the glorious ever-Virgin Mary,
Mother of our God and Lord, Jesus Christ,
† and blessed Joseph, her Spouse,
your blessed Apostles and Martyrs,
Peter and Paul, Andrew,
(James, John,
Thomas, James, Philip,

---

*Mention may be made here of the Coadjutor Bishop or Auxiliary Bishops.

Bartholomǽi, Matthǽi,
Simónis et Thaddǽi:
Lini, Cleti, Cleméntis, Xysti,
Cornélii, Cypriáni,
Lauréntii, Chrysógoni,
Ioánnis et Pauli,
Cosmæ et Damiáni)
et ómnium Sanctórum tuórum;
quorum méritis precibúsque concédas,
ut in ómnibus protectiónis tuæ muniámur auxílio.
(Per Christum Dóminum nostrum. Amen.)

PROPER FORMS OF THE COMMUNICANTES

On the Nativity of the Lord and throughout the Octave

> Communicántes,
> et (noctem sacratíssimam) diem sacratíssimum celebrántes,
> (qua) quo beátæ Maríæ intemeráta virgínitas
> huic mundo édidit Salvatórem:
> sed et memóriam venerántes,
> in primis eiúsdem gloriósæ semper Vírginis Maríæ,
> Genetrícis eiúsdem Dei et Dómini nostri Iesu Christi: †

On the Epiphany of the Lord

> Communicántes,
> et diem sacratíssimum celebrántes,
> quo Unigénitus tuus, in tua tecum glória coætérnus,
> in veritáte carnis nostræ visibíliter corporális appáruit:
> sed et memóriam venerántes,
> in primis gloriósæ semper Vírginis Maríæ,
> Genetrícis eiúsdem Dei et Dómini nostri Iesu Christi: †

From the Mass of the Easter Vigil until the Second Sunday of Easter

> Communicántes,
> et (noctem sacratíssimam) diem sacratíssimum celebrántes
> Resurrectiónis Dómini nostri Iesu Christi secúndum carnem:
> sed et memóriam venerántes,
> in primis gloriósæ semper Vírginis Maríæ,
> Genetrícis eiúsdem Dei et Dómini nostri Iesu Christi: †

Bartholomew, Matthew,
Simon and Jude;
Linus, Cletus, Clement, Sixtus,
Cornelius, Cyprian,
Lawrence, Chrysogonus,
John and Paul,
Cosmas and Damian)
and all your Saints;
we ask that through their merits and prayers,
in all things we may be defended
by your protecting help.
(Through Christ our Lord. Amen.)

PROPER FORMS OF THE COMMUNICANTES

On the Nativity of the Lord and throughout the Octave

Celebrating the most sacred night (day)
on which blessed Mary the immaculate Virgin
brought forth the Saviour for this world,
and in communion with those whose memory we venerate,
especially the glorious ever-Virgin Mary,
Mother of our God and Lord, Jesus Christ, †

On the Epiphany of the Lord

Celebrating the most sacred day
on which your Only Begotten Son,
eternal with you in your glory,
appeared in a human body, truly sharing our flesh,
and in communion with those whose memory we venerate,
especially the glorious ever-Virgin Mary,
Mother of our God and Lord, Jesus Christ, †

From the Mass of the Easter Vigil until the Second Sunday of Easter

Celebrating the most sacred night (day)
of the Resurrection of our Lord Jesus Christ in the flesh,
and in communion with those whose memory we venerate,
especially the glorious ever-Virgin Mary,
Mother of our God and Lord, Jesus Christ, †

On the Ascension of the Lord

> Communicántes,
> et diem sacratíssimum celebrántes,
> quo Dóminus noster, Unigénitus Fílius tuus,
> unítam sibi fragilitátis nostræ substántiam
> in glóriæ tuæ déxtera collocávit:
> sed et memóriam venerántes,
> in primis gloriósæ semper Vírginis Maríæ,
> Genetrícis eiúsdem Dei et Dómini nostri Iesu Christi: †

On Pentecost Sunday

> Communicántes,
> et diem sacratíssimum Pentecóstes celebrántes,
> quo Spíritus Sanctus
> Apóstolis in ígneis linguis appáruit:
> sed et memóriam venerántes,
> in primis gloriósæ semper Vírginis Maríæ,
> Genetrícis Dei et Dómini nostri Iesu Christi: †

Hanc ígitur oblatiónem servitútis nostræ,
sed et cunctæ famíliæ tuæ,
quǽsumus, Dómine, ut placátus accípias:
diésque nostros in tua pace dispónas,
atque ab ætérna damnatióne nos éripi
et in electórum tuórum iúbeas grege numerári.
(Per Christum Dóminum nostrum. Amen.)

From the Mass of the Easter Vigil until the Second Sunday of Easter

> Hanc ígitur oblatiónem servitútis nostræ,
> sed et cunctæ famíliæ tuæ,
> quam tibi offérimus
> pro his quoque, quos regeneráre dignátus es ex aqua et Spíritu Sancto,
> tríbuens eis remissiónem ómnium peccatórum,
> quǽsumus, Dómine, ut placátus accípias:
> diésque nostros in tua pace dispónas,
> atque ab ætérna damnatióne nos éripi
> et in electórum tuórum iúbeas grege numerári.
> (Per Christum Dóminum nostrum. Amen.)

On the Ascension of the Lord

Celebrating the most sacred day
on which your Only Begotten Son, our Lord,
placed at the right hand of your glory
our weak human nature,
which he had united to himself,
and in communion with those whose memory we venerate,
especially the glorious ever-Virgin Mary,
Mother of our God and Lord, Jesus Christ, †

On Pentecost Sunday

Celebrating the most sacred day of Pentecost,
on which the Holy Spirit
appeared to the Apostles in tongues of fire,
and in communion with those whose memory we venerate,
especially the glorious ever-Virgin Mary,
Mother of our God and Lord, Jesus Christ, †

Therefore, Lord, we pray:
graciously accept this oblation of our service,
that of your whole family;
order our days in your peace,
and command that we be delivered from eternal damnation
and counted among the flock of those you have chosen.
(Through Christ Our Lord. Amen.)

From the Mass of the Easter Vigil until the Second Sunday of Easter

Therefore, Lord, we pray:
graciously accept this oblation of our service,
that of your whole family,
which we make to you
also for those to whom you have been pleased to give
the new birth of water and the Holy Spirit,
granting them forgiveness of all their sins;
order our days in your peace,
and command that we be delivered from eternal damnation
and counted among the flock of those you have chosen.
(Through Christ our Lord. Amen.)

Quam oblatiónem tu, Deus, in ómnibus, quǽsumus,
benedíctam, adscríptam, ratam,
rationábilem, acceptabilémque fácere dignéris:
ut nobis Corpus et Sanguis fiat dilectíssimi Fílii tui,
Dómini nostri Iesu Christi.

Qui, prídie quam paterétur,
accépit panem in sanctas ac venerábiles manus suas,
et elevátis óculis in cælum
ad te Deum Patrem suum omnipoténtem,
tibi grátias agens benedíxit,
fregit,
dedítque discípulis suis, dicens:

ACCÍPITE ET MANDUCÁTE EX HOC OMNES:
HOC EST ENIM CORPUS MEUM,
QUOD PRO VOBIS TRADÉTUR.

Símili modo, postquam cenátum est,
accípiens et hunc præclárum cálicem
in sanctas ac venerábiles manus suas,
item tibi grátias agens benedíxit,
dedítque discípulis suis dicens:

ACCÍPITE ET BÍBITE EX EO OMNES:
HIC EST ENIM CALIX SÁNGUINIS MEI
NOVI ET ÆTÉRNI TESTAMÉNTI,
QUI PRO VOBIS ET PRO MULTIS EFFUNDÉTUR
IN REMISSIÓNEM PECCATÓRUM.
HOC FÁCITE IN MEAM COMMEMORATIÓNEM.

Be pleased, O God, we pray,
to bless, acknowledge,
and approve this offering in every respect;
make it spiritual and acceptable,
so that it may become for us
the Body and Blood of your most beloved Son,
our Lord Jesus Christ.

On the day before he was to suffer,
he took bread in his holy and venerable hands,
and with eyes raised to heaven
to you, O God, his almighty Father,
giving you thanks, he said the blessing,
broke the bread
and gave it to his disciples, saying:

TAKE THIS, ALL OF YOU, AND EAT OF IT,
FOR THIS IS MY BODY,
WHICH WILL BE GIVEN UP FOR YOU.

In a similar way, when supper was ended,
he took this precious chalice
in his holy and venerable hands,
and once more giving you thanks, he said the blessing
and gave the chalice to his disciples, saying:

TAKE THIS, ALL OF YOU, AND DRINK FROM IT,
FOR THIS IS THE CHALICE OF MY BLOOD,
THE BLOOD OF THE NEW AND ETERNAL COVENANT,
WHICH WILL BE POURED OUT FOR YOU AND FOR MANY
FOR THE FORGIVENESS OF SINS.

DO THIS IN MEMORY OF ME.

Pr. Mystérium fídei.

The people continue, acclaiming one of the following:

Mortem tu-am annunti-ámus, Dómi-ne,   et tu-am resurrecti-ó-

nem confi-témur, do-nec vé-ni-as.

1. **Mortem tuam annuntiámus, Dómine,**
et tuam resurrectiónem confitémur, donec vénias.

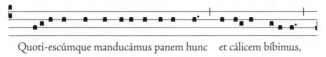

Quoti-escúmque manducámus panem hunc   et cálicem bíbimus,

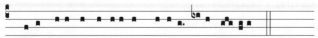

mortem tu-am annunti-ámus, Dómine, donec vé- ni-as.

2. **Quotiescúmque manducámus panem hunc**
et cálicem bíbimus,
mortem tuam annuntiámus, Dómine, donec vénias.

Salvátor mundi, salva nos, qui per crucem et resurrecti-ónem tu-am

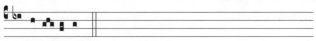

li-be-rá- sti nos.

3. **Salvátor mundi, salva nos,**
qui per crucem et resurrectiónem tuam liberásti nos.

Pr. The mystery of faith.

The people continue, acclaiming one of the following:

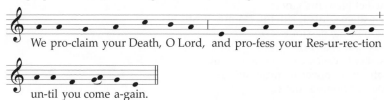

We pro-claim your Death, O Lord, and pro-fess your Res-ur-rec-tion un-til you come a-gain.

1. **We proclaim your Death, O Lord,**
and profess your Resurrection
until you come again.

When we eat this Bread and drink this Cup, we pro-claim your Death, O Lord, un-til you come a-gain.

2. **When we eat this Bread and drink this Cup,**
we proclaim your Death, O Lord,
until you come again.

Save us, Sav-iour of the world, for by your Cross and Res-ur-rec-tion you have set us free.

3. **Save us, Saviour of the world,**
for by your Cross and Resurrection
you have set us free.

Only in Ireland: 4. **My Lord and my God.**

Pr. Unde et mémores, Dómine,
nos servi tui,
sed et plebs tua sancta,
eiúsdem Christi, Fílii tui, Dómini nostri,
tam beátæ passiónis,
necnon et ab ínferis resurrectiónis,
sed et in cælos gloriósæ ascensiónis:
offérimus præcláræ maiestáti tuæ
de tuis donis ac datis
hóstiam puram,
hóstiam sanctam,
hóstiam immaculátam,
Panem sanctum vitæ ætérnæ
et Cálicem salútis perpétuæ.

Supra quæ propítio ac seréno vultu
respícere dignéris:
et accépta habére,
sícuti accépta habére dignátus es
múnera púeri tui iusti Abel,
et sacrifícium Patriárchæ nostri Abrahæ,
et quod tibi óbtulit summus sacérdos tuus Melchísedech,
sanctum sacrifícium, immaculátam hóstiam.

Súpplices te rogámus, omnípotens Deus:
iube hæc perférri per manus sancti Angeli tui
in sublíme altáre tuum,
in conspéctu divínæ maiestátis tuæ;
ut, quotquot ex hac altáris participatióne
sacrosánctum Fílii tui Corpus et Sánguinem sumpsérimus,
omni benedictióne cælésti et grátia repleámur
(Per Christum Dóminum nostrum. Amen.)

Commemoration of the Dead.

Meménto étiam, Dómine, famulórum famularúmque tuárum N. et N.,
qui nos præcessérunt cum signo fídei,
et dórmiunt in somno pacis.
Ipsis, Dómine, et ómnibus in Christo quiescéntibus,
locum refrigérii, lucis et pacis,
ut indúlgeas, deprecámur.
(Per Christum Dóminum nostrum. Amen.)

Nobis quoque peccatóribus fámulis tuis,
de multitúdine miseratiónum tuárum sperántibus,

Pr. Therefore, O Lord,
as we celebrate the memorial of the blessed Passion,
the Resurrection from the dead,
and the glorious Ascension into heaven
of Christ, your Son, our Lord,
we, your servants and your holy people,
offer to your glorious majesty
from the gifts that you have given us,
this pure victim,
this holy victim,
this spotless victim,
the holy Bread of eternal life
and the Chalice of everlasting salvation.

Be pleased to look upon these offerings
with a serene and kindly countenance,
and to accept them,
as once you were pleased to accept
the gifts of your servant Abel the just,
the sacrifice of Abraham, our father in faith,
and the offering of your high priest Melchizedek,
a holy sacrifice, a spotless victim.

In humble prayer we ask you, almighty God:
command that these gifts be borne
by the hands of your holy Angel
to your altar on high
in the sight of your divine majesty,
so that all of us, who through this participation at the altar
receive the most holy Body and Blood of your Son,
may be filled with every grace and heavenly blessing.
(Through Christ our Lord. Amen.)

Commemoration of the Dead.

Remember also, Lord, your servants N. and N.,
who have gone before us with the sign of faith
and rest in the sleep of peace.
Grant them, O Lord, we pray,
and all who sleep in Christ,
a place of refreshment, light and peace.
(Through Christ our Lord. Amen.)

To us, also, your servants, who, though sinners,
hope in your abundant mercies,

partem áliquam et societátem donáre dignéris
cum tuis sanctis Apóstolis et Martýribus:
cum Ioánne, Stéphano,
Matthía, Bárnaba,
(Ignátio, Alexándro,
Marcellíno, Petro,
Felicitáte, Perpétua,
Agatha, Lúcia,
Agnéte, Cæcília, Anastásia)
et ómnibus Sanctis tuis:
intra quorum nos consórtium,
non æstimátor mériti,
sed véniæ, quæsumus, largítor admítte.
Per Christum Dóminum nostrum.

Per quem hæc ómnia, Dómine,
semper bona creas, sanctíficas, vivíficas, benedícis,
et præstas nobis.

Pr. Per ipsum, et cum ipso, et in ipso,
est tibi Deo Patri omnipoténti,
in unitáte Spíritus Sancti,
omnis honor et glória
per ómnia sǽcula sæculórum.

A-men.
R. **Amen.**

Then follows the Communion Rite, p.120.

EUCHARISTIC PRAYER II

Pr. Dóminus vóbiscum.
R. **Et cum spíritu tuo.**
Pr. Sursum corda.
R. **Habémus ad Dóminum.**
Pr. Grátias agámus Dómino Deo nostro.
R. **Dignum et iustum est.**
Pr. Vere dignum et iustum est, æquum et salutáre, nos tibi, sancte Pater,

gracIously grant some share
and fellowship with your holy Apostles and Martyrs:
with John the Baptist, Stephen,
Matthias, Barnabas,
(Ignatius, Alexander,
Marcellinus, Peter,
Felicity, Perpetua,
Agatha, Lucy,
Agnes, Cecilia, Anastasia)
and all your Saints;
admit us, we beseech you,
into their company,
not weighing our merits,
but granting us your pardon,
through Christ our Lord.

Through whom
you continue to make all these good things, O Lord;
you sanctify them, fill them with life,
bless them, and bestow them upon us.

Pr. Through him, and with him, and in him,
O God, almighty Father,
in the unity of the Holy Spirit,
all glory and honour is yours,
for ever and ever.

A-men.

R. **Amen.**

Then follows the Communion Rite, p.121.

EUCHARISTIC PRAYER II

Pr. The Lord be with you.
R. **And with your spirit.**
Pr. Lift up your hearts.
R. **We lift them up to the Lord.**
Pr. Let us give thanks to the Lord our God.
R. **It is right and just.**
Pr. It is truly right and just, our duty and our salvation,

semper et ubíque grátias ágere
per Fílium dilectiónis tuæ Iesum Christum,
Verbum tuum per quod cuncta fecísti:
quem misísti nobis Salvatórem et Redemptórem,
incarnátum de Spíritu Sancto et ex Vírgine natum.

Qui voluntátem tuam adímplens
et pópulum tibi sanctum acquírens
exténdit manus cum paterétur,
ut mortem sólveret et resurrectiónem manifestáret.

Et ídeo cum Angelis et ómnibus Sanctis
glóriam tuam prædicámus, una voce dicéntes:

The people sing or say aloud the Sanctus.

anc-tus, * Sanc-tus, Sanc-tus Dó-mi-nus De-us Sá-ba-oth. Ple-ni
sunt cæ-li et ter-ra gló-ri-a tu-a. Ho-sán-na in ex-cél-sis. Be-ne-díc-
tus qui ve-nit in nómine Dómini. Ho-sán-na in excél-sis.

Sanctus, Sanctus, Sanctus Dóminus Deus Sábaoth.
Pleni sunt cæli et terra glória tua.
Hosánna in excélsis.
Benedíctus qui venit in nómine Dómini.
Hosánna in excélsis.

Pr. Vere Sanctus es, Dómine, fons omnis sanctitátis.

Hæc ergo dona, quæsumus,
Spíritus tui rore sanctífica,
ut nobis Corpus et ✠ Sanguis fiant
Dómini nostri Iesu Christi.

always and everywhere to give you thanks, Father most holy,
through your beloved Son, Jesus Christ,
your Word through whom you made all things,
whom you sent as our Saviour and Redeemer,
incarnate by the Holy Spirit and born of the Virgin.

Fulfilling your will and gaining for you a holy people,
he stretched out his hands as he endured his Passion,
so as to break the bonds of death and manifest the resurrection.

And so, with the Angels and all the Saints
we declare your glory,
as with one voice we acclaim:

The people sing or say aloud the Sanctus.

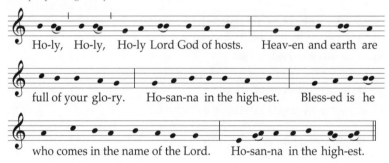

Ho-ly, Ho-ly, Ho-ly Lord God of hosts. Heav-en and earth are full of your glo-ry. Ho-san-na in the high-est. Bless-ed is he who comes in the name of the Lord. Ho-san-na in the high-est.

Holy, Holy, Holy Lord God of hosts.
Heaven and earth are full of your glory.
Hosanna in the highest.
Blessed is he who comes in the name of the Lord.
Hosanna in the highest.

Pr. You are indeed Holy, O Lord,
the fount of all holiness.

Make holy, therefore, these gifts, we pray,
by sending down your Spirit upon them like the dewfall,
so that they may become for us
the Body and ✠ Blood of our Lord Jesus Christ.

Qui cum Passióni voluntárie traderétur,
accépit panem et grátias agens fregit,
dedítque discípulis suis, dicens:

Accípite et manducáte ex hoc omnes:
hoc est enim Corpus meum,
quod pro vobis tradétur.

Símili modo, postquam cenátum est,
accípiens et cálicem,
íterum grátias agens dedit discípulis suis, dicens:

Accípite et bíbite ex eo omnes:
hic est enim calix Sánguinis mei
novi et Ætérni testaménti,
qui pro vobis et pro multis effundétur
in remissiónem peccatórum.
Hoc fácite in meam commemoratiónem.

Pr. Mystérium fídei.

The people continue, acclaiming one of the following:

Mortem tu-am annunti-ámus, Dómi-ne, et tu-am resurrecti-ó-

nem confi-témur, do-nec vé-ni-as.

1. **Mortem tuam annuntiámus, Dómine,
et tuam resurrectiónem confitémur, donec vénias.**

At the time he was betrayed
and entered willingly into his Passion,
he took bread and, giving thanks, broke it,
and gave it to his disciples, saying:

TAKE THIS, ALL OF YOU, AND EAT OF IT,
FOR THIS IS MY BODY,
WHICH WILL BE GIVEN UP FOR YOU.

In a similar way, when supper was ended,
he took the chalice
and, once more giving thanks,
he gave it to his disciples, saying:

TAKE THIS, ALL OF YOU, AND DRINK FROM IT,
FOR THIS IS THE CHALICE OF MY BLOOD,
THE BLOOD OF THE NEW AND ETERNAL COVENANT,
WHICH WILL BE POURED OUT FOR YOU AND FOR MANY
FOR THE FORGIVENESS OF SINS.
DO THIS IN MEMORY OF ME.

Pr. The mystery of faith.

The people continue, acclaiming one of the following:

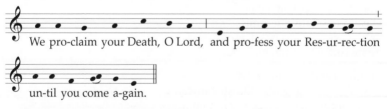

We pro-claim your Death, O Lord, and pro-fess your Res-ur-rec-tion
un-til you come a-gain.

1. We proclaim your Death, O Lord,
and profess your Resurrection
until you come again.

Quoti-escúmque manducámus panem hunc   et cálicem bíbimus,

mortem tu-am annunti-ámus, Dómine,   donec vé- ni-as.

2. **Quotiescúmque manducámus panem hunc
et cálicem bíbimus,
mortem tuam annuntiámus, Dómine, donec vénias.**

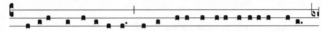

Salvátor mundi, salva nos, qui per crucem et resurrecti-ónem tu-am

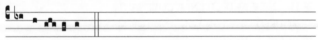

li-be-rá- sti nos.

3. **Salvátor mundi, salva nos,
qui per crucem et resurrectiónem tuam liberásti nos.**

Pr. Mémores ígitur mortis et resurrectiónis eius,
tibi, Dómine, panem vitæ
et cálicem salútis offérimus,
grátias agéntes quia nos dignos habuísti
astáre coram te et tibi ministráre.

Et súpplices deprecámur
ut Córporis et Sánguinis Christi partícipes
a Spíritu Sancto congregémur in unum.

Recordáre, Dómine, Ecclésiæ tuæ toto orbe diffúsæ,
ut eam in caritáte perfícias
una cum Papa nostro N. et Epíscopo nostro N.*
et univérso clero.

---

* Mention may be made here of the Coadjutor Bishop or Auxiliary Bishops.

When we eat this Bread and drink this Cup, we pro-claim your Death, O Lord, un-til you come a-gain.

**2. When we eat this Bread and drink this Cup,
we proclaim your Death, O Lord,
until you come again.**

Save us, Sav-iour of the world, for by your Cross and Res-ur-rec-tion you have set us free.

**3. Save us, Saviour of the world,
for by your Cross and Resurrection
you have set us free.**

Only in Ireland: **4. My Lord and my God.**

Pr. Therefore, as we celebrate
the memorial of his Death and Resurrection,
we offer you, Lord,
the Bread of life and the Chalice of salvation,
giving thanks that you have held us worthy
to be in your presence and minister to you.

Humbly we pray
that, partaking of the Body and Blood of Christ,
we may be gathered into one by the Holy Spirit.

Remember, Lord, your Church,
spread throughout the world,
and bring her to the fullness of charity,
together with N. our Pope and N. our Bishop*
and all the clergy.

---

* Mention may be made here of the Coadjutor Bishop or Auxiliary Bishops.

In Masses for the Dead, the following may be added:

Meménto fámuli tui (fámulæ tuæ) N.,
quem (quam) (hódie) ad te ex hoc mundo vocásti.
Concéde, ut, qui (quæ) complantátus (complantáta) fuit
    similitúdini mortis Fílii tui,
simul fiat et resurrectiónis ipsíus.

Meménto étiam fratrum nostrórum,
qui in spe resurrectiónis dormiérunt,
omniúmque in tua miseratióne defunctórum,
et eos in lumen vultus tui admítte.
Omnium nostrum, quǽsumus, miserére,
ut cum beáta Dei Genetríce Vírgine María,
beáto Ioseph, eius Sponso,
beátis Apostólis et ómnibus Sanctis,
qui tibi a sǽculo placuérunt,
ætérnæ vitæ mereámur esse consórtes,
et te laudémus et glorificémus
per Fílium tuum Iesum Christum.

Per ipsum, et cum ipso, et in ipso,
est tibi Deo Patri omnipoténti,
in unitáte Spíritus Sancti,
omnis honor et glória
per ómnia sǽcula sæculórum.

A-men.
R.   **Amen.**

Then follows the Communion Rite, p.120.

EUCHARISTIC PRAYER III

Pr. Vere Sanctus es, Dómine,
et mérito te laudat omnis a te cóndita creatúra,
quia per Fílium tuum,
Dóminum nostrum Iesum Christum,
Spíritus Sancti operánte virtúte,
vivíficas et sanctíficas univérsa,
et pópulum tibi congregáre non désinis,

In Masses for the Dead, the following may be added:

Remember your servant N.,
whom you have called (today)
from this world to yourself.
Grant that he (she) who was united with your Son in a death like his,
may also be one with him in his Resurrection.

Remember also our brothers and sisters
who have fallen asleep in the hope of the resurrection,
and all who have died in your mercy:
welcome them into the light of your face.
Have mercy on us all, we pray,
that with the Blessed Virgin Mary, Mother of God,
with blessed Joseph, her Spouse,
with the blessed Apostles,
and all the Saints who have pleased you throughout the ages,
we may merit to be coheirs to eternal life,
and may praise and glorify you
through your Son, Jesus Christ.

Through him, and with him, and in him,
O God, almighty Father,
in the unity of the Holy Spirit,
all glory and honour is yours,
for ever and ever.

A-men.

R. **Amen.**

Then follows the Communion Rite, p.121.

EUCHARISTIC PRAYER III

Pr. You are indeed Holy, O Lord,
and all you have created
rightly gives you praise,
for through your Son our Lord Jesus Christ,
by the power and working of the Holy Spirit,
you give life to all things and make them holy,
and you never cease to gather a people to yourself,

ut a solis ortu usque ad occásum
oblátio munda offerátur nómini tuo.

Súpplices ergo te, Dómine, deprecámur,
ut hæc múnera, quæ tibi sacránda detúlimus,
eódem Spíritu sanctificáre dignéris,
ut Corpus et ✠ Sanguis fiant
Fílii tui Dómini nostri Iesu Christi,
cuius mandáto hæc mystéria celebrámus.

Ipse enim in qua nocte tradebátur
accépit panem
et tibi grátias agens benedíxit,
fregit, dedítque discípulis suis, dicens:

ACCÍPITE ET MANDUCÁTE EX HOC OMNES:
HOC EST ENIM CORPUS MEUM,
QUOD PRO VOBIS TRADÉTUR.

Símili modo, postquam cenátum est,
accípiens cálicem,
et tibi grátias agens benedíxit,
dedítque discípulis suis, dicens:

ACCÍPITE ET BÍBITE EX EO OMNES:
HIC EST ENIM CALIX SÁNGUINIS MEI
NOVI ET ÆTÉRNI TESTAMÉNTI,
QUI PRO VOBIS ET PRO MULTIS EFFUNDÉTUR
IN REMISSIÓNEM PECCATÓRUM.
HOC FÁCITE IN MEAM COMMEMORATIÓNEM.

so that from the rising of the sun to its setting
a pure sacrifice may be offered to your name.

Therefore, O Lord, we humbly implore you:
by the same Spirit graciously make holy
these gifts we have brought to you for consecration,
that they may become the Body and ✠ Blood
of your Son our Lord Jesus Christ,
at whose command we celebrate these mysteries.

For on the night he was betrayed
he himself took bread,
and, giving you thanks, he said the blessing,
broke the bread and gave it to his disciples, saying:

TAKE THIS, ALL OF YOU, AND EAT OF IT,
FOR THIS IS MY BODY,
WHICH WILL BE GIVEN UP FOR YOU.

In a similar way, when supper was ended,
he took the chalice,
and, giving you thanks, he said the blessing,
and gave the chalice to his disciples, saying:

TAKE THIS, ALL OF YOU, AND DRINK FROM IT,
FOR THIS IS THE CHALICE OF MY BLOOD,
THE BLOOD OF THE NEW AND ETERNAL COVENANT,
WHICH WILL BE POURED OUT FOR YOU AND FOR MANY
FOR THE FORGIVENESS OF SINS.
DO THIS IN MEMORY OF ME.

Pr. Mystérium fídei.

The people continue, acclaiming one of the following:

Mortem tu-am annunti-ámus, Dómi-ne,   et tu-am resurrecti-ó-

nem confi-témur, do-nec vé-ni-as.

1. Mortem tuam annuntiámus, Dómine,
et tuam resurrectiónem confitémur, donec vénias.

Quoti-escúmque manducámus panem hunc   et cálicem bíbimus,

mortem tu-am annunti-ámus, Dómine, donec vé- ni-as.

2. Quotiescúmque manducámus panem hunc
et cálicem bíbimus,
mortem tuam annuntiámus, Dómine, donec vénias.

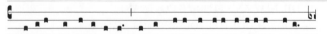

Salvátor mundi, salva nos, qui per crucem et resurrecti-ónem tu-am

li-be-rá- sti nos.

3. Salvátor mundi, salva nos,
qui per crucem et resurrectiónem tuam liberásti nos.

Pr. The mystery of faith.

The people continue, acclaiming one of the following:

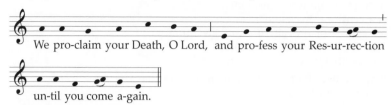

We pro-claim your Death, O Lord, and pro-fess your Res-ur-rec-tion un-til you come a-gain.

**1. We proclaim your Death, O Lord,
and profess your Resurrection
until you come again.**

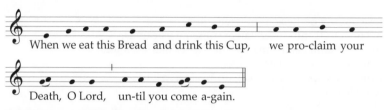

When we eat this Bread and drink this Cup, we pro-claim your Death, O Lord, un-til you come a-gain.

**2. When we eat this Bread and drink this Cup,
we proclaim your Death, O Lord,
until you come again.**

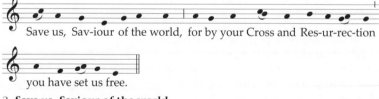

Save us, Sav-iour of the world, for by your Cross and Res-ur-rec-tion you have set us free.

**3. Save us, Saviour of the world,
for by your Cross and Resurrection
you have set us free.**

Only in Ireland: **4. My Lord and my God.**

Pr. Mémores ígitur, Dómine,
eiúsdem Fílii tui salutíferæ passiónis
necnon mirábilis resurrectiónis
et ascensiónis in cælum,
sed et præstolántes álterum eius advéntum,
offérimus tibi, grátias reféntes,
hoc sacrifícium vivum et sanctum.

Réspice, quǽsumus, in oblatiónem Ecclésiæ tuæ
et, agnóscens Hóstiam,
cuius volúisti immolatióne placári,
concéde, ut qui Córpore et Sánguine Fílii tui refícimur,
Spíritu eius Sancto repléti,
unum corpus et unus spíritus inveniámur in Christo.

Ipse nos tibi perfíciat munus ætérnum,
ut cum eléctis tuis hereditátem cónsequi valeámus,
in primis cum beátissima Vírgine, Dei Genetríce, María,
cum beáto Ioseph, eius Sponso,
cum beátis Apóstolis tuis et gloriósis Martýribus
(cum Sancto N.: the saint of the day or Patron Saint)
et ómnibus Sanctis,
quorum intercessióne
perpétuo apud te confídimus adiuvári.

Hæc Hóstia nostræ reconciliatiónis profíciat,
quǽsumus, Dómine,
ad totíus mundi pacem atque salútem.
Ecclésiam tuam, peregrinántem in terra,
in fide et caritáte firmáre dignéris
cum fámulo tuo Papa nostro N. et Epíscopo nostro N.[*],
cum episcopáli órdine et univérso clero
et omni pópulo acquisitiónis tuæ.

Votis huius famíliæ, quam tibi astáre voluísti,
adésto propítius.
Omnes fílios tuos ubíque dispérsos
tibi, clemens Pater, miserátus coniúnge.

---

[*] Mention may be made here of the Coadjutor Bishop or Auxiliary Bishops.

Pr. Therefore, O Lord, as we celebrate the memorial
of the saving Passion of your Son,
his wondrous Resurrection
and Ascension into heaven,
and as we look forward to his second coming,
we offer you in thanksgiving
this holy and living sacrifice.

Look, we pray, upon the oblation of your Church
and, recognising the sacrificial Victim by whose death
you willed to reconcile us to yourself,
grant that we, who are nourished
by the Body and Blood of your Son
and filled with his Holy Spirit,
may become one body, one spirit in Christ.

May he make of us
an eternal offering to you,
so that we may obtain an inheritance with your elect,
especially with the most Blessed Virgin Mary, Mother of God,
with blessed Joseph, her Spouse,
with your blessed Apostles and glorious Martyrs
(with Saint N.: the Saint of the day or Patron Saint)
and with all the Saints,
on whose constant intercession in your presence
we rely for unfailing help.

May this Sacrifice of our reconciliation,
we pray, O Lord,
advance the peace and salvation of all the world.
Be pleased to confirm in faith and charity
your pilgrim Church on earth,
with your servant N. our Pope and N. our Bishop*,
the Order of Bishops, all the clergy,
and the entire people you have gained for your own.

Listen graciously to the prayers of this family,
whom you have summoned before you:
in your compassion, O merciful Father,
gather to yourself all your children
scattered throughout the world.

---

*Mention may be made here of the Coadjutor Bishop or Auxiliary Bishops.

† Fratres nostros defúnctos
et omnes qui, tibi placéntes, ex hoc sǽculo transiérunt,
in regnum tuum benígnus admítte,
ubi fore sperámus,
ut simul glória tua perénniter satiémur,
per Christum Dóminum nostrum,
per quem mundo bona cuncta largíris. †

Per ipsum, et cum ipso, et in ipso,
est tibi Deo Patri omnipoténti,
in unitáte Spíritus Sancti,
omnis honor et glória
per ómnia sǽcula sæculórum.

A-men.

R.   **Amen.**

Then follows the Communion Rite, p.120.

When this Eucharistic Prayer is used in Masses for the Dead, the following may be said:

† Meménto fámuli tui (fámulæ tuæ) N.,
quem (quam) (hódie) ad te ex hoc mundo vocásti.
Concéde, ut, qui (quæ) complantátus (complantáta)
      fuit similitúdini mortis Fílii tui,
simul fiat et resurrectiónis ipsíus,
quando mórtuos suscitábit in carne de terra
et corpus humilitátis nostræ
configurábit córpori claritátis suæ.
Sed et fratres nostros defúnctos,
et omnes qui, tibi placéntes, ex hoc sǽculo transiérunt,
in regnum tuum benígnus admítte,
ubi fore sperámus,
ut simul glória tua perénniter satiémur,
quando omnem lácrimam abstérges ab óculis nostris,
quia te, sícuti es, Deum nostrum vidéntes,
tibi símiles érimus cuncta per sǽcula,
et te sine fine laudábimus,
per Christum Dóminum nostrum,
per quem mundo bona cuncta largíris. †

† To our departed brothers and sisters
and to all who were pleasing to you
at their passing from this life,
give kind admittance to your kingdom.
There we hope to enjoy for ever the fullness of your glory
through Christ our Lord,
through whom you bestow on the world all that is good. †

Through him, and with him, and in him,
O God, almighty Father,
in the unity of the Holy Spirit,
all glory and honour is yours,
for ever and ever.

A-men.

R. **Amen.**

Then follows the Communion Rite, p.121.

When this Eucharistic Prayer is used in Masses for the Dead, the following may be said:
† Remember your servant N.
whom you have called (today)
from this world to yourself.
Grant that he (she) who was united with your Son in a death like his,
may also be one with him in his Resurrection,
when from the earth
he will raise up in the flesh those who have died,
and transform our lowly body
after the pattern of his own glorious body.
To our departed brothers and sisters, too,
and to all who were pleasing to you
at their passing from this life,
give kind admittance to your kingdom.
There we hope to enjoy for ever the fullness of your glory,
when you will wipe away every tear from our eyes.
For seeing you, our God, as you are,
we shall be like you for all the ages
and praise you without end,
through Christ our Lord,
through whom you bestow on the world all that is good. †

EUCHARISTIC PRAYER IV

Pr. Dóminus vóbiscum.

R. **Et cum spíritu tuo.**

Pr. Sursum corda.

R. **Habémus ad Dóminum.**

Pr. Grátias agámus Dómino Deo nostro.

R. **Dignum et iustum est.**

Pr. Vere dignum est tibi grátias ágere,
vere iustum est te glorificáre, Pater sancte,
quia unus es Deus vivus et verus,
qui es ante sǽcula et pérmanes in ætérnum,
inaccessíbilem lucem inhábitans;
sed et qui unus bonus atque fons vitæ cuncta fecísti,
ut creatúras tuas benedictiónibus adimpléres
multásque lætificáres tui lúminis claritáte.

Et ídeo coram te innúmeræ astant turbæ Angelórum,
qui die ac nocte sérviunt tibi
et, vultus tui glóriam contemplántes,
te incessánter gloríficant.

Cum quibus et nos et, per nostram vocem,
omnis quæ sub cælo est creatúra
nomen tuum in exsultatióne confitémur, canéntes:

The people sing or say aloud the Sanctus.

Sanctus, * Sanctus, Sanctus Dóminus Deus Sábaoth. Pleni
sunt cæli et terra glória tua. Hosánna in excélsis. Benedíctus qui venit in nómine Dómini. Hosánna in excélsis.

EUCHARISTIC PRAYER IV

Pr. The Lord be with you.
R. **And with your spirit.**
Pr. Lift up your hearts.
R. **We lift them up to the Lord.**
Pr. Let us give thanks to the Lord our God.
R. **It is right and just.**

Pr. It is truly right to give you thanks,
truly just to give you glory, Father most holy,
for you are the one God living and true,
existing before all ages and abiding for all eternity,
dwelling in unapproachable light;
yet you, who alone are good, the source of life,
have made all that is,
so that you might fill your creatures with blessings
and bring joy to many of them by the glory of your light.

And so, in your presence are countless hosts of Angels,
who serve you day and night
and, gazing upon the glory of your face,
glorify you without ceasing.

With them we, too, confess your name in exultation,
giving voice to every creature under heaven,
as we acclaim:

The people sing or say aloud the Sanctus.

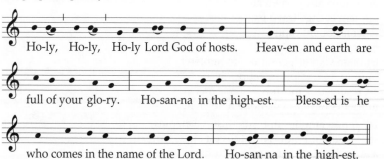

Ho-ly, Ho-ly, Ho-ly Lord God of hosts. Heav-en and earth are
full of your glo-ry. Ho-san-na in the high-est. Bless-ed is he
who comes in the name of the Lord. Ho-san-na in the high-est.

Sanctus, Sanctus, Sanctus Dóminus Deus Sábaoth.
Pleni sunt cæli et terra glória tua.
Hosánna in excélsis.
Benedíctus qui venit in nómine Dómini.
Hosánna in excélsis.

Pr. Confitémur tibi, Pater sancte,
quia magnus es et ómnia ópera tua
in sapiéntia et caritáte fecísti.
Hóminem ad tuam imáginem condidísti,
eíque commisísti mundi curam univérsi,
ut, tibi soli Creatóri sérviens,
creatúris ómnibus imperáret.
Et cum amicítiam tuam, non obœdiens, amisísset,
non eum dereliquísti in mortis império.
Omnibus enim misericórditer subvenísti,
ut te quæréntes invenírent.
Sed et fœdera plúries homínibus obtulísti
eósque per prophétas erudísti in exspectatióne salútis.

Et sic, Pater sancte, mundum dilexísti,
ut, compléta plenitúdine témporum,
Unigénitum tuum nobis mítteres Salvatórem.
Qui, incarnátus de Spíritu Sancto
et natus ex María Vírgine,
in nostra condiciónis forma est conversátus
per ómnia absque peccáto;
salútem evangelizávit paupéribus,
redemptiónem captívis,
mæstis corde lætítiam.
Ut tuam vero dispensatiónem impléret,
in mortem trádidit semetípsum
ac, resúrgens a mórtuis,
mortem destrúxit vitámque renovávit.

Et, ut non ámplius nobismetípsis viverémus,
sed sibi qui pro nobis mórtuus est atque surréxit,
a te, Pater, misit Spíritum Sanctum
primítias credéntibus,

Holy, Holy, Holy Lord God of hosts.
Heaven and earth are full of your glory.
Hosanna in the highest.
Blessed is he who comes in the name of the Lord.
Hosanna in the highest.

Pr. We give you praise, Father most holy,
for you are great
and you have fashioned all your works
in wisdom and in love.
You formed man in your own image
and entrusted the whole world to his care,
so that in serving you alone, the Creator,
he might have dominion over all creatures.
And when through disobedience he had lost your friendship,
you did not abandon him to the domain of death.
For you came in mercy to the aid of all,
so that those who seek might find you.
Time and again you offered them covenants
and through the prophets
taught them to look forward to salvation.

And you so loved the world, Father most holy,
that in the fullness of time
you sent your Only Begotten Son to be our Saviour.
Made incarnate by the Holy Spirit
and born of the Virgin Mary,
he shared our human nature
in all things but sin.
To the poor he proclaimed the good news of salvation,
to prisoners, freedom,
and to the sorrowful of heart, joy.
To accomplish your plan,
he gave himself up to death,
and, rising from the dead,
he destroyed death and restored life.

And that we might live no longer for ourselves
but for him who died and rose again for us,
he sent the Holy Spirit from you, Father,

qui, opus suum in mundo perfíciens,
omnem sanctificatiónem compléret.

Quǽsumus ígitur, Dómine,
ut idem Spíritus Sanctus
hæc múnera sanctificáre dignétur,
ut Corpus et ✠ Sanguis fiant
Dómini nostri Iesu Christi
ad hoc magnum mystérium celebrándum,
quod ipse nobis relíquit in fœdus ætérnum.

Ipse enim, cum hora venísset
ut glorificarétur a te, Pater sancte,
ac dilexísset suos qui erant in mundo,
in finem diléxit eos:
et cenántibus illis
accépit panem, benedíxit ac fregit,
dedítque discípulis suis, dicens:

Accípite et manducáte ex hoc omnes:
hoc est enim Corpus meum,
quod pro vobis tradétur.

Símili modo
accípiens cálicem, ex genímine vitis replétum,
grátias egit, dedítque discípulis suis, dicens:

Accípite et bíbite ex eo omnes:
hic est enim calix Sánguinis mei
novi et ætérni testaménti,
qui pro vobis et pro multis effundétur
in remissiónem peccatórum.
Hoc fácite in meam commemoratiónem.

Pr. Mystérium fídei.

The people continue, acclaiming one of the following:

as the first fruits for those who believe,
so that, bringing to perfection his work in the world,
he might sanctify creation to the full.

Therefore, O Lord, we pray:
may this same Holy Spirit
graciously sanctify these offerings,
that they may become
the Body and ✠ Blood of our Lord Jesus Christ
for the celebration of this great mystery,
which he himself left us
as an eternal covenant.

For when the hour had come
for him to be glorified by you, Father most holy,
having loved his own who were in the world,
he loved them to the end:
and while they were at supper,
he took bread, blessed and broke it,
and gave it to his disciples, saying:

TAKE THIS, ALL OF YOU, AND EAT OF IT,
FOR THIS IS MY BODY,
WHICH WILL BE GIVEN UP FOR YOU.

In a similar way,
taking the chalice filled with the fruit of the vine,
he gave thanks,
and gave the chalice to his disciples, saying:

TAKE THIS, ALL OF YOU, AND DRINK FROM IT,
FOR THIS IS THE CHALICE OF MY BLOOD,
THE BLOOD OF THE NEW AND ETERNAL COVENANT,
WHICH WILL BE POURED OUT FOR YOU AND FOR MANY
FOR THE FORGIVENESS OF SINS.
DO THIS IN MEMORY OF ME.

Pr. The mystery of faith.

The people continue, acclaiming one of the following:

Mortem tu-am annunti-ámus, Dómi-ne,   et tu-am resurrecti-ó-

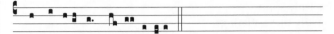

nem confi-témur, do-nec vé-ni-as.

1. Mortem tuam annuntiámus, Dómine,
et tuam resurrectiónem confitémur, donec vénias.

Quoti-escúmque manducámus panem hunc   et cálicem bíbimus,

mortem tu-am annunti-ámus, Dómine, donec vé- ni-as.

2. Quotiescúmque manducámus panem hunc
et cálicem bíbimus,
mortem tuam annuntiámus, Dómine, donec vénias.

Salvátor mundi, salva nos, qui per crucem et resurrecti-ónem tu-am

li-be-rá- sti nos.

3. Salvátor mundi, salva nos,
qui per crucem et resurrectiónem tuam liberásti nos.

Pr. Unde et nos, Dómine, redemptiónis nostræ memoriále nunc celebrántes,
mortem Christi
eiúsque descénsum ad ínferos recólimus,
eius resurrectiónem
et ascensiónem ad tuam déxteram profitémur,

We pro-claim your Death, O Lord, and pro-fess your Res-ur-rec-tion un-til you come a-gain.

1. **We proclaim your Death, O Lord,**
and profess your Resurrection
until you come again.

When we eat this Bread and drink this Cup, we pro-claim your Death, O Lord, un-til you come a-gain.

2. **When we eat this Bread and drink this Cup,**
we proclaim your Death, O Lord,
until you come again.

Save us, Sav-iour of the world, for by your Cross and Res-ur-rec-tion you have set us free.

3. **Save us, Saviour of the world,**
for by your Cross and Resurrection
you have set us free.

Only in Ireland: 4. **My Lord and my God.**

Pr. Therefore, O Lord,
as we now celebrate the memorial of our redemption,
we remember Christ's Death
and his descent to the realm of the dead,
we proclaim his Resurrection
and his Ascension to your right hand,

et, exspectántes ipsíus advéntum in glória,
offérimus tibi eius Corpus et Sánguinem,
sacrifícium tibi acceptábile et toti mundo salutáre.

Réspice, Dómine, in Hóstiam,
quam Ecclésiæ tuæ ipse parásti,
et concéde benígnus ómnibus
qui ex hoc uno pane participábunt et cálice,
ut, in unum corpus a Sancto Spíritu congregáti,
in Christo hóstia viva perficiántur,
ad laudem glóriæ tuæ.

Nunc ergo, Dómine, ómnium recordáre,
pro quibus tibi hanc oblatiónem offérimus:
in primis fámuli tui, Papæ nostri N.,
Epíscopi nostri N.*, et Episcopórum órdinis univérsi,
sed et totíus cleri, et offeréntium,
et circumstántium,
et cuncti pópuli tui,
et ómnium, qui te quærunt corde sincéro.

Meménto étiam illórum,
qui obiérunt in pace Christi tui,
et ómnium defunctórum,
quorum fidem tu solus cognovísti.

Nobis ómnibus, fíliis tuis, clemens Pater, concéde,
ut cæléstem hereditátem cónsequi valeámus
cum beáta Vírgine, Dei Genetríce, María,
cum beáto Ioseph, eius Sponso,
cum Apóstolis et Sanctis tuis
in regno tuo, ubi cum univérsa creatúra,
a corruptióne peccáti et mortis liberáta,
te glorificémus per Christum Dóminum nostrum,
per quem mundo bona cuncta largíris.

Per ipsum, et cum ipso, et in ipso,
est tibi Deo Patri omnipoténti,
in unitáte Spíritus Sancti,
omnis honor et glória
per ómnia sæcula sæculórum.

---

* Mention may be made here of the Coadjutor Bishop or Auxiliary Bishops.

and, as we await his coming in glory,
we offer you his Body and Blood,
the sacrifice acceptable to you
which brings salvation to the whole world.

Look, O Lord, upon the Sacrifice
which you yourself have provided for your Church,
and grant in your loving kindness
to all who partake of this one Bread and one Chalice
that, gathered into one body by the Holy Spirit,
they may truly become a living sacrifice in Christ
to the praise of your glory.

Therefore, Lord, remember now
all for whom we offer this sacrifice:
especially your servant N. our Pope,
N. our Bishop,* and the whole Order of Bishops,
all the clergy,
those who take part in this offering,
those gathered here before you,
your entire people,
and all who seek you with a sincere heart.

Remember also
those who have died in the peace of your Christ
and all the dead,
whose faith you alone have known.

To all of us, your children,
grant, O merciful Father,
that we may enter into a heavenly inheritance
with the Blessed Virgin Mary, Mother of God,
with blessed Joseph, her Spouse,
and with your Apostles and Saints in your kingdom.
There, with the whole of creation,
freed from the corruption of sin and death,
may we glorify you through Christ our Lord,
through whom you bestow on the world all that is good.

Through him, and with him, and in him,
O God, almighty Father,
in the unity of the Holy Spirit,
all glory and honour is yours,
for ever and ever.

---

* Mention may be made here of the Coadjutor Bishop or Auxiliary Bishops.

A-men.

R. **Amen.**

Then follows the Communion Rite.

THE COMMUNION RITE

The eating and drinking together of the Lord's Body and Blood in a Paschal meal is the culmination of the Eucharist

THE LORD'S PRAYER

After the chalice and paten have been set down, the congregation stands and the Priest says:

Pr. **Præcéptis salutáribus móniti,**
et divína institutióne formáti,
audémus dícere:

Together with the people, he continues:

Pa-ter noster, qui es in cæ-lis: sancti-fi-cé-tur nomen tu-um; advéni-at regnum tu-um; fi-at volúntas tu-a, sic-ut in cæ-lo, et in terra. Pa-nem nostrum coti-di-ánum da nobis hódi-e; et dimítte nobis débi-ta nostra, sicut et nos dimíttimus de-bi-tó-ribus nostris; et ne nos indúcas in tenta-ti-ó-nem; sed líbera nos a ma-lo.

A-men.

R. **Amen.**

Then follows the Communion Rite.

THE COMMUNION RITE

The eating and drinking together of the Lord's Body and Blood in a Paschal meal is the culmination of the Eucharist

THE LORD'S PRAYER

After the chalice and paten have been set down, the congregation stands and the Priest says:

Pr. At the Saviour's command
and formed by divine teaching,
we dare to say:

Together with the people, he continues:

Our Fa-ther, who art in heav-en, hal-lowed be thy name; thy king-dom come, thy will be done on earth as it is in heav-en. Give us this day our dai-ly bread, and for-give us our tres-pass-es, as we for-give those who tres-pass a-gainst us; and lead us not in-to temp-ta-tion, but de-liv-er us from e-vil.

R. Pater noster, qui es in cælis:
sanctificétur nomen tuum;
advéniat regnum tuum;
fiat volúntas tua, sicut in cælo, et in terra.
Panem nostrum cotidiánum da nobis hódie;
et dimítte nobis debíta nostra,
sicut et nos dimíttimus debitóribus nostris;
et ne nos indúcas in tentatiónem;
sed líbera nos a malo.

Pr. Líbera nos, quǽsumus, Dómine, ab ómnibus malis,
da propítius pacem in diébus nostris,
ut, ope misericórdiæ tuæ adiúti,
et a peccáto simus semper líberi
et ab omni perturbatióne secúri:
exspectántes beátam spem
et advéntum Salvatóris nostri Iesu Christi.

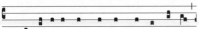

Qui-a tu-um est regnum, et po-téstas,

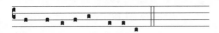

et gló- ri- a in saecu-la.

R. Quia tuum est regnum,
et potéstas, et glória
in sǽcula.

THE PEACE

Pr. Dómine Iesu Christe, qui dixísti Apostólis tuis:
Pacem relínquo vobis, pacem meam do vobis:
ne respícias peccáta nostra,
sed fidem Ecclésiæ tuæ;
eámque secúndum voluntátem tuam
pacificáre et coadunáre dignéris.
Qui vivis et regnas in sǽcula sæculórum.

R. Amen.

R. **Our Father, who art in heaven,
hallowed be thy name;
thy kingdom come,
thy will be done
on earth as it is in heaven.
Give us this day our daily bread,
and forgive us our trespasses,
as we forgive those who trespass against us;
and lead us not into temptation,
but deliver us from evil.**

Pr. Deliver us, Lord, we pray, from every evil,
graciously grant peace in our days,
that, by the help of your mercy,
we may be always free from sin
and safe from all distress,
as we await the blessed hope
and the coming of our Saviour, Jesus Christ.

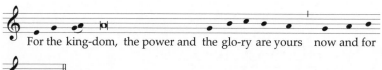

For the king-dom, the power and the glo-ry are yours   now and for

ev-er.

R. **For the kingdom,
the power and the glory are yours
now and for ever.**

THE PEACE

Pr. Lord Jesus Christ,
who said to your Apostles:
Peace I leave you, my peace I give you;
look not on our sins,
but on the faith of your Church,
and graciously grant her peace and unity
in accordance with your will.
Who live and reign for ever and ever.
R. **Amen.**

Pr. Pax Dómini sit semper vobíscum.

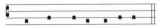

Et cum spí-ri- tu tu- o.

R. **Et cum spíritu tuo.**

Then, if appropriate, the Deacon, or the Priest, adds:

Pr. **Offérte vobis pacem.**

And all offer one another the customary sign of peace.

BREAKING OF THE BREAD

Then the Priest takes the host, breaks it over the paten, and places a small piece in the chalice. Meanwhile the following is sung or said:

A g-nus De-i, * qui tol-lis pec-cá-ta mundi:

mi-se-ré-re no-bis.

Ag-nus De-i, * qui tol-lis pec-cá-ta mundi:

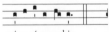

mi-se-ré-re no-bis.

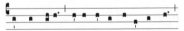

Ag-nus De-i, * qui tol-lis pec-cá-ta mun-di:

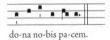

do-na no-bis pa-cem.

Pr. The peace of the Lord be with you always.

And with your spir-it.

R. **And with your spirit.**

Then, if appropriate, the Deacon, or the Priest, adds:

Pr. Let us offer each other the sign of peace.

And all offer one another the customary sign of peace.

BREAKING OF THE BREAD

Then the Priest takes the host, breaks it over the paten, and places a small piece in the chalice. Meanwhile the following is sung or said:

Lamb of God, * you take a-way the sins of the world,

have mer-cy on us.

Lamb of God, * you take a-way the sins of the world,

have mer-cy on us.

Lamb of God, * you take a-way the sins of the world,

grant us peace.

The invocation may even be repeated several times if the fraction is prolonged. Only the final time, however, is **grant us peace** said.

Agnus Dei, qui tollis peccáta mundi: miserére nobis.
Agnus Dei, qui tollis peccáta mundi: miserére nobis.
Agnus Dei, qui tollis peccáta mundi: dona nobis pacem.

Then the Priest, with hands joined, says quietly:

Domine Iesu Christe, Fili Dei vivi,
qui ex voluntate Patris,
cooperante Spiritu Sancto,
per mortem tuam mundum vivificasti:
libera me per hoc sacrosanctum Corpus et Sanguinem tuum
ab omnibus iniquitatibus meis et universis malis:
et fac me tuis semper inhærere mandatis,
et a te numquam separari permittas.

Or:

Perceptio Corporis et Sanguinis tui, Domine Iesu Christe,
non mihi proveniat in iudicium et condemnationem:
sed pro tua pietate prosit mihi
ad tutamentum mentis et corporis,
et ad medelam percipiendam.

INVITATION TO COMMUNION

All kneel. The Priest genuflects, takes the host and, holding it slightly raised above the paten or above the chalice says aloud:

Pr. Ecce Agnus Dei, ecce qui tollit peccáta mundi.
      Beáti qui ad cenam Agni vocáti sunt.

R. **Dómine, non sum dignus, ut intres sub tectum meum,**
    sed tantum dic verbo, et sanábitur ánima mea.

While the Priest is receiving the Body of Christ, the Communion Chant begins.

COMMUNION PROCESSION

After the priest has reverently consumed the Body and Blood of Christ he takes the paten or ciborium and approaches the communicants.

The Priest raises the host slightly and shows it to each of the communicants, saying:

Pr. **Corpus Christi.**
R. **Amen.**

Lamb of God, you take away the sins of the world, have mercy on us.
Lamb of God, you take away the sins of the world, have mercy on us.
Lamb of God, you take away the sins of the world, grant us peace.

Then the Priest, with hands joined, says quietly:

Lord Jesus Christ, Son of the living God,
who, by the will of the Father
and the work of the Holy Spirit,
through your Death gave life to the world,
free me by this, your most holy Body and Blood,
from all my sins and from every evil;
keep me always faithful to your commandments,
and never let me be parted from you.

Or:

May the receiving of your Body and Blood,
Lord Jesus Christ,
not bring me to judgement and condemnation,
but through your loving mercy
be for me protection in mind and body
and a healing remedy.

INVITATION TO COMMUNION

All kneel. The Priest genuflects, takes the host and, holding it slightly raised above the paten or above the chalice says aloud:

Pr. Behold the Lamb of God,
   behold him who takes away the sins of the world.
   Blessed are those called to the supper of the Lamb.

R. **Lord, I am not worthy**
   that you should enter under my roof,
   but only say the word
   and my soul shall be healed.

While the Priest is receiving the Body of Christ, the Communion Chant begins.

COMMUNION PROCESSION

After the priest has reverently consumed the Body and Blood of Christ he takes the paten or ciborium and approaches the communicants.

The Priest raises the host slightly and shows it to each of the communicants, saying:

Pr. The Body of Christ.
R. **Amen.**

When Communion is ministered from the chalice:

Pr. Sanguis Christi.

R. Amen.

After the distribution of Communion, if appropriate, a sacred silence may be observed for a while, or a psalm or other canticle of praise or a hymn may be sung.

PRAYER AFTER COMMUNION

Then, the Priest says:

Pr. Orémus.

All stand and pray in silence for a while, unless silence has just been observed. Then the Priest says the Prayer after Communion, at the end of which the people acclaim:

R. Amen.

THE CONCLUDING RITES

The Mass closes, sending the people forth to put what they have celebrated into effect in their daily lives.

Any brief announcements follow here. Then the dismissal takes place.

Pr. Dóminus vóbiscum.

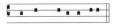

Et cum spí-ri-tu tu-o.

R. Et cum spíritu tuo.

The Priest blesses the people, saying:

**Pr. Benedícat vos omnípotens Deus,
Pater, et Fílius, ✠ et Spíritus Sanctus.**

A-men.

R. Amen.

When Communion is ministered from the chalice:

Pr. The Blood of Christ.

R. **Amen.**

After the distribution of Communion, if appropriate, a sacred silence may be observed for a while, or a psalm or other canticle of praise or a hymn may be sung.

PRAYER AFTER COMMUNION

Then, the Priest says:

Pr. Let us pray.

All stand and pray in silence for a while, unless silence has just been observed. Then the Priest says the Prayer after Communion, at the end of which the people acclaim:

R. **Amen.**

THE CONCLUDING RITES

The Mass closes, sending the people forth to put what they have celebrated into effect in their daily lives.

Any brief announcements follow here. Then the dismissal takes place.

Pr. The Lord be with you.

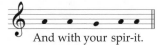
And with your spir-it.

R. **And with your spirit.**

The Priest blesses the people, saying:

Pr. May almighty God bless you,
the Father, and the Son, ✠ and the Holy Spirit.

A-men.

R. **Amen.**

Then the Deacon, or the Priest himself says the Dismissal:

Pr. Ite, missa est.

Or:

Pr. Ite, ad Evangélium Dómini annuntiándum.

Or:

Pr. Ite in pace, glorificándo vita vestra Dóminum.

De- o grá- ti-as.

R. **Deo grátias.**

Or:

Pr. Ite in pace.

De- o grá- ti- as.

R. **Deo grátias.**

Then the Priest venerates the altar as at the beginning. After making a profound bow with the ministers, he withdraws.

Then the Deacon, or the Priest himself says the Dismissal:

Pr. Go forth, the Mass is ended.

Or:

Pr. Go and announce the Gospel of the Lord.

Or:

Pr. Go in peace, glorifying the Lord by your life.

R. Thanks be to God.

R. **Thanks be to God.**

Or:

Pr. Go in peace.

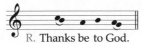

R. Thanks be to God.

R. **Thanks be to God.**

Then the Priest venerates the altar as at the beginning. After making a profound bow with the ministers, he withdraws.

SOLEMN BLESSINGS

The following blessings may be used, at the discretion of the Priest, at the end of the
celebration of Mass, or of a Liturgy of the Word, or of the Office, or of the Sacraments.

The Deacon or, in his absence, the Priest himself, says the invitation: **Inclinate vos
ad benedictionem**. Then the Priest, with hands extended over the people, says the
blessing, with all responding: **Amen**.

I. For Celebrations in the Different Liturgical Times

1. In Adventu

Omnipotens et misericors Deus, cuius Unigeniti adventum
et præteritum creditis, et futurum exspectatis,
eiusdem adventus vos illustratione sanctificet
et sua benedictione locupletet.
R. Amen.

In præsentis vitæ stadio reddat vos in fide stabiles,
spe gaudentes, et in caritate efficaces.
R. Amen.

Ut, qui de adventu Redemptoris nostri
secundum carnem devota mente lætamini,
in secundo, cum in maiestate sua venerit,
præmiis æternæ vitæ ditemini.
R. Amen.

Et benedictio Dei omnipotentis,
Patris, et Filii, ✠ et Spiritus Sancti,
descendat super vos et maneat semper.
R. Amen.

2. In Nativitate Domini

Deus infinitæ bonitatis,
qui incarnatione Filii sui mundi tenebras effugavit,
et eius gloriosa nativitate
hanc noctem (diem) sacratissimam irradiavit,
effuget a vobis tenebras vitiorum,
et irradiet corda vestra luce virtutum.
R. Amen.

Quique eius salutiferæ nativitatis gaudium magnum
pastoribus ab Angelo voluit nuntiari,
ipse mentes vestras suo gaudio impleat,
et vos Evangelii sui nuntios efficiat.
R. Amen.

SOLEMN BLESSINGS

The following blessings may be used, at the discretion of the Priest, at the end of the celebration of Mass, or of a Liturgy of the Word, or of the Office, or of the Sacraments.

The Deacon or, in his absence, the Priest himself, says the invitation: **Bow down for the blessing**. Then the Priest, with hands extended over the people, says the blessing, with all responding: **Amen**.

I. For Celebrations in the Different Liturgical Times

1. Advent

May the almighty and merciful God,
by whose grace you have placed your faith
in the First Coming of his Only Begotten Son
and yearn for his coming again,
sanctify you by the radiance of Christ's Advent
and enrich you with his blessing.
R. Amen.

As you run the race of this present life,
may he make you firm in faith,
joyful in hope and active in charity.
R. Amen.

So that, rejoicing now with devotion
at the Redeemer's coming in the flesh,
you may be endowed with the rich reward of eternal life
when he comes again in majesty.
R. Amen.

And may the blessing of almighty God,
the Father, and the Son, ✠ and the Holy Spirit,
come down on you and remain with you for ever.
R. Amen.

2. The Nativity of the Lord

May the God of infinite goodness,
who by the Incarnation of his Son has driven darkness from the world
and by that glorious Birth has illumined this most holy night (day),
drive far from you the darkness of vice
and illumine your hearts with the light of virtue.
R. Amen.

May God, who willed that the great joy
of his Son's saving Birth
be announced to shepherds by the Angel,
fill your minds with the gladness he gives
and make you heralds of his Gospel.
R. Amen.

Et, qui per eius incarnationem terrena cælestibus sociavit,
dono vos suæ pacis et bonæ repleat voluntatis,
et vos faciat Ecclesiæ consortes esse cælestis.
R. Amen.

Et benedictio Dei omnipotentis,
Patris, et Filii, ✠ et Spiritus Sancti,
descendat super vos et maneat semper.
R. Amen.

3. Initio anni

Deus, fons et origo totius benedictionis,
gratiam vobis concedat,
benedictionis suæ largitatem infundat,
atque per totum annum vos salvos et incolumes protegat.
R. Amen.

Custodiat fidei vobis integritatem,
tribuat spei longanimitatem,
perseverantem usque ad finem
cum sancta patientia caritatem.
R. Amen.

Dies et actus vestros in sua pace disponat,
preces hic et ubique exaudiat,
et ad vitam æternam feliciter vos perducat.
R. Amen.

Et benedictio Dei omnipotentis,
Patris, et Filii, ✠ et Spiritus Sancti,
descendat super vos et maneat semper.
R. Amen.

4. In Epiphania Domini

Deus, qui vos de tenebris vocavit in admirabile lumen suum,
suam vobis benedictionem benignus infundat,
et corda vestra fide, spe et caritate stabiliat.
R. Amen.

Et quia Christum sequimini confidenter,
qui hodie mundo apparuit lux relucens in tenebris,
faciat et vos lucem esse fratribus vestris.
R. Amen.

And may God, who by the Incarnation
brought together the earthly and heavenly realm,
fill you with the gift of his peace and favour
and make you sharers with the Church in heaven.
R. Amen.

And may the blessing of almighty God,
the Father, and the Son, ✠ and the Holy Spirit,
come down on you and remain with you for ever.
R. Amen.

3. The Beginning of the Year

May God, the source and origin of all blessing,
grant you grace,
pour out his blessing in abundance,
and keep you safe from harm throughout the year.
R. Amen.

May he give you integrity in the faith,
endurance in hope,
and perseverance in charity
with holy patience to the end.
R. Amen.

May he order your days and your deeds in his peace,
grant your prayers in this and in every place,
and lead you happily to eternal life.
R. Amen.

And may the blessing of almighty God,
the Father, and the Son, ✠ and the Holy Spirit,
come down on you and remain with you for ever.
R. Amen.

4. The Epiphany of the Lord

May God, who has called you
out of darkness into his wonderful light,
pour out in kindness his blessing upon you
and make your hearts firm
in faith, hope and charity.
R. Amen.

And since in all confidence you follow Christ,
who today appeared in the world
as a light shining in darkness,
may God make you, too,
a light for your brothers and sisters.
R. Amen.

Quatenus, peregrinatione peracta,
perveniatis ad eum, quem magi stella prævia quæsierunt,
et gaudio magno, lucem de luce,
Christum Dominum invenerunt.
R. Amen.

Et benedictio Dei omnipotentis,
Patris, et Filii, ✠ et Spiritus Sancti,
descendat super vos et maneat semper.
R. Amen.

5. De Passione Domini

Deus, Pater misericordiarum, qui Unigeniti sui passione
tribuit vobis caritatis exemplum,
præstet ut, per servitium Dei et hominum,
percipiatis suæ benedictionis ineffabile donum.
R. Amen.

Ut ab eo sempiternæ vitæ munus obtineatis,
per cuius temporalem mortem, æternam vos evadere creditis.
R. Amen.

Quatenus, cuius humilitatis sequimini documenta,
eius resurrectionis possideatis consortia.
R. Amen.

Et benedictio Dei omnipotentis,
Patris, et Filii, ✠ et Spiritus Sancti,
descendat super vos et maneat semper.
R. Amen.

6. Tempore paschali

Deus, qui per resurrectionem Unigeniti sui
dignatus est vobis bonum redemptionis
adoptionisque conferre,
sua benedictione vos tribuat congaudere.
R. Amen.

And so when your pilgrimage is ended,
may you come to him
whom the Magi sought as they followed the star
and whom they found with great joy, the Light from Light,
who is Christ the Lord.
R. Amen.

And may the blessing of almighty God,
the Father, and the Son, ✠ and the Holy Spirit,
come down on you and remain with you for ever.
R. Amen.

5. The Passion of the Lord
May God, the Father of mercies,
who has given you an example of love
in the Passion of his Only Begotten Son,
grant that, by serving God and your neighbour,
you may lay hold of the wondrous gift of his blessing.
R. Amen.

So that you may receive the reward of everlasting life from him,
through whose earthly Death
you believe that you escape eternal death.
R. Amen.

And by following the example of his self-abasement,
may you possess a share in his Resurrection.
R. Amen.

And may the blessing of almighty God,
the Father, and the Son, ✠ and the Holy Spirit,
come down on you and remain with you for ever.
R. Amen.

6. Easter Time
May God, who by the Resurrection of his Only Begotten Son
was pleased to confer on you
the gift of redemption and of adoption,
give you gladness by his blessing.
R. Amen.

Et quo redimente percepistis donum perpetuæ libertatis,
eo largiente hereditatis æternæ consortes effici valeatis.
R. Amen.

Et cui resurrexisti in baptismate iam credendo,
adiungi mereamini in patria cælesti nunc recte vivendo.
R. Amen.

Et benedictio Dei omnipotentis,
Patris, et Filii, ✠ et Spiritus Sancti,
descendat super vos et maneat semper.
R. Amen.

7. In Ascensione Domini

Benedicat vos omnipotens Deus,
cuius Unigenitus hodierna die cælorum alta penetravit,
et vobis, ubi est ipse, ascendendi aditum reseravit.
R. Amen.

Concedat ut, sicut Christus post resurrectionem suam
visus est discipulis manifestus,
ita vobis in iudicium veniens
appareat pro æternitate placatus.
R. Amen.

Et qui eum consedere Patri in sua creditis maiestate,
ipsum usque in finem sæculi vobiscum permanere
secundum eius promissionem læti valeatis experire.
R. Amen.

Et benedictio Dei omnipotentis,
Patris, et Filii, ✠ et Spiritus Sancti,
descendat super vos et maneat semper.
R. Amen.

8. De Spiritu Sancto

Deus, Pater luminum, qui discipulorum mentes
Spiritus Paracliti infusione dignatus est illustrare,
sua vos faciat benedictione gaudere,
et perpetuo donis eiusdem Spiritus abundare.
R. Amen.

May he, by whose redeeming work
you have received the gift of everlasting freedom,
make you heirs to an eternal inheritance.
R. Amen.

And may you, who have already risen with Christ
in Baptism through faith,
by living in a right manner on this earth,
be united with him in the homeland of heaven.
R. Amen.

And may the blessing of almighty God,
the Father, and the Son, ✠ and the Holy Spirit,
come down on you and remain with you for ever.
R. Amen.

7. The Ascension of the Lord

May almighty God bless you,
for on this very day his Only Begotten Son
pierced the heights of heaven
and unlocked for you the way
to ascend to where he is.
R. Amen.

May he grant that,
as Christ after his Resurrection
was seen plainly by his disciples,
so when he comes as Judge
he may show himself merciful to you for all eternity.
R. Amen.

And may you, who believe he is seated
with the Father in his majesty,
know with joy the fulfilment of his promise
to stay with you until the end of time.
R. Amen.

And may the blessing of almighty God,
the Father, and the Son, ✠ and the Holy Spirit,
come down on you and remain with you for ever.
R. Amen.

8. The Holy Spirit

May God, the Father of lights,
who was pleased to enlighten the disciples' minds
by the outpouring of the Spirit, the Paraclete,
grant you gladness by his blessing
and make you always abound with the gifts of the same Spirit.
R. Amen.

Ignis ille, qui super discipulos mirandus apparuit,
corda vestra ab omni malo potenter expurget,
et sui luminis infusione perlustret.
R. Amen.

Quique dignatus est in unius fidei confessione
diversitatem adunare linguarum,
in eadem fide perseverare vos faciat,
et per illam a spe ad speciem pervenire concedat.
R. Amen.

Et benedictio Dei omnipotentis,
Patris, et Filii, ✠ et Spiritus Sancti,
descendat super vos et maneat semper.
R. Amen.

9. Per annum, I
Benedicat vobis Dominus, et custodiat vos.
R. Amen.

Illuminet faciem suam super vos, et misereatur vestri.
R. Amen.

Convertat vultum suum ad vos, et donet vobis suam pacem.
R. Amen.

Et benedictio Dei omnipotentis,
Patris, et Filii, ✠ et Spiritus Sancti,
descendat super vos et maneat semper.
R. Amen.

10. Per annum, II
Pax Dei, quæ exsuperat omnem sensum,
custodiat corda vestra et intellegentias vestras
in scientia et caritate Dei,
et Filii sui, Domini nostri Iesu Christi.
R. Amen.

Et benedictio Dei omnipotentis,
Patris, et Filii, ✠ et Spiritus Sancti,
descendat super vos et maneat semper.
R. Amen.

11. Per annum, III
Omnipotens Deus sua vos clementia benedicat,
et sensum in vobis sapientiæ salutaris infundat.
R. Amen.

May the wondrous flame that appeared above the disciples,
powerfully cleanse your hearts from every evil
and pervade them with its purifying light.
R. Amen.

And may God, who has been pleased to unite many tongues
in the profession of one faith,
give you perseverance in that same faith
and, by believing, may you journey from hope to clear vision.
R. Amen.

And may the blessing of almighty God,
the Father, and the Son, ✠ and the Holy Spirit,
come down on you and remain with you for ever.
R. Amen.

9. Ordinary Time I

May the Lord bless you and keep you.
R. Amen.

May he let his face shine upon you
and show you his mercy.
R. Amen.

May he turn his countenance towards you
and give you his peace.
R. Amen.

And may the blessing of almighty God,
the Father, and the Son, ✠ and the Holy Spirit,
come down on you and remain with you for ever.
R. Amen.

10. Ordinary Time II

May the peace of God,
which surpasses all understanding,
keep your hearts and minds
in the knowledge and love of God,
and of his Son, our Lord Jesus Christ.
R. Amen.

And may the blessing of almighty God,
the Father, and the Son, ✠ and the Holy Spirit,
come down on you and remain with you for ever.
R. Amen.

11. Ordinary Time III

May almighty God bless you in his kindness
and pour out saving wisdom upon you.
R. Amen.

Fidei documentis vos semper enutriat,
et in sanctis operibus, ut perseveretis, efficiat.
R. Amen.

Gressus vestros ad se convertat,
et viam vobis pacis et caritatis ostendat.
R. Amen.

Et benedictio Dei omnipotentis,
Patris, et Filii, ✠ et Spiritus Sancti,
descendat super vos et maneat semper.
R. Amen.

12. Per annum, IV

Deus totius consolationis dies vestros in sua pace disponat,
et suæ vobis benedictionis dona concedat.
R. Amen.

Ab omni semper perturbatione vos liberet,
et corda vestra in suo amore confirmet.
R. Amen.

Quatenus donis spei, fidei et caritatis divites,
et præsentem vitam transigatis in opere efficaces,
et possitis ad æternam pervenire felices.
R. Amen.

Et benedictio Dei omnipotentis,
Patris, et Filii, ✠ et Spiritus Sancti,
descendat super vos et maneat semper.
R. Amen.

13. Per annum, V

Omnipotens Deus universa a vobis adversa semper excludat,
et suæ super vos benedictionis dona propitiatus infundat.
R. Amen.

Corda vestra efficiat divinis intenta eloquiis,
ut repleri possint gaudiis sempiternis.
R. Amen.

Quatenus, quæ bona et recta intellegentes,
viam mandatorum Dei inveniamini semper currentes,
et civium supernorum efficiamini coheredes.
R. Amen.

Et benedictio Dei omnipotentis,
Patris, et Filii, ✠ et Spiritus Sancti,
descendat super vos et maneat semper.
R. Amen.

May he nourish you always with the teachings of the faith
and make you persevere in holy deeds.
R. Amen.

May he turn your steps towards himself
and show you the path of charity and peace.
R. Amen.

And may the blessing of almighty God,
the Father, and the Son, ✠ and the Holy Spirit,
come down on you and remain with you for ever.
R. Amen.

12. Ordinary Time IV

May the God of all consolation order your days in his peace
and grant you the gifts of his blessing.
R. Amen.

May he free you always from every distress
and confirm your hearts in his love.
R. Amen.

So that on this life's journey
you may be effective in good works,
rich in the gifts of hope, faith and charity,
and may come happily to eternal life.
R. Amen.

And may the blessing of almighty God,
the Father, and the Son, ✠ and the Holy Spirit,
come down on you and remain with you for ever.
R. Amen.

13. Ordinary Time V

May almighty God always keep every adversity far from you
and in his kindness pour out upon you the gifts of his blessing.
R. Amen.

May God keep your hearts attentive to his words,
that they may be filled with everlasting gladness.
R. Amen.

And so, may you always understand what is good and right,
and be found ever hastening along
in the path of God's commands,
made coheirs with the citizens of heaven.
R. Amen.

And may the blessing of almighty God,
the Father, and the Son, ✠ and the Holy Spirit,
come down on you and remain with you for ever.
R. Amen.

14. Per annum, VI

Benedicat vos Deus omni benedictione cælesti,
sanctosque vos et puros
in conspectu suo semper efficiat;
divitias gloriæ suæ in vos abundanter effundat,
verbis veritatis instruat, Evangelio salutis erudiat,
et caritate fraterna semper locupletet.
Per Christum Dominum nostrum.
R. Amen.

Et benedictio Dei omnipotentis,
Patris, et Filii, ✠ et Spiritus Sancti,
descendat super vos et maneat semper.
R. Amen.

II. For Celebrations of the Saints

15. De beata Maria Virgine

Deus, qui per beatæ Mariæ Virginis partum
genus humanum sua voluit benignitate redimere,
sua vos dignetur benedictione ditare.
R. Amen.

Eiusque semper et ubique patrocinia sentiatis,
per quam auctorem vitæ suscipere meruistis.
R. Amen.

Et qui hodierna die devotis mentibus convenistis,
spiritalium gaudiorum cælestiumque præmiorum
vobiscum munera reportetis.
R. Amen.

Et benedictio Dei omnipotentis,
Patris, et Filii, ✠ et Spiritus Sancti,
descendat super vos et maneat semper.
R. Amen.

16. De sanctis Petro et Paulo

Benedicat vos omnipotens Deus,
qui in beati Petri confessione vos saluberrima stabilivit,
et per eam in Ecclesiæ soliditate fidei fundavit.
R. Amen.

Et quos beati Pauli instruxit indefessa prædicatione,
suo semper exemplo doceat Christo fratres lucrifacere.
R. Amen.

14. Ordinary Time VI

May God bless you with every heavenly blessing,
make you always holy and pure in his sight,
pour out in abundance upon you the riches of his glory,
and teach you with the words of truth;
may he instruct you in the Gospel of salvation,
and ever endow you with fraternal charity.
Through Christ our Lord.
R. **Amen.**

And may the blessing of almighty God,
the Father, and the Son, ✠ and the Holy Spirit,
come down on you and remain with you for ever.
R. **Amen.**

II. For Celebrations of the Saints

15. The Blessed Virgin Mary

May God, who through the childbearing of the Blessed Virgin Mary
willed in his great kindness to redeem the human race,
be pleased to enrich you with his blessing.
R. **Amen.**

May you know always and everywhere
the protection of her,
through whom you have been found worthy to receive
the author of life.
R. **Amen.**

May you, who have devoutly gathered on this day,
carry away with you the gifts of spiritual joys and heavenly rewards.
R. **Amen.**

And may the blessing of almighty God,
the Father, and the Son, ✠ and the Holy Spirit,
come down on you and remain with you for ever.
R. **Amen.**

16. Saints Peter and Paul, Apostles

May almighty God bless you,
for he has made you steadfast in Saint Peter's saving confession
and through it has set you on the solid rock of the Church's faith.
R. **Amen.**

And having instructed you
by the tireless preaching of Saint Paul,
may God teach you constantly by his example
to win brothers and sisters for Christ.
R. **Amen.**

Ut Petrus clave, Paulus verbo,
ope intercessionis uterque
in illam patriam nos certent inducere,
ad quam meruerunt illi, alter cruce, alter gladio,
feliciter pervenire.
R. Amen.

Et benedictio Dei omnipotentis,
Patris, et Filii, ✠ et Spiritus Sancti,
descendat super vos et maneat semper.
R. Amen.

17. De Apostolis

Deus, qui vos in apostolicis tribuit consistere fundamentis,
benedicere vobis dignetur
beatorum Apostolorum N. et N. (beati Apostoli N.)
meritis intercedentibus gloriosis.
R. Amen.

Et apostolicis præsidiis vos pro cunctis faciat testes veritatis,
qui vos eorum munerari documentis voluit et exemplis.
R. Amen.

Ut eorum intercessione
ad æternæ patriæ hereditatem pervenire possitis,
per quorum doctrinam fidei firmitatem possidetis.
R. Amen.

Et benedictio Dei omnipotentis,
Patris, et Filii, ✠ et Spiritus Sancti,
descendat super vos et maneat semper.
R. Amen.

18. De omnibus Sanctis

Deus, gloria et exsultatio Sanctorum,
benedicat vos benedictione perpetua,
qui vobis tribuit eximiis suffragiis roborari.
R. Amen.

Eorum intercessione a præsentibus malis liberati,
et exemplis sanctæ conversationis instructi,
in servitio Dei fratrumque inveniamini semper intenti.
R. Amen.

So that by the keys of St Peter and the words of St Paul,
and by the support of their intercession,
God may bring us happily to that homeland
that Peter attained on a cross
and Paul by the blade of a sword.
R. **Amen.**

And may the blessing of almighty God,
the Father, and the Son, ✠ and the Holy Spirit,
come down on you and remain with you for ever.
R. **Amen.**

17. The Apostles

May God, who has granted you
to stand firm on apostolic foundations,
graciously bless you through the glorious merits
of the holy Apostles N. and N. (the holy Apostle N.).
R. **Amen.**

And may he, who endowed you
with the teaching and example of the Apostles,
make you, under their protection,
witnesses to the truth before all.
R. **Amen.**

So that through the intercession of the Apostles,
you may inherit the eternal homeland,
for by their teaching you possess firmness of faith.
R. **Amen.**

And may the blessing of almighty God,
the Father, and the Son, ✠ and the Holy Spirit,
come down on you and remain with you for ever.
R. **Amen.**

18. All Saints

May God, the glory and joy of the Saints,
who has caused you to be strengthened
by means of their outstanding prayers,
bless you with unending blessings.
R. **Amen.**

Freed through their intercession from present ills
and formed by the example of their holy way of life,
may you be ever devoted
to serving God and your neighbour.
R. **Amen.**

Quatenus cum iis omnibus
valeatis illius patriæ vos gaudia possidere,
in qua filios suos supernis coniungi civibus
in pace perpetua sancta lætatur Ecclesia.
R. Amen.

Et benedictio Dei omnipotentis,
Patris, et Filii, ✠ et Spiritus Sancti,
descendat super vos et maneat semper.
R. Amen.

III. Other Blessings

19. In dedicatione ecclesiæ

Deus, Dominus cæli et terræ,
qui vos hodie ad huius domus dedicationem adunavit,
ipse vos cælesti benedictione faciat abundare.
R. Amen.

Concedatque vobis fieri templum suum
et habitaculum Spiritus Sancti,
qui omnes filios dispersos voluit in Filio suo congregari.
R. Amen.

Quatenus feliciter emundati,
habitatorem Deum in vobismetipsis possitis habere,
et æternæ beatitudinis hereditatem
cum omnibus Sanctis possidere.
R. Amen.

Et benedictio Dei omnipotentis,
Patris, et Filii, ✠ et Spiritus Sancti,
descendat super vos et maneat semper.
R. Amen.

20. In celebrationibus pro defunctis

Benedicat vos Deus totius consolationis,
qui hominem ineffabili bonitate creavit,
et in resurrectione Unigeniti sui
spem credentibus resurgendi concessit.
R. Amen.

Nobis, qui vivimus, veniam tribuat pro peccatis,
et omnibus defunctis locum concedat lucis et pacis.
R. Amen.

So that, together with all,
you may possess the joys of the homeland,
where Holy Church rejoices
that her children are admitted in perpetual peace
to the company of the citizens of heaven.
R. Amen.

And may the blessing of almighty God,
the Father, and the Son, ✠ and the Holy Spirit,
come down on you and remain with you for ever.
R. Amen.

III. Other Blessings

19. For the Dedication of a Church

May God, the Lord of heaven and earth,
who has gathered you today for the dedication of this church,
make you abound in heavenly blessings.
R. Amen.

And may he, who has willed that all his scattered children
should be gathered together in his Son,
grant that you may become his temple
and the dwelling place of the Holy Spirit.
R. Amen.

And so, when you are thoroughly cleansed,
may God dwell within you
and grant you to possess with all the Saints
the inheritance of eternal happiness.
R. Amen.

And may the blessing of almighty God,
the Father, and the Son, ✠ and the Holy Spirit,
come down on you and remain with you for ever.
R. Amen.

20. In Celebrations for the Dead

May the God of all consolation bless you,
for in his unfathomable goodness he created the human race,
and in the Resurrection of his Only Begotten Son
he has given believers the hope of rising again.
R. Amen.

To us who are alive, may God grant pardon for our sins,
and to all the dead, a place of light and peace.
R. Amen.

Ut omnes cum Christo sine fine feliciter vivamus,
quem resurrexisse a mortuis veraciter credimus.

R. Amen.

Et benedictio Dei omnipotentis,
Patris, et Filii, ✠ et Spiritus Sancti,
descendat super vos et maneat semper.

R. Amen.

So may we all live happily for ever with Christ,
whom we believe truly rose from the dead.

R. Amen.

And may the blessing of almighty God,
the Father, and the Son, ✠ and the Holy Spirit,
come down on you and remain with you for ever.

R. Amen.

THANKSGIVING AFTER MASS

Prayer of Saint Thomas Aquinas

Oratio S. Thomas Aquinatis

I give you thanks,
Lord, holy Father,
    almighty and eternal God,
who have been pleased
    to nourish me,
a sinner and your
    unworthy servant,
with the precious Body and Blood
of your Son, our Lord Jesus Christ:
this through no merits of mine,
but due solely to
    the graciousness of your mercy.

And I pray that this
    Holy Communion
may not be for me an offence
    to be punished,
but a saving plea for forgiveness.
May it be for me the armour of faith,
and the shield of good will.
May it cancel my faults,
destroy concupiscence
    and carnal passion,
increase charity and patience,
    humility and obedience
and all the virtues,
may it be a firm defence against
    the snares of all my enemies,
both visible and invisible,
the complete calming of
    my impulses,
both of the flesh and of the spirit,
a firm adherence to you,
    the one true God,
and the joyful completion of my
    life's course.

Gratias tibi ago, Domine,
sancte Pater,
    omnipotens æterne Deus,
qui me peccatorem,
    indignum famulum tuum,
nullis meis meritis, sed sola
    dignatione misericordiæ tuæ
satiare dignatus es pretioso Corpore
    et Sanguine Filii tui,
Domini nostri Iesu Christi.

Et precor,
    ut hæc sancta communio
non sit mihi reatus ad pœnam,
sed intercessio salutaris ad veniam.
Sit mihi armatura fidei,
    et scutum bonæ voluntatis.
Sit vitiorum meorum evacuatio,
concupiscentiæ
    et libidinis exterminatio,
caritatis et patientiæ,
    humilitatis et obœdientiæ,
omniumque virtutum
    augmentatio:
contra insidias
    inimicorum omnium
tam visibilium quam invisibilium,
    firma defensio:
motuum meorum, tam carnalium
    quam spiritalium,
perfecta quietatio:
in te uno ac vero Deo
    firma adhæsio,
atque finis mei felix consummatio.

And I beseech you to lead me,
  a sinner,
to that banquet beyond all telling,
where with your Son and the
  Holy Spirit
you are the true light of
  your Saints,
fullness of satisfied desire,
  eternal gladness,
consummate delight and
  perfect happiness.
Through Christ our Lord.
Amen.

Et precor te,
  ut ad illud ineffabile convivium
me peccatorem perducere digneris,
ubi tu, cum Filio tuo et
  Spiritu Sancto,
Sanctis tuis es lux vera,
  satietas plena,
gaudium sempiternum,
iucunditas consummata et
  felicitas perfecta.
Per Christum Dominum nostrum.
Amen.

Prayer to the Most Holy Redeemer

Aspirationes ad Ss.mum Redemptorem

Soul of Christ, sanctify me.
Body of Christ, save me.
Blood of Christ, embolden me.
Water from the side of Christ,
  wash me.
Passion of Christ, strengthen me.
O good Jesus, hear me.
Within your wounds hide me.
Never permit me to be parted
  from you.
From the evil Enemy defend me.
At the hour of my death call me
and bid me come to you,
that with your Saints
  I may praise you
for age upon age.
Amen.

Anima Christi, sanctifica me.
Corpus Christi, salva me.
Sanguis Christi, inebria me.
Aqua lateris Christi, lava me.

Passio Christi, conforta me.
O bone Iesu, exaudi me.
Intra tua vulnera absconde me.
Ne permittas me separari a te.

Ab hoste maligno defende me.
In hora mortis meæ voca me.
Et iube me venire ad te,
ut cum Sanctis tuis laudem te
in sæcula sæculorum.

Amen.

Prayer of Self-Offering

Oblatio sui

Receive, Lord, my entire freedom.
Accept the whole of my memory,
my intellect and my will.

Suscipe, Domine,
  universam meam libertatem.
Accipe memoriam, intellectum
  atque voluntatem omnem.

Whatever I have or possess,
it was you who gave it to me;
I restore it to you in full,
and I surrender it completely
to the guidance of your will.
Give me only love of you
together with your grace,
and I am rich enough
and ask for nothing more.
Amen.

Quidquid habeo vel possideo,
    mihi largitus es:
id tibi totum restituo,
ac tuæ prorsus voluntati
    trado gubernandum.
Amorem tui solum cum gratia tua
    mihi dones,
et dives sum satis, nec aliud
    quidquam ultra posco.
Amen.

Prayer to Our Lord Jesus Christ Crucified

Oratio ad Dominum nostrum Iesum Christum Crucifixum

Behold, O good and loving Jesus,
that I cast myself on my knees
    before you
and, with the greatest fervour
    of spirit,
I pray and beseech you to instill
    into my heart
ardent sentiments of faith,
    hope and charity,
with true repentance for my sins
and a most firm purpose
    of amendment.
With deep affection and sorrow
I ponder intimately
and contemplate in my mind
    your five wounds,
having before my eyes what
    the prophet David
had already put in your mouth
    about yourself, O good Jesus:
They have pierced my hands and
    my feet;
they have numbered all my bones
    (Ps 21:17-18).

En ego, o bone et dulcissime Iesu,
ante conspectum tuum genibus
    me provolvo,
ac maximo animi ardore te oro
    atque obtestor,
ut meum in cor vividos fidei,
    spei et caritatis sensus,
atque veram peccatorum
    meorum pœnitentiam,
eaque emendandi firmissimam
    voluntatem velis imprimere;

dum magno animi affectu et dolore
tua quinque vulnera mecum
    ipse considero
ac mente contemplor,
illud præ oculis habens,
quod iam in ore ponebat tuo David
    propheta de te, o bone Iesu:

Foderunt manus meas
    et pedes meos:
dinumeraverunt omnia ossa mea
    (Ps 21:17-18).

The Universal Prayer Attributed to Pope Clement XI

I believe, O Lord,
  but may I believe more firmly;
I hope,
  but may I hope more securely;
I love,
  but may I love more ardently;
I sorrow,
  but may I sorrow more deeply.

I adore you as my first beginning;
I long for you as my last end;
I praise you as my
  constant benefactor;
I invoke you as my
  gracious protector.

By your wisdom direct me,
by your righteousness restrain me,
by your indulgence console me,
by your power protect me.

I offer you, Lord, my thoughts to
  be directed to you,
my words, to be about you,
my deeds, to respect your will,
my trials, to be endured for you.

I will whatever you will,
I will it because you will it,
I will it in the way you will it,
I will it for as long as you will it.

Lord, enlighten my understanding,
  I pray:
arouse my will,
cleanse my heart,
sanctify my soul.

Oratio universalis sub nomine Clementis Pp. XI vulgata

Credo, Domine,
  sed credam firmius;
spero, sed sperem securius;
amo, sed amem ardentius;
doleo, sed doleam vehementius.

Adoro te ut primum principium;
desidero ut finem ultimum;
laudo ut benefactorem perpetuum;
invoco ut defensorem propitium.

Tua me sapientia dirige,
iustitia contine,
clementia solare,
potentia protege.

Offero tibi, Domine, cogitanda,
  ut sint ad te;
dicenda, ut sint de te;
facienda, ut sint secundum te;
ferenda, ut sint propter te.

Volo quidquid vis,
volo quia vis,
volo quomodo vis,
volo quamdiu vis.

Oro, Domine:
  intellectum illumines,
voluntatem inflammes,
cor emundes,
animam sanctifices.

May I weep for past sins,
repel future temptations,
correct evil inclinations,
nurture appropriate virtues.

Give me, good God,
love for you, hatred for myself,
zeal for my neighbour,
contempt for the world.

May I strive to obey superiors,
to help those dependent on me,
to have care for my friends,
forgiveness for my enemies.

May I conquer sensuality
    by austerity,
avarice by generosity,
anger by gentleness,
lukewarmness by fervour.

Render me prudent in planning,
steadfast in dangers,
patient in adversity,
humble in prosperity.

Make me, O Lord, attentive at prayer,
moderate at meals,
diligent in work,
steadfast in intent.

May I be careful to maintain
    interior innocence,
outward modesty,
exemplary behaviour,
a regular life.

May I be always watchful in
    subduing nature,
in nourishing grace,
in observing your law,
in winning salvation.

Defleam præteritas iniquitates,
repellam futuras tentationes,
corrigam vitiosas propensiones,
excolam idoneas virtutes.

Tribue mihi, bone Deus,
amorem tui, odium mei,
zelum proximi,
contemptum mundi.

Studeam superioribus obœdire,
inferioribus subvenire,
amicis consulere,
inimicis parcere.

Vincam voluptatem austeritate,
avaritiam largitate,
iracundiam lenitate,
tepiditatem fervore.

Redde me prudentem in consiliis,
constantem in periculis,
patientem in adversis,
humilem in prosperis.

Fac, Domine,
    ut sim in oratione attentus,
in epulis sobrius,
in munere sedulus,
in proposito firmus.

Curem habere innocentiam
    interiorem,
modestiam exteriorem,
conversationem exemplarem,
vitam regularem.

Assidue invigilem naturæ
    domandæ,
gratiæ fovendæ,
legi servandæ,
saluti promerendæ.

May I learn from you
how precarious are earthly things,
how great divine things,
how fleeting is time,
how lasting things eternal.

Grant that I may prepare for death,
fear judgement,
flee hell,
gain paradise.
Through Christ our Lord.
Amen.

Discam a te quam tenue quod
    terrenum,
quam grande quod divinum,
quam breve quod temporaneum,
quam durabile quod æternum.

Da, ut mortem præveniam,
iudicium pertimeam,
infernum effugiam,
paradisum obtineam.
Per Christum Dominum nostrum.
Amen.

Prayers to the Blessed Virgin Mary

Orationes ad B. Mariam Virginem

O Mary, Virgin and
    Mother most holy,
behold, I have received your
    most dear Son,
whom you conceived in
    your immaculate womb,
brought forth, nursed and
    embraced most tenderly.
Behold him at whose sight
you used to rejoice and be filled
    with all delight;
him whom, humbly and lovingly,
once again I present
and offer him to you
to be clasped in your arms,
to be loved by your heart,
and to be offered up to
    the Most Holy Trinity
as the supreme worship of adoration,
for your own honour and glory
and for my needs and for those of
    the whole world.
I ask you therefore,
    most loving Mother:

O Maria, Virgo
    et Mater sanctissima,
ecce suscepi dilectissimum
    Filium tuum,
quem immaculato utero
    tuo concepisti,
genuisti, lactasti atque suavissimis
    amplexibus strinxisti.
Ecce, cuius aspectu lætabaris
    et omnibus deliciis replebaris,
illum ipsum tibi humiliter
    et amanter repræsento et offero,

tuis bracchiis constringendum,
    tuo corde amandum,

sanctissimæque Trinitati in
    supremum latriæ cultum,
pro tui ipsius honore et gloria
et pro meis totiusque mundi
    necessitatibus, offerendum.
Rogo ergo te, piissima Mater,

entreat for me the forgiveness
   of all my sins
and, in abundant measure,
   the grace
of serving him in the future
   more faithfully,
and at the last, final grace,
so that with you I may praise him
for all the ages of ages.
Amen.

Hail, Mary, full of grace, the Lord is
   with thee;
blessed art thou amongst women,
and blessed is the fruit of thy
   womb, Jesus.
Holy Mary, Mother of God,
pray for us sinners
now and at the hour of our death.
Amen.

impetra mihi veniam omnium
   peccatorum meorum,
uberemque gratiam ipsi deinceps
   fidelius serviendi,
ac denique gratiam finalem,
ut eum tecum laudare possim
per omnia sæcula sæculorum.

Amen.

Ave Maria, gratia plena, Dominus
   tecum;
benedicta tu in mulieribus,
et benedictus fructus ventris tui,
   Iesus.
Sancta Maria, Mater Dei,
ora pro nobis peccatoribus
nunc et in hora mortis nostræ.
Amen.

AFTER HOLY COMMUNION

Act of Faith

O Jesus, I believe that I have received your Flesh to eat and your Blood to drink, because you have said it, and your word is true. All that I have and all that I am are your gift and now you have given me yourself.

Act of Adoration

O Jesus, my God, my Creator, I adore you, because from your hands I came and with you I am to be happy for ever.

Act of Humility

O Jesus, I am not worthy to receive you, and yet you have come to me that my poor heart may learn of you to be meek and humble.

Act of Love

Jesus, I love you; I love you with all my heart. You know that I love you, and wish to love you daily more and more.

Act of Thanksgiving

My good Jesus, I thank you with all my heart. How good, how kind you are to me. Blessed be Jesus in the most holy Sacrament of the Altar.

Act of Offering

O Jesus, receive my poor offering.
Jesus, you have given yourself to me,
and now let me give myself to you:
I give you my body, that I may be chaste and pure.
I give you my soul, that I may be free from sin.
I give you my heart, that I may always love you.
I give you my every breath that I shall breathe,
and especially my last.
I give you myself in life and in death,
that I may be yours for ever and ever.

For Yourself

O Jesus, wash away my sins with your Precious Blood.

O Jesus, the struggle against temptation is not yet finished. My Jesus, when temptation comes near me, make me strong against it. In the moment of temptation may I always say: "My Jesus, mercy! Mary, help!"

O Jesus, may I lead a good life; may I die a happy death. May I receive you before I die. May I say when I am dying: "Jesus, Mary and Joseph, I give you my heart and my soul".

Listen now for a moment to Jesus Christ; perhaps he has something to say to you. Answer Jesus in your heart, and tell him all your troubles. Then say:

For Perseverance

Jesus, I am going away for a time, but, I trust, not without you. You are with me by your grace. I resolve never to leave you by mortal sin. Although I am so weak I have such hope in you. Give me grace to persevere. Amen.

IF I CAN'T GET TO MASS

Spiritual Communion

Spiritual Communion is the heartfelt desire to receive Our Lord, even when we are unable because of the distance or for some other reason. This desire to receive him through spiritual Communion is an act of love which prolongs our thanksgiving even when we are not in the Eucharistic presence of Our Lord. The wish to live constantly in his presence can be fuelled by acts of love and desire to be united with him and is a means of drawing more deeply from the life of the Holy Spirit dwelling within our souls in the state of grace. 'The effects of a sacrament can be received by desire. Although in such a case the sacrament is not received physically . . . nevertheless the actual reception of the sacrament itself brings with it fuller effect than receiving it through desire alone' (St Thomas Aquinas). The writings of the saints reveal many formulae for making a spiritual Communion:

Acts of Spiritual Communion

My Jesus, I believe that You are truly present in the Most Holy Sacrament. I love You above all things, and I desire to receive You into my soul. Since I cannot at this moment receive You sacramentally, come at least spiritually into my heart. I embrace You as being already there and unite myself wholly to You. Never permit me to be separated from You. Amen.

(St Alphonsus Liguori)

I wish, my Lord, to receive You with the purity, humility and devotion with which your Most Holy Mother received You, with the spirit and fervour of the saints. Come, Lord Jesus.

Give me, good Lord, a longing to be with You ... give me warmth, delight and quickness in thinking upon You. And give me Your grace to long for Your holy sacraments, and specially to rejoice in the presence of Your very blessed Body, Sweet Saviour Christ, in the Holy Sacrament of the altar.

(St Thomas More)

5 April

PALM SUNDAY OF THE PASSION OF THE LORD

Why does Jesus enter Jerusalem? Or better: how does Jesus enter Jerusalem? The crowds acclaim him as King. And he does not deny it, he does not tell them to be silent. But what kind of a King is Jesus? Let us take a look at him: he is riding on a donkey, he is not accompanied by a court, he is not surrounded by an army as a symbol of power. He is received by humble people, simple folk who have the sense to see something more in Jesus; they have that sense of the faith which says: here is the Saviour. Jesus does not enter the Holy City to receive the honours reserved to earthly kings, to the powerful, to rulers; he enters to be scourged, insulted and abused, as Isaiah foretold in the First Reading. He enters to receive a crown of thorns, a staff, a purple robe: his kingship becomes an object of derision. He enters to climb Calvary, carrying his burden of wood. Jesus enters Jerusalem in order to die on the Cross. And it is precisely here that his kingship shines forth in godly fashion: his royal throne is the wood of the Cross! It reminds me of what Benedict XVI said to the Cardinals: you are princes, but of a king crucified.

(Pope Francis)

On this day the Church recalls the entrance of Christ the Lord into Jerusalem to accomplish his Paschal Mystery. Accordingly, the memorial of this entrance of the Lord takes place at all Masses, by means of the Procession or the Solemn Entrance before the principal Mass or the Simple Entrance before other Masses. The Solemn Entrance, but not the Procession, may be repeated before other Masses that are usually celebrated with a large gathering of people.

It is desirable that, where neither the Procession nor the Solemn Entrance can take place, there be a sacred celebration of the Word of God on the messianic entrance and on the Passion of the Lord, either on Saturday evening or on Sunday at a convenient time.

The Commemoration of the Lord's Entrance into Jerusalem

First Form: The Procession

At an appropriate hour, a gathering takes place at a smaller church or other suitable place other than inside the church to which the procession will go. The faithful hold branches in their hands.

Wearing the red sacred vestments as for Mass, the Priest and the Deacon, accompanied by other ministers, approach the place where the people are gathered.

Instead of the chasuble, the Priest may wear a cope, which he leaves aside when the procession is over, and puts on a chasuble.

Meanwhile, the following antiphon or another appropriate chant is sung.

Ant.	Mt 21:9	Ant.

Hosanna to the Son of David;
blessed is he who comes
in the name of the Lord,
the King of Israel.
Hosanna in the highest.

Hosanna filio David:
benedictus qui venit
    in nomine Domini.
Rex Israel:
Hosanna in excelsis.

After this, the Priest and people sign themselves, while the Priest says: **In the name of the Father, and of the Son, and of the Holy Spirit**. Then he greets the people in the usual way. A brief address is given, in which the faithful are invited to participate actively and consciously in the celebration of this day, in these or similar words:

Dear brethren (brothers and sisters),
since the beginning of Lent until now
we have prepared our hearts
    by penance and charitable works.
Today we gather together to herald
    with the whole Church
the beginning of the celebration
of our Lord's Paschal Mystery,
that is to say, of his Passion
    and Resurrection.
For it was to accomplish this mystery
that he entered his own city
    of Jerusalem.
Therefore, with all faith
    and devotion,
let us commemorate
the Lord's entry into the city
    for our salvation,
following in his footsteps,
so that, being made by his grace
    partakers of the Cross,
we may have a share also in his
    Resurrection and in his life.

Fratres carissimi,
postquam iam ab initio
    Quadragesimæ corda nostra
pænitentia et operibus
    caritatis præparavimus,
hodierna die congregamur,
ut cum tota Ecclesia præludamus
paschale Domini nostri mysterium,
eius nempe passionem
    atque resurrectionem,
ad quod implendum
ipse ingressus est civitatem
    suam Ierusalem.
Quare cum omni fide et devotione
    memoriam agentes
huius salutiferi ingressus,
    sequamur Dominum,
ut, per gratiam consortes
    effecti crucis,
partem habeamus resurrectionis
    et vitæ.

After the address, the Priest says one of the following prayers with hands extended.

Let us pray.

Almighty ever-living God,
sanctify ✠ these branches
   with your blessing,
that we, who follow Christ the King
   in exultation,
may reach the eternal Jerusalem
   through him.
Who lives and reigns
   for ever and ever.
℟. Amen.

Or:

Increase the faith of those who
   place their hope in you, O God,
and graciously hear the prayers
   of those who call on you,
that we, who today hold high
   these branches
to hail Christ in his triumph,
may bear fruit for you by good
   works accomplished in him.
Who lives and reigns
for ever and ever.
℟. Amen.

Oremus.

Omnipotens sempiterne Deus,
hos palmites tua
   benedictione ✠ sanctifica,
ut nos, qui Christum Regem
   exsultando prosequimur,
per ipsum valeamus ad æternam
   Ierusalem pervenire.
Qui vivit et regnat
   in sæcula sæculorum.
℟. Amen.

Vel:

Auge fidem in te sperantium, Deus,
et supplicum preces
   clementer exaudi,
ut, qui hodie Christo triumphanti
   palmites exhibemus,
in ipso fructus tibi bonorum
   operum afferamus.
Qui vivit et regnat
   in sæcula sæculorum.
℟. Amen.

He sprinkles the branches with holy water without saying anything.

Then a Deacon or, if there is no Deacon, a Priest, proclaims in the usual way the Gospel concerning the Lord's entrance according to one of the four Gospels. If appropriate, incense may be used.

GOSPEL

A reading from the holy Gospel according to Matthew   21:1-11

'Blessed is he who comes in the name of the Lord.'

When they drew near to Jerusalem
and came to Bethphage, to the Mount of Olives,
Jesus sent two disciples, saying to them,
'Go into the village opposite you,
and immediately you will find an ass tied,
and a colt with her; untie them and bring them to me.
If any one says anything to you, you shall say,
"The Lord has need of them,"
and he will send them immediately.'
This took place to fulfil
what was spoken by the prophet, saying,

'Tell the daughter of Sion,
Behold, your king is coming to you,
humble, and mounted on an ass,
and on a colt, the foal of an ass.'

The disciples went and did as Jesus had directed them;
they brought the ass and the colt,
and put their garments on them, and he sat thereon.
Most of the crowd spread their garments on the road,
and others cut branches from the trees
and spread them on the road.
And the crowds that went before him
and that followed him shouted,
'Hosanna to the Son of David!
Blessed is he who comes in the name of the Lord!
Hosanna in the highest!'
And when he entered Jerusalem,
all the city was stirred, saying, 'Who is this?'
And the crowds said,
'This is the prophet Jesus from Nazareth of Galilee.'

The Gospel of the Lord.

After the Gospel, a brief homily may be given. Then, to begin the Procession, an invitation may be given by a Priest or a Deacon or a lay minister, in these or similar words:

Dear brethren (brothers and sisters), like the crowds who acclaimed
   Jesus in Jerusalem,
let us go forth in peace.

Imitemur, fratres carissimi,
   turbas acclamantes Iesum,
et procedamus in pace.

Or:

Vel:

Let us go forth in peace.

Procedamus in pace.

In this latter case, all respond:

In the name of Christ. Amen.
In nomine Christi. Amen.

The Procession to the church where Mass will be celebrated then sets off in the usual way. If incense is used, the thurifer goes first, carrying a thurible with burning incense, then an acolyte or another minister, carrying a cross decorated with palm branches according to local custom, between two ministers with lighted candles. Then follow the Deacon carrying the Book of the Gospels, the Priest with the ministers, and, after them, all the faithful carrying branches.

As the Procession moves forward, the following or other suitable chants in honour of Christ the King are sung by the choir and people.

Antiphon 1

Antiphona 1

The children of the Hebrews,
   carrying olive branches,
went to meet the Lord,
   crying out and saying:
Hosanna in the highest.

Pueri Hebræorum,
   portantes ramos olivarum,
obviaverunt Domino,
   clamantes et dicentes:
Hosanna in excelsis.

If appropriate, this antiphon is repeated between the strophes of the following Psalm.

PSALM 23

The Lord's is the earth
   and its fullness,*
the world, and those who dwell in it.
It is he who set it on the seas;*
on the rivers he made it firm. Ant.

Domini est terra et plenitudo eius,*
orbis terrarum et qui habitant in eo.
Quia ipse super maria fundavit eum*
et super flumina firmavit eum. Ant.

Who shall climb the mountain
    of the Lord?*
The clean of hands and pure of heart,
whose soul is not set on vain things,†
who has not sworn
    deceitful words.* Ant.

Quis ascendet in montem Domini,*
aut quis stabit in loco sancto eius?
Innocens manibus et mundo corde,†
qui non levavit ad vana
    animam suam,*
nec iuravit in dolum. Ant.

Blessings from the Lord
    shall he receive,*
and right reward from the God
    who saves him.
Such are the people who seek him,*
who seek the face of the God
    of Jacob. Ant.

Hic accipiet benedictionem
    a Domino*
et iustificationem a Deo salutari suo.
Hæc est generatio
    quærentium eum,*
quærentium faciem Dei Iacob. Ant.

O gates, lift high your heads,†
grow higher, ancient doors.*
Let him enter, the king of glory!
Who is this king of glory?*
The Lord, the mighty, the valiant;
the Lord, the valiant in war. Ant.

Attollite, portæ, capita vestra,†
et elevamini, portæ æternales,*
et introibit rex gloriæ.
Quis est iste rex gloriæ?*
Dominus fortis et potens,
Dominus potens in prœlio. Ant.

O gates, lift high your heads;†
grow higher, ancient doors.*
Let him enter, the king of glory!
Who is this king of glory?*
He, the Lord of hosts,
he is the king of glory. Ant.

Attollite, portæ, capita vestra, †
et elevamini, portæ æternales,*
et introibit rex gloriæ.
Quis est iste rex gloriæ?*
Dominus virtutum ipse est
    rex gloriæ. Ant.

Antiphon 2

The children of the Hebrews spread
    their garments on the road,
crying out and saying:
    Hosanna to the Son of David;
blessed is he who comes
    in the name of the Lord.

Antiphona 2

Pueri Hebræorum vestimenta
    prosternebant in via,
et clamabant dicentes:
    Hosanna filio David;
benedictus, qui venit
    in nomine Domini.

If appropriate, this antiphon is repeated between the strophes of the following Psalm.

PSALM 46

All peoples, clap your hands.*
Cry to God with shouts of joy!
For the Lord, the Most High,
　　is awesome,*
the great king over all the earth. Ant.

He humbles peoples under us*
and nations under our feet.
Our heritage he chose for us,*
the pride of Jacob whom he loves.
God goes up with shouts of joy.*
The Lord goes up
　　with trumpet blast. Ant.

Sing praise for God; sing praise!*
Sing praise to our king; sing praise!
God is king of all earth.*
Sing praise with all your skill. Ant.

God reigns over the nations.*
God sits upon his holy throne.
The princes of the peoples
　　are assembled
with the people of the God
　　of Abraham. †
The rulers of the earth belong
　　to God,*
who is greatly exalted. Ant.

Omnes gentes, plaudite manibus,*
iubilate Deo in voce exsultationis,
quoniam Dominus Altissimus,
　　terribilis,*
rex magnus super omnem terram. Ant.

Subiecit populos nobis,*
et gentes sub pedibus nostris.
Elegit nobis hereditatem nostram,*
gloriam Iacob, quem dilexit.
Ascendit Deus in iubilo,*
et Dominus in voce tubæ. Ant.

Psallite Deo, psallite;*
psallite regi nostro, psallite.
Quoniam rex omnis terræ Deus,*
psallite sapienter. Ant.

Regnavit Deus super gentes,*
Deus sedet super sedem
　　sanctam suam.
Principes populorum congregati sunt
cum populo Dei Abraham,†
quoniam Dei sunt scuta terræ:*
vehementer elevatus est. Ant.

Hymn to Christ the King
Chorus:

Glory and honour and praise be to
　　you, Christ, King and Redeemer,
to whom young children cried out
　　loving Hosannas with joy.
All repeat: Glory and honour. . .
Chorus:

Israel's King are you, King David's
　　magnificent offspring;
you are the ruler who come blest
　　in the name of the Lord.
All repeat: Glory and honour. . .

Hymnus ad Christum Regem

Gloria, laus et honor tibi sit,
　　rex Christe redemptor,
cui puerile decus prompsit
　　Hosanna pium.
Omnes repetunt: Gloria, laus. . .

Israel es tu rex, Davidis
　　et inclita proles,
nomine qui in Domini,
　　rex benedicte, venis.
Omnes repetunt: Gloria, laus. . .

Chorus:

Heavenly hosts on high unite
   in singing your praises;
men and women on earth
   and all creation join in.
All repeat: Glory and honour. . .

Chorus:

Bearing branches of palm, Hebrews
   came crowding to greet you;
see how with prayers and hymns
   we come to pay you our vows.
All repeat: Glory and honour. . .

Chorus:

They offered gifts of praise to you,
   so near to your Passion;
see how we sing this song now
   to you reigning on high.
All repeat: Glory and honour. . .

Chorus:

Those you were pleased to accept;
   now accept our gifts of devotion,
good and merciful King,
   lover of all that is good.
All repeat: Glory and honour. . .

Cœtus in excelsis te laudat
   cælicus omnis,
et mortalis homo,
   et cuncta creata simul.
Omnes repetunt: Gloria, laus. . .

Plebs Hebræa tibi cum palmis
   obvia venit;
cum prece, voto,
   hymnis adsumus ecce tibi.
Omnes repetunt: Gloria, laus. . .

Hi tibi passuro solvebant
   munia laudis;
nos tibi regnanti
   pangimus ecce melos.
Omnes repetunt: Gloria, laus. . .

Hi placuere tibi,
   placeat devotio nostra:
rex bone, rex clemens,
   cui bona cuncta placent.
Omnes repetunt: Gloria, laus. . .

As the procession enters the church, there is sung the following responsory or another chant, which should speak of the Lord's entrance.

R. As the Lord entered the holy city,
the children of the Hebrews
proclaimed the resurrection of life.
*Waving their branches of palm,
   they cried:
Hosanna in the Highest.

V. When the people heard that
   Jesus was coming to Jerusalem,
   they went out to meet him.

*Waving their branches. . .

R. Ingrediente Domino
   in sanctam civitatem,
Hebræorum pueri, resurrectionem
   vitæ pronuntiantes,
*Cum ramis palmarum:
Hosanna, clamabant, in excelsis.

V. Cum audisset populus, quod
   Iesus veniret Hierosolymam,
   exierunt obviam ei.

*Cum ramis. . .

When the Priest arrives at the altar, he venerates it and, if appropriate, incenses it. Then he goes to the chair, where he puts aside the cope, if he has worn one, and puts on the chasuble. Omitting the other Introductory Rites of the Mass and, if appropriate, the **Kyrie** (**Lord, have mercy**), he says the Collect of the Mass, and then continues the Mass in the usual way.

Second Form: The Solemn Entrance

When a procession outside the church cannot take place, the entrance of the Lord is celebrated inside the church by means of a Solemn Entrance before the principal Mass.

Holding branches in their hands, the faithful gather either outside, in front of the church door, or inside the church itself. The Priest and ministers and a representative group of the faithful go to a suitable place in the church outside the sanctuary, where at least the greater part of the faithful can see the rite.

While the Priest approaches the appointed place, the antiphon **Hosanna** or another appropriate chant is sung. Then the blessing of branches and the proclamation of the Gospel of the Lord's entrance into Jerusalem take place. After the Gospel, the Priest processes solemnly with the ministers and the representative group of the faithful through the church to the sanctuary, while the responsory **As the Lord entered** or another appropriate chant is sung.

Arriving at the altar, the Priest venerates it. He then goes to the chair and, omitting the Introductory Rites of the Mass and, if appropriate, the **Kyrie** (**Lord, have mercy**), he says the Collect of the Mass, and then continues the Mass in the usual way.

Third Form: The Simple Entrance

At all other Masses of this Sunday at which the Solemn Entrance is not held, the memorial of the Lord's entrance into Jerusalem takes place by means of a Simple Entrance.

While the Priest proceeds to the altar, the Entrance Antiphon with its Psalm or another chant on the same theme is sung. Arriving at the altar, the Priest venerates it and goes to the chair. After the Sign of the Cross, he greets the people and continues the Mass in the usual way.

At other Masses, in which singing at the entrance cannot take place, the Priest, as soon as he has arrived at the altar and venerated it, greets the people, reads the Entrance Antiphon, and continues the Mass in the usual way.

Entrance Antiphon Cf. Jn 12:1,12-13; Ps 23:9-10 | Ant. ad introitum

SIX days before the Passover,
when the Lord came into
   the city of Jerusalem,
the children ran to meet him;
in their hands they carried
   palm branches
and with a loud voice cried out:

*Hosanna in the highest!
Blessed are you, who have come
   in your abundant mercy!

O gates, lift high your heads;
grow higher, ancient doors.
Let him enter, the king of glory!
Who is this king of glory?
He, the Lord of hosts,
   he is the king of glory.

*Hosanna in the highest!
Blessed are you, who have come
   in your abundant mercy!

ANTE sex dies sollemnis Paschæ,
   quando venit Dominus
   in civitatem Ierusalem,
occurrerunt ei pueri:
et in manibus portabant
   ramos palmarum
et clamabant voce magna, dicentes:

*Hosanna in excelsis:
Benedictus, qui venisti
   in multitudine misericordiæ tuæ.
Attollite, portæ, capita vestra,
et elevamini, portæ æternales,
et introibit rex gloriæ.
Quis est iste rex gloriæ?
Dominus virtutum ipse est
   rex gloriæ.

*Hosanna in excelsis:
Benedictus, qui venisti
   in multitudine misericordiæ tuæ.

At the Mass

After the Procession or Solemn Entrance the Priest begins the Mass with the Collect.

Collect | Collecta

Almighty ever-living God,
who as an example of humility
   for the human race to follow
caused our Saviour to take flesh
   and submit to the Cross,
graciously grant that we may heed
   his lesson of patient suffering
and so merit a share
   in his Resurrection.
Who lives and reigns with you
   in the unity of the Holy Spirit,
one God, for ever and ever.

Omnipotens sempiterne Deus,
qui humano generi, ad imitandum
   humilitatis exemplum,
Salvatorem nostrum carnem sumere,
et crucem subire fecisti,
concede propitius,
ut et patientiæ ipsius
   habere documenta
et resurrectionis consortia mereamur.
Qui tecum vivit et regnat
   in unitate Spiritus Sancti,
Deus, per omnia sæcula sæculorum.

FIRST READING

A reading from the prophet Isaiah   50:4-7

I did not cover my face against insult - I know I shall not be shamed.

The Lord has given me
a disciple's tongue.
So that I may know how to reply to the wearied
he provides me with speech.
Each morning he wakes me to hear,
to listen like a disciple.
The Lord has opened my ear.
For my part, I made no resistance,
neither did I turn away.
I offered my back to those who struck me,
my cheeks to those who tore at my beard;
I did not cover my face
against insult and spittle.
The Lord comes to my help,
so that I am untouched by the insults.
So, too, I set my face like flint,
I know I shall not be shamed.

The word of the Lord.

Responsorial Psalm   Ps 21:8-9,17-20,23-24. R. v.2

R. **My God, my God, why have you forsaken me?**

All who see me deride me.
They curl their lips, they toss their heads.
'He trusted in the Lord, let him save him;
let him release him if this is his friend.' R.

Many dogs have surrounded me,
a band of the wicked beset me.
They tear holes in my hands and my feet.
I can count every one of my bones. R.

They divide my clothing among them.
They cast lots for my robe.
O Lord, do not leave me alone,
my strength, make haste to help me! R.

I will tell of your name to my brethren
and praise you where they are assembled.
'You who fear the Lord give him praise;
all sons of Jacob, give him glory.
Revere him, Israel's sons.' R.

SECOND READING

A reading from the letter of St Paul to the Philippians 2:6-11

He humbled himself, but God raised him high.

His state was divine,
yet Christ Jesus did not cling
to his equality with God
but emptied himself
to assume the condition of a slave,
and became as men are;
and being as all men are,
he was humbler yet,
even to accepting death,
death on a cross.
But God raised him high
and gave him the name
which is above all other names
so that all beings
in the heavens, on earth and in the underworld,
should bend the knee at the name of Jesus
and that every tongue should acclaim
Jesus Christ as Lord,
to the glory of God the Father.

The word of the Lord.

Gospel Acclamation Ph 2:8-9

R. **Praise to you, O Christ, king of eternal glory.**
Christ was humbler yet,
even to accepting death, death on a cross.
But God raised him high
and gave him the name which is above all names.
R. **Praise to you, O Christ, king of eternal glory.**

The narrative of the Lord's Passion is read without candles and without incense, with no greeting or signing of the book. It is read by a Deacon or, if there is no Deacon, by a Priest. It may also be read by readers, with the part of Christ, if possible, reserved to a Priest.

Deacons, but not others, ask for the blessing of the Priest before singing the Passion, as at other times before the Gospel.

GOSPEL

The passion of our Lord Jesus Christ according to Matthew   26:14-27:66

The symbols in the following passion narrative represent:

N Narrator   J Jesus   O Other single speaker
C Crowd, or more than one speaker

N One of the Twelve, the man called Judas Iscariot, went to the chief priests and said:
O What are you prepared to give me if I hand him over to you?
N They paid him thirty silver pieces, and from that moment he looked for an opportunity to betray him.
    Now on the first day of Unleavened Bread the disciples came to Jesus to say,
C Where do you want us to make the preparations for you to eat the Passover?
N He replied:
J Go to so-and-so in the city and say to him, 'The Master says: My time is near. It is at your house that I am keeping Passover with my disciples.'
N The disciples did what Jesus told them and prepared the Passover. When the evening came he was at table with the twelve disciples. And while they were eating he said:
J I tell you solemnly, one of you is about to betray me.
N They were greatly distressed and started asking him in turn,
C Not I, Lord, surely?
N He answered:
J Someone who has dipped his hand into the dish with me, will betray me. The Son of Man is going to his fate, as the scriptures say he will, but alas for that man by whom the Son of Man is betrayed! Better for that man if he had never been born!
N Judas, who was to betray him, asked in his turn,
O Not I, Rabbi, surely?
N Jesus answered:
J They are your own words.
N Now as they were eating, Jesus took some bread, and when he had said the blessing he broke it and gave it to the disciples and said:
J Take it and eat; this is my body.
N Then he took a cup, and when he had returned thanks he gave it to them saying:
J Drink all of you from this, for this is my blood, the blood of the covenant, which is to be poured out for many for the forgiveness of

sins. From now on, I tell you, I shall not drink wine until the day I drink the new wine with you in the kingdom of my Father.

N   After psalms had been sung they left for the Mount of Olives. Then Jesus said to them,

J   You will all lose faith in me this night, for the scripture says: I shall strike the shepherd and the sheep of the flock will be scattered. But after my resurrection I shall go before you to Galilee.

N   At this, Peter said:

O   Though all lose faith in you, I will never lose faith.

N   Jesus answered him,

J   I tell you solemnly, this very night, before the cock crows, you will have disowned me three times.

N   Peter said to him,

O   Even if I have to die with you, I will never disown you.

N   And all the disciples said the same.
     Then Jesus came with them to a small estate called Gethsemane; and he said to his disciples,

J   Stay here while I go over there to pray.

N   He took Peter and the two sons of Zebedee with him. And sadness came over him, and great distress. Then he said to them:

J   My soul is sorrowful to the point of death. Wait here and keep awake with me.

N   And going on a little further he fell on his face and prayed:

J   My Father, if it is possible let this cup pass me by. Nevertheless, let it be as you, not I, would have it.

N   He came back to the disciples and found them sleeping, and he said to Peter:

J   So you had not the strength to keep awake with me one hour? You should be awake, and praying not to be put to the test. The spirit is willing, but the flesh is weak.

N   Again, a second time, he went away and prayed:

J   My Father, if this cup cannot pass by without my drinking it, your will be done!

N   And he came again back and found them sleeping, their eyes were so heavy. Leaving them there, he went away again and prayed for the third time, repeating the same words. Then he came back to the disciples and said to them,

J   You can sleep on now and take your rest. Now the hour has come when the Son of Man is to be betrayed into the hands of sinners. Get up! Let us go! My betrayer is already close at hand.

N   He was still speaking when Judas, one of the Twelve, appeared, and with him a large number of men armed with swords and clubs, sent by the chief priests and elders of the people Now the traitor had arranged a sign with them. He had said:

O   'The one I kiss, he is the man. Take him in charge.'

N   So he went straight up to Jesus and said:

O   Greetings, Rabbi,

N   and kissed him. Jesus said to him,

J   My friend, do what you are here for.

N   Then they came forward, seized Jesus and took him in charge. At that, one of the followers of Jesus grasped his sword and drew it; he struck out at the high priest's servant and cut off his ear. Jesus then said:

J   Put your sword back, for all who draw the sword will die by the sword. Or do you think that I cannot appeal to my Father who would promptly send more than twelve legions of angels to my defence? But then, how would the scriptures be fulfilled that say this is the way it must be?

N   It was at this time that Jesus said to the crowds:

J   Am I a brigand, that you had to set out to capture me with swords and clubs? I sat teaching in the Temple day after day and you never laid hands on me.

N   Now all this happened to fulfil the prophecies in scripture. Then all the disciples deserted him and ran away.

      The men who had arrested Jesus led him off to Caiaphas the high priest, where the scribes and the elders were assembled. Peter followed him at a distance, and when he reached the high priest's palace, he went in and sat down with the attendants to see what the end would be.

      The chief priests and the whole Sanhedrin were looking for evidence against Jesus, however false, on which they might pass the death-sentence. But they could not find any, though several lying witnesses came forward. Eventually two stepped forward and made a statement,

O   This man said: 'I have power to destroy the Temple of God and in three days build it up.'

N   The high priest then stood up and said to him:

O   Have you no answer to that? What is this evidence these men are bringing against you?

N   But Jesus was silent. And the high priest said to him:

O   I put you on oath by the living God to tell us if you are the Christ, the Son of God.

N   Jesus answered:

J   The words are your own. Moreover, I tell you that from this time onward you will see the Son of Man seated at the right hand of the Power and coming on the clouds of heaven.

N   At this, the high priest tore his clothes and said:

O   He has blasphemed. What need of witnesses have we now? There! You have just heard the blasphemy. What is your opinion?

N   They answered:

C   He deserves to die

N   Then they spat in his face and hit him with their fists; others said as they struck him:

C   Play the prophet, Christ! Who hit you then?

N   Meanwhile Peter was sitting outside in the courtyard, and a servant-girl came up to him and said:

O   You too were with Jesus the Galilean.

N   But he denied it in front of them all, saying:

O   I do not know what you are talking about.

N   When he went out to the gateway another servant-girl saw him and said to the people there:

O   This man was with Jesus the Nazarene.

N   And again, with an oath, he denied it,

O   I do not know the man.

N   A little later the bystanders came up and said to Peter:

C   You are one of them for sure! Why, your accent gives you away.

N   Then he started calling down curses on himself and swearing:

O   I do not know the man.

N   At that moment the cock crew, and Peter remembered what Jesus had said, 'Before the cock crows you will have disowned me three times.' And he went outside and wept bitterly.

When morning came, all the chief priests and the elders of the people met in council to bring about the death of Jesus. They had him bound, and led him away to hand him over to Pilate, the governor. When he found that Jesus had been condemned, Judas his betrayer was filled with remorse and took the thirty pieces of silver back to the chief priests and elders, saying:

O   I have sinned. I have betrayed innocent blood.
N   They replied:
C   What is that to us? That is your concern.
N   And flinging down the silver pieces in the sanctuary he made off, and
    went and hanged himself. The chief priests picked up the silver pieces
    and said:
C   It is against the Law to put this into the treasury; it is blood money.
N   So they discussed the matter and bought the potter's field with it as a
    graveyard for foreigners, and this is why the field is called the Field of
    Blood today. The words of the prophet Jeremiah were then fulfilled:
    And they took the thirty silver pieces, the sum at which the precious
    One was priced by children of Israel, and they gave them for the
    potter's field, just as the Lord directed me.
    [Jesus, then, was brought before the governor, and the governor put to
    him this question:
O   Are you the king of the Jews?
N   Jesus replied:
J   It is you who say it.
N   But when he was accused by the chief priests and the elders he refused
    to answer at all. Pilate then said to him:
O   Do you not hear how many charges they have brought against you?
N   But to the governor's complete amazement, he offered no reply to any
    of the charges.
        At festival time it was the governor's practice to release a prisoner
    for the people, anyone they chose. Now there was at that time a
    notorious prisoner whose name was Barabbas. So when the crowd
    gathered, Pilate said to them,
O   Which do you want me to release for you: Barabbas or Jesus who is
    called Christ?
N   For Pilate knew it was out of jealousy that they had handed him over.
    Now as he was seated in the chair of judgement, his wife sent him a message,
O   Have nothing to do with that man; I have been upset all day by a dream
    I had about him.
N   The chief priests and the elders, however, had persuaded the crowd to
    demand the release of Barabbas and the execution of Jesus. So when
    the governor spoke and asked them:
O   Which of the two do you want me to release for you?
N   They said:

C Barabbas.

N Pilate said to them:

O What am I to do with Jesus who is called Christ?

N They all said:

C Let him be crucified!

N Pilate asked:

O Why? What harm has he done?

N But they shouted all the louder,

C Let him be crucified!

N Then Pilate saw that he was making no impression, that in fact a riot was imminent. So he took some water, washed his hands in front of the crowd and said:

O I am innocent of this man's blood. It is your concern.

N And the people, to a man, shouted back:

C His blood be on us and on our children!

N Then he released Barabbas for them. He ordered Jesus to be first scourged and then handed over to be crucified.

The governor's soldiers took Jesus with them into the Praetorium and collected the whole cohort round him. Then they stripped him and made him wear a scarlet cloak, and having twisted some thorns into a crown they put this on his head and placed a reed in his right hand. To make fun of him they knelt to him saying:

C Hail, king of the Jews!

N And they spat on him and took the reed and struck him on the head with it. And when they had finished making fun of him, they took off the cloak and dressed him in his own clothes and led him away to crucify him.

On their way out, they came across a man from Cyrene, Simon by name, and enlisted him to carry his cross. When they had reach a place called Golgotha, that is, the place of the skull, they gave him wine to drink. When they had finished crucifying him they shared out his clothing by casting lots, and then sat down and stayed there keeping guard over him. Above his head was placed the charge against him; it read: 'This is Jesus, the King of the Jews.' At the same time two robbers were crucified with him, one on the right and one on the left.

The passers-by jeered at him; they shook their heads and said:

C So you would destroy the Temple and rebuild it in three days! Then save yourself! If you are God's son, come down from the cross!

N   The chief priests with the scribes and elders mocked him in the same way, saying:

C   He saved others; he cannot save himself. He is the King of Israel; let him come down from the cross now, and we will believe in him. He put his trust in God; now let God rescue him if he wants him. For he did say, 'I am the son of God.'

N   Even the robbers who were crucified with him taunted him in the same way.

From the sixth hour there was darkness over all the land until the ninth hour. And about the ninth hour, Jesus cried out in a loud voice:

J   Eli, Eli, lama sabachthani?

N   That is: 'My God, my God, why have you deserted me?' When some of those who stood there heard this, they said:

C   The man is calling on Elijah,

N   and one of them quickly ran to get a sponge which he dipped in vinegar and, putting it on a reed, gave it him to drink. The rest of them said:

C   Wait! See if Elijah will come to save him.

N   But Jesus, again crying out in a loud voice, yielded up his spirit.

All kneel and pause a moment.

N   At that, the veil of the Temple was torn in two from top to bottom; the earth quaked; the rocks were split; the tombs opened and the bodies of many holy men rose from the dead, and these, after his resurrection, came out of the tombs, entered the Holy City and appeared to a number of people.

Meanwhile the centurion, together with the others guarding Jesus, had seen the earthquake and all that was taking place, and they were terrified and said:

C   In truth this was a son of God.]

N   And many women were there, watching from a distance, the same women who had followed Jesus from Galilee and looked after him. Among them were Mary of Magdala, Mary the mother of James and Joseph, and the mother of Zebedee's sons.

When it was evening, there came a rich man of Arimathaea called Joseph, who had himself become a disciple of Jesus. This man went to Pilate and asked for the body of Jesus. Pilate thereupon ordered it to be handed over. So Joseph took the body, wrapped it in a clean shroud and put it in his own new tomb which he had hewn out of the rock. He then rolled a large stone across the entrance of the tomb and went away. Now Mary of Magdala and the other Mary were there, sitting opposite the sepulchre.

Next day, that is, when Preparation Day was over, the chief priests and the Pharisees went in a body to Pilate and said to him,

C Your Excellency, we recall that this impostor said, while he was still alive, 'After three days I shall rise again.' Therefore give the order to have the sepulchre kept secure until the third day, for fear his disciples come and steal him away and tell the people, 'He has risen from the dead.' This last piece of fraud would be worse than what went before.

N Pilate said to them:

O You may have your guards. Go and make all as secure as you know how.

N So they went and made the sepulchre secure, putting seals on the stone and mounting a guard.

| [The Gospel of the Lord.]

Shorter Form, verses 27:11-54. Read between [ ]

After the narrative of the Passion, a brief homily should take place, if appropriate. A period of silence may also be observed.

The Creed is said, and the Universal Prayer takes place.

Prayer over the Offerings

Through the Passion of your Only Begotten Son, O Lord,
may our reconciliation with you be near at hand,
so that, though we do not merit it by our own deeds,
yet by this sacrifice made once for all,
we may feel already the effects of your mercy.
Through Christ our Lord.

Super oblata

Per Unigeniti tui passionem placatio tua nobis, Domine, sit propinqua,
quam, etsi nostris operibus non meremur,
interveniente sacrificio singulari,
tua percipiamus miseratione prӕventi.
Per Christum Dominum nostrum.

Preface: The Passion of the Lord.

It is truly right and just,
our duty and our salvation,
always and everywhere to give you thanks,
Lord, holy Father, almighty and eternal God,
through Christ our Lord.

Prӕfatio: De dominica Passione.

Vere dignum et iustum est,
ӕquum et salutare,
nos tibi semper et ubique gratias agere:
Domine, sancte Pater, omnipotens ӕterne Deus:
per Christum Dominum nostrum.

For, though innocent, he suffered
willingly for sinners
and accepted unjust condemnation
to save the guilty.
His Death has washed away our sins,
and his Resurrection has purchased
our justification.

And so, with all the Angels,
we praise you, as in joyful
celebration we acclaim:

Holy, Holy, Holy Lord God of hosts...

| Qui pati pro impiis dignatus
est innocens,
et pro sceleratis
indebite condemnari.
Cuius mors delicta nostra detersit,
et iustificationem nobis
resurrectio comparavit.

Unde et nos cum omnibus Angelis
te laudamus,
iucunda celebratione clamantes:

Sanctus, Sanctus, Sanctus. . .

Communion Antiphon   Mt 26:42

Father, if this chalice cannot pass
without my drinking it,
your will be done.

Ant. ad communionem

Pater, si non potest
hic calix transire,
nisi bibam illum, fiat voluntas tua.

Prayer after Communion

Nourished with these sacred gifts,
we humbly beseech you, O Lord,
that, just as through the death
of your Son
you have brought us to hope
for what we believe,
so by his Resurrection
you may lead us to where you call.
Through Christ our Lord.

Post communionem

Sacro munere satiati,
supplices te, Domine, deprecamur,
ut, qui fecisti nos
morte Filii tui sperare
quod credimus,
facias nos, eodem resurgente,
pervenire quo tendimus.
Per Christum Dominum nostrum.

Prayer over the People

Look, we pray, O Lord,
on this your family,
for whom our Lord Jesus Christ
did not hesitate to be delivered
into the hands of the wicked
and submit to the agony
of the Cross.
Who lives and reigns
for ever and ever.

Oratio super populum

Respice, quæsumus, Domine,
super hanc familiam tuam,
pro qua Dominus noster
Iesus Christus
non dubitavit manibus
tradi nocentium,
et crucis subire tormentum.
Qui vivit et regnat
in sæcula sæculorum.

THE SACRED PASCHAL TRIDUUM

In the Sacred Triduum, the Church solemnly celebrates the greatest mysteries of our redemption, keeping by means of special celebrations the memorial of her Lord, crucified, buried, and risen.

The Paschal Fast should also be kept sacred. It is to be celebrated everywhere on the Friday of the Lord's Passion and, where appropriate, prolonged also through Holy Saturday as a way of coming, with spirit uplifted, to the joys of the Lord's Resurrection.

For a fitting celebration of the Sacred Triduum, a sufficient number of lay ministers is required, who must be carefully instructed as to what they are to do.

The singing of the people, the ministers, and the Priest Celebrant has a special importance in the celebrations of these days, for when texts are sung, they have their proper impact.

Pastors should, therefore, not fail to explain to the Christian faithful, as best they can, the meaning and order of the celebrations and to prepare them for active and fruitful participation.

The celebrations of the Sacred Triduum are to be carried out in cathedral and parochial churches and only in those churches in which they can be performed with dignity, that is, with a good attendance of the faithful, an appropriate number of ministers, and the means to sing at least some of the parts.

Consequently, it is desirable that small communities, associations, and special groups of various kinds join together in these churches to carry out the sacred celebrations in a more noble manner.

9 April

THURSDAY OF THE LORD'S SUPPER
(MAUNDY THURSDAY)

Actions speak louder than images and words. There are, in this Word of God that we have read, two acts: Jesus who serves, who washes feet.... He, who was the "master", washes the feet of others, his disciples, of the least. An act. The second act: Judas who goes to Jesus' enemies, to those who do not want peace with Jesus, in order to take the money for which he betrayed him, thirty pieces of silver... Today, at this moment, as I perform the same act as Jesus by washing the feet of you twelve, we are all engaged in the act of brotherhood, and we are all saying: "We are diverse, we are different, we have different cultures and religions, but we are brothers and sisters and we want to live in peace". This is the act that I carry out with you. Each of us has a history on our shoulders: so many crosses, so much pain, but also an open heart that wants brotherhood.

(Pope Francis)

In accordance with a most ancient tradition of the Church, on this day all Masses without the people are forbidden.

At the Evening Mass

The Mass of the Lord's Supper is celebrated in the evening, at a convenient time, with the full participation of the whole local community and with all the Priests and ministers exercising their office.

All Priests may concelebrate even if they have already concelebrated the Chrism Mass on this day, or if they have to celebrate another Mass for the good of the Christian faithful.

Where a pastoral reason requires it, the local Ordinary may permit another Mass to be celebrated in churches and oratories in the evening and, in case of genuine necessity, even in the morning, but only for the faithful who are in no way able to participate in the evening Mass. Care should, nevertheless, be taken that celebrations of this sort do not take place for the advantage of private persons or special small groups, and do not prejudice the evening Mass.

Holy Communion may only be distributed to the faithful during Mass; but it may be brought to the sick at any hour of the day.

The altar may be decorated with flowers with a moderation that accords with the character of this day. The tabernacle should be entirely empty; but a sufficient amount of bread should be consecrated in this Mass for the Communion of the clergy and the people on this and the following day.

Entrance Antiphon Cf. Ga 6:14	Ant. ad introitum

WE should glory in the Cross
of our Lord Jesus Christ,
in whom is our salvation,
  life and resurrection,
through whom we are saved
  and delivered.

NOS autem gloriari oportet
in cruce Domini nostri
  Iesu Christi,
in quo est salus,
  vita et resurrectio nostra,
per quem salvati et liberati sumus.

The **Gloria in excelsis** (Glory to God in the highest) is said. While the hymn is being sung, bells are rung, and when it is finished, they remain silent until the **Gloria in excelsis** of the Easter Vigil, unless, if appropriate, the Diocesan Bishop has decided otherwise. Likewise, during this same period, the organ and other musical instruments may be used only so as to support the singing.

Collect	Collecta

O God, who have called us
  to participate
in this most sacred Supper,
in which your Only Begotten Son,
when about to hand himself over
  to death,
entrusted to the Church a sacrifice
  new for all eternity,
the banquet of his love,
grant, we pray,
that we may draw from so great
  a mystery,
the fullness of charity and of life.
Through our Lord Jesus Christ,
  your Son,
who lives and reigns with you
  in the unity of the Holy Spirit,
one God, for ever and ever.

Sacratissimam, Deus,
  frequentantibus Cenam,
in qua Unigenitus tuus,
  morti se traditurus,
novum in sæcula sacrificium
dilectionisque suæ convivium
  Ecclesiæ commendavit,
da nobis, quæsumus,
  ut ex tanto mysterio
plenitudinem caritatis hauriamus
  et vitæ.
Per Dominum nostrum Iesum
  Christum Filium tuum,
qui tecum vivit et regnat
  in unitate Spiritus Sancti,
Deus, per omnia sæcula sæculorum.

FIRST READING

A reading from the book of Exodus   12:1-8,11-14

Instructions concerning the Passover meal.

The Lord said to Moses and Aaron in the land of Egypt, 'This month is to be the first of all the others for you, the first month of your year. Speak to the whole community of Israel and say, "On the tenth day of this month each man must take an animal from the flock, one for each family: one animal for each household. If the household is too small to eat the animal, a man must join with his neighbour, the nearest to his house, as the number of persons requires. You must take into account what each can eat in deciding the number for the animal. It must be an animal without blemish, a male one year old; you may take it from either sheep or goats. You must keep it till the fourteenth day of the month when the whole assembly of the community of Israel shall slaughter it between the two evenings. Some of the blood must then be taken and put on the two doorposts and the lintel of the houses where it is eaten. That night, the flesh is to be eaten, roasted over the fire; it must be eaten with unleavened bread and bitter herbs. You shall eat it like this: with a girdle round your waist, sandals on your feet, a staff in your hand. You shall eat it hastily; it is a passover in honour of the Lord. That night, I will go through the land of Egypt and strike down all the first-born in the land of Egypt, man and beast alike, and I shall deal out punishment to all the gods of Egypt, I am the Lord. The blood shall serve to mark the houses that you live in. When I see the blood I will pass over you and you shall escape the destroying plague when I strike the land of Egypt. This day is to be a day of remembrance for you, and you must celebrate it as a feast in the Lord's honour. For all generations you are to declare it a day of festival, for ever.'"

The word of the Lord.

Responsorial Psalm   Ps 115:12-13,15-18. R. Cf. 1 Co 10:16

R. **The blessing-cup that we bless**
   is a communion with the blood of Christ.

How can I repay the Lord
for his goodness to me?
The cup of salvation I will raise;
I will call on the Lord's name. R.

O precious in the eyes of the Lord
is the death of his faithful.
Your servant, Lord, your servant am I;
you have loosened my bonds. R.

A thanksgiving sacrifice I make:
I will call on the Lord's name.
My vows to the Lord I will fulfil
before all his people. R.

SECOND READING

A reading from the first letter of St Paul to the Corinthians   11:23-26

Every time you eat this bread and drink this cup, you are proclaiming the death of the Lord.

This is what I received from the Lord, and in turn passed on to you: that on the same night that he was betrayed, the Lord Jesus took some bread, and thanked God for it and broke it, and he said, 'This is my body, which is for you; do this as a memorial of me.' In the same way he took the cup after supper, and said,'This cup is the new covenant in my blood. Whenever you drink it, do this as a memorial of me.' Until the Lord comes, therefore, every time you eat this bread and drink this cup, you are proclaiming his death.

The word of the Lord.

Gospel Acclamation   Jn 13:34

R. **Praise and honour to you, Lord Jesus!**
I give you a new commandment:
love one another just as I have loved you, says the Lord.
R. **Praise and honour to you, Lord Jesus!**

GOSPEL

A reading from the holy Gospel according to John   13:1-15

Now he showed how perfect his love was.

It was before the festival of the Passover, and Jesus knew that the hour had come for him to pass from this world to the Father. He had always loved those who were his in the world, but now he showed how perfect his love was.

They were at supper, and the devil had already put it into the mind of Judas Iscariot son of Simon, to betray him. Jesus knew that the Father had put everything into his hands, and that he had come from God and was returning to God, and he got up from table, removed his outer garment and, taking a towel, wrapped it round his waist; he then poured water into a basin and began to wash the disciples' feet and to wipe them with the towel he was wearing.

He came to Simon Peter, who said to him, 'Lord, are you going to wash my feet?' Jesus answered, 'At the moment you do not know what I am doing, but later you will understand.' 'Never!' said Peter 'You shall never wash my feet.' Jesus replied, 'If I do not wash you, you can have nothing in common with me.' 'Then, Lord,' said Simon Peter 'not only my feet, but my hands and my head as well!' Jesus said, 'No one who has taken a bath needs washing, he is clean all over. You too are clean, though not all of you are.' He knew who was going to betray him, that was why he said, 'though not all of you are.'

When he had washed their feet and put on his clothes again he went back to the table. 'Do you understand' he said 'what I have done to you? You call me Master and Lord, and rightly; so I am. If I, then, the Lord and Master, have washed your feet, you should wash each other's feet. I have given you an example so that you may copy what I have done to you.'

The Gospel of the Lord.

After the proclamation of the Gospel, the Priest gives a homily in which light is shed on the principal mysteries that are commemorated in this Mass, namely, the institution of the Holy Eucharist and of the priestly Order, and the commandment of the Lord concerning fraternal charity.

The Washing of Feet

After the Homily, where a pastoral reason suggests it, the Washing of Feet follows.

Those who have been chosen are led by the ministers to seats prepared in a suitable place. Then the Priest (removing his chasuble if necessary) goes to each one, and, with the help of the ministers, pours water over each one's feet and then dries them. Meanwhile some of the following antiphons or other appropriate chants are sung.

Antiphon 1 Cf. Jn 13:4,5,15	Antiphona 1
After the Lord had risen from supper, he poured water into a basin and began to wash the feet of his disciples: he left them this example.	Postquam surrexit Dominus a cena, misit aquam in pelvim, et cœpit lavare pedes discipulorum: hoc exemplum reliquit eis.

Antiphon 2 Cf. Jn 13:12,13,15	Antiphona 2
The Lord Jesus, after eating supper with his disciples, washed their feet and said to them: Do you know what I, your Lord and Master, have done for you? I have given you an example, that you should do likewise.	Dominus Iesus, postquam cenavit cum discipulis suis, lavit pedes eorum, et ait illis: 'Scitis quid fecerim vobis ego, Dominus et Magister? Exemplum dedi vobis, ut et vos ita faciatis.'

Antiphon 3   Jn 13:6,7,8

Lord, are you to wash my feet?
   Jesus said to him in answer:
If I do not wash your feet,
   you will have no share with me.

V. So he came to Simon Peter
   and Peter said to him:
– Lord, are you to wash my feet?. . .

V. What I am doing,
   you do not know for now,
   but later you will come to know.
– Lord, are you to wash my feet?. . .

Antiphon 4   Cf. Jn 13:14

If I, your Lord and Master,
   have washed your feet,
how much more should you wash
   each other's feet?

Antiphon 5   Jn 13:35

This is how all will know that you
   are my disciples:
if you have love for one another.

V. Jesus said to his disciples:
– This is how all will know. . .

Antiphon 6   Jn 13:34

I give you a new commandment,
that you love one another
as I have loved you, says the Lord.

Antiphon 7   1 Co 13:13

Let faith, hope and charity,
   these three, remain among you,
but the greatest of these is charity.

V. Now faith, hope and charity,
   these three, remain;
but the greatest of these is charity.
– Let faith, hope and charity. . .

Antiphona 3

Domine, tu mihi lavas pedes?
   Respondit Iesus et dixit ei:
Se non lavero tibi pedes,
   non habebis partem mecum.

V. Venit ergo ad Simonem Petrum,
   et dixit ei Petrus:
– Domine, tu mihi lavas pedes?. . .

V. Quod ego facio,
   tu nescis modo:
   scies autem postea.
– Domine, tu mihi lavas pedes?. . .

Antiphona 4

Si ego, Dominus et Magister vester,
   lavi vobis pedes:
quanto magis debetis alter alterius
   lavare pedes?

Antiphona 5

In hoc cognoscent omnes,
   quia discipuli mei estis,
si dilectionem habueritis
   ad invicem.

V. Dixit Iesus discipulis suis.
– In hoc cognoscent omnes. . .

Antiphona 6

Mandatum novum do vobis,
   ut diligatis invicem,
sicut dilexi vos, dicit Dominus.

Antiphona 7

Maneant in vobis fides, spes,
   caritas, tria hæc:
maior autem horum est caritas.

V. Nunc autem manent fides, spes,
   caritas, tria hæc:
maior horum est caritas.
– Maneant in vobis fides. . .

After the Washing of Feet, the Priest washes and dries his hands, puts the chasuble back on, and returns to the chair, and from there he directs the Universal Prayer.

The Creed is not said.

The Liturgy of the Eucharist

At the beginning of the Liturgy of the Eucharist, there may be a procession of the faithful in which gifts for the poor may be presented with the bread and wine.

Meanwhile the following, or another appropriate chant, is sung.

Ant.   Where true charity is dwelling,
        God is present there.

V. By the love of Christ we have
        been brought together:

V. let us find in him our gladness
        and our pleasure;

V. may we love him and revere him,
        God the living,

V. and in love respect each other
        with sincere hearts.

Ant. Where true charity is dwelling,
        God is present there.

V. So when we as one are gathered
        all together,

V. let us strive to keep our minds
        free of division;

V. may there be an end to malice,
        strife and quarrels,

V. and let Christ our God
        be dwelling here among us.

Ant. Where true charity is dwelling,
        God is present there.

V. May your face thus be our vision,
        bright in glory,

V. Christ our God, with all
        the blessed Saints in heaven:

V. such delight is pure and faultless,
        joy unbounded,

V. which endures through
        countless ages
        world without end. Amen.

Ant.   Ubi caritas est vera,
        Deus ibi est.

V. Exsultemus et in
        ipso iucundemur.

V. Congregavit nos in unum
        Christi amor.

V. Timeamus et amemus
        Deum vivum.

V. Et ex corde diligamus nos sincero

Ant. Ubi caritas est vera,
        Deus ibi est.

V. Simul ergo cum in
        unum congregamur:

V. Ne nos mente dividamur,
        caveamus.

V. Cessent iurgia maligna,
        cessent lites.

V. Et in medio nostri sit
        Christus Deus.

Ant. Ubi caritas est vera,
        Deus ibi est.

V. Simul quoque cum beatis
        videamus

V. Glorianter vultum tuum,
        Christe Deus:

V. Gaudium, quod est immensum
        atque probum,

V. Sæcula per infinita sæculorum.
        Amen.

Prayer over the Offerings

Grant us, O Lord, we pray,
that we may participate worthily
    in these mysteries,
for whenever the memorial
    of this sacrifice is celebrated
the work of our redemption
    is accomplished.
Through Christ our Lord.

Super oblata

Concede nobis,
    quæsumus, Domine,
hæc digne frequentare mysteria,
quia, quoties huius hostiæ
    commemoratio celebratur,
opus nostræ redemptionis exercetur.
Per Christum Dominum nostrum.

Preface I of the Most Holy Eucharist, pp.68-69.
If the Roman Canon is said, the following special forms are used.

Celebrating the most sacred day
on which our Lord Jesus Christ
was handed over for our sake,
and in communion with those
    whose memory we venerate,
especially the glorious
    ever-Virgin Mary,
Mother of our God and Lord,
    Jesus Christ,
and blessed Joseph, her Spouse,
your blessed Apostles and Martyrs,
Peter and Paul, Andrew,
(James, John,
Thomas, James, Philip,
Bartholomew, Matthew,
Simon and Jude;
Linus, Cletus, Clement, Sixtus,
Cornelius, Cyprian,
Lawrence, Chrysogonus,
John and Paul,
Cosmas and Damian)
and all your Saints;
we ask that through their merits
    and prayers,
in all things we may be defended
by your protecting help.
(Through Christ our Lord. Amen.)

Communicantes, et diem
    sacratissimum celebrantes,
quo Dominus noster Iesus Christus
pro nobis est traditus,
sed et memoriam venerantes,
in primis gloriosæ semper
    Virginis Mariæ,
Genetricis eiusdem Dei et Domini
    nostri Iesu Christi:
sed et beati Ioseph,
    eiusdem Virginis Sponsi,
et beatorum Apostolorum ac
    Martyrum tuorum,
Petri et Pauli, Andreæ,
(Iacobi, Ioannis,
Thomæ, Iacobi, Philippi,
Bartholomæi, Matthæi,
Simonis et Thaddæi:
Lini, Cleti, Clementis, Xysti,
Cornelii, Cypriani,
Laurentii, Chrysogoni,
Ioannis et Pauli,
Cosmæ et Damiani)
et omnium Sanctorum tuorum;
quorum meritis precibusque concedas,
ut in omnibus protectionis tuæ
    muniamur auxilio.
(Per Christum Dominum nostrum.
    Amen.)

Therefore, Lord, we pray:
graciously accept this oblation of
    our service,
that of your whole family,
which we make to you
as we observe the day
on which our Lord Jesus Christ
handed on the mysteries
    of his Body and Blood
for his disciples to celebrate;
order our days in your peace,
and command that we be delivered
    from eternal damnation
and counted among the flock of
    those you have chosen.
(Through Christ our Lord. Amen.)

Be pleased, O God, we pray,
to bless, acknowledge,
and approve this offering
    in every respect;
make it spiritual and acceptable,
so that it may become for us
the Body and Blood of your most
    beloved Son,
our Lord Jesus Christ.

On the day before he was to suffer
for our salvation and the salvation
    of all,
that is today,
he took bread in his holy
    and venerable hands,
and with eyes raised to heaven
to you, O God, his almighty Father,
giving you thanks,
    he said the blessing,
broke the bread
and gave it to his disciples, saying:

TAKE THIS, ALL OF YOU,
    AND EAT OF IT,
FOR THIS IS MY BODY,
WHICH WILL BE GIVEN UP FOR YOU.

Hanc igitur oblationem
    servitutis nostræ,
sed et cunctæ familiæ tuæ,
quam tibi offerimus ob diem,
in qua Dominus noster Iesus Christus
tradidit discipulis suis
Corporis et Sanguinis
    sui mysteria celebranda,
quæsumus, Domine,
    ut placatus accipias:
diesque nostros in tua pace
    disponas,
atque ab æterna damnatione
    nos eripi
et in electorum tuorum iubeas
    grege numerari.
(Per Christum Dominum nostrum.
    Amen.)

Quam oblationem tu, Deus,
    in omnibus, quæsumus,
benedictam, adscriptam, ratam,
rationabilem, acceptabilemque
    facere digneris:
ut nobis Corpus et Sanguis fiat
    dilectissimi Filii tui,
Domini nostri Iesu Christi.

Qui, pridie quam pro nostra
omniumque salute pateretur,
hoc est hodie,
accepit panem in sanctus ac
    venerabiles manus suas,
et elevatis oculis in cælum
ad te Deum Patrem
    suum omnipotentem,
tibi gratias agens benedixit,
fregit, deditque discipulis suis, dicens:

ACCIPITE ET MANDUCATE
    EX HOC OMNES:
HOC EST ENIM CORPUS MEUM,
QUOD PRO VOBIS TRADETUR.

Then follows the remainder of the Roman Canon as usual (see pp.86-93) and the Communion Rite, pp.120-121.

At an appropriate moment during Communion, the Priest entrusts the Eucharist from the table of the altar to Deacons or acolytes or other extraordinary ministers, so that afterwards it may be brought to the sick who are to receive Holy Communion at home.

Communion Antiphon 1 Co 11:24-25	Ant. ad communionem
This is the Body that will be given up for you;	Hoc Corpus, quod pro vobis tradetur:
this is the Chalice of the new covenant in my Blood, says the Lord;	hic calix novi testamenti est in meo Sanguine, dicit Dominus;
do this, whenever you receive it, in memory of me.	hoc facite, quotiescumque sumitis, in meam commemorationem.

After the distribution of Communion, the ciborium with hosts for Communion on the following day is left on the altar. The Priest, standing at the chair, says the Prayer after Communion.

Prayer after Communion	Post communionem
Grant, almighty God, that, just as we are renewed by the Supper of your Son in this present age, so we may enjoy his banquet for all eternity. Who lives and reigns for ever and ever.	Concede nobis, omnipotens Deus, ut, sicut Cena Filii tui reficimur temporali, ita satiari mereamur æterna. Per Christum Dominum nostrum.

The Transfer of the Most Blessed Sacrament

After the Prayer after Communion, the Priest puts incense in the thurible while standing, blesses it and then, kneeling, incenses the Blessed Sacrament three times. Then, having put on a white humeral veil, he rises, takes the ciborium, and covers it with the ends of the veil.

A procession is formed in which the Blessed Sacrament, accompanied by torches and incense, is carried through the church to a place of repose prepared in a part of the church or in a chapel suitably decorated. A lay minister with a cross, standing between two other ministers with lighted candles leads off. Others carrying lighted candles follow. Before the Priest carrying the Blessed Sacrament comes the thurifer with a smoking thurible. Meanwhile, the hymn **Pange, lingua** (exclusive of the last two stanzas) or another eucharistic chant is sung.

When the procession reaches the place of repose, the Priest, with the help of the Deacon if necessary, places the ciborium in the tabernacle, the door of which remains open. Then he puts incense in the thurible and, kneeling, incenses the Blessed Sacrament, while **Tantum ergo Sacramentum** or another eucharistic chant is sung. Then the Deacon or the Priest himself places the Sacrament in the tabernacle and closes the door.

After a period of adoration in silence, the Priest and ministers genuflect and return to the sacristy.

At an appropriate time, the altar is stripped and, if possible, the crosses are removed from the church. It is expedient that any crosses which remain in the church be veiled.

Vespers (Evening Prayer) is not celebrated by those who have attended the Mass of the Lord's Supper.

The faithful are invited to continue adoration before the Blessed Sacrament for a suitable length of time during the night, according to local circumstances, but after midnight the adoration should take place without solemnity.

If the celebration of the Passion of the Lord on the following Friday does not take place in the same church, the Mass is concluded in the usual way and the Blessed Sacrament is placed in the tabernacle.

10 April

FRIDAY OF THE PASSION OF THE LORD
(GOOD FRIDAY)

The Cross is the word through which God has responded to evil in the world. Sometimes it may seem as though God does not react to evil, as if he is silent. And yet, God has spoken, he has replied, and his answer is the Cross of Christ: a word which is love, mercy, forgiveness. It is also reveals a judgement, namely that God, in judging us, loves us. Let us remember this: God judges us by loving us. If I embrace his love then I am saved, if I refuse it, then I am condemned, not by him, but my own self, because God never condemns, he only loves and saves. Tthe word of the Cross is also the answer which Christians offer in the face of evil, the evil that continues to work in us and around us. Christians must respond to evil with good, taking the Cross upon themselves as Jesus did.

(Pope Francis)

On this and the following day, by a most ancient tradition, the Church does not celebrate the Sacraments at all, except for Penance and the Anointing of the Sick.

On this day, Holy Communion is distributed to the faithful only within the celebration of the Lord's Passion; but it may be brought at any hour of the day to the sick who cannot participate in this celebration.

The altar should be completely bare: without a cross, without candles and without cloths.

The Celebration of the Passion of the Lord

On the afternoon of this day, about three o'clock (unless a later hour is chosen for a pastoral reason), there takes place the celebration of the Lord's Passion consisting of three parts, namely, the Liturgy of the Word, the Adoration of the Cross, and Holy Communion.

The Priest and the Deacon, if a Deacon is present, wearing red vestments as for Mass, go to the altar in silence and, after making a reverence to the altar, prostrate themselves or, if appropriate, kneel and pray in silence for a while. All others kneel.

Then the Priest, with the ministers, goes to the chair where, facing the people, who are standing, he says, with hands extended, one of the following prayers, omitting the invitation **Let us pray**.

Prayer

Remember your mercies, O Lord,
and with your eternal protection
   sanctify your servants,
for whom Christ your Son,
by the shedding of his Blood,
established the Paschal Mystery.
Who lives and reigns
   for ever and ever.
R. Amen.

Or:

O God, who by the Passion
   of Christ your Son, our Lord,
abolished the death inherited
   from ancient sin
by every succeeding generation,
grant that just as,
   being conformed to him,
we have borne by the law of nature
the image of the man of earth,
so by the sanctification of grace
we may bear the image of the Man
   of heaven.
Through Christ our Lord.
R. Amen.

Oratio

Reminiscere miserationum
   tuarum, Domine,
et famulos tuos æterna
   protectione sanctifica,
pro quibus Christus, Filius tuus,
per suum cruorem instituit
   paschale mysterium.
Qui vivit et regnat
   in sæcula sæculorum.
R. Amen.

Vel:

Deus, qui peccati veteris
   hereditariam mortem,
in qua posteritatis genus
   omne successerat,
Christi Filii tui, Domini nostri,
   passione solvisti,
da, ut conformes eidem facti,
sicut imaginem terreni hominis
naturæ necessitate portavimus,
ita imaginem cælestis
gratiæ sanctificatione portemus.
Per Christum Dominum nostrum.
R. Amen.

FIRST PART:

The Liturgy of the Word

FIRST READING

A reading from the prophet Isaiah   52:13-53:12

He was pierced through our faults.

See, my servant will prosper,
he shall be lifted up, exalted, rise to great heights.

As the crowds were appalled on seeing him
 – so disfigured did he look
that he seemed no longer human –
so will the crowds be astonished at him,
and kings stand speechless before him;
for they shall see something never told
and witness something never heard before:
'Who could believe what we have heard,
and to whom has the power of the Lord been revealed?'

Like a sapling he grew up in front of us,
like a root in arid ground.
Without beauty, without majesty (we saw him),
no looks to attract our eyes;
a thing despised and rejected by men,
a man of sorrows and familiar with suffering,
a man to make people screen their faces;
he was despised and we took no account of him.

And yet ours were the sufferings he bore,
ours the sorrows he carried.
But we, we thought of him as someone punished,
struck by God, and brought low.
Yet he was pierced through for our faults,
crushed for our sins.
On him lies a punishment that brings us peace,
and through his wounds we are healed.

We had all gone astray like sheep,
each taking his own way,
and the Lord burdened him
with the sins of all of us.

Harshly dealt with, he bore it humbly,
he never opened his mouth,
like a lamb that is led to the slaughter-house,
like a sheep that is dumb before its shearers
never opening its mouth.

By force and by law he was taken;
would anyone plead his cause?
Yes, he was torn away from the land of the living;
for our faults struck down in death.
They gave him a grave with the wicked,
a tomb with the rich,
though he had done no wrong
and there had been no perjury in his mouth.
The Lord has been pleased to crush him with suffering.
If he offers his life in atonement,
he shall see his heirs, he shall have a long life
and through him what the Lord wishes will be done.

His soul's anguish over
he shall see the light and be content.
By his sufferings shall my servant justify many,
taking their faults on himself.

Hence I will grant whole hordes for his tribute,
he shall divide the spoil with the mighty,
for surrendering himself to death
and letting himself be taken for a sinner,
while he was bearing the faults of many
and praying all the time for sinners.

    The word of the Lord.

Responsorial Psalm   Ps 30:2,6,12-13,15-17,25. R. Lk 23:46

R. **Father, into your hands I commend my spirit.**

    In you, O Lord, I take refuge.
    Let me never be put to shame.
    In your justice, set me free.
    Into your hands I commend my spirit.
    It is you who will redeem me, Lord.   R.

In the face of all my foes
I am a reproach,
an object of scorn to my neighbours
and of fear to my friends. R.

Those who see me in the street
run far away from me.
I am like a dead man, forgotten in men's hearts,
like a thing thrown away. R.

But as for me, I trust in you, Lord,
I say: 'You are my God.'
My life is in your hands, deliver me
from the hands of those who hate me. R.

Let your face shine on your servant.
Save me in your love.
Be strong, let your heart take courage,
all who hope in the Lord. R.

R. **Father, into your hands I commend my spirit.**

SECOND READING

A reading from the letter to the Hebrews   4:14-16; 5:7-9

He learnt to obey through suffering and became for all who obey him the source of eternal salvation.

Since in Jesus, the Son of God, we have the supreme high priest who has gone through to the highest heaven, we must never let go of the faith that we have professed. For it is not as if we had a high priest who was incapable of feeling our weaknesses with us; but we have one who has been tempted in every way that we are, though he is without sin. Let us be confident, then, in approaching the throne of grace, that we shall have mercy from him and find grace when we are in need of help.

During his life on earth, he offered up prayer and entreaty, aloud and in silent tears, to the one who had the power to save him out of death, and he submitted so humbly that his prayer was heard. Although he was Son, he learnt to obey through suffering; but having been made perfect, he became for all who obey him the source of eternal salvation.

The word of the Lord.

Gospel Acclamation   Ph 2:8-9

R. **Glory and praise to you, O Christ!**
Christ was humbler yet,
even accepting death, death on a cross.
But God raised him high
and gave him the name which is above all names.
R. **Glory and praise to you, O Christ!**

GOSPEL

The symbols in the following passion narrative represent:

N Narrator   J Jesus   O Other single speaker
C Crowd, or more than one speaker

The passion of our Lord Jesus Christ according to John   18:1-19:42

N Jesus left with his disciples and crossed the Kedron valley. There was a garden there, and he went into it with his disciples. Judas the traitor knew the place well, since Jesus had often met his disciples there, and he brought the cohort to this place together with a detachment of guards sent by the chief priests and the Pharisees, all with lanterns and torches and weapons. Knowing everything that was going to happen to him, Jesus then came forward and said,

J Who are you looking for?

N They answered,

C Jesus the Nazarene.

N He said,

J I am he.

N Now Judas the traitor was standing among them. When Jesus said, 'I am he', they moved back and fell to the ground. He asked them a second time,

J Who are you looking for?

N They said,

C Jesus the Nazarene.

N Jesus replied,

J I have told you that I am he. If I am the one you are looking for, let these others go.

N This was to fulfil the words he has spoken: 'Not one of those you gave me have I lost.'

Simon Peter, who carried a sword, drew it and wounded the high priest's servant, cutting off his right ear. The servant's name was Malchus. Jesus said to Peter,

J   Put your sword back in its scabbard; am I not to drink the cup that the Father has given me?

N   The cohort and its captain and the Jewish guards seized Jesus and bound him. They took him first to Annas, because Annas was the father-in-law of Caiaphas, who was high priest that year. It was Caiaphas who had suggested to the Jews, 'It is better for one man to die for the people.'

      Simon Peter, with another disciple, followed Jesus. This disciple, who was known to the high priest, went with Jesus into the high priest's palace, but Peter stayed outside the door. So the other disciple, the one known to the high priest, went out, spoke to the woman who was keeping the door and brought Peter in. The maid on duty at the door said to Peter,

O   Aren't you another of that man's disciples?

N   He answered,

O   I am not.

N   Now it was cold, and the servants and guards had lit a charcoal fire and were standing there warming themselves; so Peter stood there too, warming himself with the others.

      The high priest questioned Jesus about his disciples and his teaching. Jesus answered,

J   I have spoken openly for all the world to hear; I have always taught in the synagogue and in the Temple where all the Jews meet together: I have said nothing in secret. But why ask me? Ask my hearers what I taught: they know what I said.

N   At these words, one of the guards standing by gave Jesus a slap in the face, saying,

O   Is that the way to answer the high priest?

N   Jesus replied,

J   If there is something wrong in what I said, point it out; but if there is no offence in it, why do you strike me?

N   Then Annas sent him, still bound, to Caiaphas, the high priest. As Simon Peter stood there warming himself, someone said to him,

O   Aren't you another of his disciples?

N   He denied it saying,

O   I am not.

N   One of the high priest's servants, a relation of the man whose ear Peter had cut off, said,

O   Didn't I see you in the garden with him?

N   Again Peter denied it, and at once a cock crew.

They then led Jesus from the house of Caiaphas to the Praetorium. It was now morning. They did not go into the Praetorium themselves or they would be defiled and unable to eat the passover. So Pilate came outside to them and said,

O What charge do you bring against this man?

N They replied,

C If he were not a criminal, we should not be handing him over to you.

N Pilate said,

O Take him yourselves, and try him by your own Law.

N The Jews answered,

C We are not allowed to put a man to death.

N This was to fulfil the words Jesus had spoken indicating the way he was going to die.

So Pilate went back into the Praetorium and called Jesus to him, and asked,

O Are you the king of Jews?

N Jesus replied,

J Do you ask this of your own accord, or have others spoken to you about me?

N Pilate answered,

O Am I a Jew? It is your own people and the chief priests who have handed you over to me: what have you done?

N Jesus replied,

J Mine is not a kingdom of this world; if my kingdom were of this world, my men would have fought to prevent me being surrendered to the Jews. But my kingdom is not of this kind.

N Pilate said,

O So you are the king then?

N Jesus answered,

J It is you who say it. Yes, I am a king. I was born for this; I came into the world for this; to bear witness to the truth, and all who are on the side of truth listen to my voice.

N Pilate said,

O Truth? What is that?

N And with that he went out again to the Jews and said,

O I find no case against him. But according to a custom of yours I should release one prisoner at the Passover; would you like me, then, to release the king of Jews?

N At this they shouted:

C   Not this man, but Barabbas.

N   Barabbas was a brigand.

     Pilate then had Jesus taken away and scourged; and after this, the soldiers twisted some thorns into a crown and put it on his head, and dressed him in a purple robe. They kept coming up to him and saying,

C   Hail, king of the Jews!

N   and they slapped him in the face.

     Pilate came outside again and said to them,

O   Look, I am going to bring him out to you to let you see that I find no case.

N   Jesus then came out wearing the crown of thorns and the purple robe. Pilate said,

O   Here is the man.

N   When they saw him the chief priests and the guards shouted,

C   Crucify him! Crucify him!

N   Pilate said,

O   Take him yourselves and crucify him: I can find no case against him

N   The Jews replied,

C   We have a Law, and according to the Law he ought to die, because he has claimed to be the son of God.

N   When Pilate heard them say this his fears increased. Re-entering the Praetorium, he said to Jesus,

O   Where do you come from?

N   But Jesus made no answer. Pilate then said to him,

O   Are you refusing to speak to me? Surely you know I have power to release you and I have power to crucify you?

N   Jesus replied,

J   You would have no power over me if it had not been given you from above; that is why the one who handed me over to you has the greater guilt.

N   From that moment Pilate was anxious to set him free, but the Jews shouted,

C   If you set him free you are no friend of Caesar's; anyone who makes himself king is defying Caesar.

N   Hearing these words, Pilate had Jesus brought out, and seated himself on the chair of judgement at a place called the Pavement, in Hebrew Gabbatha. It was Passover Preparation Day, about the sixth hour. Pilate said to the Jews,

O   Here is your king.

N   They said,

C   Take him away, take him away. Crucify him!

N Pilate said,

O Do you want me to crucify your king?

N The chief priests answered,

C We have no king except Caesar.

N So in the end Pilate handed him over to them to be crucified.

They then took charge of Jesus, and carrying his own cross he went out of the city to the place of the skull, or, as it was called in Hebrew, Golgotha, where they crucified him with two others, one on either side with Jesus in the middle. Pilate wrote out a notice and had it fixed to the cross; it ran: 'Jesus the Nazarene, King of the Jews.' This notice was read by many of the Jews, because the place where Jesus was crucified was not far from the city, and the writing was in Hebrew, Latin and Greek. So the Jewish chief priests said to Pilate,

C You should not write 'King of the Jews', but 'This man said: I am King of the Jews'.

N Pilate answered,

O What I have written, I have written.

N When the soldiers had finished crucifying Jesus they took his clothing and divided it into four shares, one for each soldier. His undergarment was seamless, woven in one piece from neck to hem; so they said to one another,

C Instead of tearing it, let's throw dice to decide who is to have it.

N In this way the words of scripture were fulfilled:

They shared out my clothing among them.

They cast lots for my clothes.

This is exactly what the soldiers did.

Near the cross of Jesus stood his mother and his mother's sister, Mary the wife of Clopas, and Mary of Magdala. Seeing his mother and the disciple he loved standing near her, Jesus said to his mother,

J Woman, this is your son.

N Then to the disciple he said,

J This is your mother.

N And from that moment the disciple made a place for her in his home.

After this, Jesus knew that everything had now been completed, and to fulfil the scripture perfectly he said:

J I am thirsty.

N A jar full of vinegar stood there, so putting a sponge soaked in vinegar on a hyssop stick they held it up to his mouth. After Jesus had taken the vinegar he said,

J   It is accomplished;

N   and bowing his head he gave up the spirit.

All kneel and pause a moment.

N   It was Preparation Day, and to prevent the bodies remaining on the cross during the sabbath – since that sabbath was a day of special solemnity – the Jews asked Pilate to have the legs broken and the bodies taken away. Consequently the soldiers came and broke the legs of the first man who had been crucified with him and then of the other. When they came to Jesus, they found that he was already dead, and so instead of breaking his legs one of the soldiers pierced his side with a lance; and immediately there came out blood and water. This is the evidence of one who saw it – trustworthy evidence, and he knows he speaks the truth – and he gives it so that you may believe as well. Because all this happened to fulfil the words of scripture:

Not one bone of his will be broken,

and again, in another place scripture says:

They will look on the one whom they have pierced.

After this, Joseph of Arimathaea, who was a disciple of Jesus – though a secret one because he was afraid of the Jews – asked Pilate to let him remove the body of Jesus. Pilate gave permission, so they came and took it away. Nicodemus came as well – the same one who had first come to Jesus at night – time – and he brought a mixture of myrrh and aloes, weighing about a hundred pounds. They took the body of Jesus and wrapped it with the spices in linen cloths, following the Jewish burial custom. At the place where he had been crucified there was a garden, and in the garden a new tomb in which no one had yet been buried. Since it was the Jewish Day of Preparation and the tomb was near at hand, they laid Jesus there.

The Gospel of the Lord.

After the reading of the Lord's Passion, the Priest gives a brief homily and, at its end, the faithful may be invited to spend a short time in prayer.

The Solemn Intercessions

The Liturgy of the Word concludes with the Solemn Intercessions, which take place in this way: the Deacon, if a Deacon is present, or if he is not, a lay minister, stands at the ambo, and sings or says the invitation in which the intention is expressed. Then all pray in silence for a while, and afterwards the Priest, standing at the chair or, if appropriate, at the altar, with hands extended, sings or says the prayer.

The faithful may remain either kneeling or standing throughout the entire period of the prayers.

Before the Priest's prayer, in accord with tradition, it is permissible to use the Deacon's invitations **Let us kneel – Let us stand**, (**Flectamus genua – Levate**), with all kneeling for silent prayer.

The Conferences of Bishops may provide other invitations to introduce the prayer of the Priest.

In a situation of grave public need, the Diocesan Bishop may permit or order the addition of a special intention.

The prayer is sung in the simple tone or, if the invitations **Let us kneel – Let us stand**, (**Flectamus genua – Levate**), are used, in the solemn tone.

I. For Holy Church

Let us pray, dearly beloved,
    for the holy Church of God,
that our God and Lord be pleased
    to give her peace,
to guard her and to unite her
    throughout the whole world
and grant that, leading our life
    in tranquillity and quiet,
we may glorify God
    the Father almighty.

Prayer in silence. Then the Priest says:

Almighty ever-living God,
who in Christ revealed your glory
    to all the nations,
watch over the works of your mercy,
that your Church, spread
    throughout all the world,
may persevere with steadfast faith
    in confessing your name.
Through Christ our Lord.
R. Amen.

II. For the Pope

Let us pray also for our most
    Holy Father Pope N.,
that our God and Lord,
who chose him for the
    Order of Bishops,

I. Pro sancta Ecclesia

Oremus, dilectissimi nobis,
    pro Ecclesia sancta Dei,
ut eam Deus et Dominus noster
pacificare, adunare
    et custodire dignetur
toto orbe terrarum,
detque nobis, quietam et tranquillam
    vitam degentibus,
glorificare Deum
    Patrem omnipotentem.

Omnipotens sempiterne Deus,
qui gloriam tuam omnibus
    in Christo gentibus revelasti:
custodi opera misericordiæ tuæ,
ut Ecclesia tua, toto orbe diffusa,
stabili fide in confessione
    tui nominis perseveret.
Per Christum Dominum nostrum.
R. Amen.

II. Pro Papa

Oremus et pro beatissimo
    Papa nostro N.,
ut Deus et Dominus noster,
qui elegit eum
    in ordine episcopatus,

may keep him safe and unharmed
    for the Lord's holy Church,
to govern the holy People of God.

Prayer in silence. Then the Priest says:

Almighty ever-living God,
by whose decree all things
    are founded,
look with favour on our prayers
and in your kindness protect
    the Pope chosen for us,
that, under him,
    the Christian people,
governed by you their maker,
may grow in merit by reason
    of their faith.
Through Christ our Lord.
R. Amen.

III. For all orders and degrees of the faithful

Let us pray also for our Bishop N.,
for all Bishops, Priests,
    and Deacons of the Church
and for the whole
    of the faithful people.

Prayer in silence. Then the Priest says:

Almighty ever-living God,
by whose Spirit the whole body
    of the Church
is sanctified and governed,
hear our humble prayer
    for your ministers,
that, by the gift of your grace,
all may serve you faithfully.
Through Christ our Lord.
R. Amen.

salvum atque incolumem custodiat
    Ecclesiæ suæ sanctæ,
ad regendum populum
    sanctum Dei.

Omnipotens sempiterne Deus,
cuius iudicio universa fundantur,
respice propitius ad preces nostras,
et electum nobis Antistitem
    tua pietate conserva,
ut christiana plebs,
    quæ te gubernatur auctore,
sub ipso Pontifice,
    fidei suæ meritis augeatur.
Per Christum Dominum nostrum.
R. Amen.

III. Pro omnibus ordinibus gradibusque fidelium

Oremus et pro Episcopo nostro N.,
pro omnibus Episcopis, presbyteris,
    diaconis Ecclesiæ,
et universa plebe fidelium.

Omnipotens sempiterne Deus,
cuius Spiritu totum corpus Ecclesiæ
sanctificatur et regitur,
exaudi nos pro ministris
    tuis supplicantes,
ut, gratiæ tuæ munere, ab omnibus
    tibi fideliter serviatur.
Per Christum Dominum nostrum.
R. Amen.

IV. For catechumens

Let us pray also
    for (our) catechumens,
that our God and Lord
may open wide the ears
    of their inmost hearts
and unlock the gates of his mercy,
that, having received forgiveness
    of all their sins
through the waters of rebirth,
they, too, may be one with Christ
    Jesus our Lord.

Prayer in silence. Then the Priest says:

Almighty ever-living God,
who make your Church ever
    fruitful with new offspring,
increase the faith and understanding
    of (our) catechumens,
that, reborn in the font of Baptism,
they may be added to the number
    of your adopted children.
Through Christ our Lord.
R. Amen.

V. For the unity of Christians

Let us pray also for all our brothers
    and sisters who believe in Christ,
that our God and Lord may
    be pleased,
as they live the truth,
to gather them together and keep
    them in his one Church.

Prayer in silence. Then the Priest says:

Almighty ever-living God,
who gather what is scattered
and keep together what you
    have gathered,
look kindly on the flock of your Son,

IV. Pro catechumenis

Oremus et pro
    catechumenis (nostris),
ut Deus et Dominus noster
adaperiat aures
    præcordiorum ipsorum
ianuamque misericordiæ,
ut, per lavacrum regenerationis
accepta remissione
    omnium peccatorum,
et ipsi inveniantur in Christo Iesu
    Domino nostro.

Omnipotens sempiterne Deus,
qui Ecclesiam tuam nova semper
    prole fecundas,
auge fidem et intellectum
    catechumenis (nostris),
ut, renati fonte baptismatis,
adoptionis tuæ filiis aggregentur.
Per Christum Dominum nostrum.
R. Amen.

V. Pro unitate Christianorum

Oremus et pro universis fratribus
    in Christum credentibus,
ut Deus et Dominus noster eos,
    veritatem facientes,
in una Ecclesia sua congregare
    et custodire dignetur.

Omnipotens sempiterne Deus,
qui dispersa congregas
    et congregata conservas,
ad gregem Filii tui placatus intende,
ut, quos unum baptisma sacravit,

that those whom one Baptism
   has consecrated
may be joined together by integrity
   of faith
and united in the bond of charity.
Through Christ our Lord.
R. Amen.

eos et fidei iungat integritas
et vinculum societ caritatis.
Per Christum Dominum nostrum.
R. Amen.

VI. For the Jewish people

VI. Pro Iudæis

Let us pray also for the Jewish people,
to whom the Lord our God
   spoke first,
that he may grant them to advance
   in love of his name
and in faithfulness to his covenant.

Oremus et pro Iudæis,
ut, ad quos prius locutus est
   Dominus Deus noster,
eis tribuat in sui nominis amore
et in sui fœderis fidelitate proficere.

Prayer in silence. Then the Priest says:

Almighty ever-living God,
who bestowed your promises on
   Abraham and his descendants,
graciously hear the prayers
   of your Church,
that the people you first made
   your own
may attain the fullness
   of redemption.
Through Christ our Lord.
R. Amen.

Omnipotens sempiterne Deus,
qui promissiones tuas Abrahæ
   eiusque semini contulisti,
Ecclesiæ tuæ preces
   clementer exaudi,
ut populus acquisitionis prioris
ad redemptionis mereatur
   plenitudinem pervenire.
Per Christum Dominum nostrum.
R. Amen.

VII. For those who do not believe
in Christ

VII. Pro iis qui Christum
non credunt

Let us pray also for those who
   do not believe in Christ,
that, enlightened by the Holy Spirit,
they, too, may enter on the way
   of salvation.

Oremus et pro iis qui in Christum
   non credunt,
ut, luce Sancti Spiritus illustrati,
viam salutis et ipsi valeant introire.

Prayer in silence. Then the Priest says:

Almighty ever-living God,
grant to those who do not
   confess Christ
that, by walking before you
   with a sincere heart,

Omnipotens sempiterne Deus,
fac ut qui Christum
   non confitentur,
coram te sincero corde ambulantes,
   inveniant veritatem,

they may find the truth,
and that we ourselves, being
    constant in mutual love
and striving to understand more
    fully the mystery of your life,
may be made more perfect witnesses
    to your love in the world.
Through Christ our Lord. R. Amen.

nosque, mutuo proficientes
    semper amore
et ad tuæ vitæ mysterium plenius
    percipiendum sollicitos,
perfectiores effice tuæ testes
    caritatis in mundo.
Per Christum Dominum nostrum.
R. Amen.

VIII. For those who do not believe
in God

Let us pray also for those who
    do not acknowledge God,
that, following what is right
    in sincerity of heart,
they may find the way
    to God himself.

VIII. Pro iis qui in Deum
non credunt

Oremus et pro iis qui Deum
    non agnoscunt,
ut, quæ recta sunt sincero
    corde sectantes,
ad ipsum Deum
    pervenire mereantur.

Prayer in silence. Then the Priest says:

Almighty ever-living God,
who created all people
to seek you always by desiring you
and, by finding you, come to rest,
grant, we pray,
that, despite every harmful obstacle,
all may recognise the signs
    of your fatherly love
and the witness of the good works
done by those who believe in you,
and so in gladness confess you,
the one true God and Father
    of our human race.
Through Christ our Lord. R. Amen.

Omnipotens sempiterne Deus,
qui cunctos homines condidisti,
ut te semper desiderando quærerent
et inveniendo quiescerent,
præsta, quæsumus,
ut inter noxia quæque obstacula
omnes, tuæ signa pietatis
et in te credentium testimonium
bonorum operum percipientes,
te solum verum Deum nostrique
    generis Patrem
gaudeant confiteri.
Per Christum Dominum nostrum.
R. Amen.

IX. For those in public office

Let us pray also for those
    in public office,
that our God and Lord
may direct their minds and hearts
    according to his will
for the true peace and freedom of all.

IX. Pro rempublicam moderantibus

Oremus et pro omnibus
    rempublicam moderantibus,
ut Deus et Dominus noster
mentes et corda eorum secundum
    voluntatem suam dirigat
ad veram omnium pacem
    et libertatem.

Prayer in silence. Then the Priest says:

Almighty ever-living God,
in whose hand lies every
    human heart
and the rights of peoples,
look with favour, we pray,
on those who govern
    with authority over us,
that throughout the whole world,
the prosperity of peoples,
the assurance of peace,
and freedom of religion
may through your gift
    be made secure.
Through Christ our Lord. R. Amen.

Omnipotens sempiterne Deus,
in cuius manu sunt hominum
    corda et iura populorum,
respice benignus ad eos,
    qui nos in potestate moderantur,
ut ubique terrarum populorum
    prosperitas,
pacis securitas et religionis libertas,
te largiente, consistant.
Per Christum Dominum nostrum.
R. Amen.

X. For those in tribulation

X. Pro tribulatis

Let us pray, dearly beloved,
to God the Father almighty,
that he may cleanse the world
    of all errors,
banish disease, drive out hunger,
unlock prisons, loosen fetters,
granting to travellers safety,
    to pilgrims return,
health to the sick,
    and salvation to the dying.

Oremus, dilectissimi nobis,
    Deum Patrem omnipotentem,
ut cunctis mundum
    purget erroribus,
morbos auferat, famem depellat,
aperiat carceres, vincula solvat,
viatoribus securitatem,
    peregrinantibus reditum,
infirmantibus sanitatem
atque morientibus
    salutem indulgeat.

Prayer in silence. Then the Priest says:

Almighty ever-living God,
comfort of mourners,
    strength of all who toil,
may the prayers of those who cry out
    in any tribulation
come before you,
that all may rejoice,
because in their hour of need
your mercy was at hand.
Through Christ our Lord.
R. Amen.

Omnipotens sempiterne Deus,
mæstorum consolatio,
    laborantium fortitudo,
perveniant ad te preces
de quacumque
    tribulatione clamantium,
ut omnes sibi in necessitatibus suis
misericordiam tuam
    gaudeant affuisse.
Per Christum Dominum nostrum.
R. Amen.

SECOND PART:

THE ADORATION OF THE HOLY CROSS

After the Solemn Intercessions, the solemn Adoration of the Holy Cross takes place. Of the two forms of the showing of the Cross presented here, the more appropriate one, according to pastoral needs, should be chosen.

The Showing of the Holy Cross

First Form

The Deacon accompanied by ministers, or another suitable minister, goes to the sacristy, from which, in procession, accompanied by two ministers with lighted candles, he carries the Cross, covered with a violet veil, through the church to the middle of the sanctuary.

The Priest, standing before the altar and facing the people, receives the Cross, uncovers a little of its upper part and elevates it while beginning the **Ecce lignum Crucis** (**Behold the wood of the Cross**). He is assisted in singing by the Deacon or, if need be, by the choir. All respond, **Come, let us adore**. At the end of the singing, all kneel and for a brief moment adore in silence, while the Priest stands and holds the Cross raised.

Behold the wood of the Cross, on which hung the salvation of the world.	Ecce lignum Crucis, in quo salus mundi pependit.
R. Come, let us adore.	R. Venite, adoremus.

Then the Priest uncovers the right arm of the Cross and again, raising up the Cross, begins, **Behold the wood of the Cross** and everything takes place as above.

Finally, he uncovers the Cross entirely and, raising it up, he begins the invitation **Behold the wood of the Cross** a third time and everything takes place like the first time.

Second Form

The Priest or the Deacon accompanied by ministers, or another suitable minister, goes to the door of the church, where he receives the unveiled Cross, and the ministers take lighted candles; then the procession sets off through the church to the sanctuary. Near the door, in the middle of the church, and before the entrance of the sanctuary, the one who carries the Cross elevates it, singing, **Behold the wood of the Cross**, to which all respond, **Come, let us adore**. After each response all kneel and for a brief moment adore in silence, as above.

The Adoration of the Holy Cross

Then, accompanied by two ministers with lighted candles, the Priest or the Deacon carries the Cross to the entrance of the sanctuary or to another suitable place and there puts it down or hands it over to the ministers to hold. Candles are placed on the right and left sides of the Cross.

For the Adoration of the Cross, first the Priest Celebrant alone approaches, with the chasuble and his shoes removed, if appropriate. Then the clergy, the lay ministers, and the faithful approach, moving as if in procession, and showing reverence to the Cross by a simple genuflection or by some other sign appropriate to the usage of the region, for example, by kissing the Cross.

Only one Cross should be offered for adoration. If, because of the large number of people, it is not possible for all to approach individually, the Priest, after some of the clergy and faithful have adored, takes the Cross and, standing in the middle before the altar, invites the people in a few words to adore the Holy Cross and afterwards holds the Cross elevated higher for a brief time, for the faithful to adore it in silence.

While the adoration of the Holy Cross is taking place, the antiphon **Crucem tuam adoramus** (**We adore your Cross, O Lord**), the Reproaches, the hymn **Crux fidelis** (**Faithful Cross**) or other suitable chants are sung, during which all who have already adored the Cross remain seated.

Chants to be Sung
during the Adoration of the Holy Cross

Ant. We adore your Cross, O Lord,
we praise and glorify your
    holy Resurrection,
for behold, because of the wood
    of a tree
joy has come to the whole world.

Ant. Crucem tuam
    adoramus, Domine,
et sanctam resurrectionem tuam
    laudamus et glorificamus:
ecce enim propter lignum
venit gaudium in universo mundo.

Cf. Ps 66:2

May God have mercy on us
    and bless us;
may he let his face shed its light
    upon us
and have mercy on us.

Deus misereatur nostri,
    et benedicat nobis:
illuminet vultum suum super nos,
et misereatur nostri.

And the antiphon is repeated:

We adore. . .

Crucem tuam. . .

THE REPROACHES

Parts assigned to one of the two choirs separately are indicated by the numbers 1 (first choir) and 2 (second choir); parts sung by both choirs together are marked: 1 and 2. Some of the verses may also be sung by two cantors.

1 and 2 My people,
    what have I done to you?
Or how have I grieved you?
    Answer me!

1 et 2 Popule meus,
    quid feci tibi?
Aut in quo contristavi te?
    Responde mihi!

1   Because I led you out of the land
    of Egypt,
you have prepared a Cross
    for your Saviour.

1   Hagios o Theos,
2   Holy is God,
1   Hagios Ischyros,
2   Holy and Mighty,
1   Hagios Athanatos,
    eleison himas.
2   Holy and Immortal One,
    have mercy on us.

1 and 2 Because I led you out
    through the desert forty years
and fed you with manna and
    brought you into a land of plenty,
you have prepared a Cross
    for your Saviour.

1   Hagios o Theos,
2   Holy is God,
1   Hagios Ischyros,
2   Holy and Mighty,
1   Hagios Athanatos, eleison himas.
2   Holy and Immortal One,
    have mercy on us.

1 and 2 What more should I have
    done for you and have not done?
Indeed, I planted you as my most
    beautiful chosen vine
and you have turned very bitter
    for me,
for in my thirst you gave me
    vinegar to drink
and with a lance you pierced your
    Saviour's side.

1   Hagios o Theos,
2   Holy is God,

---

1   Quia eduxi te de terra Ægypti:
parasti Crucem Salvatori tuo.

1   Hagios o Theos.
2   Sanctus Deus.
1   Hagios Ischyros.
2   Sanctus Fortis.
1   Hagios Athanatos,
    eleison himas.
2   Sanctus Immortalis,
    miserere nobis.

1 et 2 Quia eduxi te per desertum
    quadraginta annis,
et manna cibavi te,
et introduxi te in terram
    satis bonam:
parasti Crucem Salvatori tuo.

1   Hagios o Theos.
2   Sanctus Deus.
1   Hagios Ischyros.
2   Sanctus Fortis.
1   Hagios Athanatos, eleison himas.
2   Sanctus Immortalis,
    miserere nobis.

1 et 2 Quid ultra debui facere tibi,
    et non feci?
Ego quidem plantavi te
vineam electam
    meam speciosissimam:
et tu facta es mihi nimis amara:
aceto namque sitim meam potasti,
et lancea perforasti latus
    Salvatori tuo.

1   Hagios o Theos.
2   Sanctus Deus.

1	Hagios Ischyros,		1	Hagios Ischyros.
2	Holy and Mighty,		2	Sanctus Fortis.
1	Hagios Athanatos, eleison himas.		1	Hagios Athanatos, eleison himas.
2	Holy and Immortal One, have mercy on us.		2	Sanctus Immortalis, miserere nobis.

II

Cantors:

I scourged Egypt for your sake
    with its firstborn sons,
and you scourged me and handed
    me over.

1 and 2 repeat:

My people, what have I done to you?
Or how have I grieved you?
Answer me!

Cantors:

I led you out from Egypt as Pharaoh
    lay sunk in the Red Sea,
and you handed me over
    to the chief priests.

1 and 2 repeat:

My people. . .

Cantors:

I opened up the sea before you,
and you opened my side with a lance.

1 and 2 repeat:

My people. . .

Cantors:

I went before you in a pillar of cloud,
and you led me into Pilate's palace.

1 and 2 repeat:

My people. . .

Cantores:

Ego propter te flagellavi Ægyptum
cum primogenitis suis:
et tu me flagellatum tradidisti.

1 et 2 repetunt:

Popule meus, quid feci tibi?
Aut in quo contristavi te?
Responde mihi!

Cantores:

Ego eduxi te de Ægypto,
demerso Pharaone in Mare Rubrum:
et tu me tradidisti
    principibus sacerdotum.

1 et 2 repetunt:

Popule meus. . .

Cantores:

Ego ante te aperui mare:
et tu aperuisti lancea latus meum.

1 et 2 repetunt:

Popule meus. . .

Cantores:

Ego ante te præivi in columna nubis:
et tu me duxisti ad prætorium Pilati.

1 et 2 repetunt:

Popule meus. . .

Cantors:
I fed you with manna in the desert,
and on me you rained blows
    and lashes.

Cantores:
Ego te pavi manna per desertum:
et tu me cecidisti alapis et flagellis.

1 and 2 repeat:
My people. . .

1 et 2 repetunt:
Popule meus. . .

Cantors:
I gave you saving water
    from the rock to drink,
and for drink you gave me gall
    and vinegar.

Cantores:
Ego te potavi aqua salutis de petra:
et tu me potasti felle et aceto.

1 and 2 repeat:
My people. . .

1 et 2 repetunt:
Popule meus. . .

Cantors:
I struck down for you the kings
    of the Canaanites,
and you struck my head with a reed.

Cantores:
Ego propter te Chananæorum
    reges percussi:
et tu percussisti arundine
    caput meum.

1 and 2 repeat:
My people. . .

1 et 2 repetunt:
Popule meus. . .

Cantors:
I put in your hand a royal sceptre,
and you put on my head
    a crown of thorns.

Cantores:
Ego dedi tibi sceptrum regale:
et tu dedisti capiti meo spineam
    coronam.

1 and 2 repeat:
My people. . .

1 et 2 repetunt:
Popule meus. . .

Cantors:
I exalted you with great power,
and you hung me on the scaffold
    of the Cross.

Cantores:
Ego te exaltavi magna virtute:
et tu me suspendisti
    in patibulo Crucis.

1 and 2 repeat:
My people. . .

1 et 2 repetunt:
Popule meus. . .

HYMN

All:

Faithful Cross the Saints rely on,
Noble tree beyond compare!
Never was there such a scion,
Never leaf or flower so rare.
Sweet the timber, sweet the iron,
Sweet the burden that they bear!

Cantors:

Sing, my tongue, in exultation
Of our banner and device!
Make a solemn proclamation
Of a triumph and its price:
How the Saviour of creation
Conquered by his sacrifice!

All:

Faithful Cross the Saints rely on,
Noble tree beyond compare!
Never was there such a scion,
Never leaf or flower so rare.

Cantors:

For, when Adam first offended,
Eating that forbidden fruit,
Not all hopes of glory ended
With the serpent at the root:
Broken nature would be mended
By a second tree and shoot.

All:

Sweet the timber, sweet the iron,
Sweet the burden that they bear!

Cantors:

Thus the tempter was outwitted
By a wisdom deeper still:
Remedy and ailment fitted,
Means to cure and means to kill;
That the world might be acquitted,
Christ would do his Father's will.

Omnes:

Crux fidelis, inter omnes
    arbor una nobilis,
Nulla talem silva profert,
    flore, fronde, germine!
Dulce lignum dulci clavo
    dulce pondus sustinens!

Cantores:

Pange, lingua, gloriosi
    prœlium certaminis,
Et super crucis tropæo
    dic triumphum nobilem,
Qualiter Redemptor orbis
    immolatus vicerit.

Omnes:

Crux fidelis, inter omnes
    arbor una nobilis,
Nulla talem silva profert,
    flore, fronde, germine!

Cantores:

De parentis protoplasti
    fraude factor condolens,
Quando pomi noxialis
    morte morsu corruit,
Ipse lignum tunc notavit,
    damna ligni ut solveret.

Omnes:

Dulce lignum dulci clavo
    dulce pondus sustinens!

Cantores:

Hoc opus nostræ salutis
    ordo depoposcerat,
Multiformis perditoris
    arte ut artem falleret,
Et medelam ferret inde,
    hostis unde læserat.

All:

Faithful Cross the Saints rely on,
Noble tree beyond compare!
Never was there such a scion,
Never leaf or flower so rare.

Cantors:

So the Father, out of pity
For our self-inflicted doom,
Sent him from the heavenly city
When the holy time had come:
He, the Son and the Almighty,
Took our flesh in Mary's womb.

All:

Sweet the timber, sweet the iron,
Sweet the burden that they bear!

Cantors:

Hear a tiny baby crying,
Founder of the seas and strands;
See his virgin Mother tying
Cloth around his feet and hands;
Find him in a manger lying
Tightly wrapped in swaddling-bands!

All:

Faithful Cross the Saints rely on,
Noble tree beyond compare!
Never was there such a scion,
Never leaf or flower so rare.

Cantors:

So he came, the long-expected,
Not in glory, not to reign;
Only born to be rejected,
Choosing hunger, toil and pain,
Till the scaffold was erected
And the Paschal Lamb was slain.

All:

Sweet the timber, sweet the iron,
Sweet the burden that they bear!

Cantors:

No disgrace was too abhorrent:
Nailed and mocked and

Omnes:

Crux fidelis, inter omnes
    arbor una nobilis,
Nulla talem silva profert,
    flore, fronde, germine!

Cantores:

Quando venit ergo sacri
    plenitudo temporis,
Missus est ab arce Patris
Natus, orbis conditor,
Atque ventre virginali
    carne factus prodiit.

Omnes:

Dulce lignum dulci clavo
    dulce pondus sustinens!

Cantores:

Vagit infans inter arta
    conditus præsepia,
Membra pannis involuta
    Virgo Mater alligat,
Et manus pedesque et crura
    stricta cingit fascia.

Omnes:

Crux fidelis, inter omnes
    arbor una nobilis,
Nulla talem silva profert,
    flore, fronde, germine!

Cantores:

Lustra sex qui iam peracta,
    tempus implens corporis,
se volente, natus ad hoc,
    passioni deditus,
agnus in crucis levatur
    immolandus stipite.

Omnes:

Dulce lignum dulci clavo
    dulce pondus sustinens!

Cantores:

En acetum, fel, arundo,
Mite corpus perforatur,

parched he died;
Blood and water, double warrant,
Issue from his wounded side,
Washing in a mighty torrent
Earth and stars and oceantide.

All:

Faithful Cross the Saints rely on,
Noble tree beyond compare!
Never was there such a scion,
Never leaf or flower so rare.

Cantors:

Lofty timber,
    smooth your roughness,
Flex your boughs for blossoming;
Let your fibres lose their toughness,
Gently let your tendrils cling;
Lay aside your native gruffness,
Clasp the body of your King!

All:

Sweet the timber, sweet the iron,
Sweet the burden that they bear!

Cantors:

Noblest tree of all created,
Richly jewelled and embossed:
Post by Lamb's blood consecrated;
Spar that saves the tempest-tossed;
Scaffold-beam which, elevated,
Carries what the world has cost!

All:

Faithful Cross the Saints rely on,
Noble tree beyond compare!
Never was there such a scion,
Never leaf or flower so rare.

sputa, clavi, lancea;
sanguis unde profluit;
Terra, pontus, astra, mundus
    quo lavantur flumine!

Omnes:

Crux fidelis, inter omnes
    arbor una nobilis,
Nulla talem silva profert,
    flore, fronde, germine!

Cantores:

Flecte ramos, arbor alta,
    tensa laxa viscera,
Et rigor lentescat ille,
    quem dedit nativitas,
Ut superni membra Regis
    miti tendas stipite.

Omnes:

Dulce lignum dulci clavo
    dulce pondus sustinens!

Cantores:

Sola digna tu fuisti
    ferre sæcli pretium
Atque portum præparare
    nauta mundo naufrago,
Quem sacer cruor perunxit
    fusus Agni corpore.

Omnes:

Crux fidelis, inter omnes
    arbor una nobilis,
Nulla talem silva profert,
    flore, fronde, germine!

The following conclusion is never to be omitted:

All:

Wisdom, power, and adoration
To the blessed Trinity

Omnes:

Æqua Patri Filioque,
    inclito Paraclito,

For redemption and salvation
Through the Paschal Mystery,
Now, in every generation,
And for all eternity. Amen.

Sempiterna sit beatæ
    Trinitati gloria;
cuius alma nos redemit
    atque servat gratia. Amen.

In accordance with local circumstances or popular traditions and if it is pastorally appropriate, the **Stabat Mater** may be sung, as found in the Graduale Romanum, or another suitable chant in memory of the compassion of the Blessed Virgin Mary.

When the adoration has been concluded, the Cross is carried by the Deacon or a minister to its place at the altar. Lighted candles are placed around or on the altar or near the Cross.

THIRD PART:

Holy Communion

A cloth is spread on the altar, and a corporal and the Missal put in place. Meanwhile the Deacon or, if there is no Deacon, the Priest himself, putting on a humeral veil, brings the Blessed Sacrament back from the place of repose to the altar by a shorter route, while all stand in silence. Two ministers with lighted candles accompany the Blessed Sacrament and place their candlesticks around or upon the altar.

When the Deacon, if a Deacon is present, has placed the Blessed Sacrament upon the altar and uncovered the ciborium, the Priest goes to the altar and genuflects.

Then the Priest, with hands joined, says aloud:

At the Saviour's command
and formed by divine teaching,
we dare to say:

Præceptis salutaribus moniti,
et divina institutione formati,
audemus dicere:

The Priest, with hands extended says, and all present continue:

Our Father, who art in heaven,
hallowed be thy name;
thy kingdom come,
thy will be done
on earth as it is in heaven.
Give us this day our daily bread,
and forgive us our trespasses,
as we forgive those who trespass
    against us;
and lead us not into temptation,
but deliver us from evil.

Pater noster, qui es in cælis:
sanctificetur nomen tuum;
adveniat regnum tuum;
fiat voluntas tua, sicut in cælo,
    et in terra.
Panem nostrum cotidianum
    da nobis hodie;
et dimitte nobis debita nostra,
sicut et nos dimittimus
    debitoribus nostris;
et ne nos inducas in tentationem;
sed libera nos a malo.

With hands extended, the Priest continues alone:

Deliver us, Lord, we pray,
    from every evil,

Libera nos, quæsumus, Domine,
    ab omnibus malis,

graciously grant peace in our days,	da propitius pacem in diebus nostris,
that, by the help of your mercy,	ut, ope misericordiæ tuæ adiuti,
and safe from all distress,	we may be always free from sin
as we await the blessed hope	et a peccato simus semper liberi
and the coming of our Saviour,	et ab omni perturbatione securi:
Jesus Christ.	exspectantes beatam spem
	et adventum Salvatoris nostri
	Iesu Christi.

He joins his hands.

The people conclude the prayer, acclaiming:

For the kingdom,	Quia tuum est regnum,
the power and the glory are yours	et potestas,
now and for ever.	et gloria in sæcula.

Then the Priest, with hands joined, says quietly:

May the receiving of your Body and Blood,	Perceptio Corporis tui, Domine Iesu Christe,
Lord Jesus Christ,	non mihi proveniat in iudicium
not bring me to judgement and condemnation,	et condemnationem:
but through your loving mercy	sed pro tua pietate prosit mihi
be for me protection in mind and body	ad tutamentum mentis et corporis,
and a healing remedy.	et ad medelam percipiendam.

The Priest then genuflects, takes a particle, and, holding it slightly raised over the ciborium, while facing the people, says aloud:

Behold the Lamb of God,	Ecce Agnus Dei, ecce qui tollit
behold him who takes away the sins of the world.	peccata mundi.
Blessed are those called to the supper of the Lamb.	Beati qui ad cenam Agni vocati sunt.

And together with the people he adds once:

Lord, I am not worthy	Domine, non sum dignus,
that you should enter under my roof,	ut intres sub tectum meum,
but only say the word	sed tantum dic verbo,
and my soul shall be healed.	et sanabitur anima mea.

And facing the altar, he reverently consumes the Body of Christ, saying quietly:

May the Body of Christ keep me safe for eternal life.	Corpus Christi custodiat me in vitam æternam.

He then proceeds to distribute Communion to the faithful. During Communion, Psalm 21 or another appropriate chant may be sung.

When the distribution of Communion has been completed, the ciborium is taken by the Deacon or another suitable minister to a place prepared outside the church or, if circumstances so require, it is placed in the tabernacle.

Then the Priest says: **Let us pray**, and, after a period of sacred silence, if circumstances so suggest, has been observed, he says the Prayer after Communion.

Almighty ever-living God, who have restored us to life by the blessed Death and Resurrection of your Christ, preserve in us the work of your mercy, that, by partaking of this mystery, we may have a life unceasingly devoted to you. Through Christ our Lord. R. Amen.	Omnipotens sempiterne Deus, qui nos Christi tui beata morte et resurrectione reparasti, conserva in nobis opus misericordiæ tuæ, ut huius mysterii participatione perpetua devotione vivamus. Per Christum Dominum nostrum. R. Amen.

For the Dismissal the Deacon or, if there is no Deacon, the Priest himself, may say the invitation **Bow down for the blessing**.

Then the Priest, standing facing the people and extending his hands over them, says this Prayer over the People:

May abundant blessing, O Lord, we pray, descend upon your people, who have honoured the Death of your Son in the hope of their resurrection: may pardon come, comfort be given, holy faith increase, and everlasting redemption be made secure. Through Christ our Lord. R. Amen.	Super populum tuum, quæsumus, Domine, qui mortem Filii tui in spe suæ resurrectionis recoluit, benedictio copiosa descendat, indulgentia veniat, consolatio tribuatur, fides sancta succrescat, redemptio sempiterna firmetur. Per Christum Dominum nostrum. R. Amen.

And all, after genuflecting to the Cross, depart in silence.

After the celebration, the altar is stripped, but the Cross remains on the altar with two or four candlesticks.

Vespers (Evening Prayer) is not celebrated by those who have been present at the solemn afternoon liturgical celebration.

EASTER SUNDAY OF THE RESURRECTION OF THE LORD

11 April

THE EASTER VIGIL IN THE HOLY NIGHT

The news spread: Jesus is risen as he said. And then there was his command to go to Galilee. Galilee is the place where they were first called, where everything began! For each of us, too, there is a "Galilee" at the origin of our journey with Jesus. "To go to Galilee" means something beautiful, it means rediscovering our baptism as a living fountainhead, drawing new energy from the sources of our faith and our Christian experience...In the life of every Christian, after baptism there is also another "Galilee", a more existential "Galilee": the experience of a personal encounter with Jesus Christ who called me to follow him and to share in his mission. In this sense, returning to Galilee means treasuring in my heart the living memory of that call, when Jesus passed my way, gazed at me with mercy and asked me to follow him. To return there means reviving the memory of that moment when his eyes met mine, the moment when he made me realize that he loved me. Today, tonight, each of us can ask: What is my Galilee? I need to remind myself, to go back and remember. Have I forgotten it? Seek and you will find it! There the Lord is waiting for you...Lord, help me: tell me what my Galilee is; for you know that I want to return there to encounter you and to let myself be embraced by your mercy. Do not be afraid, do not fear, return to Galilee!

(Pope Francis)

By most ancient tradition, this is the night of keeping vigil for the Lord (Ex 12:42), in which, following the Gospel admonition (Lk 12:35-37), the faithful, carrying lighted lamps in their hands, should be like those looking for the Lord when he returns, so that at his coming he may find them awake and have them sit at his table.

Of this night's Vigil, which is the greatest and most noble of all solemnities, there is to be only one celebration in each church. It is arranged, moreover, in such a way that after the Lucernarium and Easter Proclamation (which constitutes the first part of this Vigil), Holy Church meditates on the wonders the Lord God has done for his people from the beginning, trusting in his word and promise (the second part, that is, the Liturgy of the Word) until, as day approaches, with new members reborn in Baptism (the third part), the Church is called to the table the Lord has prepared for his people, the memorial of his Death and Resurrection until he comes again (the fourth part).

The entire celebration of the Easter Vigil must take place during the night, so that it begins after nightfall and ends before daybreak on the Sunday.

The Mass of the Vigil, even if it is celebrated before midnight, is a paschal Mass of the Sunday of the Resurrection.

Anyone who participates in the Mass of the night may receive Communion again at Mass during the day. A Priest who celebrates or concelebrates the Mass of the night may again celebrate or concelebrate Mass during the day.

The Easter Vigil takes the place of the Office of Readings.

The Priest is usually assisted by a Deacon. If, however, there is no Deacon, the duties of his Order, except those indicated below, are assumed by the Priest Celebrant or by a concelebrant.

The Priest and Deacon vest as at Mass, in white vestments.

Candles should be prepared for all who participate in the Vigil. The lights of the church are extinguished.

FIRST PART:

THE SOLEMN BEGINNING OF THE VIGIL OR LUCERNARIUM

The Blessing of the Fire and Preparation of the Candle

A blazing fire is prepared in a suitable place outside the church. When the people are gathered there, the Priest approaches with the ministers, one of whom carries the paschal candle. The processional cross and candles are not carried.

Where, however, a fire cannot be lit outside the church, the rite is carried out as below.

The Priest and faithful sign themselves while the Priest says: **In the name of the Father, and of the Son, and of the Holy Spirit**, and then he greets the assembled people in the usual way and briefly instructs them about the night vigil in these or similar words:

Dear brethren (brothers and sisters), on this most sacred night, in which our Lord Jesus Christ passed over from death to life, the Church calls upon her sons and daughters, scattered throughout the world, to come together to watch and pray. If we keep the memorial of the Lord's paschal solemnity in this way, listening to his word and celebrating his mysteries, then we shall have the sure hope of sharing his triumph over death and living with him in God.	Fratres carissimi, hac sacratissima nocte, in qua Dominus noster Iesus Christus de morte transivit ad vitam, Ecclesia invitat filios dispersos per orbem terrarum, ut ad vigilandum et orandum conveniant. Si ita memoriam egerimus Paschatis Domini, audientes verbum et celebrantes mysteria eius, spem habebimus participandi triumphum eius de morte et vivendi cum ipso in Deo.

Then the Priest blesses the fire, saying with hands extended:

Let us pray.

O God, who through your Son
bestowed upon the faithful the fire
   of your glory,
sanctify ✠ this new fire, we pray,
and grant that,
by these paschal celebrations,
we may be so inflamed
   with heavenly desires,
that with minds made pure
we may attain festivities
   of unending splendour.
Through Christ our Lord.
R. Amen.

Oremus.

Deus, qui per Filium tuum
claritatis tuæ ignem
   fidelibus contulisti,
novum hunc ignem ✠ sanctifica,
et concede nobis,
ita per hæc festa paschalia
cælestibus desideriis inflammari,
ut ad perpetuæ claritatis
puris mentibus valeamus
   festa pertingere.
Per Christum Dominum nostrum.
R. Amen.

After the blessing of the new fire, one of the ministers brings the paschal candle to the Priest, who cuts a cross into the candle with a stylus. Then he makes the Greek letter Alpha above the cross, the letter Omega below, and the four numerals of the current year between the arms of the cross, saying meanwhile:

1. Christ yesterday and today
2. the Beginning and the End
3. the Alpha
4. and the Omega
5. All time belongs to him
6. and all the ages
7. To him be glory and power
8. through every age and for ever.
   Amen

1. Christus heri et hodie
2. Principium et Finis
3. Alpha
4. et Omega
5. Ipsius sunt tempora
6. et sæcula
7. Ipsi gloria et imperium
8. per universa æternitatis sæcula.
   Amen

When the cutting of the cross and of the other signs has been completed, the Priest may insert five grains of incense into the candle in the form of a cross, meanwhile saying:

1. By his holy
2. and glorious wounds,
3. may Christ the Lord
4. guard us
5. and protect us. Amen.

1. Per sua sancta vulnera
2. gloriosa
3. custodiat
4. et conservet nos
5. Christus Dominus. Amen.

Where, because of difficulties that may occur, a fire is not lit, the blessing of fire is adapted to the circumstances. When the people are gathered in the church as on other occasions, the Priest comes to the door of the church, along with the ministers carrying the paschal candle. The people, insofar as is possible, turn to face the Priest.

The greeting and address take place as above; then the fire is blessed and the candle is prepared, as above.

The Priest lights the paschal candle from the new fire, saying:

May the light of Christ rising in glory dispel the darkness of our hearts and minds.	Lumen Christi gloriose resurgentis dissipet tenebras cordis et mentis.

As regards the preceding elements, Conferences of Bishops may also establish other forms more adapted to the culture of the different peoples.

Procession

When the candle has been lit, one of the ministers takes burning coals from the fire and places them in the thurible, and the Priest puts incense into it in the usual way. The Deacon or, if there is no Deacon, another suitable minister, takes the paschal candle and a procession forms. The thurifer with the smoking thurible precedes the Deacon or other minister who carries the paschal candle. After them follows the Priest with the ministers and the people, all holding in their hands unlit candles.

At the door of the church the Deacon, standing and raising up the candle, sings:

The Light of Christ.	Lumen Christi.

And all reply:

Thanks be to God.	Deo gratias.

The Priest lights his candle from the flame of the paschal candle.

Then the Deacon moves forward to the middle of the church and, standing and raising up the candle, sings a second time:

The Light of Christ.	Lumen Christi.

And all reply:

Thanks be to God.	Deo gratias.

All light their candles from the flame of the paschal candle and continue in procession.

When the Deacon arrives before the altar, he stands facing the people, raises up the candle and sings a third time:

The Light of Christ.	Lumen Christi.

And all reply:

Thanks be to God.	Deo gratias.

Then the Deacon places the paschal candle on a large candlestand prepared next to the ambo or in the middle of the sanctuary.

And lights are lit throughout the church, except for the altar candles.

The Easter Proclamation (Exsultet)

Arriving at the altar, the Priest goes to his chair, gives his candle to a minister, puts incense into the thurible and blesses the incense as at the Gospel at Mass. The Deacon goes to the Priest and saying, **Your blessing, Father**, asks for and receives a blessing from the Priest, who says in a low voice:

May the Lord be in your heart and on your lips,	Dominus sit in corde tuo et in labiis tuis,
that you may proclaim his paschal praise worthily and well,	ut digne et competenter annunties suum paschale præconium:
in the name of the Father and of the Son, ✠ and of the Holy Spirit.	in nomine Patris, et Filii, ✠ et Spiritus Sancti.
The Deacon replies: **Amen.**	Amen.

This blessing is omitted if the Proclamation is made by someone who is not a Deacon.

The Deacon, after incensing the book and the candle, proclaims the Easter Proclamation (Exsultet) at the ambo or at a lectern, with all standing and holding lighted candles in their hands.

The Easter Proclamation may be made, in the absence of a Deacon, by the Priest himself or by another concelebrating Priest. If, however, because of necessity, a lay cantor sings the Proclamation, the words **Therefore, dearest friends** up to the end of the invitation are omitted, along with the greeting **The Lord be with you**.

The Proclamation may also be sung in the shorter form p.230.

Longer Form of the Easter Proclamation

Exult, let them exult, the hosts of heaven, exult, let Angel ministers of God exult, let the trumpet of salvation sound aloud our mighty King's triumph!	Exsultet iam angelica turba cælorum: exsultent divina mysteria: et pro tanti Regis victoria tuba insonet salutaris.
Be glad, let earth be glad, as glory floods her, ablaze with light from her eternal King, let all corners of the earth be glad, knowing an end to gloom and darkness.	Gaudeat et tellus tantis irradiata fulgoribus: et, æterni Regis splendore illustrata, totius orbis se sentiat amisisse caliginem.

Rejoice, let Mother Church
    also rejoice,
arrayed with the lightning
    of his glory,
let this holy building shake with joy,
filled with the mighty voices
    of the peoples.

(Therefore, dearest friends,
standing in the awesome glory
    of this holy light,
invoke with me, I ask you,
the mercy of God almighty,
that he, who has been pleased
    to number me,
though unworthy, among the Levites,
may pour into me his light
    unshadowed,
that I may sing this candle's
    perfect praises.)

(V. The Lord be with you.
R. And with your spirit.)

V. Lift up your hearts.
R. We lift them up to the Lord.
V. Let us give thanks to the Lord
    our God.
R. It is right and just.

It is truly right and just,
with ardent love of mind and heart
and with devoted service of our voice,
to acclaim our God invisible,
    the almighty Father,
and Jesus Christ, our Lord, his Son,
    his Only Begotten.

Who for our sake paid Adam's debt
    to the eternal Father,
and, pouring out his own dear Blood,
wiped clean the record of our
    ancient sinfulness.

Lætetur et mater Ecclesia,
tanti luminis adornata fulgoribus:
et magnis populorum vocibus hæc
    aula resultet.

(Quapropter astantes vos,
    fratres carissimi,
ad tam miram huius sancti
    luminis claritatem,
una mecum, quæso,
Dei omnipotentis
    misericordiam invocate.
Ut, qui me non meis meritis
intra Levitarum numerum dignatus
    est aggregare,
luminis sui claritatem infundens,
cerei huius laudem
    implere perficiat.)

(V. Dominus vobiscum.
R. Et cum spiritu tuo.)

V. Sursum corda.
R. Habemus ad Dominum.
V. Gratias agamus Domino
    Deo nostro.
R. Dignum et iustum est.

Vere dignum et iustum est,
invisibilem Deum
    Patrem omnipotentem
Filiumque eius Unigenitum,
Dominum nostrum
    Iesum Christum,
toto cordis ac mentis affectu
    et vocis ministerio personare.

Qui pro nobis æterno Patri Adæ
    debitum solvit,
et veteris piaculi cautionem
    pio cruore detersit.

These then are the feasts of Passover,
in which is slain the Lamb,
    the one true Lamb,
whose Blood anoints the doorposts
    of believers.

This is the night,
when once you led our forebears,
    Israel's children,
from slavery in Egypt
and made them pass dry-shod
    through the Red Sea.

This is the night
that with a pillar of fire
banished the darkness of sin.

This is the night
that even now, throughout the world,
sets Christian believers apart
    from worldly vices
and from the gloom of sin,
leading them to grace
and joining them to his holy ones.

This is the night,
when Christ broke the prison-bars
    of death
and rose victorious
    from the underworld.

Our birth would have been no gain,
had we not been redeemed.
O wonder of your humble care for us!
O love, O charity beyond all telling,
to ransom a slave you gave away
    your Son!

O truly necessary sin of Adam,
destroyed completely by the Death
    of Christ!

Hæc sunt enim festa paschalia,
in quibus verus ille Agnus occiditur,
cuius sanguine postes
    fidelium consecrantur.

Hæc nox est,
in qua primum patres nostros,
filios Israel eductos de Ægypto,
Mare Rubrum sicco vestigio
    transire fecisti.

Hæc igitur nox est,
quæ peccatorum tenebras columnæ
    illuminatione purgavit.

Hæc nox est,
quæ hodie per universum mundum
    in Christo credentes,
a vitiis sæculi et caligine
    peccatorum segregatos,
reddit gratiæ, sociat sanctitati.

Hæc nox est,
in qua, destructis vinculis mortis,
Christus ab inferis victor ascendit.

Nihil enim nobis nasci profuit,
    nisi redimi profuisset.
O mira circa nos tuæ pietatis
    dignatio!
O inæstimablilis dilectio caritatis:
ut servum redimeres,
    Filium tradidisti!

O certe necessarium
    Adæ peccatum,
quod Christi morte deletum est!

O happy fault
that earned so great,
    so glorious a Redeemer!

O truly blessed night,
worthy alone to know the time
    and hour
when Christ rose
    from the underworld!

This is the night
of which it is written:
The night shall be as bright as day,
dazzling is the night for me,
and full of gladness.

The sanctifying power of this night
dispels wickedness,
    washes faults away,
restores innocence to the fallen,
    and joy to mourners,
drives out hatred, fosters concord,
    and brings down the mighty.

On this, your night of grace,
    O holy Father,
accept this candle, a solemn offering,
the work of bees and of your
    servants' hands,
an evening sacrifice of praise,
this gift from your most holy Church.

But now we know the praises
    of this pillar,
which glowing fire ignites
    for God's honour,
a fire into many flames divided,
yet never dimmed by sharing
    of its light,
for it is fed by melting wax,
drawn out by mother bees
to build a torch so precious.

O felix culpa,
quæ talem ac tantum meruit
    habere Redemptorem!

O vere beata nox,
quæ sola meruit scire tempus
    et horam,
in qua Christus ab inferis resurrexit!

Hæc nox est, de qua scriptum est:
Et nox sicut dies illuminabitur:
et nox illuminatio mea
    in deliciis meis.

Huius igitur sanctificatio noctis
    fugat scelera, culpas lavat:
et reddit innocentiam lapsis
    et mæstis lætitiam.
Fugat odia, concordiam parat
    et curvat imperia.

In huius igitur noctis gratia,
suscipe, sancte Pater, laudis huius
    sacrificium vespertinum,
quod tibi in hac cerei
    oblatione sollemni,
per ministrorum manus
de operibus apum,
    sacrosancta reddit Ecclesia.

Sed iam columnæ huius
    præconia novimus,
quam in honorem Dei rutilans
    ignis accendit.
Qui, licet sit divisus in partes,
mutuati tamen luminis detrimenta
    non novit.
Alitur enim liquantibus ceris,
quas in substantiam pretiosæ
    huius lampadis
apis mater eduxit.

O truly blessed night,
when things of heaven are wed
    to those of earth,
and divine to the human.

O vere beata nox,
in qua terrenis cælestia,
    humanis divina iunguntur!

Therefore, O Lord,
we pray you that this candle,
hallowed to the honour of
    your name,
may persevere undimmed,
to overcome the darkness
    of this night.
Receive it as a pleasing fragrance,
and let it mingle with
    the lights of heaven.
May this flame be found still burning
by the Morning Star:
the one Morning Star who never sets,
Christ your Son,
who, coming back
    from death's domain,
has shed his peaceful light
    on humanity,
and lives and reigns
    for ever and ever.
R. Amen.

Oramus ergo te, Domine,
ut cereus iste in honorem tui
    nominis consecratus,
ad noctis huius
    caliginem destruendam,
indeficiens perseveret.

Et in odorem suavitatis acceptus,
supernis luminaribus misceatur.
Flammas eius lucifer
    matutinus inveniat:

Ille, inquam, lucifer,
    qui nescit occasum:
Christus Filius tuus,
qui, regressus ab inferis, humano
    generi serenus illuxit,
et vivit et regnat
    in sæcula sæculorum.

R. Amen.

Shorter Form of the Easter Proclamation

Exult, let them exult,
    the hosts of heaven,
exult, let Angel ministers
    of God exult,
let the trumpet of salvation
sound aloud our mighty
    King's triumph!

Exsultet iam angelica
    turba cælorum:
exsultent divina mysteria:
et pro tanti Regis victoria tuba
    insonet salutaris.

Be glad, let earth be glad, as glory
    floods her,
ablaze with light from her
    eternal King,
let all corners of the earth be glad,
knowing an end to gloom
    and darkness.

Gaudeat et tellus tantis
    irradiata fulgoribus:
et, æterni Regis splendore illustrata,
totius orbis se sentiat
    amisisse caliginem.

Rejoice, let Mother Church
    also rejoice,
arrayed with the lightning
    of his glory,
let this holy building shake with joy,
filled with the mighty voices
    of the peoples.

(V. The Lord be with you.
R. And with your spirit.)

V. Lift up your hearts.
R. We lift them up to the Lord.
V. Let us give thanks to the Lord
    our God.
R. It is right and just.

It is truly right and just,
with ardent love of mind and heart
and with devoted service of our voice,
to acclaim our God invisible,
    the almighty Father,
and Jesus Christ, our Lord, his Son,
    his Only Begotten.

Who for our sake paid Adam's debt
    to the eternal Father,
and, pouring out his own dear Blood,
wiped clean the record
    of our ancient sinfulness.

These then are the feasts of Passover,
in which is slain the Lamb,
    the one true Lamb,
whose Blood anoints the doorposts
    of believers.

This is the night,
when once you led our forebears,
    Israel's children,
from slavery in Egypt
and made them pass dry-shod
    through the Red Sea.

Lætetur et mater Ecclesia,
tanti luminis adornata fulgoribus:
et magnis populorum vocibus hæc
    aula resultet.

(V. Dominus vobiscum.
R. Et cum spiritu tuo.)

V. Sursum corda.
R. Habemus ad Dominum.
V. Gratias agamus Domino
    Deo nostro.
R. Dignum et iustum est.

Vere dignum et iustum est,
invisibilem Deum
    Patrem omnipotentem
Filiumque eius Unigenitum,
Dominum nostrum
    Iesum Christum,
toto cordis ac mentis affectu
    et vocis ministerio personare.

Qui pro nobis æterno Patri Adæ
    debitum solvit,
et veteris piaculi cautionem pio
    cruore detersit.

Hæc sunt enim festa paschalia,
in quibus verus ille
    Agnus occiditur,
cuius sanguine postes
    fidelium consecrantur.

Hæc nox est,
in qua primum patres nostros,
    filios Israel
eductos de Ægypto,
Mare Rubrum sicco vestigio
    transire fecisti.

This is the night
that with a pillar of fire
banished the darkness of sin.

Hæc igitur nox est,
quæ peccatorum tenebras columnæ
    illuminatione purgavit.

This is the night
that even now, throughout the world,
sets Christian believers apart
    from worldly vices
and from the gloom of sin,
leading them to grace
and joining them to his holy ones.

Hæc nox est,
quæ hodie per universum mundum
    in Christo credentes,
a vitiis sæculi et caligine
peccatorum segregatos,
reddit gratiæ, sociat sanctitati.

This is the night,
when Christ broke the prison-bars
    of death
and rose victorious
    from the underworld.

Hæc nox est,
in qua, destructis vinculis mortis,
Christus ab inferis victor ascendit.

O wonder of your humble care for us!
O love, O charity beyond all telling,
to ransom a slave you gave away
    your Son!

O mira circa nos tuæ
    pietatis dignatio!
O inæstimablilis dilectio caritatis:
ut servum redimeres,
    Filium tradidisti!

O truly necessary sin of Adam,
destroyed completely by the Death
    of Christ!

O certe necessarium Adæ peccatum,
quod Christi morte deletum est!

O happy fault
that earned so great,
    so glorious a Redeemer!

O felix culpa,
quæ talem ac tantum meruit
    habere Redemptorem!

The sanctifying power of this night
dispels wickedness,
    washes faults away,
restores innocence to the fallen,
    and joy to mourners.

Huius igitur sanctificatio noctis
    fugat scelera, culpas lavat:
et reddit innocentiam lapsis
    et mæstis lætitiam.

O truly blessed night,
when things of heaven are wed
    to those of earth,
and divine to the human.

O vere beata nox,
in qua terrenis cælestia,
    humanis divina iunguntur!

On this, your night of grace,
    O holy Father,
accept this candle, a solemn offering,
the work of bees and of your

In huius igitur noctis gratia,
suscipe, sancte Pater, laudis huius
    sacrificium vespertinum,
quod tibi in hac cerei

servants' hands,
an evening sacrifice of praise,
this gift from your most
    holy Church.

Therefore, O Lord,
we pray you that this candle,
hallowed to the honour
    of your name,
may persevere undimmed,
to overcome the darkness
    of this night.
Receive it as a pleasing fragrance,
and let it mingle with the lights
    of heaven.
May this flame be found
    still burning
by the Morning Star:
the one Morning Star who never sets,
Christ your Son,
who, coming back from
    death's domain,
has shed his peaceful light
    on humanity,
and lives and reigns
    for ever and ever.
R. Amen.

oblatione sollemni,
per ministrorum manus
de operibus apum,
    sacrosancta reddit Ecclesia.

Oramus ergo te, Domine,
ut cereus iste in honorem tui
    nominis consecratus,
ad noctis huius
    caliginem destruendam,
indeficiens perseveret.
Et in odorem suavitatis acceptus,
supernis luminaribus misceatur.
Flammas eius lucifer
    matutinus inveniat:
Ille, inquam, lucifer,
    qui nescit occasum:
Christus Filius tuus,
qui, regressus ab inferis,
    humano generi serenus illuxit,
et vivit et regnat
    in sæcula sæculorum.
R. Amen.

SECOND PART:

The Liturgy of the Word

In this Vigil, the mother of all Vigils, nine readings are provided, namely seven from the Old Testament and two from the New (the Epistle and Gospel), all of which should be read whenever this can be done, so that the character of the Vigil, which demands an extended period of time, may be preserved.

Nevertheless, where more serious pastoral circumstances demand it, the number of readings from the Old Testament may be reduced, always bearing in mind that the reading of the Word of God is a fundamental part of this Easter Vigil. At least three readings should be read from the Old Testament, both from the Law and from the Prophets, and their respective Responsorial Psalms should be sung. Never, moreover, should the reading of chapter 14 of Exodus with its canticle be omitted.

After setting aside their candles, all sit. Before the readings begin, the Priest instructs the people in these or similar words:

Dear brethren (brothers and sisters),	Vigiliam sollemniter ingressi, fratres carissimi,

Dear brethren (brothers and
    sisters),
now that we have begun
    our solemn Vigil,
let us listen with quiet hearts
    to the Word of God.
Let us meditate on how God in
    times past saved his people
and in these, the last days, has sent
    us his Son as our Redeemer.
Let us pray that our God may
    complete this paschal work
    of salvation
by the fullness of redemption.

Vigiliam sollemniter ingressi,
    fratres carissimi,
quieto corde nunc verbum
    Dei audiamus.
Meditemur, quomodo Deus
    populum suum
elapsis temporibus salvum fecerit,
et novissime nobis Filium suum
    miserit Redemptorem.
Oremus, ut Deus noster hoc
    paschale salvationis opus
ad plenam redemptionem perficiat.

Then the readings follow. A reader goes to the ambo and proclaims the reading. Afterwards a psalmist or a cantor sings or says the Psalm with the people making the response. Then all rise, the Priest says, Let us pray and, after all have prayed for a while in silence, he says the prayer corresponding to the reading. In place of the Responsorial Psalm a period of sacred silence may be observed, in which case the pause after **Let us pray** *is omitted.*

FIRST READING

A reading from the book of Genesis   1:1-2:2

God saw all he made, and indeed it was very good.

[In the beginning God created the heavens and the earth.] Now the earth was a formless void, there was darkness over the deep, and God's spirit hovered over the water.

    God said, 'Let there be light,' and there was light. God saw that light was good, and God divided light from darkness. God called light 'day', and darkness he called 'night'. Evening came and morning came: the first day.

God said, 'Let there be a vault in the waters to divide the waters in two.' And so it was. God made the vault, and it divided the waters above the vault from the waters under the vault. God called the vault 'heaven'. Evening came and morning came: the second day.

    God said, 'Let the waters under heaven come together into a single mass, and let dry land appear.' And so it was. God called the dry land 'earth' and the mass of waters 'seas', and God saw that it was good.

    God said, 'Let the earth produce vegetation: seed-bearing plants, and fruit trees bearing fruit with their seed inside, on the earth.' And so it was.

The earth produced vegetation: plants bearing seed in their several kinds, and trees bearing fruit with their seed inside in their several kinds. God saw that it was good. Evening came and morning came: the third day.

God said, 'Let there be lights in the vault of heaven to divide day from night, and let them indicate festivals, days and years. Let them be lights in the vault of heaven to shine on the earth.' And so it was. God made the two great lights: the greater light to govern the day, the smaller light to govern the night, and the stars. God set them in the vault of heaven to shine on the earth, to govern the day and the night and to divide light from darkness. God saw that it was good. Evening came and morning came: the fourth day.

God said, 'Let the waters teem with living creatures, and let birds fly above the earth within the vault of heaven.' And so it was. God created great sea-serpents and every kind of living creature with which the waters teem, and every kind of winged creature. God saw that it was good. God blessed them, saying, 'Be fruitful, multiply, and fill the waters of the seas, and let the birds multiply upon the earth.' Evening came and morning came: the fifth day.

God said, 'Let the earth produce every kind of living creature: cattle, reptiles, and every kind of wild beast.' And so it was. God made every kind of wild beast, every kind of cattle, and every kind of land reptile. God saw that it was good.

[God said, 'Let us make man in our own image, in the likeness of ourselves, and let them be masters of the fish of the sea, the birds of heaven, the cattle, all the wild beasts and all the reptiles that crawl upon the earth.'

God created man in the image of himself,
in the image of God he created him,
male and female he created them.

God blessed them, saying to them, 'Be fruitful, multiply, fill the earth and conquer it. Be masters of the fish of the sea, the birds of heaven and all living animals on the earth.' God said, 'See, I give you all the seed-bearing plants that are upon the whole earth, and all the trees with seed-bearing fruit; this shall be your food. To all wild beasts, all birds of heaven and all living reptiles on the earth I give all the foliage of plants for food.' And so it was. God saw all he had made, and indeed it was very good. Evening came and morning came: the sixth day.

Thus heaven and earth were completed with all their array. On the seventh day God completed the work he had been doing. He rested on the seventh day after all the work he had been doing.

The word of the Lord.]

Shorter Form, verses 1, 26-31. Read between [ ]

Responsorial Psalm   Ps 103:1-2,5-6,10,12-14,24,35. R. Cf. v.30

R. **Send forth your spirit, O Lord,**
   and renew the face of the earth.
   Bless the Lord, my soul!
   Lord God, how great you are,
   clothed in majesty and glory,
   wrapped in light as in a robe! R.

You founded the earth on its base,
to stand firm from age to age.
You wrapped it with the ocean like a cloak:
the waters stood higher than the mountains. R.

You make springs gush forth in the valleys:
they flow in between the hills.
On their banks dwell the birds of heaven;
from the branches they sing their song. R.

From your dwelling you water the hills;
earth drinks its fill of your gift.
You make the grass grow for the cattle
and the plants to serve man's needs. R.

How many are your works, O Lord!
In wisdom you have made them all.
The earth is full of your riches.
Bless the Lord, my soul! R.

Alternative Psalm   Ps 32:4-7,12-13,20,22. R. v.5

R. **The Lord fills the earth with his love.**

The word of the Lord is faithful
and all his works to be trusted.
The Lord loves justice and right
and fills the earth with his love. R.

By his word the heavens were made,
by the breath of his mouth all the stars.
He collects the waves of the ocean;
he stores up the depths of the sea. R.

They are happy, whose God is the Lord,
the people he has chosen as his own.
From the heavens the Lord looks forth,
he sees all the children of men. R.

Our soul is waiting for the Lord.
The Lord is our help and our shield.
May your love be upon us, O Lord,
as we place all our hope in you. R.

Prayer

Let us pray.

Oremus.

Almighty ever-living God,
who are wonderful in the ordering
    of all your works,
may those you have
    redeemed understand
that there exists nothing
    more marvellous
than the world's creation
    in the beginning
except that, at the end of the ages,
Christ our Passover
    has been sacrificed.
Who lives and reigns
    for ever and ever.
R. Amen.

Omnipotens sempiterne Deus,
qui es in omnium operum tuorum
    dispensatione mirabilis,
intellegant redempti tui,
    non fuisse excellentius,
quod initio factus est mundus,
quam quod in fine sæculorum
Pascha nostrum immolatus
    est Christus.
Qui vivit et regnat
    in sæcula sæculorum.
R. Amen.

Or, On the creation of man:

O God, who wonderfully created
    human nature
and still more wonderfully
    redeemed it,
grant us, we pray,
to set our minds against
    the enticements of sin,
that we may merit to attain
    eternal joys.
Through Christ our Lord.
R. Amen.

Deus, qui mirabiliter creasti hominem
et mirabilius redemisti,
da nobis, quæsumus,
contra oblectamenta peccati mentis
    ratione persistere,
ut mereamur ad æterna
    gaudia pervenire.
Per Christum Dominum nostrum.
R. Amen.

SECOND READING

A reading from the book of Genesis   22:1-18

The sacrifice of Abraham, our father in faith.

[God put Abraham to the test. 'Abraham, Abraham,' he called. 'Here I am'
he replied. 'Take your son,' God said 'your only child Isaac, whom you

love, and go to the land of Moriah. There you shall offer him as a burnt offering, on a mountain I will point out to you.']

Rising early next morning Abraham saddled his ass and took with him two of his servants and his son Isaac. He chopped wood for the burnt offering and started on his journey to the place God had pointed out to him. On the third day Abraham looked up and saw the place in the distance. Then Abraham said to his servants, 'Stay here with the donkey. The boy and I will go over there; we will worship and come back to you.'

Abraham took the wood for the burnt offering, loaded it on Isaac, and carried in his own hands the fire and the knife. Then the two of them set out together. Isaac spoke to his father Abraham, 'Father' he said. 'Yes, my son' he replied. 'Look,' he said 'here are the fire and the wood, but where is the lamb for the burnt offering?' Abraham answered, 'My son, God himself will provide the lamb for the burnt offering.' Then the two of them went on together.

[When they arrived at the place God had pointed out to him, Abraham built an altar there, and arranged the wood. Then he bound his son Isaac and put him on the altar on top of the wood. Abraham stretched out his hand and seized the knife to kill his son.

But the angel of the Lord called to him from heaven. 'Abraham, Abraham' he said. 'I am here' he replied. 'Do not raise your hand against the boy' the angel said. 'Do not harm him, for now I know you fear God. You have not refused me your son, your only son.' Then looking up, Abraham saw a ram caught by its horns in a bush. Abraham took the ram and offered it as a burnt-offering in place of his son.] Abraham called this place 'The Lord provides', and hence the saying today: On the mountain the Lord provides.

[The angel of the Lord called Abraham a second time from heaven. 'I swear by my own self – it is the Lord who speaks – because you have done this, because you have not refused me your son, your only son, I will shower blessings on you, I will make your descendants as many as the stars of heaven and the grains of sand on the seashore. Your descendants shall gain possession of the gates of their enemies. All the nations of the earth shall bless themselves by your descendants, as a reward for your obedience.

The word of the Lord.]

Shorter Form, verses 1-2,9-13,15-18. Read between [ ]

Responsorial Psalm   Ps 15:5,8-11, R. v.1

R. **Preserve me, God, I take refuge in you.**

O Lord, it is you who are my portion and cup;
it is you yourself who are my prize.
I keep the Lord ever in my sight:
since he is at my right hand, I shall stand firm. R.

And so my heart rejoices, my soul is glad;
even my body shall rest in safety.
For you will not leave my soul among the dead,
nor let your beloved know decay. R.

You will show me the path of life,
the fullness of joy in your presence,
at your right hand happiness for ever. R.

Prayer

Let us pray.

O God, supreme Father
    of the faithful,
who increase the children
    of your promise
by pouring out the grace
    of adoption
throughout the whole world
and who through the Paschal Mystery
make your servant Abraham father
    of nations,
as once you swore,
grant, we pray,
that your peoples may enter worthily
into the grace to which you call them.
Through Christ our Lord.
R. Amen.

Oremus.

Deus, Pater summe fidelium,
qui promissionis tuæ filios diffusa
    adoptionis gratia
in toto terrarum orbe multiplicas,
et per paschale sacramentum
Abraham puerum tuum
universarum, sicut iurasti,
    gentium efficis patrem,
da populis tuis digne ad gratiam
    tuæ vocationis intrare.
Per Christum Dominum nostrum.
R. Amen.

The following reading must always be read.

THIRD READING

A reading from book of Exodus   14:15-15:1

The sons of Israel went on dry ground right into the sea.

The Lord said to Moses, 'Why do you cry to me so? Tell the sons of Israel to march on. For yourself, raise your staff and stretch out your hand over the sea and part it for the sons of Israel to walk through the sea on dry ground. I for my part will make the heart of the Egyptians so stubborn that they will follow them. So shall I win myself glory at the expense of Pharaoh, of all his army, his chariots, his horsemen. And when I have won glory for myself, at the expense of Pharaoh and his chariots and his army, the Egyptians will learn that I am the Lord.'

Then the angel of the Lord, who marched at the front of the army of Israel, changed station and moved to their rear. The pillar of cloud changed station from the front to the rear of them, and remained there. It came between the camp of the Egyptians and the camp of Israel. The cloud was dark, and the night passed without the armies drawing any closer the whole night long. Moses stretched out his hand over the sea. The Lord drove back the sea with a strong easterly wind all night, and he made dry land of the sea. The waters parted and the sons of Israel went on dry ground right into the sea, walls of water to right and to left of them. The Egyptians gave chase: after them they went, right into the sea, all Pharaoh's horses, his chariots, and his horsemen. In the morning watch, the Lord looked down on the army of the Egyptians from the pillar of fire and of cloud, and threw the army into confusion. He so clogged their chariot wheels that they could scarcely make headway. 'Let us flee from the Israelites,' the Egyptians cried 'the Lord is fighting for them against the Egyptians!' 'Stretch out your hand over the sea,' the Lord said to Moses 'that the waters may flow back on the Egyptians and their chariots and their horsemen.' Moses stretched out his hand over the sea and, as day broke, the sea returned to its bed. The fleeing Egyptians marched right into it, and the Lord overthrew the Egyptians in the very middle of the sea. The returning waters overwhelmed the chariots and the horsemen of Pharaoh's whole army, which had followed the Israelites into the sea; not a single one of them was left. But the sons of Israel had marched through the sea on dry ground, walls of water to right and to left of them. That day, the Lord rescued Israel from the Egyptians, and Israel saw the Egyptians lying dead on the shore. Israel witnessed the great act that the Lord had performed against the Egyptians, and the people venerated the Lord; they put their faith in the Lord and in Moses, his servant.

It was then that Moses and the sons of Israel sang this song in honour of the Lord:

The choir takes up the Responsorial Psalm immediately.

Responsorial Psalm   Ex 15:1-6,17-18. R. v.1

R. **I will sing to the Lord, glorious his triumph!**

> I will sing to the Lord, glorious his triumph!
> Horse and rider he has thrown into the sea!
> The Lord is my strength, my song, my salvation.
> This is my God and I extol him,
> my father's God and I give him praise. R.

> The Lord is a warrior! The Lord is his name.
> The chariots of Pharaoh he hurled into the sea,
> the flower of his army is drowned in the sea.
> The deeps hide them; they sank like a stone. R.

> Your right hand, Lord, glorious in its power,
> your right hand, Lord, has shattered the enemy.
> In the greatness of your glory you crushed the foe. R.

> You will lead your people and plant them on your mountain,
> the place, O Lord, where you have made your home,
> the sanctuary, Lord, which your hands have made.
> The Lord will reign for ever and ever. R.

Prayer

Let us pray.
O God, whose ancient wonders
remain undimmed in splendour
   even in our day,
for what you once bestowed
   on a single people,
freeing them from
   Pharaoh's persecution
by the power of your right hand,
now you bring about as the salvation
   of the nations
through the waters of rebirth,
grant, we pray,
   that the whole world
may become children of Abraham
and inherit the dignity
   of Israel's birthright.
Through Christ our Lord.
R. Amen.

Oremus.
Deus, cuius antiqua miracula
etiam nostris temporibus
   coruscare sentimus,
dum, quod uni populo
a persecutione Pharaonis liberando
dexteræ tuæ potentia contulisti,
id in salutem gentium
per aquam regenerationis operaris,
præsta, ut in Abrahæ filios
et in Israeliticam dignitatem
totius mundi transeat plenitudo.
Per Christum Dominum nostrum.
R. Amen.

Or:	Vel:
O God, who by the light of the New Testament have unlocked the meaning of wonders worked in former times, so that the Red Sea prefigures the sacred font and the nation delivered from slavery foreshadows the Christian people, grant, we pray, that all nations, obtaining the privilege of Israel by merit of faith, may be reborn by partaking of your Spirit. Through Christ our Lord. R. Amen.	Deus, qui primis temporibus impleta miracula novi testamenti luce reserasti, ut et Mare Rubrum forma sacri fontis exsisteret, et plebs a servitute liberata christiani populi sacramenta præferret, da, ut omnes gentes, Israelis privilegium merito fidei consecutæ, Spiritus tui participatione regenerentur. Per Christum Dominum nostrum. R. Amen.

FOURTH READING

A reading from the prophet Isaiah   54:5-14

With everlasting love the Lord your redeemer has taken pity on you.

Now your creator will be your husband,
his name, the Lord of hosts;
your redeemer will be the Holy One of Israel,
he is called the God of the whole earth.
Yes, like a forsaken wife, distressed in spirit,
the Lord calls you back.
Does a man cast off the wife of his youth?
says your God.

I did forsake you for a brief moment,
but with great love will I take you back.
In excess of anger, for a moment
I hid my face from you.
But with everlasting love I have taken pity on you,
says the Lord, your redeemer.

I am now as I was in the days of Noah
when I swore that Noah's waters
should never flood the world again.
So now I swear concerning my anger with you
and the threats I made against you;

for the mountains may depart,
the hills be shaken,
but my love for you will never leave you;
and my covenant of peace with you will never be shaken,
says the Lord who takes pity on you.

Unhappy creature, storm-tossed, disconsolate,
see, I will set your stones on carbuncles
and your foundations on sapphires.
I will make rubies your battlements,
your gates crystal,
and your entire wall precious stones.
Your sons will all be taught by the Lord.
The prosperity of your sons will be great.
You will be founded on integrity;
remote from oppression, you will have nothing to fear;
remote from terror, it will not approach you.

The word of the Lord.

Responsorial Psalm   Ps 29:2,4-6,11-13. R. v.2

R. **I will praise you, Lord, you have rescued me.**

I will praise you, Lord, you have rescued me
and have not let my enemies rejoice over me.
O Lord, you have raised my soul from the dead,
restored me to life from those who sink into the grave. R.

Sing psalms to the Lord, you who love him,
give thanks to his holy name.
His anger lasts but a moment; his favour through life.
At night there are tears, but joy comes with dawn. R.

The Lord listened and had pity.
The Lord came to my help.
For me you have changed my mourning into dancing,
O Lord my God, I will thank you for ever. R.

Prayer

Let us pray.
Almighty ever-living God,
surpass, for the honour of your name,
what you pledged to the Patriarchs
    by reason of their faith,
and through sacred adoption increase
    the children of your promise,
	Oremus.
	Omnipotens sempiterne Deus,
	multiplica in honorem nominis tui
	quod patrum fidei spopondisti,
	et promissionis filios sacra
	    adoptione dilata,
	ut, quod priores sancti non

so that what the Saints of old never
   doubted would come to pass
your Church may now see in great
   part fulfilled.
Through Christ our Lord. R. Amen.

dubitaverunt futurum,
Ecclesia tua magna ex parte iam
   cognoscat impletum.
Per Christum Dominum nostrum.
R. Amen.

Alternatively, other prayers may be used from among those which follow the readings that have been omitted.

FIFTH READING

A reading from the prophet Isaiah   55:1-11

Come to me and your soul will live, and I will make an everlasting covenant with you.

Thus says the Lord:
    Oh, come to the water all you who are thirsty;
    though you have no money, come!
    Buy corn without money, and eat,
    and, at no cost, wine and milk.
    Why spend money on what is not bread,
    your wages on what fails to satisfy?
    Listen, listen to me, and you will have good things to eat
    and rich food to enjoy.
    Pay attention, come to me;
    and your soul will live.

    With you I will make an everlasting covenant
    out of the favours promised to David.
    See, I have made of you a witness to the peoples,
    a leader and a master of the nations.
    See, you will summon a nation you never knew,
    those unknown will come hurrying to you,
    for the sake of the Lord your God,
    of the Holy One of Israel who will glorify you.

    Seek the Lord while he is still to be found,
    call to him while he is still near.
    Let the wicked man abandon his way,
    the evil man his thoughts.
    Let him turn back to the Lord who will take pity on him,
    to our God who is rich in forgiving;
    for my thoughts are not your thoughts,
    my ways not your ways – it is the Lord who speaks.
    Yes, the heavens are as high above earth
    as my ways are above your ways,
    my thoughts above your thoughts.

Yes, as the rain and the snow come down from the heavens and do not return without watering the earth, making it yield and giving growth to provide seed for the sower and bread for the eating, so the word that goes from my mouth does not return to me empty, without carrying out my will and succeeding in what it was sent to do.

The word of the Lord.

Responsorial Psalm

Is 12:2-6. R. v.3

R. **With joy you will draw water from the wells of salvation.**

Truly God is my salvation,
I trust, I shall not fear.
For the Lord is my strength, my song,
he became my saviour.
With joy you will draw water
from the wells of salvation. R.

Give thanks to the Lord, give praise to his name!
Make his mighty deeds known to the peoples,
declare the greatness of his name. R.

Sing a psalm to the Lord
for he has done glorious deeds,
make them known to all the earth!
People of Zion, sing and shout for joy
for great in your midst is the Holy One of Israel. R.

Prayer

Let us pray.

Almighty ever-living God,
sole hope of the world,
who by the preaching
   of your Prophets
unveiled the mysteries
   of this present age,
graciously increase the longing
   of your people,
for only at the prompting
   of your grace
do the faithful progress in any
   kind of virtue.
Through Christ our Lord.
R. Amen.

Oremus.

Omnipotens sempiterne Deus,
spes unica mundi,
qui prophetarum tuorum præconio
præsentium temporum
   declarasti mysteria,
auge populi tui vota placatus,
quia in nullo fidelium nisi ex tua
   inspiratione proveniunt
quarumlibet incrementa virtutum.
Per Christum Dominum nostrum.
R. Amen.

SIXTH READING

A reading from the prophet Baruch   3:9-15,32-4:4

In the radiance of the Lord make your way to light.

Listen, Israel, to commands that bring life;
hear, and learn what knowledge means.
Why, Israel, why are you in the country of your enemies,
growing older and older in an alien land,
sharing defilement with the dead,
reckoned with those who go to Sheol?
Because you have forsaken the fountain of wisdom.
Had you walked in the way of God,
you would have lived in peace for ever.
Learn where knowledge is, where strength,
where understanding, and so learn
where length of days is, where life,
where the light of the eyes and where peace.
But who has found out where she lives,
who has entered her treasure house?

But the One who knows all knows her,
he has grasped her with his own intellect,
he has set the earth firm for ever
and filled it with four-footed beasts,
he sends the light – and it goes,
he recalls it – and trembling it obeys;
the stars shine joyfully at their set times:
when he calls them, they answer, 'Here we are';
they gladly shine for their creator.
It is he who is our God,
no other can compare with him.
He has grasped the whole way of knowledge,
and confided it to his servant Jacob,
to Israel his well-beloved;
so causing her to appear on earth
and move among men.

This is the book of the commandments of God,
the Law that stands for ever;
those who keep her live,
those who desert her die.

Turn back, Jacob, seize her,
in her radiance make your way to light:
do not yield your glory to another,
your privilege to a people not your own.
Israel, blessed are we:
what pleases God has been revealed to us.

The word of the Lord.

Responsorial Psalm   Ps 18:8-11. R. Jn 6:69

R. **You have the message of eternal life, O Lord.**

The law of the Lord is perfect,
it revives the soul.
The rule of the Lord is to be trusted,
it gives wisdom to the simple. R.

The precepts of the Lord are right,
they gladden the heart.
The command of the Lord is clear,
it gives light to the eyes. R.

The fear of the Lord is holy,
abiding for ever.
The decrees of the Lord are truth
and all of them just. R.

They are more to be desired than gold,
than the purest of gold
and sweeter are they than honey,
than honey from the comb. R.

Prayer

Let us pray.

O God, who constantly increase
    your Church
by your call to the nations,
graciously grant
to those you wash clean
    in the waters of Baptism
the assurance of your
    unfailing protection.
Through Christ our Lord.
R. Amen.

Oremus.

Deus, qui Ecclesiam tuam
semper gentium
    vocatione multiplicas,
concede propitius,
ut, quos aqua baptismatis abluis,
continua protectione tuearis.
Per Christum Dominum nostrum.
R. Amen.

SEVENTH READING

A reading from the prophet Ezekiel   36:16-28

I shall pour clean water over you, and I shall give you a new heart.

The word of the Lord was addressed to me as follows: 'Son of man, the members of the House of Israel used to live in their own land, but they defiled it by their conduct and actions. I then discharged my fury at them because of the blood they shed in their land and the idols with which they defiled it. I scattered them among the nations and dispersed them in foreign countries. I sentenced them as their conduct and actions deserved. And now they have profaned my holy name among the nations where they have gone, so that people say of them, "These are the people of the Lord; they have been exiled from his land." But I have been concerned about my holy name, which the House of Israel has profaned among the nations where they have gone. And so, say to the House of Israel, "The Lord says this: I am not doing this for my sake, House of Israel, but for the sake of my holy name, which you have profaned among the nations where you have gone. I mean to display the holiness of my great name, which has been profaned among the nations, which you have profaned among them. And the nations will learn that I am the Lord – it is the Lord who speaks – when I display my holiness for your sake before their eyes. Then I am going to take you from among the nations and gather you together from all the foreign countries, and bring you home to your own land. I shall pour clean water over you and you will be cleansed; I shall cleanse you of all your defilement and all your idols. I shall give you a new heart, and put a new spirit in you; I shall remove the heart of stone from your bodies and give you a heart of flesh instead. I shall put my spirit in you, and make you keep my laws and sincerely respect my observances. You will live in the land which I gave your ancestors. You shall be my people and I will be your God."'

The word of the Lord.

Responsorial Psalm   Pss 41:3,5; 42:3,4. R. Ps 41:1

R. **Like the deer that yearns for running streams,**
   so my soul is yearning for you, my God.

My soul is thirsting for God.
the God of my life;
when can I enter and see
the face of God? R.

These things I will remember
as I pour out my soul:
how I would lead the rejoicing crowd
into the house of God,
amid cries of gladness and thanksgiving,
the throng wild with joy. R.

O send forth your light and your truth;
let these be my guide.
Let them bring me to your holy mountain
to the place where you dwell. R.

And I will come to the altar of God,
the God of my joy.
My redeemer, I will thank you on the harp,
O God, my God. R.

If a Baptism takes place the Responsorial Psalm which follows the Fifth Reading (see p.244), is used, or Psalm 50 as follows.

Responsorial Psalm   Ps 50:12-15,18,19. R. v.12

R. **A pure heart create for me, O God.**

A pure heart create for me, O God,
put a steadfast spirit within me.
Do not cast me away from your presence,
nor deprive me of your holy spirit. R.

Give me again the joy of your help;
with a spirit of fervour sustain me,
that I may teach transgressors your ways
and sinners may return to you. R.

For in sacrifice you take no delight,
burnt offering from me you would refuse,
my sacrifice, a contrite spirit.
A humbled, contrite heart you will not spurn. R.

Prayer

Let us pray.

O God of unchanging power
   and eternal light,
look with favour on the wondrous
   mystery of the whole Church

Oremus.

Deus, incommutabilis virtus
   et lumen æternum,
respice propitius ad totius
   Ecclesiæ mirabile sacramentum,

and serenely accomplish the work
of human salvation,
which you planned from all eternity;
may the whole world know and see
that what was cast down is raised up,
what had become old is made new,
and all things are restored
   to integrity through Christ,
just as by him they came into being.
Who lives and reigns
   for ever and ever.
R. Amen.

et opus salutis humanæ
perpetuæ dispositionis effectu
tranquillius operare;
totusque mundus experiatur
   et videat
deiecta erigi, inveterata renovari
et per ipsum Christum redire
   omnia in integrum,
a quo sumpsere principium.
Qui vivit et regnat
   in sæcula sæculorum.
R. Amen.

Or:

Vel:

O God, who by the pages
   of both Testaments
instruct and prepare us to celebrate
   the Paschal Mystery,
grant that we may comprehend
   your mercy,
so that the gifts we receive
   from you this night
may confirm our hope of the gifts
   to come.
Through Christ our Lord.
R. Amen.

Deus, qui nos ad celebrandum
   paschale sacramentum
utriusque Testamenti
   paginis instruis,
da nobis intellegere
   misericordiam tuam,
ut ex perceptione
   præsentium munerum
firma sit exspectatio futurorum.
Per Christum Dominum nostrum.
R. Amen.

After the last reading from the Old Testament with its Responsorial Psalm and its prayer, the altar candles are lit, and the Priest intones the hymn **Gloria in excelsis Deo** (Glory to God in the highest), which is taken up by all, while bells are rung, according to local custom.

The complete musical setting of the Latin text is found in the Graduale Romanum.

When the hymn is concluded, the Priest says the Collect in the usual way.

Collect

Collecta

Let us pray.

Oremus.

O God, who make this most sacred
   night radiant
with the glory
   of the Lord's Resurrection,
stir up in your Church a spirit
   of adoption,

Deus, qui hanc
   sacratissimam noctem
gloria dominicæ
   resurrectionis illustras,
excita in Ecclesia tua
   adoptionis spiritum,

so that, renewed in body and mind,	ut, corpore et mente renovati,
we may render you undivided service.	puram tibi exhibeamus servitutem.
Through our Lord Jesus Christ, your Son,	Per Dominum nostrum Iesum Christum Filium tuum,
who lives and reigns with you in the unity of the Holy Spirit,	qui tecum vivit et regnat in unitate Spiritus Sancti,
one God, for ever and ever.	Deus, per omnia sæcula sæculorum.

FIRST READING

A reading from the letter of St Paul to the Romans   6:3-11

Christ, having been raised from the dead, will never die again.

When we were baptised in Christ Jesus we were baptised in his death; in other words, when we were baptised we went into the tomb with him and joined him in death, so that as Christ was raised from the dead by the Father's glory, we too might live a new life.

If in union with Christ we have imitated his death, we shall also imitate him in his resurrection. We must realise that our former selves have been crucified with him to destroy this sinful body and to free us from the slavery of sin. When a man dies, of course, he has finished with sin.

But we believe that having died with Christ we shall return to life with him: Christ, as we know, having been raised from the dead will never die again. Death has no power over him any more. When he died, he died, once for all, to sin, so his life now is life with God; and in that way, you too must consider yourselves to be dead to sin but alive for God in Christ Jesus.

The word of the Lord.

After the Epistle has been read, all rise, then the Priest solemnly intones the **Alleluia** *three times, raising his voice by a step each time, with all repeating it. If necessary, the psalmist intones the* **Alleluia***.*

Responsorial Psalm   Ps 117:1-2,16-17,22-23

R. **Alleluia, alleluia, alleluia!**

> Give thanks to the Lord for he is good,
> for his love has no end.
> Let the sons of Israel say:
> 'His love has no end.' R.

The Lord's right hand has triumphed;
his right hand raised me.
I shall not die, I shall live
and recount his deeds. R.

The stone which the builders rejected
has become the corner stone.
This is the work of the Lord,
a marvel in our eyes. R.

R. **Alleluia, alleluia, alleluia!**

The Priest, in the usual way, puts incense in the thurible and blesses the Deacon. At the Gospel lights are not carried, but only incense.

GOSPEL

A reading from the holy Gospel according to Matthew   28:1-10

He has risen from the dead and now he is going before you into Galilee.

After the sabbath, and towards dawn on the first day of the week, Mary of Magdala and the other Mary went to visit the sepulchre. And all at once there was a violent earthquake, for the angel of the Lord, descending from heaven, came and rolled away the stone and sat on it. His face was like lightning, his robe white as snow. The guards were so shaken, so frightened of him, that they were like dead men. But the angel spoke; and he said to the women, 'There is no need for you to be afraid. I know you are looking for Jesus, who was crucified. He is not here, for he has risen, as he said he would. Come and see the place where he lay, then go quickly and tell his disciples, "He has risen from the dead and now he is going before you to Galilee; it is there you will see him." Now I have told you.' Filled with awe and great joy, the women came quickly away from the tomb and ran to tell the disciples.

And there, coming to meet them, was Jesus. 'Greetings' he said. And the women came up to him and, falling down before him, clasped his feet. Then Jesus said to them, 'Do not be afraid; go and tell my brothers that they must leave for Galilee; they will see me there.'

The Gospel of the Lord.

After the Gospel, the Homily, even if brief, is not to be omitted.

THIRD PART:

Baptismal Liturgy

After the Homily the Baptismal Liturgy begins. The Priest goes with the ministers to the baptismal font, if this can be seen by the faithful. Otherwise a vessel with water is placed in the sanctuary.

Catechumens, if there are any, are called forward and presented by their godparents in front of the assembled Church or, if they are small children, are carried by their parents and godparents.

Then, if there is to be a procession to the baptistery or to the font, it forms immediately. A minister with the paschal candle leads off, and those to be baptised follow him with their godparents, then the ministers, the Deacon, and the Priest. During the procession, the Litany is sung. When the Litany is completed, the Priest gives the address.

If, however, the Baptismal Liturgy takes place in the sanctuary, the Priest immediately makes an introductory statement in these or similar words.

If there are candidates to be baptised:

Dearly beloved, with one heart and one soul, let us by our prayers come to the aid of these our brothers and sisters in their blessed hope, so that, as they approach the font of rebirth, the almighty Father may bestow on them all his merciful help.	Precibus nostris, carissimi, fratrum nostrorum beatam spem unanimes adiuvemus, ut Pater omnipotens ad fontem regenerationis euntes omni misericordiæ suæ auxilio prosequatur.

If the font is to be blessed, but no one is to be baptised:

Dearly beloved, let us humbly invoke upon this font the grace of God the almighty Father, that those who from it are born anew may be numbered among the children of adoption in Christ.	Dei Patris omnipotentis gratiam, carissimi, super hunc fontem supplices invocemus, ut qui ex eo renascentur adoptionis filiis in Christo aggregentur.

The Litany

The Litany is sung by two cantors, with all standing (because it is Easter Time) and responding.

If, however, there is to be a procession of some length to the baptistery, the Litany is sung during the procession; in this case, those to be baptised are called forward before the procession begins, and the procession takes place led by the paschal candle, followed by the catechumens with their godparents, then the ministers, the Deacon, and the Priest. The address should occur before the Blessing of Water.

If no one is to be baptised and the font is not to be blessed, the Litany is omitted, and the Blessing of Water takes place at once.

In the Litany the names of some Saints may be added, especially the Titular Saint of the church and the Patron Saints of the place and of those to be baptised.

Lord, have mercy.		Kyrie, eleison.	
	Lord, have mercy.		Kyrie, eleison.
Christ, have mercy.		Christe, eleison.	
	Christ, have mercy.		Christe, eleison.
Lord, have mercy.		Kyrie, eleison.	
	Lord have mercy.		Kyrie, eleison.
Holy Mary,		Sancta Maria,	
Mother of God,	pray for us.	Mater Dei,	ora pro nobis.
Saint Michael,	pray for us.	Sancte Michael,	ora pro nobis.
Holy Angels of God,	pray for us.	Sancti Angeli Dei,	orate pro nobis.
Saint John the Baptist,	pray for us.	Sancte Ioannes Baptista,	ora pro nobis.
Saint Joseph,	pray for us.	Sancte Ioseph,	ora pro nobis.
Saint Peter and Saint Paul,	pray for us.	Sancti Petre et Paule,	orate pro nobis.
Saint Andrew,	pray for us.	Saint Augustine,	pray for us.
Saint John,	pray for us.	Sancte Andrea,	ora pro nobis.
Saint Mary Magdalene,	pray for us.	Sancte Ioannes,	ora pro nobis.
		Sancta Maria Magdalena,	ora pro nobis.
Saint Stephen,	pray for us.	Sancte Stephane,	ora pro nobis.
Saint Ignatius of Antioch,	pray for us.	Sancte Ignati Antiochene,	ora pro nobis.
Saint Lawrence,	pray for us.	Sancte Laurenti,	ora pro nobis.
Saint Perpetua and Saint Felicity,	pray for us.	Sanctæ Perpetua et Felicitas,	orate pro nobis.
Saint Agnes,	pray for us.	Sancta Agnes,	ora pro nobis.
Saint Gregory,	pray for us.		

Sancte Gregori, ora pro nobis.	Sancte Augustine, ora pro nobis.
Saint Athanasius, pray for us.	Sancte Athanasi, ora pro nobis.
Saint Basil, pray for us.	Sancte Basili, ora pro nobis.
Saint Martin, pray for us.	Sancte Martine, ora pro nobis.
Saint Benedict, pray for us.	Sancte Benedicte, ora pro nobis.
Saint Francis and Saint Dominic, pray for us.	Sancti Francisce et Dominice, orate pro nobis.
Saint Francis Xavier, pray for us.	Sancte Francisce (Xavier), ora pro nobis.
Saint John Vianney, pray for us.	Sancte Ioannes Maria (Vianney), ora pro nobis.
Saint Catherine of Siena, pray for us.	Sancta Catharina (Senensis), ora pro nobis.
Saint Teresa of Jesus, pray for us.	Sancta Teresia a Iesu, ora pro nobis.
All holy men and women, Saints of God, pray for us.	Omnes Sancti et Sanctæ Dei, orate pro nobis.
Lord, be merciful Lord, deliver us, we pray.	Propitius esto, libera nos, Domine.
From all evil, Lord, deliver us, we pray.	Ab omni malo, libera nos, Domine.
From every sin, Lord, deliver us, we pray.	Ab omni peccato, libera nos, Domine.
From everlasting death, Lord, deliver us, we pray.	A morte perpetua, libera nos, Domine.
By your Incarnation, Lord, deliver us, we pray.	Per incarnationem tuam, libera nos, Domine.
By your Death and Resurrection, Lord, deliver us, we pray.	Per mortem et resurrectionem tuam, libera nos, Domine.
By the out-pouring of the Holy Spirit, Lord, deliver us, we pray.	Per effusionem Spiritus Sancti, libera nos, Domine.
Be merciful to us sinners, Lord we ask you to hear our prayer.	Peccatores, te rogamus, audi nos.

If there are candidates to be baptised

Bring these chosen ones to new birth through the grace of Baptism, Lord, we ask you, hear our prayer.	Ut hos electos per gratiam Baptismi regenerare digneris te rogamus, audi nos.

If there is no one to be baptised:

Make this font holy by your grace
    for the new birth of your children,
    Lord, we ask you, hear our prayer.
	Ut hunc fontem,
	    regenerandis tibi filiis,
	    gratia tua sanctificare digneris
	            te rogamus, audi nos.

Jesus, Son of the Living God,
    Lord, we ask you, hear our prayer.
	Iesu, Fili Dei vivi,
	            te rogamus, audi nos.

Christ, hear us.   Christ, hear us.
Christ, graciously hear us.
      Christ graciously hear us.
	Christe, audi nos. Christe, audi nos.
	Christe, exaudi nos.
	          Christe, exaudi nos.

If there are candidates to be baptised, the Priest, with hands extended, says the following prayer:

Almighty ever-living God,
be present by the mysteries of your
    great love
and send forth the spirit of adoption
to create the new peoples
brought to birth for you in the font
    of Baptism,
so that what is to be carried out
    by our humble service
may be brought to fulfilment
    by your mighty power.
Through Christ our Lord.
R. Amen.
	Omnipotens sempiterne Deus,
	adesto magnæ pietatis
	    tuæ sacramentis,
	et ad recreandos novos populos,
	quos tibi fons baptismatis parturit,
	spiritum adoptionis emitte,
	ut, quod nostræ humilitatis
	    gerendum est ministerio,
	virtutis tuæ impleatur effectu.
	Per Christum Dominum nostrum.
	R. Amen.

Blessing of Baptismal Water

The Priest then blesses the baptismal water, saying the following prayer with hands extended:

O God, who by invisible power
accomplish a wondrous effect
through sacramental signs
and who in many ways have
    prepared water, your creation,
to show forth the grace of Baptism;
	Deus, qui invisibili potentia
	per sacramentorum signa
	    mirabilem operaris effectum,
	et creaturam aquæ multis
	    modis præparasti,
	ut baptismi gratiam demonstraret;

O God, whose Spirit
in the first moments
    of the world's creation
hovered over the waters,
	Deus, cuius Spiritus
	super aquas inter ipsa mundi
	    primordia ferebatur,
	ut iam tunc virtutem sanctificandi

so that the very substance of water
would even then take to itself
   the power to sanctify;

O God, who by the outpouring
   of the flood
foreshadowed regeneration,
so that from the mystery of one
   and the same element of water
would come an end to vice
   and a beginning of virtue;

O God, who caused the children
   of Abraham
to pass dry-shod through the Red Sea,
so that the chosen people,
set free from slavery to Pharaoh,
would prefigure the people
   of the baptised;

O God, whose Son,
baptised by John in the waters
   of the Jordan,
was anointed with the Holy Spirit,
and, as he hung upon the Cross,
gave forth water from his side
   along with blood,
and after his Resurrection,
   commanded his disciples:
'Go forth, teach all nations,
   baptising them
in the name of the Father and of the
   Son and of the Holy Spirit',
look now, we pray, upon the face
   of your Church
and graciously unseal for her
   the fountain of Baptism.

May this water receive
   by the Holy Spirit
the grace of your Only Begotten Son,

aquarum natura conciperet;

Deus, qui regenerationis speciem
in ipsa diluvii effusione signasti,
ut unius eiusdemque
   elementi mysterio
et finis esset vitiis et origo virtutum;

Deus, qui Abrahæ filios
per Mare Rubrum sicco vestigio
   transire fecisti,
ut plebs, a Pharaonis
   servitute liberata,
populum baptizatorum
   præfiguraret;

Deus, cuius Filius, in aqua Iordanis
   a Ioanne baptizatus,
Sancto Spiritu est inunctus,
et, in cruce pendens,
una cum sanguine aquam de latere
   suo produxit,
ac, post resurrectionem suam,
   discipulis iussit:

'Ite, docete omnes gentes,
   baptizantes eos
in nomine Patris et Filii
   et Spiritus Sancti':
respice in faciem Ecclesiæ tuæ,
eique dignare fontem
   baptismatis aperire.

Sumat hæc aqua Unigeniti tui
   gratiam de Spiritu Sancto,
ut homo, ad imaginem

so that human nature,
    created in your image,
and washed clean through
    the Sacrament of Baptism
from all the squalor of the life of old,
may be found worthy to rise
    to the life of newborn children
through water and the Holy Spirit.

tuam conditus,
sacramento baptismatis
a cunctis squaloribus
    vetustatis ablutus,
in novam infantiam
ex aqua et Spiritu Sancto
    resurgere mereatur.

And, if appropriate, lowering the paschal candle into the water either once or three times, he continues:

May the power of the Holy Spirit,
O Lord, we pray,
come down through your Son
into the fullness of this font,

Descendat, quæsumus, Domine,
in hanc plenitudinem fontis
per Filium tuum virtus
    Spiritus Sancti,

and, holding the candle in the water, he continues:

so that all who have been buried
    with Christ
by Baptism into death
may rise again to life with him.
Who lives and reigns with you
    in the unity of the Holy Spirit,
one God, for ever and ever.
R. **Amen.**

ut omnes, cum Christo consepulti
per baptismum in mortem,
ad vitam cum ipso resurgant.
Qui tecum vivit et regnat
    in unitate Spiritus Sancti,
Deus, per omnia sæcula sæculorum.
R. **Amen.**

Then the candle is lifted out of the water, as the people acclaim:

Springs of water, bless the Lord;
praise and exalt him above all
    for ever.

Benedicite, fontes, Domino,
laudate et superexaltate eum
    in sæcula.

After the blessing of baptismal water and the acclamation of the people, the Priest, standing, puts the prescribed questions to the adults and the parents or godparents of the children, as is set out in the respective Rites of the Roman Ritual, in order for them to make the required renunciation.

If the anointing of the adults with the Oil of Catechumens has not taken place beforehand, as part of the immediately preparatory rites, it occurs at this moment.

Then the Priest questions the adults individually about the faith and, if there are children to be baptised, he requests the triple profession of faith from all the parents and godparents together, as is indicated in the respective Rites.

Where many are to be baptised on this night, it is possible to arrange the rite so that, immediately after the response of those to be baptised and of the godparents and the parents, the Celebrant asks for and receives the renewal of baptismal promises of all present.

When the interrogation is concluded, the Priest baptises the adult elect and the children.

After the Baptism, the Priest anoints the infants with chrism. A white garment is given to each, whether adults or children. Then the Priest or Deacon receives the paschal candle from the hand of the minister, and the candles of the newly baptised are lighted. For infants the rite of Ephphetha is omitted.

Afterwards, unless the baptismal washing and the other explanatory rites have occurred in the sanctuary, a procession returns to the sanctuary, formed as before, with the newly baptised or the godparents or parents carrying lighted candles. During this procession, the baptismal canticle **Vidi aquam** (I saw water) or another appropriate chant is sung.

If adults have been baptised, the Bishop or, in his absence, the Priest who has conferred Baptism, should at once administer the Sacrament of Confirmation to them in the sanctuary, as is indicated in the Roman Pontifical or Roman Ritual.

The Blessing of Water

If no one present is to be baptised and the font is not to be blessed, the Priest introduces the faithful to the blessing of water, saying:

Dear brothers and sisters,
let us humbly beseech the Lord
    our God
to bless this water he has created,
which will be sprinkled upon us
as a memorial of our Baptism.
May he graciously renew us,
that we may remain faithful
    to the Spirit
whom we have received.

Dominum Deum nostrum,
    fratres carissimi,
suppliciter exoremus,
ut hanc creaturam aquæ
    benedicere dignetur,
super nos aspergendam in nostri
    memoriam baptismi.
Ipse autem nos adiuvare dignetur,
ut Spiritui, quem accepimus,
    fideles maneamus.

And after a brief pause in silence, he proclaims the following prayer, with hands extended:

Lord our God,
in your mercy be present
    to your people
who keep vigil on this most
    sacred night,
and, for us who recall the wondrous
    work of our creation

Domine Deus noster,
populo tuo hac nocte
    sacratissima vigilanti
adesto propitius;
et nobis, mirabile nostræ
    creationis opus,
sed et redemptionis nostræ

and the still greater work
  of our redemption,
graciously bless this water.
For you created water to make
  the fields fruitful
and to refresh and cleanse our bodies.
You also made water the instrument
  of your mercy:
for through water you freed
  your people from slavery
and quenched their thirst
  in the desert;
through water the Prophets
  proclaimed the new covenant
you were to enter upon
  with the human race;
and last of all,
through water, which Christ made
  holy in the Jordan,
you have renewed our
  corrupted nature
in the bath of regeneration.
Therefore, may this water be for us
a memorial of the Baptism
  we have received,
and grant that we may share
in the gladness of our brothers
  and sisters,
who at Easter have received
  their Baptism.
Through Christ our Lord.
R. Amen.

mirabilius, memorantibus,
hanc aquam benedicere tu dignare.

Ipsam enim tu fecisti,
ut et arva fecunditate donaret,
et levamen corporibus nostris
  munditiamque præberet.

Aquam etiam tuæ ministram
  misericordiæ condidisti;
nam per ipsam solvisti tui
  populi servitutem
illiusque sitim in deserto sedasti;
per ipsam novum fœdus
  nuntiaverunt prophetæ,
quod eras cum hominibus initurus;
per ipsam denique, quam Christus
  in Iordane sacravit,
corruptam naturæ
  nostræ substantiam
in regenerationis lavacro renovasti.

Sit igitur hæc aqua nobis suscepti
  baptismatis memoria,
et cum fratribus nostris,
  qui sunt in Paschate baptizati,
gaudia nos tribuas sociare.
Per Christum Dominum nostrum.
R. Amen.

The Renewal of Baptismal Promises

When the Rite of Baptism (and Confirmation) has been completed or, if this has not taken place, after the blessing of water, all stand, holding lighted candles in their hands, and renew the promise of baptismal faith, unless this has already been done together with those to be baptised.

The Priest addresses the faithful in these or similar words:

Dear brethren (brothers and sisters),
through the Paschal Mystery
we have been buried with Christ
  in Baptism,
so that we may walk with him
  in newness of life.
And so, now that our Lenten
  observance is concluded,
let us renew the promises
  of Holy Baptism,
by which we once renounced Satan
  and his works
and promised to serve God
  in the holy Catholic Church.
And so I ask you:

Priest: Do you renounce Satan?
All: **I do.**

Priest: And all his works?
All: **I do.**

Priest: And all his empty show?
All: **I do.**

Or:

Priest: Do you renounce sin,
so as to live in the freedom
  of the children of God?
All: **I do.**

Priest: Do you renounce the lure
  of evil,
so that sin may have no mastery
  over you?
All: **I do.**

Priest: Do you renounce Satan,
the author and prince of sin?
All: **I do.**

Per paschale mysterium,
  fratres carissimi,
in baptismo consepulti sumus
  cum Christo,
ut cum eo in novitate
  vitæ ambulemus.
Quapropter, quadragesimali
  observatione absoluta,
sancti baptismatis
  promissiones renovemus,
quibus olim Satanæ et operibus
  eius abrenuntiavimus,
et Deo in sancta Ecclesia catholica
  servire promisimus.
Quapropter:

Sacerdos: Abrenutiatis Satanæ?
Omnes: **Abrenuntio.**

Sacerdos: Et omnibus operibus eius?
Omnes: **Abrenuntio.**

Sacerdos: Et omnibus pompis eius?
Omnes: **Abrenuntio.**

Vel:

Sacerdos: Abrenuntiatis peccato,
ut in libertate filiorum Dei vivatis?
Omnes: **Abrenuntio.**

Sacerdos: Abrenuntiatis
  seductionibus iniquitatis,
ne pecccatum vobis dominetur?
Omnes: **Abrenuntio.**

Sacerdos: Abrenuntiatis Satanæ,
qui est auctor et princeps peccati?
Omnes: **Abrenuntio.**

If the situation warrants, this second formula may be adapted by Conferences of Bishops according to local needs.

Then the Priest continues:

Priest: Do you believe in God, the Father almighty, Creator of heaven and earth?
All: **I do.**

Priest: Do you believe in Jesus Christ, his only Son, our Lord, who was born of the Virgin Mary, suffered death and was buried, rose again from the dead and is seated at the right hand of the Father?
All: **I do.**

Priest: Do you believe in the Holy Spirit, the holy Catholic Church, the communion of saints, the forgiveness of sins, the resurrection of the body, and life everlasting?
All: **I do.**

And the Priest concludes:

And may almighty God, the Father of our Lord Jesus Christ, who has given us new birth by water and the Holy Spirit and bestowed on us forgiveness of our sins, keep us by his grace, in Christ Jesus our Lord, for eternal life.
All: Amen.

The Priest sprinkles the people with the blessed water, while all sing:

Antiphon

I saw water flowing from the Temple, from its right-hand side, alleluia; and all to whom this water came were saved and shall say: Alleluia, alleluia.

Sacerdos: Creditis in Deum Patrem omnipotentem, creatorem cæli et terræ?
Omnes: **Credo.**

Sacerdos: Creditis in Iesum Christum, Filium eius unicum, Dominum nostrum, natum ex Maria Virgine, passum et sepultum, qui a mortuis resurrexit et sedet ad dexteram Patris?
Omnes: **Credo.**

Sacerdos: Creditis in Spiritum Sanctum, sanctam Ecclesiam catholicam, sanctorum communionem, remissionem peccatorum, carnis resurrectionem et vitam æternam?
Omnes: **Credo.**

Et Deus omnipotens, Pater Domini nostri Iesu Christi, qui nos regeneravit ex aqua et Spiritu Sancto, quique nobis dedit remissionem peccatorum, ipse nos custodiat gratia sua, in Christo Iesu Domino nostro, in vitam æternam.
Omnes: Amen.

Vidi aquam egredientem de templo, a latere dextro, alleluia; et omnes, ad quos pervenit aqua ista, salvi facti sunt et dicent: Alleluia, alleluia.

Another chant that is baptismal in character may also be sung.

Meanwhile the newly baptised are led to their place among the faithful.

If the blessing of baptismal water has not taken place in the baptistery, the Deacon and the ministers reverently carry the vessel of water to the font.

If the blessing of the font has not occurred, the blessed water is put aside in an appropriate place.

After the sprinkling, the Priest returns to the chair where, omitting the Creed, he directs the Universal Prayer, in which the newly baptised participate for the first time.

FOURTH PART:
The Liturgy of the Eucharist

The Priest goes to the altar and begins the Liturgy of the Eucharist in the usual way.

It is desirable that the bread and wine be brought forward by the newly baptised or, if they are children, by their parents or godparents.

Prayer over the Offerings	Super oblata
Accept, we ask, O Lord,	Suscipe, quæsumus, Domine,
the prayers of your people	preces populi tui
with the sacrificial offerings,	cum oblationibus hostiarum,
that what has begun	ut, paschalibus initiata mysteriis,
in the paschal mysteries	ad æternitatis nobis medelam,
may, by the working of your power,	te operante, proficiant.
bring us to the healing of eternity.	Per Christum Dominum nostrum.
Through Christ our Lord.	

Preface I of Easter: The Paschal Mystery (. . .on this night above all. . .), pp.52-55.

In the Eucharistic Prayer, a commemoration is made of the baptised and their godparents in accord with the formulas which are found in the Roman Missal and Roman Ritual for each of the Eucharistic Prayers.

Before the **Ecce Agnus Dei (Behold the Lamb of God)**, the Priest may briefly address the newly baptised about receiving their first Communion and about the excellence of this great mystery, which is the climax of Initiation and the centre of the whole of Christian life.

It is desirable that the newly baptised receive Holy Communion under both kinds, together with their godfathers, godmothers, and Catholic parents and spouses, as well as their lay catechists. It is even appropriate that, with the consent of the Diocesan Bishop, where the occasion suggests this, all the faithful be admitted to Holy Communion under both kinds.

Communion Antiphon 1 Co 5:7-8	Ant. ad communionem
Christ our Passover	Pascha nostrum immolatus
has been sacrificed;	est Christus;
therefore let us keep the feast	itaque epulemur in azymis
with the unleavened bread	sinceritatis et veritatis, alleluia.
of purity and truth, alleluia.	

Psalm 117 may appropriately be sung.

Prayer after Communion

Pour out on us, O Lord,
   the Spirit of your love,
and in your kindness make those
   you have nourished
by this paschal Sacrament
one in mind and heart.
Through Christ our Lord.

Solemn Blessing

May almighty God bless you
through today's Easter Solemnity
and, in his compassion,
defend you from every assault of sin.
R. Amen.

And may he, who restores you
   to eternal life
in the Resurrection
   of his Only Begotten,
endow you with the prize
   of immortality.
R. Amen.

Now that the days of the Lord's
   Passion have drawn to a close,
may you who celebrate
   the gladness of the Paschal Feast
come with Christ's help,
   and exulting in spirit,
to those feasts that are celebrated
   in eternal joy.
R. Amen.

And may the blessing
   of almighty God,
the Father, and the Son,
   ✠ and the Holy Spirit,
come down on you and remain
   with you for ever.
R. Amen.

Post communionem

Spiritum nobis, Domine,
   tuæ caritatis infunde,
ut, quos sacramentis
   paschalibus satiasti,
tua facias pietate concordes.
Per Christum Dominum nostrum.

Benedictio sollemnis

Benedicat vos omnipotens Deus,
hodierna interveniente
   sollemnitate paschali,
et ab omni miseratus defendat
   incursione peccati.
R. Amen.

Et qui ad æternam vitam
in Unigeniti sui resurrectione
   vos reparat,
vos præmiis
   immortalitatis adimpleat.
R. Amen.

Et qui, expletis passionis
   dominicæ diebus,
paschalis festi gaudia celebratis,
ad ea festa, quæ lætitiis
   peraguntur æternis,
ipso opitulante, exsultantibus
animis veniatis.
R. Amen.

Et benedictio Dei omnipotentis,
Patris, et Filii, ✠ et Spiritus Sancti,
descendat super vos
   et maneat semper.
R. Amen.

The final blessing formula from the Rite of Baptism of Adults or of Children may also be used, according to circumstances.

To dismiss the people the Deacon or, if there is no Deacon, the Priest himself sings or says:

Go forth, the Mass is ended, alleluia, alleluia.	Ite, missa est, alleluia, alleluia.
Or:	Vel:
Go in peace, alleluia, alleluia.	Ite in pace, alleluia, alleluia
All reply:	Omnes respondent:
Thanks be to God, alleluia, alleluia.	Deo gratias, alleluia, alleluia.

This practice is observed throughout the Octave of Easter.
The paschal candle is lit in all the more solemn liturgical celebrations of this period.

12 April

At the Mass during the Day

As St Paul wrote to the Corinthians, "If Christ has not been raised, then our preaching is in vain and your faith is in vain" (1 Co 15:14). Therefore on these days it is important to reinterpret the narratives of Christ's Resurrection which we find in the four Gospels. They are accounts which present in different ways the meetings of the disciples with the Risen Jesus and thereby permit us to meditate on this wonderful event which has transformed history and gives meaning to the existence of every person. The event of the Resurrection as such is not described by the Evangelists: it remains mysterious, not in the sense of being less real, but hidden, beyond the scope of our knowledge: like a light so bright that we cannot look at it or we should be blinded. The narratives begin instead when, towards dawn on the day after Saturday, the women went to the tomb and found it open and empty. In those times, in Israel the testimony of women could not possess any official or juridical value, but the women had had an experience of a special bond with the Lord, which was fundamental for the practical life of the Christian community, and this is always the case in every epoch and not only when the Church was taking her first steps.

(Pope Benedict XVI)

Entrance Antiphon Cf. Ps 138:18,5-6	Ant. ad introitum
I HAVE risen, and I am with you still, alleluia.	RESURREXI, et adhuc tecum sum, alleluia:
You have laid your hand upon me, alleluia.	posuisti super me manum tuam, alleluia:
Too wonderful for me, this knowledge, alleluia, alleluia.	mirabilis facta est scientia tua, alleluia, alleluia.

Or: Lk 24:34; Cf. Rv 1:6

The Lord is truly risen, alleluia.
To him be glory and power
for all the ages of eternity, alleluia,
     alleluia.

Vel:

Surrexit Dominus vere, alleluia.
Ipsi gloria et imperium
per universa æternitatis sæcula,
     alleluia, alleluia.

The Gloria in excelsis (Glory to God in the highest) is said.

Collect

O God, who on this day,
through your Only Begotten Son,
have conquered death
and unlocked for us the path
     to eternity,
grant, we pray, that we who keep
the solemnity of
     the Lord's Resurrection
may, through the renewal brought
     by your Spirit,
rise up in the light of life.
Through our Lord Jesus Christ,
     your Son,
who lives and reigns with you
     in the unity of the Holy Spirit,
one God, for ever and ever.

Collecta

Deus, qui hodierna die,
     per Unigenitum tuum,
æternitatis nobis aditum,
     devicta morte, reserasti,
da nobis, quæsumus,
ut, qui resurrectionis dominicæ
     sollemnia colimus,
per innovationem tui Spiritus
in lumine vitæ resurgamus.
Per Dominum nostrum Iesum
     Christum Filium tuum,
qui tecum vivit et regnat
     in unitate Spiritus Sancti,
Deus, per omnia sæcula sæculorum.

FIRST READING

A reading from the Acts of the Apostles   10:34,37-43

We have eaten and drunk with him after his resurrection.

Peter addressed Cornelius and his household: 'You must have heard about the recent happenings in Judaea; about Jesus of Nazareth and how he began in Galilee, after John had been preaching baptism. God had anointed him with the Holy Spirit and with power, and because God was with him, Jesus went about doing good and curing all who had fallen into the power of the devil. Now I, and those with me, can witness to everything he did throughout the countryside of Judaea and in Jerusalem itself: and also to the fact that they killed him by hanging him on a tree, yet three days afterwards God raised him to life and allowed him to be seen, not by the whole people but only by certain witnesses God had chosen beforehand. Now we are those witnesses – we have eaten and drunk with him after his resurrection from the dead – and he has ordered us to proclaim this to his people and to tell them that God has appointed him to judge everyone, alive or dead. It is to him that all the prophets bear this witness: that all who believe in Jesus will have their sins forgiven through his name.'

The word of the Lord.

Responsorial Psalm   Ps 117:1-2,16-17,22-23. R. v. 24

R. **This day was made by the Lord;**
   we rejoice and are glad.
   Or: **Alleluia, alleluia, alleluia!**

Give thanks to the Lord for he is good,
for his love has no end.
Let the sons of Israel say:
'His love has no end.' R.

The Lord's right hand has triumphed;
his right hand raised me.
I shall not die, I shall live
and recount his deeds. R.

The stone which the builders rejected
has become the corner stone.
This is the work of the Lord,
a marvel in our eyes. R.

SECOND READING

A reading from the letter of St Paul to the Colossians   3:1-4

You must look for the things that are in heaven, where Christ is.

Since you have been brought back to true life with Christ, you must look for the things that are in heaven, where Christ is, sitting at God's right hand. Let your thoughts be on heavenly things, not on the things that are on the earth, because you have died, and now the life you have is hidden with Christ in God. But when Christ is revealed – and he is your life – you too will be revealed in all your glory with him.

The word of the Lord.

ALTERNATIVE SECOND READING

A reading from the first letter of St Paul to the Corinthians   5:6-8

Get rid of the old yeast, and make yourselves into a completely new batch of bread.

You must know how even a small amount of yeast is enough to leaven all the dough, so get rid of all the old yeast, and make yourselves into a completely new batch of bread, unleavened as you are meant to be. Christ, our Passover, has been sacrificed; let us celebrate the feast, by getting rid of all the old yeast of evil and wickedness, having only the unleavened bread of sincerity and truth.

The word of the Lord.

The sequence is said or sung on this day. On the weekdays of the Octave of Easter, its use is optional.

SEQUENCE

Christians, to the Paschal Victim
    offer sacrifice and praise.
The sheep are ransomed
    by the Lamb;
and Christ, the undefiled,
hath sinners to his Father reconciled.
	Victimæ paschali laudes
	    immolent Christiani.
	Agnus redemit oves:
	    Christus innocens Patri
	    reconciliavit peccatores.

Death with life contended:
    combat strangely ended!
Life's own Champion, slain,
    yet lives to reign.
	Mors et vita duello
	    conflixere mirando:
	    dux vitæ mortuus regnat vivus.

Tell us, Mary:
    say what thou didst see
    upon the way.
	Dic nobis, Maria,
	    quid vidisti in via?

The tomb the Living did enclose; I saw Christ's glory as he rose!	Sepulcrum Christi viventis, gloriam vidi resurgentis.

The angels there attesting;
shroud with grave-clothes resting.
Christ, my hope, has risen:
he goes before you into Galilee.
	Angelicos testes,
	    sudarium et vestes.
	Surrexit Christus spes mea:
	    præcedet vos in Galilæam.

That Christ is truly risen
    from the dead we know.
Victorious king, thy mercy show!
	Scimus Christum surrexisse
	    a mortuis vere:
	tu nobis, victor Rex, miserere.

Gospel Acclamation   1 Co 5:7-8

R. **Alleluia, alleluia!**
Christ, our passover, has been sacrificed;
let us celebrate the feast then, in the Lord.
R. **Alleluia!**

GOSPEL
A reading from the holy Gospel according to John   20:1-9
He must rise from the dead.

It was very early on the first day of the week and still dark, when Mary of Magdala came to the tomb. She saw that the stone had been moved away from the tomb and came running to Simon Peter and the other disciple, the one Jesus loved. 'They have taken the Lord out of the tomb' she said 'and we don't know where they have put him.'

So Peter set out with the other disciple to go to the tomb. They ran together, but the other disciple, running faster than Peter, reached the tomb first; he bent down and saw the linen cloths lying on the ground, but did not go in. Simon Peter who was following now came up, went right into the tomb, saw the linen cloths on the ground, and also the cloth that had been over his head; this was not with the linen cloths but rolled up in a place by itself. Then the other disciple who had reached the tomb first also went in; he saw and he believed. Till this moment they had failed to understand the teaching of scripture, that he must rise from the dead.

The Gospel of the Lord.

The Creed is said. However, in Easter Sunday Masses which are celebrated with a congregation, the rite of the renewal of baptismal promises may take place after the homily, according to the text used at the Easter Vigil (pp.260-263). In that case the Creed is omitted.

Prayer over the Offerings

Exultant with paschal gladness,
    O Lord,
we offer the sacrifice
by which your Church
is wondrously reborn and nourished.
Through Christ our Lord.

Super oblata

Sacrificia, Domine,
    paschalibus gaudiis
exsultantes offerimus,
quibus Ecclesia tua
mirabiliter renascitur et nutritur.
Per Christum Dominum nostrum.

Preface I of Easter, The Paschal Mystery, pp.52-55.

When the Roman Canon is used, the proper forms of the **Communicantes** (In communion with those) and **Hanc igitur** (Therefore, Lord, we pray) are said.

Communion Antiphon 1 Co 5:7-8

Christ our Passover has been
    sacrificed, alleluia;
therefore let us keep the feast
    with the unleavened bread
of purity and truth, alleluia, alleluia.

Ant. ad communionem

Pascha nostrum immolatus
    est Christus, alleluia;
itaque epulemur
    in azymis sinceritatis
et veritatis, alleluia, alleluia.

Prayer after Communion

Look upon your Church, O God,
with unfailing love and favour,
so that, renewed by the paschal
    mysteries,
she may come to the glory
    of the resurrection.
Through Christ our Lord.

Post communionem

Perpetuo, Deus, Ecclesiam tuam
    pio favore tuere,
ut, paschalibus renovata mysteriis,
ad resurrectionis perveniat claritatem.
Per Christum Dominum nostrum.

To impart the blessing at the end of Mass, the Priest may appropriately use the formula of Solemn Blessing for the Mass of the Easter Vigil, p.264.

For the dismissal of the people, the following is sung or said:

Go forth, the Mass is ended, alleluia, alleluia.	Ite, missa est, alleluia, alleluia.
Or:	Vel:
Go in peace, alleluia, alleluia.	Ite in pace, alleluia, alleluia
R. Thanks be to God, alleluia, alleluia.	R. Deo gratias, alleluia, alleluia.

19 April

SECOND SUNDAY OF EASTER

(or of Divine Mercy)

At the heart of this Sunday, which concludes the Octave of Easter, are the glorious wounds of the risen Jesus...The wounds of Jesus are a scandal, a stumbling block for faith, yet they are also the test of faith. That is why on the body of the risen Christ the wounds never pass away: they remain, for those wounds are the enduring sign of God's love for us. They are essential for believing in God. Not for believing that God exists, but for believing that God is love, mercy and faithfulness. St Peter, quoting Isaiah, writes to Christians: "by his wounds you have been healed".

(Pope Francis)

Entrance Antiphon 1 P 2:2	Ant. ad introitum
LIKE newborn infants, you must long for the pure, spiritual milk, that in him you may grow to salvation, alleluia.	QUASI modo geniti infantes, rationabile, sine dolo lac concupiscite, ut in eo crescatis in salutem, alleluia.
Or: 4 Esdr 2:36-37	Vel:
Receive the joy of your glory, giving thanks to God, who has called you into the heavenly kingdom, alleluia.	Accipite iucunditatem gloriæ vestræ, gratias agentes Deo, qui vos ad cælestia regna vocavit, alleluia.

The Gloria in excelsis (Glory to God in the highest) is said.

Collect	Collecta

God of everlasting mercy,
who, in the very recurrence
   of the paschal feast
kindle the faith of the people you
   have made your own,
increase, we pray, the grace you
   have bestowed,
that all may grasp
   and rightly understand
in what font they have been washed,
by whose Spirit they have
   been reborn,
by whose Blood they have
   been redeemed.
Through our Lord Jesus Christ,
   your Son,
who lives and reigns with you
   in the unity of the Holy Spirit,
one God, for ever and ever.
	Deus misericordiæ sempiternæ,
	qui in ipso paschalis festi recursu
	fidem sacratæ tibi plebis accendis,
	auge gratiam quam dedisti,
	ut digna omnes
	   intellegentia comprehendant,
	quo lavacro abluti,
	   quo Spiritu regenerati,
	quo sanguine sunt redempti.
	Per Dominum nostrum Iesum
	   Christum Filium tuum,
	qui tecum vivit et regnat
	   in unitate Spiritus Sancti,
	Deus, per omnia sæcula sæculorum.

FIRST READING

A reading from the Acts of the Apostles   2:42-47

The faithful all lived together and owned everything in common.

The whole community remained faithful to the teaching of the apostles, to the brotherhood, to the breaking of bread and to the prayers.

The many miracles and signs worked through the apostles made a deep impression on everyone.

The faithful all lived together and owned everything in common; they sold their goods and possessions and shared out the proceeds among themselves according to what each one needed.

They went as a body to the Temple every day but met in their houses for the breaking of bread; they shared their food gladly and generously; they praised God and were looked up to by everyone. Day by day the Lord added to their community those destined to be saved.

The word of the Lord.

Responsorial Psalm   Ps 117:2-4,13-15,22-24. R. v.1

R. **Give thanks to the Lord for he is good,**
   for his love has no end.
   Or: **Alleluia, alleluia, alleluia!**

Let the sons of Israel say:
'His love has no end.'
Let the sons of Aaron say:
'His love has no end.'
Let those who fear the Lord say:
'His love has no end.' R.

I was thrust, thrust down and falling
but the Lord was my helper.
The Lord is my strength and my song;
he was my saviour.
There are shouts of joy and victory
in the tents of the just. R.

The stone which the builders rejected
has become the corner stone.
This is the work of the Lord
a marvel in our eyes.
This day was made by the Lord;
we rejoice and are glad. R.

SECOND READING

A reading from the first letter of St Peter   1:3-9

In his great mercy he has given us a new birth as his sons by raising Jesus from the dead.

Blessed be God the Father of our Lord Jesus Christ, who in his great mercy
has given us a new birth as his sons, by raising Jesus Christ from the dead,
so that we have a sure hope and the promise of an inheritance that can
never be spoilt or soiled and never fade away, because it is being kept for
you in the heavens. Through your faith, God's power will guard you until
the salvation which had been prepared is revealed at the end of time. This
is a cause of great joy for you, even though you may for a short time have
to bear being plagued by all sorts of trials; so that, when Jesus Christ is
revealed, your faith will have been tested and proved like gold – only it
is more precious than gold, which is corruptible even though it bears
testing by fire – and then you will have praise and glory and honour. You
did not see him, yet you love him; and still without seeing him, you are

already filled with a joy so glorious that it cannot be described, because you believe; and you are sure of the end to which your faith looks forward, that is, the salvation of your souls.

The word of the Lord.

Easter Sequence can be sung here, see p.268.

Gospel Acclamation   Jn 20:29

R. **Alleluia, alleluia!**
Jesus said: 'You believe because you can see me.
Happy are those who have not seen and yet believe.'
R. **Alleluia!**

GOSPEL

A reading from the holy Gospel according to John   20:19-31

Eight days later, Jesus came.

In the evening of that same day, the first day of the week, the doors were closed in the room where the disciples were, for fear of the Jews. Jesus came and stood among them. He said to them, 'Peace be with you,' and showed them his hands and his side. The disciples were filled with joy when they saw the Lord, and he said to them again,

'Peace be with you.
As the Father sent me,
so am I sending you.'

After saying this he breathed on them and said:

'Receive the Holy Spirit.
For those whose sins you forgive,
they are forgiven;
for those whose sins you retain,
they are retained.'

Thomas, called the Twin, who was one of the Twelve, was not with them when Jesus came. When the disciples said, 'We have seen the Lord,' he answered, 'Unless I see the holes that the nails made in his hands and can put my finger into the holes they made, and unless I can put my hand into his side, I refuse to believe.' Eight days later the disciples were in the house again and Thomas was with them. The doors were closed, but Jesus came in and stood among them. 'Peace be with you,' he said. Then he spoke to Thomas, 'Put your finger here; look, here are my hands. Give me your hand; put it into my side. Doubt no longer but believe.' Thomas replied, 'My Lord and my God!'

Jesus said to him:

'You believe because you can see me.
Happy are those who have not seen and yet believe.'

There were many other signs that Jesus worked and the disciples saw, but they are not recorded in this book. These are recorded so that you may believe that Jesus is the Christ, the Son of God, and that believing this you may have life through his name.

The Gospel of the Lord.

The Creed is said.

Prayer over the Offerings	Super oblata
Accept, O Lord, we pray,	Suscipe, quæsumus, Domine,
the oblations of your people	plebis tuæ
(and of those you have brought	(et tuorum renatorum) oblationes,
to new birth),	ut, confessione tui nominis
that, renewed by confession of your	et baptismate renovati,
name and by Baptism,	sempiternam beatitudinem
they may attain unending happiness.	consequantur.
Through Christ our Lord.	Per Christum Dominum nostrum.

Preface I of Easter: The Paschal Mystery (. . .on this day above all. . .), pp.52-55.
When the Roman Canon is used, the proper forms of the Communicantes (In communion with those) and Hanc igitur (Therefore, Lord, we pray) are said.

Communion Antiphon Cf. Jn 20:27	Ant. ad communionem
Bring your hand and feel the place	Mitte manum tuam, et cognosce
of the nails,	loca clavorum,
and do not be unbelieving	et noli esse incredulus, sed fidelis,
but believing, alleluia.	alleluia.

Prayer after Communion	Post communionem
Grant, we pray, almighty God,	Concede, quæsumus,
that our reception of this paschal	omnipotens Deus,
Sacrament	ut paschalis perceptio sacramenti
may have a continuing effect	continua in nostris
in our minds and hearts.	mentibus perseveret.
Through Christ our Lord.	Per Christum Dominum nostrum.

A formula of Solemn Blessing, pp.136-139, may be used.
For the dismissal of the people, the following is sung or said: Go forth, the Mass is ended, alleluia, alleluia. Or: Go in peace, alleluia, alleluia. The people respond: Thanks be to God, alleluia, alleluia.

In England

23 April

SAINT GEORGE, MARTYR, PATRON OF ENGLAND

The Church's action is credible and effective only to the extent to which those who belong to her are prepared to pay in person for their fidelity to Christ in every circumstance. When this readiness is lacking, the crucial argument of truth on which the Church herself depends is also absent. Dear brothers and sisters, as in early times, today too Christ needs apostles ready to sacrifice themselves. He needs witnesses and martyrs.

(Pope Benedict XVI)

Solemnity

Entrance Antiphon   Cf. Mt 25:34

REJOICE, you Saints, in the presence of the Lamb;
a kingdom has been prepared for you
from the foundation of the world, alleluia.

Or: Ps 90:13

On the asp and the viper you will tread,
and trample the young lion and the dragon, alleluia.

The Gloria in excelsis (Glory to God in the highest) is said.

Collect

God of hosts,
who so kindled the fire of charity
in the heart of Saint George your martyr
that he bore witness to the risen Lord
both by his life and by his death,
grant us through his intercession, we pray,
the same faith and power of love,
that we who rejoice in his triumph
may be led to share with him
in the fullness of the resurrection.
Through our Lord Jesus Christ, your Son,
who lives and reigns with you in the unity of the Holy Spirit,
one God, for ever and ever.

FIRST READING

A reading from the book of the Apocalypse   12:10-12

In the face of death they would not cling to life.

I, John, heard a voice shout from heaven, 'Victory and power and empire for ever have been won by our God, and all authority for his Christ, now that the persecutor, who accused our brothers day and night before our God, has been brought down. They have triumphed over him by the blood of the Lamb and by the witness of their martyrdom, because even in the face of death they would not cling to life. Let the heavens rejoice and all who live there.'

The word of the Lord.

Responsorial Psalm   Ps 30

R. **Those who are sowing in tears
will sing when they reap.**

When the Lord delivered Zion from bondage,
it seemed like a dream.
Then was our mouth filled with laughter,
on our lips there were songs. R.

The heathens themselves said: 'What marvels
the Lord worked for them!'
What marvels the Lord worked for us!
Indeed we were glad. R.

Deliver us, O Lord, from our bondage
as streams in dry land.
Those who are sowing in tears
will sing when they reap. R.

They go out, they go out, full of tears,
carrying seed for the sowing;
they come back, they come back, full of song,
carrying their sheaves. R.

A second reading is chosen from the Common of Martyrs.

Gospel Acclamation   Mt 23:9-10

R. **Alleluia, alleluia!**
Happy the man who stands firm,
for he has proved himself,
and will win the crown of life.
R. **Alleluia!**

GOSPEL

A reading from the holy Gospel according to John   15:18-21
If they persecuted me, they will persecute you.

Jesus said to his disciples:
  'If the world hates you,
  remember that it hated me before you.
  If you belonged to the world,
  the world would love you as its own;
  but because you do not belong to the world,
  because my choice withdrew you from the world,
  therefore the world hates you.
  Remember the words I said to you:
  A servant is not greater than his master.
  If they persecuted me,
  they will persecute you too;
  if they kept my word,
  they will keep yours as well.
  But it will be on my account that they will do all this,
  because they do not know the one who sent me.'

  The Gospel of the Lord.

ALTERNATIVE GOSPEL

A reading from the holy Gospel according to John   15:1-8

Whoever remains in me, with me in him, bears fruit in plenty.

Jesus said to his disciples:
'I am the true vine,
and my Father is the vinedresser.
Every branch in me that bears no fruit
he cuts away,
and every branch that does bear fruit he prunes
to make it bear even more.
You are pruned already,
by means of the word that I have spoken to you.
Make your home in me, as I make mine in you.
As a branch cannot bear fruit all by itself,
but must remain part of the vine,
neither can you unless you remain in me.
I am the vine,
you are the branches.
Whoever remains in me, with me in him,
bears fruit in plenty;
for cut off from me you can do nothing.
Anyone who does not remain in me
is like a branch that has been thrown away
– he withers;
these branches are collected and thrown on the fire,
and they are burnt.
If you remain in me
and my words remain in you,
you may ask what you will
and you shall get it.
It is to the glory of my Father that you should bear much fruit,
and then you will be my disciples.'

The Gospel of the Lord.

The Creed is said.

Prayer over the Offerings

Receive, we pray, O Lord,
the sacrifice of conciliation and praise,
which we offer to your majesty
in commemoration of the blessed Martyr Saint George,
that it may lead us to forgiveness
and confirm us in constant thanksgiving.
Through Christ our Lord.

Preface I or II of Holy Martyrs, pp.72-73.

Communion Antiphon   Cf. 2 Tm 2:11-12

If we have died with Christ, we shall also live with him;
if we persevere, we shall also reign with him, alleluia.

Prayer after Communion

Rejoicing on this festival day, O Lord,
we have received your heavenly gifts;
grant, we pray,
that we who in this divine banquet
proclaim the death of your Son
may merit with Saint George to be partakers
in his resurrection and glory.
Through Christ our Lord.

---

26 April

THIRD SUNDAY OF EASTER

The Gospel from this Sunday is that of the disciples of Emmaus. The road to Emmaus becomes a symbol of our journey of faith: the Scriptures and the Eucharist are the indispensable elements for encountering the Lord. We too often go to Sunday Mass with our worries, difficulties and disappointments... Life sometimes wounds us and we go away feeling sad, towards our "Emmaus", turning our backs on God's plan. We distance ourselves from God. But the Liturgy of the Word welcomes us: Jesus explains the Scriptures to us and rekindles in our hearts the warmth of faith and hope, and in Communion he gives us strength.

(Pope Francis)

Entrance Antiphon   Cf. Ps 65:1-2

CRY out with joy to God,
all the earth;
O sing to the glory of his name.
O render him glorious praise,
alleluia.

Ant. ad introitum

IUBILATE Deo, omnis terra,
psalmum dicite nomini eius,
date gloriam laudi eius, alleluia.

The Gloria in excelsis (Glory to God in the highest) is said.

Collect

May your people exult for ever,
    O God,
in renewed youthfulness of spirit,
so that, rejoicing now in the restored
    glory of our adoption,
we may look forward
    in confident hope
to the rejoicing of the day
    of resurrection.
Through our Lord Jesus Christ,
    your Son,
who lives and reigns with you
    in the unity of the Holy Spirit,
one God, for ever and ever.

Collecta

Semper exsultet populus tuus, Deus,
renovata animæ iuventute,
ut, qui nunc lætatur in adoptionis
    se gloriam restitutum,
resurrectionis diem spe certæ
    gratulationis exspectet.
Per Dominum nostrum Iesum
    Christum Filium tuum,
qui tecum vivit et regnat
    in unitate Spiritus Sancti,
Deus, per omnia sæcula sæculorum.

FIRST READING

A reading from the Acts of the Apostles   2:14,22-33

It was impossible for him to be held in the power of Hades.

On the day of Pentecost Peter stood up with the Eleven and addressed the crowd in a loud voice: 'Men of Israel, listen to what I am going to say: Jesus the Nazarene was a man commended to you by God by the miracles and portents and signs that God worked through him when he was among you, as you all know. This man, who was put into your power by the deliberate intention and foreknowledge of God, you took and had crucified by men outside the Law. You killed him, but God raised him to life, freeing him from the pangs of Hades; for it was impossible for him to be held in its power since, as David says of him:

I saw the Lord before me always,
    for with him at my right hand nothing can shake me.

So my heart was glad
and my tongue cried out with joy;
my body, too, will rest in the hope
that you will not abandon my soul to Hades
nor allow your holy one to experience corruption.
You have made known the way of life to me,
you will fill me with gladness through your presence.

'Brothers, no one can deny that the patriarch David himself is dead and buried: his tomb is still with us. But since he was a prophet, and knew that God had sworn him an oath to make one of his descendants succeed him on the throne, what he foresaw and spoke about was the resurrection of the Christ: he is the one who was not abandoned to Hades, and whose body did not experience corruption. God raised this man Jesus to life, and all of us are witnesses to that. Now raised to the heights by God's right hand, he has received from the Father the Holy Spirit, who was promised, and what you see and hear is the outpouring of that Spirit.'

The word of the Lord.

Responsorial Psalm   Ps 15:1-2,5,7-11. R. v.11

R. **Show us, Lord, the path of life.**
Or: **Alleluia!**

Preserve me, God, I take refuge in you.
I say to the Lord: 'You are my God.
O Lord, it is you who are my portion and cup;
it is you yourself who are my prize.' R.

I will bless the Lord who gives me counsel,
who even at night directs my heart.
I keep the Lord ever in my sight:
since he is at my right hand, I shall stand firm. R.

And so my heart rejoices, my soul is glad;
even my body shall rest in safety.
For you will not leave my soul among the dead,
nor let your beloved know decay. R.

You will show me the path of life,
the fullness of joy in your presence,
at your right hand happiness for ever. R.

SECOND READING

A reading from the first letter of St Peter   1:17-21

Your ransom was paid in the precious blood of a lamb without spot or stain, namely, Christ.

If you are acknowledging as your Father one who has no favourites and judges everyone according to what he has done, you must be scrupulously careful as long as you are living away from your home. Remember, the ransom that was paid to free you from the useless way of life your ancestors handed down was not paid in anything corruptible, neither in silver nor gold, but in the precious blood of a lamb without spot or stain, namely Christ; who though known since before the world was made, has been revealed only in our time, the end of the ages, for your sake. Through him you now have faith in God, who raised him from the dead and gave him glory for that very reason – so that you would have faith and hope in God.

The word of the Lord.

Gospel Acclamation   Cf. Lk 24:32

R. **Alleluia, alleluia!**
Lord Jesus, explain the scriptures to us.
Make our hearts burn within us as you talk to us.
R. **Alleluia!**

GOSPEL

A reading from the holy Gospel according to Luke   24:13-35

They recognised him at the breaking of bread.

Two of the disciples of Jesus were on their way to a village called Emmaus, seven miles from Jerusalem, and they were talking together about all that had happened. Now as they talked this over, Jesus himself came up and walked by their side; but something prevented them from recognising him. He said to them, 'What matters are you discussing as you walk along?' They stopped short, their faces downcast.

Then one of them, called Cleopas, answered him, 'You must be the only person staying in Jerusalem who does not know the things that have been happening there these last few days.' 'What things?' he asked. 'All about Jesus of Nazareth' they answered 'who proved he was a great prophet by the things he said and did in the sight of God and of the whole people; and how our chief priests and our leaders handed him over to be sentenced to death, and had him crucified. Our own hope had been that he would be the one to set Israel free. And this is not all: two whole days have gone by since it all happened; and some women from our group have astounded us: they went to the tomb in the early morning, and when they did not find the body, they came back to tell us they had seen a vision of angels who declared he was alive. Some of our friends went to the tomb and found everything exactly as the women had reported, but of him they saw nothing.'

Then he said to them, 'You foolish men! So slow to believe the full message of the prophets! Was it not ordained that the Christ should suffer and so enter into his glory?' Then, starting with Moses and going through all the prophets, he explained to them the passages throughout the scriptures that were about himself.

When they drew near to the village to which they were going, he made as if to go on; but they pressed him to stay with them. 'It is nearly evening' they said 'and the day is almost over.' So he went in to stay with them. Now while he was with them at table, he took the bread and said the blessing; then he broke it and handed it to them. And their eyes were opened and they recognised him; but he had vanished from their sight. Then they said to each other, 'Did not our hearts burn within us as he talked to us on the road and explained the scriptures to us?'

They set out that instant and returned to Jerusalem. There they found the Eleven assembled together with their companions, who said to them, 'Yes, it is true. The Lord has risen and has appeared to Simon.' Then they told their story of what had happened on the road and how they had recognised him at the breaking of bread.

The Gospel of the Lord.

The Creed is said.

Prayer over the Offerings | Super oblata

Receive, O Lord, we pray,
 these offerings of your
  exultant Church,
and, as you have given her cause
  for such great gladness,
grant also that the gifts we bring
may bear fruit in perpetual happiness.
Through Christ our Lord.

Suscipe munera, Domine,
 quæsumus, exsultantis Ecclesiæ,
et cui causam tanti gaudii præstitisti,
perpetuæ fructum concede lætitiæ.
Per Christum Dominum nostrum.

Preface of Easter, pp.52-57.

Communion Antiphon Lk 24:35	Ant. ad communionem

The disciples recognised
    the Lord Jesus
in the breaking of the bread, alleluia.
	Cognoverunt discipuli
	    Dominum Iesum
	in fractione panis, alleluia.

Prayer after Communion	Post communionem

Look with kindness upon
    your people, O Lord,
and grant, we pray,
that those you were pleased
    to renew by eternal mysteries
may attain in their flesh
the incorruptible glory
    of the resurrection.
Through Christ our Lord.
	Populum tuum, quæsumus,
	    Domine, intuere benignus,
	et, quem æternis dignatus
	    es renovare mysteriis,
	ad incorruptibilem glorificandæ
	    carnis resurrectionem
	pervenire concede.
	Per Christum Dominum nostrum.

A formula of Solemn Blessing, pp.136-139, may be used.

3 May

FOURTH SUNDAY OF EASTER

The Evangelist John presents us, on this Fourth Sunday of the Easter Season, with the image of Jesus the Good Shepherd. In contemplating this, we can understand the kind of relationship that Jesus had with his disciples: a relationship based on tenderness, love, mutual knowledge and the promise of an immeasurable gift...St Caesarius of Arles, a father of the first centuries of the Church, explained how the People of God must help the pastor, and he gave this example: when a calf is hungry it goes to the cow, its mother, to get milk. The cow, however, does not give it right away: it seems that she withholds it. And what does the calf do? It knocks with its nose at the cow's udder, so that the milk will come. It is a beautiful image! "So also you must be with your pastors", this saint said: always knock at their door, at their hearts, that they may give you the milk of doctrine, the milk of grace and the milk of guidance.

(Pope Francis)

Entrance Antiphon Cf. Ps 32:5-6	Ant. ad introitum

THE merciful love of the Lord
fills the earth;
by the word of the Lord
   the heavens were made, alleluia.

MISERICORDIA Domini plena
est terra;
verbo Domini cæli firmati sunt,
   alleluia.

The Gloria in excelsis (Glory to God in the highest) is said.

Collect	Collecta

Almighty ever-living God,
lead us to a share in the joys
   of heaven,
so that the humble flock may reach
where the brave Shepherd
   has gone before.
Who lives and reigns with you
   in the unity of the Holy Spirit,
one God, for ever and ever.

Omnipotens sempiterne Deus,
deduc nos ad societatem
   cælestium gaudiorum,
ut eo perveniat humilitas gregis,
quo processit fortitudo pastoris.
Per Dominum nostrum Iesum
   Christum Filium tuum,
qui tecum vivit et regnat
   in unitate Spiritus Sancti,
Deus, per omnia sæcula sæculorum.

FIRST READING

A reading from the Acts of the Apostles   2:14,36-41

God has made him both Lord and Christ.

On the day of Pentecost Peter stood up with the Eleven and addressed the crowd with a loud voice: 'The whole House of Israel can be certain that God has made this Jesus whom you crucified both Lord and Christ.'

Hearing this, they were cut to the heart and said to Peter and the apostles, 'What must we do, brothers?' 'You must repent,' Peter answered 'and every one of you must be baptised in the name of Jesus Christ for the forgiveness of your sins, and you will receive the gift of the Holy Spirit. The promise that was made is for you and your children, and for all those who are far away, for all those whom the Lord our God will call to himself.' He spoke to them for a long time using many arguments, and he urged them, 'Save yourselves from this perverse generation.' They were convinced by his arguments, and they accepted what he said and were baptised. That very day about three thousand were added to their number.

The word of the Lord.

Responsorial Psalm   Ps 22:1-6. R. v.1

R. **The Lord is my shepherd;**
   there is nothing I shall want.
   Or: **Alleluia!**

   The Lord is my shepherd;
   there is nothing I shall want.
   Fresh and green are the pastures
   where he gives me repose.
   Near restful waters he leads me,
   to revive my drooping spirit. R.

   He guides me along the right path;
   he is true to his name.
   If I should walk in the valley of darkness
   no evil would I fear.
   You are there with your crook and your staff;
   with these you give me comfort. R.

   You have prepared a banquet for me
   in the sight of my foes.
   My head you have anointed with oil;
   my cup is overflowing. R.

   Surely goodness and kindness shall follow me
   all the days of my life.

In the Lord's own house shall I dwell
for ever and ever. R.

SECOND READING

A reading from the first letter of St Peter   2:20-25

You have come back to the shepherd of your souls.

The merit, in the sight of God, is in bearing punishment patiently when
you are punished after doing your duty.

This, in fact, is what you were called to do, because Christ suffered for
you and left an example for you to follow the way he took. He had not
done anything wrong, and there had been no perjury in his mouth. He
was insulted and did not retaliate with insults; when he was tortured he
made no threats but he put his trust in the righteous judge. He was bearing
our faults in his own body on the cross, so that we might die to our faults
and live for holiness; through his wounds you have been healed. You had
gone astray like sheep but now you have come back to the shepherd and
guardian of your souls.

The word of the Lord.

Gospel Acclamation   Jn 10:14

R. **Alleluia, alleluia!**
I am the good shepherd, says the Lord;
I know my own sheep and my own know me.
R. **Alleluia!**

GOSPEL

A reading from the holy Gospel according to John   10:1-10

I am the gate of the sheepfold.

Jesus said: 'I tell you most solemnly, anyone who does not enter the
sheepfold through the gate, but gets in some other way is a thief and a
brigand. The one who enters through the gate is the shepherd of the flock;
the gatekeeper lets him in, the sheep hear his voice, one by one he calls
his own sheep and leads them out. When he has brought out his flock, he
goes ahead of them, and the sheep follow because they know his voice.
They never follow a stranger but run away from him: they do not recognise
the voice of strangers.'

Jesus told them this parable but they failed to understand what he
meant by telling it to them.

So Jesus spoke to them again:

'I tell you most solemnly,
I am the gate of the sheepfold.

All others who have come
are thieves and brigands;
but the sheep took no notice of them.
I am the gate.
Anyone who enters through me will be safe:
he will go freely in and out
and be sure of finding pasture.
The thief comes
only to steal and kill and destroy.
I have come so that they may have life
and have it to the full.'

The Gospel of the Lord.

The Creed is said.

Prayer over the Offerings

Grant, we pray, O Lord,
that we may always find delight
    in these paschal mysteries,
so that the renewal constantly
    at work within us
may be the cause of our unending joy.
Through Christ our Lord.

Preface of Easter, pp.52-57.

Super oblata

Concede, quæsumus, Domine,
semper nos per hæc mysteria
    paschalia gratulari,
ut continua nostræ
    reparationis operatio
perpetuæ nobis fiat causa lætitiæ.
Per Christum Dominum nostrum.

Communion Antiphon

The Good Shepherd has risen,
who laid down his life for his sheep
and willingly died for his flock,
    alleluia.

Ant. ad communionem

Surrexit Pastor bonus, qui animam
    suam posuit pro ovibus suis,
et pro grege suo mori dignatus est,
    alleluia.

Prayer after Communion

Look upon your flock,
    kind Shepherd,
and be pleased to settle
    in eternal pastures
the sheep you have redeemed
by the Precious Blood of your Son.
Who lives and reigns
    for ever and ever.

Post communionem

Gregem tuum, Pastor bone,
    placatus intende,
et oves, quas pretioso Filii
    tui sanguine redemisti,
in æternis pascuis collocare digneris.
Per Christum Dominum nostrum.

A formula of Solemn Blessing, pp.136-139, may be used.

10 May

FIFTH SUNDAY OF EASTER

Today the reading from the Acts of the Apostles enables us to see that the first tensions and the first dissension also arose in the early Church. There are conflicts in life, the question is how we confront them...Faced with this conflict, the Apostles take the situation into their own hands: they call a meeting that is also open to the disciples, and they discuss the matter together. Problems, in fact, are not resolved by pretending that they do not exist! Conflicts in the Church are resolved by facing one other, by discussing and praying, with the certainty that gossip, envy, jealousy can never bring us to concord, harmony or peace. There, too, it was the Holy Spirit who crowned this understanding, and this enables us to understand that when we let ourselves to be guided by the Holy Spirit, he brings us to harmony, unity and respect for various gifts and talents.

(Pope Francis)

Entrance Antiphon Cf. Ps 97:1-2	Ant. ad introitum

O SING a new song to the Lord,
   for he has worked wonders;
in the sight of the nations
he has shown his deliverance,
   alleluia.

C ANTATE Domino
   canticum novum,
quia mirabilia fecit Dominus;
ante conspectum gentium revelavit
   iustitiam suam, alleluia.

The Gloria in excelsis (Glory to God in the highest) is said.

Collect | Collecta

Almighty ever-living God,
constantly accomplish the Paschal
   Mystery within us,
that those you were pleased
   to make new in Holy Baptism
may, under your protective care,
   bear much fruit
and come to the joys of life eternal.
Through our Lord Jesus Christ,
   your Son,
who lives and reigns with you
   in the unity of the Holy Spirit,
one God, for ever and ever.

Omnipotens sempiterne Deus,
semper in nobis paschale
   perfice sacramentum,
ut, quos sacro baptismate dignatus
   es renovare,
sub tuæ protectionis auxilio multos
   fructus afferant,
et ad æternæ vitæ gaudia
   pervenire concedas.
Per Dominum nostrum Iesum
   Christum Filium tuum,
qui tecum vivit et regnat
   in unitate Spiritus Sancti,
Deus, per omnia sæcula sæculorum.

FIRST READING

A reading from the Acts of the Apostles   6:1-7

They elected seven men full of the Holy Spirit.

About this time, when the number of disciples was increasing, the Hellenists made a complaint against the Hebrews: in the daily distribution their own widows were being overlooked. So the Twelve called a full meeting of the disciples and addressed them, 'It would not be right for us to neglect the word of God so as to give out food; you, brothers, must select from among yourselves seven men of good reputation, filled with the Spirit and with wisdom; we will hand over this duty to them, and continue to devote ourselves to prayer and to the service of the word.' The whole assembly approved of this proposal and elected Stephen, a man full of faith and of the Holy Spirit, together with Philip, Prochorus, Nicanor, Timon, Parmenas, and Nicolaus of Antioch, a convert to Judaism. They presented these to the apostles, who prayed and laid their hands on them.

The word of the Lord continued to spread: the number of disciples in Jerusalem was greatly increased, and a large group of priests made their submission to the faith.

The word of the Lord.

Responsorial Psalm   Ps 32:1-2,4-5,18-19. R. v.22

R. **May your love be upon us, O Lord,**
   as we place all our hope in you.
   Or: **Alleluia!**

   Ring out your joy to the Lord, O you just;
   for praise is fitting for loyal hearts.
   Give thanks to the Lord upon the harp,
   with a ten-stringed lute sing him songs. R.

   For the word of the Lord is faithful
   and all his works to be trusted.
   The Lord loves justice and right
   and fills the earth with his love. R.

   The Lord looks on those who revere him,
   on those who hope in his love,
   to rescue their souls from death,
   to keep them alive in famine. R.

SECOND READING

A reading from the first letter of St Peter   2:4-9

But you are a chosen race, a royal priesthood.

The Lord is the living stone, rejected by men but chosen by God and precious to him; set yourselves close to him so that you too, the holy priesthood that offers the spiritual sacrifices which Jesus Christ has made acceptable to God, may be living stones making a spiritual house. As scripture says: See how I lay in Zion a precious cornerstone that I have chosen and the man who rests his trust on it will not be disappointed. That means that for you who are believers, it is precious; but for unbelievers, the stone rejected by the builders has proved to be the keystone, a stone to stumble over, a rock to bring men down. They stumble over it because they do not believe in the word; it was the fate in store for them.

But you are a chosen race, a royal priesthood, a consecrated nation, a people set apart to sing the praises of God who called you out of the darkness into his wonderful light.

The word of the Lord.

Gospel Acclamation   Jn 14:6

R. **Alleluia, alleluia!**
Jesus said: 'I am the Way, the Truth, and the Life.
No one can come to the Father except through me.'
R. **Alleluia!**

GOSPEL

A reading from the holy Gospel according to John   14:1-12

I am the Way, the Truth and the Life.

Jesus said to his disciples:

'Do not let your hearts be troubled.
Trust in God still, and trust in me.
There are many rooms in my Father's house;
if there were not, I should have told you.
I am going now to prepare a place for you,
and after I have gone and prepared you a place,
I shall return to take you with me;
so that where I am
you may be too.
You know the way to the place where I am going.'

Thomas said, 'Lord, we do not know where you are going, so how can we know the way?' Jesus said:

'I am the Way, the Truth and the Life.
No one can come to the Father except through me.
If you know me, you know my Father too.
From this moment you know him and have seen him.'

Philip said, 'Lord, let us see the Father and then we shall be satisfied.'
'Have I been with you all this time, Philip,' said Jesus to him 'and you still
do not know me?

'To have seen me is to have seen the Father,
so how can you say, "Let us see the Father"?
Do you not believe
that I am in the Father and the Father is in me?
The words I say to you I do not speak as from myself:
it is the Father, living in me, who is doing this work.
You must believe me when I say
that I am in the Father and the Father is in me;
believe it on the evidence of this work, if for no other reason.

'I tell you most solemnly,
whoever believes in me
will perform the same works as I do myself,
he will perform even greater works,
because I am going to the Father.'

The Gospel of the Lord.

The Creed is said.

Prayer over the Offerings

O God, who by the wonderful
    exchange effected in this sacrifice
have made us partakers of the one
    supreme Godhead,
grant, we pray,
that, as we have come to know
    your truth,
we may make it ours by a worthy
    way of life.
Through Christ our Lord.

Preface of Easter, pp.52-57.

Super oblata

Deus, qui nos, per huius sacrificii
    veneranda commercia,
unius summæque divinitatis
    participes effecisti,
præsta, quæsumus,
ut, sicut tuam cognovimus veritatem,
sic eam dignis moribus assequamur.
Per Christum Dominum nostrum.

Communion Antiphon Cf. Jn 15:1,5	Ant. ad communionem
I am the true vine and you are the branches, says the Lord. Whoever remains in me, and I in him, bears fruit in plenty, alleluia.	Ego sum vitis vera et vos palmites, dicit Dominus; qui manet in me et ego in eo, hic fert fructum multum, alleluia.
Prayer after Communion	Post communionem
Graciously be present to your people, we pray, O Lord, and lead those you have imbued with heavenly mysteries to pass from former ways to newness of life. Through Christ our Lord.	Populo tuo, quæsumus, Domine, adesto propitius, et, quem mysteriis cælestibus imbuisti, fac ad novitatem vitæ de vetustate transire. Per Christum Dominum nostrum.

A formula of Solemn Blessing, pp.136-139, may be used.

17 May

SIXTH SUNDAY OF EASTER

The Holy Spirit anointed Jesus inwardly and he anoints his disciples, so that they can have the mind of Christ and thus be disposed to live lives of peace and communion. Through the anointing of the Spirit, our human nature is sealed with the holiness of Jesus Christ and we are enabled to love our brothers and sisters with the same love which God has for us. We ought, therefore, to show concrete signs of humility, fraternity, forgiveness and reconciliation. These signs are the prerequisite of a true, stable and lasting peace...Thus, by putting aside our grievances and divisions, we can show fraternal love for one another. This is what Jesus asks of us in the Gospel: "If you love me, you will keep my commandments. And I will pray the Father, and he will give you another Paraclete, to be with you for ever".

(Pope Francis)

Entrance Antiphon Cf. Is 48:20	Ant. ad introitum
PROCLAIM a joyful sound and let it be heard; proclaim to the ends of the earth: The Lord has freed his people, alleluia.	VOCEM iucunditatis annuntiate, et audiatur, annuntiate usque ad extremum terræ: liberavit Dominus populum suum, alleluia.

The Gloria in excelsis (Glory to God in the highest) is said.

Collect

Grant, almighty God,
that we may celebrate with heartfelt
   devotion these days of joy,
which we keep in honour
   of the risen Lord,
and that what we relive
   in remembrance
we may always hold to in what we do.
Through our Lord Jesus Christ,
   your Son,
who lives and reigns with you
   in the unity of the Holy Spirit,
one God, for ever and ever.

Collecta

Fac nos, omnipotens Deus,
   hos lætitiæ dies,
quos in honorem Domini
   resurgentis exsequimur,
affectu sedulo celebrare,
ut quod recordatione percurrimus
semper in opere teneamus.
Per Dominum nostrum Iesum
   Christum Filium tuum,
qui tecum vivit et regnat
   in unitate Spiritus Sancti,
Deus, per omnia sæcula sæculorum.

FIRST READING

A reading from the Acts of the Apostles   8:5-8,14-17

They laid hands on them, and they received the Holy Spirit.

Philip went to a Samaritan town and proclaimed the Christ to them. The people united in welcoming the message Philip preached, either because they had heard of the miracles he worked or because they saw them for themselves. There were, for example, unclean spirits that came shrieking out of many who were possessed, and several paralytics and cripples were cured. As a result there was great rejoicing in that town.

When the apostles in Jerusalem heard that Samaria had accepted the word of God, they sent Peter and John to them, and they went down there, and prayed for the Samaritans to receive the Holy Spirit, for as yet he had not come down on any of them: they had only been baptised in the name of the Lord Jesus. Then they laid hands on them, and they received the Holy Spirit.

The word of the Lord.

Responsorial Psalm   Ps 65:1-7,16,20. R. v.1

R. **Cry out with joy to God all the earth.**
   Or: **Alleluia!**

   Cry out with joy to God all the earth,
   O sing to the glory of his name.
   O render him glorious praise.
   Say to God: 'How tremendous your deeds! R.

'Before you all the earth shall bow;
shall sing to you, sing to your name!'
Come and see the works of God,
tremendous his deeds among men. R.

He turned the sea into dry land,
they passed through the river dry-shod.
Let our joy then be in him;
he rules for ever by his might. R.

Come and hear, all who fear God.
I will tell what he did for my soul:
Blessed be God who did not reject my prayer
nor withhold his love from me. R.

SECOND READING

A reading from the first letter of St Peter   3:15-18

In the body he was put to death, in the spirit he was raised to life.

Reverence the Lord Christ in your hearts, and always have your answer ready
for people who ask you the reason for the hope that you all have. But give
it with courtesy and respect and with a clear conscience, so that those who
slander you when you are living a good life in Christ may be proved wrong
in the accusations that they bring. And if it is the will of God that you should
suffer, it is better to suffer for doing right than for doing wrong.

Why, Christ himself, innocent though he was, had died once for sins,
died for the guilty, to lead us to God. In the body he was put to death, in
the spirit he was raised to life.

The word of the Lord.

Gospel Acclamation   Jn 14:23

R. **Alleluia, alleluia!**
Jesus said: 'If anyone loves me he will keep my word,
and my Father will love him, and we shall come to him.'
R. **Alleluia.**

GOSPEL

A reading from the holy Gospel according to John   14:15-21

I shall ask the Father, and he will give you another Advocate.

Jesus said to his disciples:

'If you love me you will keep my commandments.
I shall ask the Father,
and he will give you another Advocate

to be with you for ever,
that Spirit of truth
whom the world can never receive
since it neither sees nor knows him,
but you know him,
because he is with you, he is in you.
I will not leave you orphans;
I will come back to you.
In a short time the world will no longer see me;
but you will see me,
because I live and you will live.
On that day
you will understand that I am in my Father
and you in me and I in you.
Anybody who receives my commandments and keeps them
will be one who loves me;
and anybody who loves me will be loved by my Father,
and I shall love him and show myself to him.'

   The Gospel of the Lord.

When the Ascension is celebrated on the Seventh Sunday of Easter, the Second
Reading and Gospel assigned to the Seventh Sunday may be read on the Sixth Sunday.

The Creed is said.

Prayer over the Offerings

May our prayers rise up to you,
    O Lord,
together with the sacrificial offerings,
so that, purified by
    your graciousness,
we may be conformed to the
    mysteries of your mighty love.
Through Christ our Lord.

Preface of Easter, pp.52-57.

Super oblata

Ascendant ad te, Domine,
    preces nostræ
cum oblationibus hostiarum,
ut, tua dignatione mundati,
sacramentis magnæ
    pietatis aptemur.
Per Christum Dominum nostrum.

Communion Antiphon Jn 14:15-16

If you love me, keep my
    commandments, says the Lord,
and I will ask the Father and he will
    send you another Paraclete,
to abide with you for ever, alleluia.

Ant. ad communionem

Si diligitis me, mandata mea
    servate, dicit Dominus.
Et ego rogabo Patrem,
    et alium Paraclitum dabit vobis,
ut maneat vobiscum in æternum,
    alleluia.

Prayer after Communion	Post communionem
Almighty ever-living God, who restore us to eternal life in the Resurrection of Christ, increase in us, we pray, the fruits of this paschal Sacrament and pour into our hearts the strength of this saving food. Through Christ our Lord.	Omnipotens sempiterne Deus, qui ad æternam vitam in Christi resurrectione nos reparas, fructus in nobis paschalis multiplica sacramenti, et fortitudinem cibi salutaris nostris infunde pectoribus. Per Christum Dominum nostrum.

A formula of Solemn Blessing, pp.136-139, may be used.

In England, Wales & Scotland

21 May

In Ireland

24 May

THE ASCENSION OF THE LORD

When Jesus returns to Heaven, he brings the Father a gift. What is the gift? His wounds. He shows him the wounds and says: "behold Father, this is the price of the pardon you have granted". Beholding the wounds of Jesus, the Father becomes most merciful. This is the beauty that urges us not to be afraid to ask forgiveness...Jesus's last message to his disciples is the mandate to depart: "Go therefore and make disciples of all nations". It is a clear mandate, not just an option! To his missionary disciples Jesus says: "I am with you always, to the close of the age". Alone, without Jesus, we can do nothing! Without the presence of the Lord and the power of his Spirit our work, though it may be well organized, winds up being ineffective. And thus, we go to tell the nations who Jesus is.

(Pope Francis)

Solemnity

Where the Solemnity of the Ascension is not to be observed as a Holyday of Obligation, it is assigned to the Seventh Sunday of Easter as its proper day.

At the Vigil Mass

This Mass is used on the evening of the day before the Solemnity, either before or after First Vespers (Evening Prayer I) of the Ascension.

Entrance Antiphon   Ps 67:33,35 | Ant. ad introitum

YOU kingdoms of the earth,
   sing to God;
praise the Lord, who ascends above
   the highest heavens;
his majesty and might
   are in the skies, alleluia.

REGNA terræ cantate Deo,
   psallite Domino,
qui ascendit super cælum cæli;
magnificentia et virtus eius
   in nubibus, alleluia.

The Gloria in excelsis (Glory to God in the highest) is said.

Collect | Collecta

O God, whose Son today ascended
   to the heavens
as the Apostles looked on,
grant, we pray, that, in accordance
   with his promise,
we may be worthy for him to live
   with us always on earth,
and we with him in heaven.
Who lives and reigns with you
   in the unity of the Holy Spirit,
one God, for ever and ever.

Deus, cuius Filius hodie in cælos,
Apostolis astantibus, ascendit,
concede nobis, quæsumus,
ut secundum eius promissionem
et ille nobiscum semper in terris
et nos cum eo in cælo
   vivere mereamur.
Qui tecum vivit et regnat
   in unitate Spiritus Sancti,
Deus, per omnia sæcula sæculorum.

FIRST READING

A reading from the Acts of the Apostles   1:1-11

He was lifted up while they looked on.

In my earlier work, Theophilus, I dealt with everything Jesus had done and taught from the beginning until the day he gave his instructions to the apostles he had chosen through the Holy Spirit, and was taken up to heaven. He had shown himself alive to them after his Passion by many demonstrations: for forty days he had continued to appear to them and tell them about the kingdom of God. When he had been at table with them, he had told them not to leave Jerusalem, but to wait there for what the Father had promised. 'It is' he had said 'what you have heard me speak about: John baptised with water but you, not many days from now, will be baptised with the Holy Spirit.'

Now having met together, they asked him, 'Lord, has the time come? Are you going to restore the kingdom to Israel?' He replied, 'It is not for you to know times or dates that the Father has decided by his own authority, but you will receive power when the Holy Spirit comes on you, and then you will be my witnesses not only in Jerusalem but throughout Judaea and Samaria, and indeed to the ends of the earth.'

As he said this he was lifted up while they looked on, and a cloud took him from their sight. They were still staring into the sky when suddenly two men in white were standing near them and they said, 'Why are you men from Galilee standing here looking into the sky? Jesus who has been taken up from you into heaven, this same Jesus will come back in the same way as you have seen him go there.'

The word of the Lord.

Responsorial Psalm   Ps 46:2-3,6-9. R. v.6

R. **God goes up with shouts of joy;**
   the Lord goes up with trumpet blast.
   Or: **Alleluia!**

All peoples, clap your hands,
cry to God with shouts of joy!
For the Lord, the Most High, we must fear,
great king over all the earth. R.

God goes up with shouts of joy;
the Lord goes up with trumpet blast.
Sing praise for God, sing praise,
sing praise to our king, sing praise. R.

God is king of all the earth.
Sing praise with all your skill.
God is king over the nations;
God reigns on his holy throne. R.

SECOND READING

A reading from the letter of St Paul to the Ephesians   1:17-23

He made him sit at his right hand in heaven.

May the God of our Lord Jesus Christ, the Father of glory, give you a spirit of wisdom and perception of what is revealed, to bring you to full knowledge of him. May he enlighten the eyes of your mind so that you can see what hope his call holds for you, what rich glories he has promised the saints will inherit and how infinitely great is the power that he has exercised for us believers. This you can tell from the strength of his power at work in Christ, when he used it to raise him from the dead and to make him sit at his right hand, in heaven, far above every Sovereignty, Authority, Power, or Domination, or any other name that can be named, not only in this age, but also in the age to come. He has put all things under his feet, and made him as the ruler of everything, the head of the Church; which is his body, the fullness of him who fills the whole creation.

The word of the Lord.

Gospel Acclamation   Mt 28:19,20

R. **Alleluia, alleluia!**
Go, make disciples of all the nations;
I am with you always; yes, to the end of time.
R. **Alleluia!**

GOSPEL

A reading from the holy Gospel according to Matthew   28:16-20

All authority in heaven and earth has been given to me.

The eleven disciples set out for Galilee, to the mountain where Jesus had arranged to meet them. When they saw him they fell down before him, though some hesitated. Jesus came up and spoke to them. He said, 'All authority in heaven and on earth has been given to me. Go, therefore, make disciples of all the nations; baptise them in the name of the Father and of the Son and of the Holy Spirit, and teach them to observe all the commands I gave you. And know that I am with you always; yes, to the end of time.'

The Gospel of the Lord.

The Creed is said.

Prayer over the Offerings

O God, whose Only Begotten Son,
  our High Priest,
is seated ever-living at your right
  hand to intercede for us,
grant that we may approach with
  confidence the throne of grace
and there obtain your mercy.
Through Christ our Lord.

Super oblata

Deus, cuius Unigenitus,
  Pontifex noster,
semper vivens sedet
  ad dexteram tuam
ad interpellandum pro nobis,
concede nos adire cum fiducia ad
  thronum gratiæ,
ut misericordiam tuam consequamur.
Per Christum Dominum nostrum.

Preface I or II of the Ascension of the Lord, pp.58-59.

When the Roman Canon is used, the proper form of the **Communicantes** (**In communion with those**) is said.

Communion Antiphon Cf. Heb 10:12

Christ, offering a single sacrifice
  for sins,
is seated for ever at God's right hand,
  alleluia.

Ant. ad communionem

Christus, unam pro peccatis
  offerens hostiam,
in sempiternum sedet in dextera Dei,
  alleluia.

Prayer after Communion

May the gifts we have received
  from your altar, Lord,
kindle in our hearts a longing
  for the heavenly homeland
and cause us to press forward,
  following in the
  Saviour's footsteps,
to the place where for our sake he
  entered before us.
Who lives and reigns
  for ever and ever.

Post communionem

Quæ ex altari tuo, Domine,
  dona percepimus,
accendant in cordibus nostris
  cælestis patriæ desiderium,
et quo præcursor pro nobis
  introivit Salvator,
faciant nos, eius vestigia
  sectantes, contendere.
Qui vivit et regnat
  in sæcula sæculorum.

A formula of Solemn Blessing, pp.138-139, may be used.

At the Mass during the Day

Entrance Antiphon   Ac 1:11 | Ant. ad introitum

MEN of Galilee, why gaze
in wonder at the heavens?
This Jesus whom you saw ascending
    into heaven
will return as you saw him go,
    alleluia.

VIRI Galilæi, quid admiramini
aspicientes in cælum?
Quemadmodum vidistis eum
    ascendentem in cælum,
    ita veniet, alleluia.

The Gloria in excelsis (Glory to God in the highest) is said.

Collect | Collecta

Gladden us with holy joys,
    almighty God,
and make us rejoice with
    devout thanksgiving,
for the Ascension of Christ your Son
is our exaltation,
and, where the Head has gone
    before in glory,
the Body is called to follow in hope.
Through our Lord Jesus Christ,
    your Son,
who lives and reigns with you
    in the unity of the Holy Spirit,
one God, for ever and ever.

Fac nos, omnipotens Deus,
    sanctis exsultare gaudiis,
et pia gratiarum actione lætari,
quia Christi Filii tui ascensio
    est nostra provectio,
et quo processit gloria capitis,
    eo spes vocatur et corporis.
Per Dominum nostrum Iesum
    Christum Filium tuum,
qui tecum vivit et regnat
    in unitate Spiritus Sancti,
Deus, per omnia sæcula sæculorum.

Or: | Vel:

Grant, we pray, almighty God,
that we, who believe that your Only
    Begotten Son, our Redeemer,
ascended this day to the heavens,
may in spirit dwell already
    in heavenly realms.
Who lives and reigns with you
    in the unity of the Holy Spirit,
one God, for ever and ever.

Concede, quæsumus,
    omnipotens Deus,
ut, qui hodierna die
Unigenitum tuum
    Redemptorem nostrum
ad cælos ascendisse credimus,
ipsi quoque mente in
    cælestibus habitemus.
Qui tecum vivit et regnat
    in unitate Spiritus Sancti,
Deus, per omnia sæcula sæculorum.

FIRST READING

A reading from the Acts of the Apostles   1:1-11

He was lifted up while they looked on.

In my earlier work, Theophilus, I dealt with everything Jesus had done and taught from the beginning until the day he gave his instructions to the apostles he had chosen through the Holy Spirit, and was taken up to heaven. He had shown himself alive to them after his Passion by many demonstrations: for forty days he had continued to appear to them and tell them about the kingdom of God. When he had been at table with them, he had told them not to leave Jerusalem, but to wait there for what the Father had promised. 'It is' he had said 'what you have heard me speak about: John baptised with water but you, not many days from now, will be baptised with the Holy Spirit.'

Now having met together, they asked him, 'Lord, has the time come? Are you going to restore the kingdom to Israel?' He replied, 'It is not for you to know times or dates that the Father has decided by his own authority, but you will receive power when the Holy Spirit comes on you, and then you will be my witnesses not only in Jerusalem but throughout Judaea and Samaria, and indeed to the ends of the earth.'

As he said this he was lifted up while they looked on, and a cloud took him from their sight. They were still staring into the sky when suddenly two men in white were standing near them and they said, 'Why are you men from Galilee standing here looking into the sky? Jesus who has been taken up from you into heaven, this same Jesus will come back in the same way as you have seen him go there.'

The word of the Lord.

Responsorial Psalm   Ps 46:2-3,6-9. R. v.6

R. **God goes up with shouts of joy;**
   the Lord goes up with trumpet blast.
   Or: **Alleluia!**

All peoples, clap your hands,
cry to God with shouts of joy!
For the Lord, the Most High, we must fear,
great king over all the earth. R.

God goes up with shouts of joy;
the Lord goes up with trumpet blast.
Sing praise for God, sing praise,
sing praise to our king, sing praise. R.

God is king of all the earth.
Sing praise with all your skill.
God is king over the nations;
God reigns on his holy throne. R.

R. **God goes up with shouts of joy;**
   the Lord goes up with trumpet blast.
   Or: **Alleluia!**

SECOND READING

A reading from the letter of St Paul to the Ephesians   1:17-23
He made him sit at his right hand in heaven.

May the God of our Lord Jesus Christ, the Father of glory, give you a spirit of
wisdom and perception of what is revealed, to bring you to full knowledge
of him. May he enlighten the eyes of your mind so that you can see what
hope his call holds for you, what rich glories he has promised the saints
will inherit and how infinitely great is the power that he has exercised for
us believers. This you can tell from the strength of his power at work in
Christ, when he used it to raise him from the dead and to make him sit at
his right hand, in heaven, far above every Sovereignty, Authority, Power, or
Domination, or any other name that can be named, not only in this age,
but also in the age to come. He has put all things under his feet, and made
him as the ruler of everything, the head of the Church; which is his body,
the fullness of him who fills the whole creation.

   The word of the Lord.

Gospel Acclamation   Mt 28:19.20

R. **Alleluia, alleluia!**
Go, make disciples of all the nations;
I am with you always; yes, to the end of time.
R. **Alleluia!**

GOSPEL

A reading from the holy Gospel according to Matthew   28:16-20
All authority in heaven and earth has been given to me.

The eleven disciples set out for Galilee, to the mountain where Jesus had
arranged to meet them. When they saw him they fell down before him,
though some hesitated. Jesus came up and spoke to them. He said, 'All
authority in heaven and on earth has been given to me. Go, therefore,
make disciples of all the nations; baptise them in the name of the Father

and of the Son and of the Holy Spirit, and teach them to observe all the commands I gave you. And know that I am with you always; yes, to the end of time.'

The Gospel of the Lord.

The Creed is said.

Prayer over the Offerings | Super oblata

We offer sacrifice now
  in supplication, O Lord,
to honour the wondrous Ascension
  of your Son:
grant, we pray,
that through this most holy exchange
we, too, may rise up
  to the heavenly realms.
Through Christ our Lord.

Sacrificium, Domine,
  pro Filii tui supplices
venerabili nunc
  ascensione deferimus:
præsta, quæsumus,
  ut his commerciis sacrosanctis
ad cælestia consurgamus.
Per Christum Dominum nostrum.

Preface I or II of the Ascension of the Lord, pp.58-59.

When the Roman Canon is used, the proper form of the **Communicantes** (In communion with those) is said.

Communion Antiphon Mt 28:20 | Ant. ad communionem

Behold, I am with you always,
even to the end of the age, alleluia.

Ecce ego vobiscum sum
  omnibus diebus,
usque ad consummationem sæculi,
  alleluia.

Prayer after Communion | Post communionem

Almighty ever-living God,
who allow those on earth
  to celebrate divine mysteries,
grant, we pray,
that Christian hope may draw
  us onward
to where our nature is united
  with you.
Through Christ our Lord.

Omnipotens sempiterne Deus,
qui in terra constitutos divina
  tractare concedis,
præsta, quæsumus,
ut illuc tendat christianæ
  devotionis affectus,
quo tecum est nostra substantia.
Per Christum Dominum nostrum.

A formula of Solemn Blessing, pp.138-139, may be used.

In England, Wales & Scotland

24 May

SEVENTH SUNDAY OF EASTER

In his farewell discourses to the disciples, Jesus stressed the importance of his "return to the Father", the culmination of his whole mission: indeed, he came into the world to bring man back to God, not on the ideal level – like a philosopher or a master of wisdom – but really, like a shepherd who wants to lead his sheep back to the fold. It was for our sake that he came down from Heaven and for our sake that he ascended to it, after making himself in all things like men, humbling himself even to death on a cross and after having touched the abyss of the greatest distance from God. For this very reason the Father was pleased with him and "highly exalted" him (Ph 2:9), restoring to him the fullness of his glory, but now with our humanity. God in man – man in God: this is even now a reality, not a theoretical truth.

(Pope Benedict XVI)

Entrance Antiphon   Cf. Ps 26:7-9

O LORD, hear my voice,
for I have called to you;
of you my heart has spoken:
Seek his face;
hide not your face from me, alleluia.

Ant. ad introitum

EXAUDI, Domine, vocem meam,
qua clamavi ad te.
Tibi dixit cor meum,
quæsivi vultum tuum,
vultum tuum requiram;
ne avertas faciem tuam a me, alleluia.

The Gloria in excelsis (Glory to God in the highest) is said.

Collect

Graciously hear our supplications,
O Lord,
so that we, who believe that
the Saviour of the human race
is with you in your glory,
may experience, as he promised,
until the end of the world,
his abiding presence among us.
Who lives and reigns with you
in the unity of the Holy Spirit,
one God, for ever and ever.

Collecta

Supplicationibus nostris, Domine,
adesto propitius,
ut, sicut humani generis Salvatorem
tecum in tua credimus maiestate,
ita eum usque ad
consummationem sæculi
manere nobiscum,
sicut ipse promisit, sentiamus.
Qui tecum vivit et regnat
in unitate Spiritus Sancti,
Deus, per omnia sæcula sæculorum.

FIRST READING

A reading from the Acts of the Apostles 1:12-14

All joined in continuous prayer.

After Jesus was taken up into heaven, the apostles went back from the Mount of Olives, as it is called, to Jerusalem, a short distance away, no more than a sabbath walk; and when they reached the city they went to the upper room where they were staying; there were Peter and John, James and Andrew, Philip and Thomas, Bartholomew and Matthew, James son of Alphaeus and Simon the Zealot, and Jude son of James. All these joined in continuous prayer, together with several women, including Mary the mother of Jesus, and with his brothers.

The word of the Lord.

Responsorial Psalm Ps 26:1,4,7-8. R. v.13

R. **I am sure I shall see the Lord's goodness**
in the land of the living.
Or: **Alleluia!**

The Lord is my light and my help;
whom shall I fear?
The Lord is the stronghold of my life;
before whom shall I shrink? R.

There is one thing I ask of the Lord,
for this I long,
to live in the house of the Lord,
all the days of my life,
to savour the sweetness of the Lord,
to behold his temple. R.

O Lord, hear my voice when I call;
have mercy and answer.
Of you my heart has spoken;
'Seek his face.' R.

SECOND READING

A reading from the first letter of St Peter 4:13-16

It is a blessing for you when they insult you for bearing the name of Christ.

If you can have some share in the sufferings of Christ, be glad, because you will enjoy a much greater gladness when his glory is revealed. It is a blessing for you when they insult you for bearing the name of Christ, because it means that you have the Spirit of glory, the Spirit of God resting on you. None of you should ever deserve to suffer for being a murderer, a thief, a criminal or an informer; but if anyone of you should suffer for being a Christian, then he is not to be ashamed of it; he should thank God that he has been called one.

The word of the Lord.

Gospel Acclamation   Cf. Jn 14:18

R. **Alleluia, alleluia!**
I will not leave you orphans, says the Lord;
I will come back to you, and your hearts will be full of joy.
R. **Alleluia!**

GOSPEL

A reading from the holy Gospel according to John   17:1-11

Father, glorify your Son.

Jesus raised his eyes to heaven and said:

'Father, the hour has come:
glorify your Son
so that your Son may glorify you;
and, through the power over all mankind that you have given him,
let him give eternal life to all those you have entrusted to him.
And eternal life is this:
to know you,
the only true God,
and Jesus Christ whom you have sent.
I have glorified you on earth
and finished the work
that you gave me to do.
Now, Father, it is time for you to glorify me
with that glory I had with you
before ever the world was.
I have made your name known
to the men you took from the world to give me.
They were yours and you gave them to me,
and they have kept your word.
Now at last they know
that all you have given me comes indeed from you;
for I have given them
the teaching you gave to me,
and they have truly accepted this, that I came from you,
and have believed that it was you who sent me.

I pray for them;
I am not praying for the world
but for those you have given me,
because they belong to you:
all I have is yours
and all you have is mine,
and in them I am glorified.
I am not in the world any longer,
but they are in the world,
and I am coming to you.'

The Gospel of the Lord.

The Creed is said.

Prayer over the Offerings

Accept, O Lord, the prayers
    of your faithful
with the sacrificial offerings,
that through these acts
    of devotedness
we may pass over to the glory
    of heaven.
Through Christ our Lord.

Super oblata

Suscipe, Domine, fidelium preces
cum oblationibus hostiarum,
ut, per hæc piæ devotionis officia,
ad cælestem gloriam transeamus.
Per Christum Dominum nostrum.

Preface of Easter, or of the Ascension, pp.52-59.

Communion Antiphon   Jn 17:22

Father, I pray that they may be one
as we also are one, alleluia.

Ant. ad communionem

Rogo, Pater, ut sint unum,
sicut et nos unum sumus, alleluia.

Prayer after Communion

Hear us, O God our Saviour,
and grant us confidence,
that through these sacred mysteries
there will be accomplished
    in the body of the whole Church
what has already come to pass
    in Christ her Head.
Who lives and reigns
    for ever and ever.

Post communionem

Exaudi nos, Deus, salutaris noster,
ut per hæc sacrosancta mysteria
in totius Ecclesiæ confidamus
    corpore faciendum,
quod eius præcessit in capite.
Per Christum Dominum nostrum.

A formula of Solemn Blessing, pp.136-139, may be used.

31 May

PENTECOST SUNDAY

If the Church is alive, she must always surprise. It is incumbent upon the living Church to astound. A Church which is unable to astound is a Church that is weak, sick, dying, and that needs admission to the intensive care unit as soon as possible! Some in Jerusalem would have liked for Jesus's disciples, frozen in fear, to remain locked inside so as not to create confusion. Even today, many would like this from the Christians. Instead, the risen Lord pushes them into the world: "As the Father has sent me, even so I send you". The Church of the Pentecost is a Church that won't submit to being powerless. She doesn't want to be a decoration. She is a Church that doesn't hesitate to go out, meet the people, proclaim the message that's been entrusted to her, even if that message disturbs or unsettles the conscience, even if that message perhaps brings problems and sometimes leads to martyrdom...We Christians are free, and the Church wants us free!

(Pope Francis)

Solemnity

At the Vigil Mass

EXTENDED FORM

This Vigil Mass may be celebrated on the Saturday evening, either before or after First Vespers (Evening Prayer I) of Pentecost Sunday.

In churches where the Vigil Mass is celebrated in an extended form, this may be done as follows.

a) If First Vespers (Evening Prayer I) celebrated in choir or in common immediately precede Mass, the celebration may begin either from the introductory verse and the hymn (**Veni, creator Spiritus**) or else from the singing of the Entrance Antiphon with the procession and greeting of the Priest; in either case the Penitential Act is omitted (Cf. General Instruction of the Liturgy of the Hours, nos. 94 and 96).

Then the Psalmody prescribed for Vespers follows, up to but not including the Short Reading.

After the Psalmody, omitting the Penitential Act, and if appropriate, the **Kyrie** (**Lord, have mercy**), the Priest says the prayer **Grant, we pray, almighty God, that the splendour**, as at the Vigil Mass.

b) If Mass is begun in the usual way, after the **Kyrie** (**Lord, have mercy**), the Priest says the prayer **Grant, we pray, almighty God, that the splendour**, as at the Vigil Mass.

Then the Priest may address the people in these or similar words:

Dear brethren (brothers and sisters), we have now begun our Pentecost Vigil, after the example of the Apostles and disciples who with Mary, the Mother of Jesus, persevered in prayer, awaiting the Spirit promised by the Lord; like them, let us, too, listen with quiet hearts to the Word of God. Let us meditate on how many great deeds God in times past did for his people and let us pray that the Holy Spirit, whom the Father sent as the first fruits for those who believe, may bring to perfection his work in the world.

Vigiliam Pentecostes ingressi, fratres carissimi, ad exemplum Apostolorum et discipulorum qui, cum Maria, Matre Iesu, instabant in oratione, exspectantes Spiritum a Domino promissum, quieto corde nunc verbum Dei audiamus. Meditemur quanta fecit Deus populo suo et oremus, ut Spiritus Sanctus quem Pater misit primitias credentibus, opus suum in mundo perficiat.

Then follow the readings proposed as options in the Lectionary. A reader goes to the ambo and proclaims the reading. Afterwards a psalmist or a cantor sings or says the Psalm with the people making the response. Then all rise, the Priest says, **Let us pray** and, after all have prayed for a while in silence, he says the prayer corresponding to the reading. In place of the Responsorial Psalm a period of sacred silence may be observed, in which case the pause after **Let us pray** is omitted.

FIRST READING

A reading from the book of Genesis
11:1-9

It was named Babel because there the language of the whole earth was confused.

Throughout the earth men spoke the same language, with the same vocabulary. Now as they moved eastwards they found a plain in the land of Shinar where they settled. They said to one another, 'Come, let us make bricks and bake them in the fire.' – For stone they used bricks, and for mortar they used bitumen. – 'Come,' they said 'let us build ourselves a town and a tower with its top reaching heaven. Let us make a name for ourselves, so that we may not be scattered about the whole earth.'

Now the Lord came down to see the town and the tower that the sons of man had built. 'So they are all a single people with a single language!' said the Lord. 'This is but the start of their undertakings! There will be nothing too hard for them to do. Come, let us go down and confuse their language on the spot so that they can no longer understand one another.'

The Lord scattered them thence over the whole face of the earth, and they stopped building the town. It was named Babel therefore, because there the Lord confused the language of the whole earth. It was from there that the Lord scattered them over the whole face of the earth.

The word of the Lord.

Responsorial Psalm   Ps 32:10-11,12-13,14-15 R. v.12b

R. **Happy the people the Lord has chosen as his own.**

He frustrates the designs of the nations,
he defeats the plans of the peoples.
His own designs shall stand for ever,
the plans of his heart from age to age. R.

They are happy, whose God is the Lord,
the people he has chosen as his own.
From the heavens the Lord looks forth,
he sees all the children of men. R.

From the place where he dwells he gazes
on all the dwellers on the earth,
he who shapes the hearts of them all
and considers all their deeds. R.

Prayer

Let us pray.	Oremus.
Grant, we pray, almighty God,	Concede, quæsumus,
that your Church may always	omnipotens Deus,
remain that holy people,	ut Ecclesia tua semper ea plebs
formed as one by the unity	sancta permaneat
of Father, Son and Holy Spirit,	de unitate Patris et Filii
which manifests to the world	et Spiritus Sancti adunata,
the Sacrament of your holiness	quce tuce sanctitatis
and unity	et unitatis sacramentum
and leads it to the perfection	mundo manifestet
of your charity.	et ipsum ad perfectionem
Through Christ our Lord.	tuce conducat caritatis.
R. Amen.	Per Christum Dominum nostrum.
	R. Amen.

SECOND READING

A reading from the book of Exodus   19:3-8,16-20

The Lord came down on the mountain of Sinai before all the people.

Moses went up to God, and the Lord called to him from the mountain, saying, 'Say this to the House of Jacob, declare this to the sons of Israel,

"You yourselves have seen what I did with the Egyptians, how I carried you on eagle's wings and brought you to myself. From this you know that now, if you obey my voice and hold fast to my covenant, you of all the nations shall be my very own, for all the earth is mine. I will count you a kingdom of priests, a consecrated nation." Those are the words you are to speak to the sons of Israel.' So Moses went and summoned the elders of the people, putting before them all that the Lord had bidden him. Then all the people answered as one, 'All that the Lord has said, we will do.'

Now at daybreak on the third day there were peals of thunder on the mountain and lightning flashes, a dense cloud, and a loud trumpet blast, and inside the camp all the people trembled. Then Moses led the people out of the camp to meet God; and they stood at the bottom of the mountain. The mountain of Sinai was entirely wrapped in smoke, because the Lord had descended on it in the form of fire. Like smoke from a furnace the smoke went up, and the whole mountain shook violently. Louder and louder grew the sound of the trumpet. Moses spoke, and God answered him with peals of thunder. The Lord came down on the mountain of Sinai, on the mountain top, and the Lord called Moses to the top of the mountain.

The word of the Lord.

Responsorial Psalm   Dn 3:52,53,54,55,56. R. v.52b

R. **To you glory and praise for evermore.**

You are blest, Lord God of our fathers. R.
Blest your glorious holy name. R.
You are blest in the temple of your glory. R.
You are blest on the throne of your kingdom. R.
You are blest who gaze into the depths. R.
You are blest in the firmament of heaven. R.

Or   Ps 18:8,9,10,11. R. Jn v.6:68c

R. **You have the message of eternal life, O Lord.**

The law of the Lord is perfect,
it revives the soul.
The rule of the Lord is to be trusted,
it gives wisdom to the simple. R.

The precepts of the Lord are right,
they gladden the heart.
The command of the Lord is clear,
it gives light to the eyes. R.

The fear of the Lord is holy,
abiding for ever.

The decrees of the Lord are truth
and all of them just. R.

They are more to be desired than gold,
than the purest of gold
and sweeter are they than honey,
than honey from the comb. R.

R. **You have the message of eternal life, O Lord.**

Prayer

Let us pray.

O God, who in fire and lightning
gave the ancient Law to Moses
  on Mount Sinai
and on this day manifested
  the new covenant
in the fire of the Spirit,
grant, we pray,
that we may always be aflame
  with that same Spirit
whom you wondrously poured out
  on your Apostles,
and that the new Israel,
gathered from every people,
may receive with rejoicing
the eternal commandment
  of your love.
Through Christ our Lord.
R. Amen.

Oremus.

Deus, qui in fulgure ignis
  in monte Sinai
legem antiquam Moysi dedisti
et fœdus novum in igne Spiritus
hoc die manifestasti,
presta, quæsumus,
ut ilio iugiter Spiritu ferveamus,
quem Apostolis tuis
  ineffabiliter infudisti,

et novus Israel,
ex omni populo congregatus,
mandatum æternum tui amoris
  lætanter accipiat.
Per Christum Dominum nostrum.
R. Amen.

THIRD READING

A reading from the prophet Ezekiel   37:1-14

Dry bones, I am going to make the breath enter you, and you will live.

The hand of the Lord was laid on me, and he carried me away by the
spirit of the Lord and set me down in the middle of a valley, a valley full
of bones. He made me walk up and down among them. There were vast
quantities of these bones on the ground the whole length of the valley;
and they were quite dried up. He said to me, 'Son of man, can these bones
live?' I said, 'You know, Lord.' He said, 'Prophesy over these bones. Say,
"Dry bones, hear the word of the Lord. The Lord says this to these bones:
I am now going to make the breath enter you, and you will live. I shall put

sinews on you, I shall make flesh grow on you, I shall cover you with skin and give you breath, and you will live, and you will learn that I am the Lord."' I prophesied as I had been ordered. While I was prophesying, there was a noise, a sound of clattering; and the bones joined together. I looked, and saw that they were covered with sinews; flesh was growing on them and skin was covering them, but there was no breath in them. He said to me, 'Prophesy to the breath; prophesy, son of man. Say to the breath, "The Lord says this: Come from the four winds, breath; breathe on these dead; let them live!"' I prophesied as he had ordered me, and the breath entered them; they came to life again and stood up on their feet, a great, an immense army.

Then he said, 'Son of man, these bones are the whole House of Israel. They keep saying, "Our bones are dried up, our hope has gone; we are as good as dead." So prophesy. Say to them, "The Lord says this: I am now going to open your graves; I mean to raise you from your graves, my people, and lead you back to the soil of Israel. And you will know that I am the Lord, when I open your graves and raise you from your graves, my people. And I shall put my spirit in you, and you will live, and I shall resettle you on your own soil; and you will know that I, the Lord have said and done this – it is the Lord who speaks."'

The word of the Lord.

Responsorial Psalm   Ps 106:2-3,4-5,6–7,8–9. R. v.1

R. **O give thanks to the Lord, for he is good;**
   for his love has no end.
   Or: **Alleluia!**

Let them say this, the Lord's redeemed,
whom he redeemed from the hand of the foe
and gathered from far-off lands,
from east and west, north and south. R.

Some wandered in the desert, in the wilderness,
finding no way to a city they could dwell in.
Hungry they were and thirsty;
their soul was fainting within them. R.

Then they cried to the Lord in their need
and he rescued them from their distress
and he led them along the right way,
to reach a city they could dwell in. R.

Let them thank the Lord for his love,
for the wonders he does for men.

For he satisfies the thirsty soul;
he fills the hungry with good things. R.

R. **O give thanks to the Lord, for he is good;**
   for his love has no end.
   Or: **Alleluia!**

Prayer

Let us pray.
Lord, God of power,
who restore what has fallen
and preserve what you have restored,
increase, we pray, the peoples
to be renewed by the sanctification
     of your name,
that all who are washed clean
     by holy Baptism
may always be directed
     by your prompting.
Through Christ our Lord.
R. Amen.

Or:

O God, who have brought us
     to rebirth by the word of life,
pour out upon us your Holy Spirit,
that, walking in oneness of faith,
we may attain in our flesh
the incorruptible glory
     of the resurrection.
Through Christ our Lord.
R. Amen.

Or:

May your people exult for ever,
     O God,
in renewed youthfulness of spirit,
so that, rejoicing now in the restored
     glory of our adoption,
we may look forward
in confident hope

Oremus.
Domine, Deus virtutum,
qui collapsa reparas
     et reparata conservas,
auge populos in tui nominis
     sanctificatione renovandos,
ut omnes, qui sacro
     Baptismate diluuntur,
tua semper inspiratione dirigantur.
Per Christum Dominum nostrum.
R. Amen.

Vel:

Deus, qui nos verbo vitæ regenerasti,
effunde super nos
     Spiritum Sanctum tuum,
ut, in unitate fidei ambulantes,
ad incorruptibilem glorificandæ
     carnis resurrectionem
pervenire mereamur.
Per Christum Dominum nostrum.
R. Amen.

Vel:

Semper exsultet populus
     tuus, Deus,
Spiritu Sancto tuo renovata
     animæ iuventute,
ut, qui nunc lætatur in adoptionis
     se gloriam restitutum,
resurrectionis diem spe certæ

to the rejoicing of the day
    of resurrection.
Through Christ our Lord.
R. Amen.

gratulationis exspectet.
Per Christum Dominum nostrum.
R. Amen.

FOURTH READING

A reading from the prophet Joel   3:1-5

I will pour out my spirit on all people.

Thus says the Lord:

'I will pour out my spirit on all mankind.
Your sons and daughters shall prophesy,
your old men shall dream dreams,
and your young men see visions.
Even on the slaves, men and women,
will I pour out my spirit in those days.
I will display portents in heaven and on earth,
blood and fire and columns of smoke.'

The sun will be turned into darkness,
and the moon into blood,
before the day of the Lord dawns,
that great and terrible day.
All who call on the name of the Lord will be saved,
for on Mount Zion there will be some who have escaped,
as the Lord has said,
and in Jerusalem some survivors whom the Lord will call.

The word of the Lord.

Responsorial Psalm   Ps 103:1-2a,24,35c,27-28,29bc-30. R. v.30

R. **Send forth your Spirit, O Lord,**
   and renew the face of the earth.
   Or: **Alleluia!**

Bless the Lord, my soul!
Lord God, how great you are,
clothed in majesty and glory,
wrapped in light as in a robe! R.

How many are your works, O Lord!
In wisdom you have made them all.
The earth is full of your riches.
Bless the Lord, my soul. R.

All of these look to you
to give them their food in due season.
You give it, they gather it up:
you open your hand, they have their fill. R.

You take back your spirit, they die,
returning to the dust from which they came.
You send forth your spirit, they are created;
and you renew the face of the earth. R.

R. **Send forth your Spirit, O Lord,
and renew the face of the earth.**

Or: **Alleluia!**

Prayer

Let us pray.	Oremus.
Fulfil for us your gracious promise,	Promissionem tuam,
O Lord, we pray,	quæsumus, Domine,
so that by his coming	super nos propitiatus adimple,
the Holy Spirit may make us	ut Spiritus Sanctus adveniens
witnesses before the world	nos coram mundo testes efficiat
to the Gospel of our Lord Jesus Christ.	Evangelii Domini nostri
Who lives and reigns	Iesu Christi.
for ever and ever.	Qui tecum vivit et regnat
R. Amen.	in sæcula sæculorum.
	R. Amen.

Then the Priest intones the hymn **Gloria in excelsis Deo** (Glory to God in the highest).

When the hymn is concluded, the Priest says the Collect in the usual way: **Almighty ever-living God, who willed**, as here below (p.319).

Then the reader proclaims the reading from the Apostle (Rm 8:22-27) pp.320-321, and Mass continues in the usual way.

If Vespers (Evening Prayer) are joined to Mass, after Communion with the Communion Antiphon (**On the last day**), the Magnificat is sung, with its Vespers antiphon (**Veni, Sancte Spiritus**); then the Prayer after Communion is said and the rest follows as usual.

At the Vigil Mass
SIMPLE FORM

This Mass is used on the Saturday evening, either before or after First Vespers (Evening Prayer I) of Pentecost Sunday.

Entrance Antiphon Rm 5:5; Cf. 8:11

THE love of God has been poured into our hearts through the Spirit of God dwelling within us, alleluia.

Ant. ad introitum

CARITAS Dei diffusa est in cordibus nostris per inhabitantem Spiritum eius in nobis, alleluia.

The Gloria in excelsis (Glory to God in the highest) is said.

Collect

Almighty ever-living God,
who willed the Paschal Mystery
to be encompassed as a sign
    in fifty days,
grant that from out
    of the scattered nations
the confusion of many tongues
may be gathered by heavenly grace
into one great confession
    of your name.
Through our Lord Jesus Christ,
    your Son,
who lives and reigns with you
    in the unity of the Holy Spirit,
one God, for ever and ever.

Collecta

Omnipotens sempiterne Deus,
qui paschale sacramentum
quinquaginta dierum voluisti
    mysterio contineri,
præsta, ut, gentium
    facta dispersione,
divisiones linguarum ad unam
    confessionem tui nominis
cælesti munere congregentur.
Per Dominum nostrum Iesum
    Christum Filium tuum,
qui tecum vivit et regnat
    in unitate Spiritus Sancti,
Deus, per omnia sæcula sæculorum.

Or:

Grant, we pray, almighty God,
that the splendour of your glory
may shine forth upon us
and that, by the bright rays
    of the Holy Spirit,
the light of your light may confirm
    the hearts
of those born again by your grace.

Vel:

Præsta, quæsumus,
    omnipotens Deus,
ut claritatis tuæ super nos
    splendor effulgeat,
et lux tuæ lucis corda eorum,
qui per tuam gratiam sunt renati,
Sancti Spiritus
    illustratione confirmet.

Through our Lord Jesus Christ, your Son, who lives and reigns with you in the unity of the Holy Spirit, one God, for ever and ever.	Per Dominum nostrum Iesum Christum Filium tuum, qui tecum vivit et regnat in unitate Spiritus Sancti, Deus, per omnia sæcula sæculorum.

FIRST READING

There is a choice of four texts for the First Reading: Either Genesis 11:1-9 (On Babel), p.311; or Exodus 19:3-8,16-20 (On God's descent on Mount Sinai), p.312; or Ezekiel 37:1-14 (On the dry bones and God's spirit), p.314; or Joel 3:1-5 (On the outpouring of the Spirit), p.317.

Responsorial Psalm   Ps 103:1-2,24,27-30,35. R. Cf. v.30

R. **Send forth your spirit, O Lord,
   and renew the face of the earth.**
   Or: **Alleluia!**

Bless the Lord, my soul!
Lord God, how great you are,
clothed in majesty and glory,
wrapped in light as in a robe! R.

How many are your works, O Lord!
In wisdom you have made them all.
The earth is full of your riches.
Bless the Lord, my soul. R.

All of these look to you
to give them their food in due season.
You give it, they gather it up:
you open your hand, they have their fill. R.

You take back your spirit, they die,
returning to the dust from which they came.
You send forth your spirit, they are created;
and you renew the face of the earth. R.

SECOND READING

A reading from the letter of St Paul to the Romans   8:22-27

The Spirit himself expresses our plea in a way that could never be put into words.

From the beginning till now the entire creation, as we know, has been groaning in one great act of giving birth; and not only creation, but all of us who possess the first-fruits of the Spirit, we too groan inwardly as we wait for our bodies to be set free. For we must be content to hope that we shall be saved – our salvation is not in sight, we should not have to be hoping for it if it were – but, as I say, we must hope to be saved since we are not saved yet – it is something we must wait for with patience.

The Spirit too comes to help us in our weakness. For when we cannot choose words in order to pray properly, the Spirit himself expresses our plea in a way that could never be put into words, and God who knows everything in our hearts knows perfectly well what he means, and that the pleas of the saints expressed by the Spirit are according to the mind of God.

The word of the Lord.

Gospel Acclamation

R. **Alleluia, alleluia!**
Come, Holy Spirit, fill the hearts of your faithful
and kindle in them the fire of your love.
R. **Alleluia!**

GOSPEL

A reading from the holy Gospel according to John   7:37-39
From his breast shall flow fountains of living water.

On the last day and greatest day of the festival, Jesus stood there and cried out:

'If any man is thirsty, let him come to me!
Let the man come and drink who believes in me!'

As scripture says: From his breast shall flow fountains of living water.

He was speaking of the Spirit which those who believed in him were to receive; for there was no Spirit as yet because Jesus had not yet been glorified.

The Gospel of the Lord.
The Creed is said.

Prayer over the Offerings	Super oblata

Pour out upon these gifts
    the blessing of your Spirit,
we pray, O Lord,
so that through them your Church
    may be imbued with such love
that the truth of your saving mystery
may shine forth for the whole world.
Through Christ our Lord.
	Præsentia munera,
	    quæsumus, Domine,
	Spiritus tui benedictione perfunde,
	ut per ipsa Ecclesiæ tuæ
	    ea dilectio tribuatur,
	per quam salutaris mysterii toto
	    mundo veritas enitescat.
	Per Christum Dominum nostrum.

Preface: The Mystery of Pentecost.

It is truly right and just,
    our duty and our salvation,
always and everywhere
    to give you thanks,
Lord, holy Father,
    almighty and eternal God.

For, bringing your Paschal Mystery
    to completion,
you bestowed the Holy Spirit today
on those you made
    your adopted children
by uniting them to your Only
    Begotten Son.
This same Spirit,
    as the Church came to birth,
opened to all peoples
    the knowledge of God
and brought together the many
    languages of the earth
in profession of the one faith.

Therefore, overcome with paschal joy,
every land, every people exults
    in your praise
and even the heavenly Powers,
    with the angelic hosts,
sing together the unending hymn
    of your glory,
as they acclaim:

Holy, Holy, Holy Lord God of hosts...

Præfatio: De mysterio Pentecostes.

Vere dignum et iustum est,
    æquum et salutare,
nos tibi semper et ubique
    gratias agere:
Domine, sancte Pater,
    omnipotens æterne Deus.

Tu enim, sacramentum
    paschale consummans,
quibus, per Unigeniti tui consortium,
filios adoptionis esse tribuisti,
hodie Spiritum Sanctum es largitus;
qui, principio nascentis Ecclesiæ,
et cunctis gentibus scientiam
    indidit deitatis,
et linguarum diversitatem in unius
    fidei confessione sociavit.

Quapropter, profusis
    paschalibus gaudiis,
totus in orbe terrarum
    mundus exsultat.
Sed et supernæ virtutes atque
    angelicæ potestates
hymnum gloriæ tuæ concinunt,
    sine fine dicentes:

Sanctus, Sanctus, Sanctus. . .

When the Roman Canon is used, the proper form of the **Communicantes** (In communion with those) is said.

Communion Antiphon   Jn 7:37

On the last day of the festival,
    Jesus stood and cried out:
If anyone is thirsty, let him come
    to me and drink, alleluia.

Ant. ad communionem

Ultimo festivitatis die, stabat Iesus
    et clamabat dicens:
Si quis sitit, veniat ad me et bibat,
    alleluia.

Prayer after Communion

May these gifts we have consumed
benefit us, O Lord,
that we may always be aflame
with the same Spirit,
whom you wondrously poured out
on your Apostles.
Through Christ our Lord.

Post communionem

Hæc nobis, Domine,
munera sumpta proficiant,
ut illo iugiter Spiritu ferveamus,
quem Apostolis tuis
ineffabiliter infudisti.
Per Christum Dominum nostrum.

A formula of Solemn Blessing, pp.138-141, may be used.

To dismiss the people the Deacon or, if there is no Deacon, the Priest himself sings or says:

Go forth, the Mass is ended,
alleluia, alleluia.

Ite, missa est, alleluia, alleluia.

Or:

Vel:

Go in peace, alleluia, alleluia.

Ite in pace, alleluia, alleluia.

And the people reply:

Omnes respondent:

Thanks be to God, alleluia, alleluia.

R. Deo gratias, alleluia, alleluia.

At the Mass during the Day

Entrance Antiphon   Ws 1:7

THE Spirit of the Lord has filled
the whole world
and that which contains all things
understands what is said, alleluia.

Ant. ad introitum

SPIRITUS Domini replevit
orbem terrarum,
et hoc quod continet omnia
scientiam habet vocis, alleluia.

Or: Rm 5:5; Cf. 8:11

The love of God has been poured
into our hearts
through the Spirit of God dwelling
within us, alleluia.

Vel:

Caritas Dei diffusa
est in cordibus nostris
per inhabitantem Spiritum eius
in nobis, alleluia.

The Gloria in excelsis (Glory to God in the highest) is said.

Collect

O God, who by the mystery
of today's great feast
sanctify your whole Church
in every people and nation,

Collecta

Deus, qui sacramento
festivitatis hodiernæ
universam Ecclesiam tuam
in omni gente et natione sanctificas,

pour out, we pray, the gifts
   of the Holy Spirit
across the face of the earth
and, with the divine grace that
   was at work
when the Gospel
   was first proclaimed,
fill now once more the hearts
   of believers.
Through our Lord Jesus Christ,
   your Son,
who lives and reigns with you
   in the unity of the Holy Spirit,
one God, for ever and ever.

in totam mundi latitudinem
   Spiritus Sancti dona defunde,
et, quod inter ipsa evangelicæ
   prædicationis exordia
operata est divina dignatio,
nunc quoque per credentium
   corda perfunde.
Per Dominum nostrum Iesum
   Christum Filium tuum,
qui tecum vivit et regnat
   in unitate Spiritus Sancti,
Deus, per omnia sæcula sæculorum.

FIRST READING

A reading from the Acts of the Apostles   2:1-11

They were all filled with the Holy Spirit and began to speak.

When Pentecost day came round, the apostles had all met in one room, when suddenly they heard what sounded like a powerful wind from heaven, the noise of which filled the entire house in which they were sitting; and something appeared to them that seemed like tongues of fire; these separated and came to rest on the head of each of them. They were all filled with the Holy Spirit, and began to speak foreign languages as the Spirit gave them the gift of speech.

Now there were devout men living in Jerusalem from every nation under heaven, and at this sound they all assembled, each one bewildered to hear these men speaking his own language. They were amazed and astonished. 'Surely' they said 'all these men speaking are Galileans? How does it happen that each of us hears them in his own native language? Parthians, Medes and Elamites; people from Mesopotamia, Judaea and Cappadocia, Pontus and Asia, Phrygia and Pamphylia, Egypt and the parts of Libya round Cyrene; as well as visitors from Rome – Jews and proselytes alike – Cretans and Arabs; we hear them preaching in our own language about the marvels of God.'

The word of the Lord.

Responsorial Psalm   Ps 103:1,24,29-31,34. R. Cf. v.30

R. **Send forth your Spirit, O Lord,**
   and renew the face of the earth.
   Or: **Alleluia!**

Bless the Lord, my soul!
Lord God, how great you are.
How many are your works, O Lord!
The earth is full of your riches. R.

You take back your spirit, they die,
returning to the dust from which they came.
You send forth your spirit, they are created;
and you renew the face of the earth. R.

May the glory of the Lord last for ever!
May the Lord rejoice in his works!
May my thoughts be pleasing to him.
I find my joy in the Lord. R.

SECOND READING

A reading from the first letter of St Paul to the Corinthians   12:3-7,12-13

In the one Spirit we were all baptised.

No one can say, 'Jesus is Lord' unless he is under the influence of the Holy Spirit.

There is a variety of gifts but always the same Spirit; there are all sorts of service to be done, but always to the same Lord; working in all sorts of different ways in different people, it is the same God who is working in all of them. The particular way in which the Spirit is given to each person is for a good purpose.

Just as a human body, though it is made up of many parts, is a single unit because all these parts, though many, make one body, so it is with Christ. In the one Spirit we were all baptised, Jews as well as Greeks, slaves as well as citizens, and one Spirit was given to us all to drink.

The word of the Lord.

SEQUENCE

The sequence may be said or sung.

Holy Spirit, Lord of light,
From the clear celestial height
Thy pure beaming radiance give.

Veni, Sancte Spiritus,
et emitte cælitus
lucis tuæ radium.

Come, thou Father of the poor,
Come with treasures which endure;
Come, thou light of all that live!

Veni, pater pauperum,
veni, dator munerum,
veni, lumen cordium.

Thou, of all consolers best,
Thou, the soul's delightful guest,
Dost refreshing peace bestow.

Consolator optime,
dulcis hospes animæ,
dulce refrigerium.

Thou in toil art comfort sweet;
Pleasant coolness in the heat;
Solace in the midst of woe.

In labore requies,
in æstu temperies,
in fletu solacium.

Light immortal, light divine,
Visit thou these hearts of thine,
And our inmost being fill:

O lux beatissima,
reple cordis intima
tuorum fidelium.

If thou take thy grace away,
Nothing pure in man will stay;
All his good is turned to ill.

Sine tuo numine,
nihil est in homine,
nihi est innoxium.

Heal our wounds,
our strength renew;
On our dryness pour thy dew;
Wash the stains of guilt away.

Lava quod est sordidum,
riga quod est aridum,
sana quod est saucium.

Bend the stubborn heart and will;
Melt the frozen, warm the chill;
Guide the steps that go astray.

Flecte quod est rigidum,
fove quod est frigidum,
rege quod est devium.

Thou, on us who evermore
Thee confess and thee adore,
thy sevenfold gifts descend:

Da tuis fidelibus,
in te confidentibus,
sacrum septenarium.

Give us comfort when we die,
Give us life with thee on high;
Give us joys that never end.

Da virtutis meritum
da salutis exitum,
da perenne gaudium.

Gospel Acclamation

R. **Alleluia, alleluia!**
Come, Holy Spirit, fill the hearts of your faithful
and kindle in them the fire of your love.
R. **Alleluia!**

GOSPEL

A reading from the holy Gospel according to John   20:19-23

As the Father sent me, so am I sending you: receive the Holy Spirit.

In the evening of the first day of the week, the doors were closed in the room where the disciples were, for fear of the Jews. Jesus came and stood among them. He said to them, 'Peace be with you,' and showed them his hands and his side. The disciples were filled with joy when they saw the Lord, and he said to them again, 'Peace be with you.

'As the Father sent me,
so am I sending you.'

After saying this he breathed on them and said:

'Receive the Holy Spirit.
For those whose sins you forgive,
they are forgiven;
for those whose sins you retain,
they are retained.'

The Gospel of the Lord.

The Creed is said.

Prayer over the Offerings	Super oblata

Grant, we pray, O Lord,
that, as promised by your Son,
the Holy Spirit may reveal to us
    more abundantly
the hidden mystery of this sacrifice
and graciously lead us into all truth.
Through Christ our Lord.
	Præsta, quæsumus, Domine,
	ut, secundum promissionem
	    Filii tui,
	Spiritus Sanctus huius nobis sacrificii
	copiosius revelet arcanum,
	et omnem propitius reseret veritatem.
	Per Christum Dominum nostrum.

Preface: The Mystery of Pentecost.	Præfatio: De mysterio Pentecostes.

It is truly right and just,
    our duty and our salvation,
always and everywhere
    to give you thanks,
Lord, holy Father,
    almighty and eternal God.
	Vere dignum et iustum est,
	    æquum et salutare,
	nos tibi semper et ubique
	    gratias agere:
	Domine, sancte Pater,
	    omnipotens æterne Deus.

For, bringing your Paschal Mystery
    to completion,
you bestowed the Holy Spirit today
	Tu enim, sacramentum
	    paschale consummans,
	quibus, per Unigeniti tui consortium,

on those you made
  your adopted children
by uniting them to your Only
  Begotten Son.
This same Spirit,
  as the Church came to birth,
opened to all peoples
  the knowledge of God
and brought together the many
  languages of the earth
in profession of the one faith.

Therefore, overcome with paschal joy,
every land, every people exults
  in your praise
and even the heavenly Powers,
  with the angelic hosts,
sing together the unending hymn
  of your glory,
as they acclaim:

Holy, Holy, Holy Lord God of hosts...

filios adoptionis esse tribuisti,
hodie Spiritum Sanctum es largitus;
qui, principio nascentis Ecclesiæ,
et cunctis gentibus scientiam
  indidit deitatis,
et linguarum diversitatem in unius
  fidei confessione sociavit.

Quapropter, profusis
  paschalibus gaudiis,
totus in orbe terrarum
  mundus exsultat.
Sed et supernæ virtutes atque
  angelicæ potestates
hymnum gloriæ tuæ concinunt,
sine fine dicentes:

Sanctus, Sanctus, Sanctus. . .

When the Roman Canon is used, the proper form of the **Communicantes** (In communion with those) is said.

Communion Antiphon Ac 2:4,11
They were all filled
  with the Holy Spirit
and spoke of the marvels of God,
alleluia.

Ant. ad communionem
Repleti sunt omnes Spiritu Sancto,
loquentes magnalia Dei, alleluia.

Prayer after Communion
O God, who bestow heavenly gifts
  upon your Church,
safeguard, we pray, the grace you
  have given,
that the gift of the Holy Spirit
  poured out upon her
may retain all its force
and that this spiritual food
may gain her abundance
  of eternal redemption.
Through Christ our Lord.

Post communionem
Deus, qui Ecclesiæ tuæ cælestia
  dona largiris,
custodi gratiam quam dedisti,
ut Spiritus Sancti vigeat semper
  munus infusum,
et ad æternæ
  redemptionis augmentum
spiritalis esca proficiat.
Per Christum Dominum nostrum.

A formula of Solemn Blessing, pp.138-141, may be used.
To dismiss the people the Deacon or, if there is no Deacon, the Priest himself sings
or says:

Go forth, the Mass is ended, alleluia, alleluia.	Ite, missa est, alleluia, alleluia.
Or:	Vel:
Go in peace, alleluia, aleluia.	Ite in pace, alleluia, alleluia.
And the people reply:	Omnes respondent:
Thanks be to God, alleluia, alleluia.	Deo gratias, alleluia, alleluia.

With Easter Time now concluded, the paschal candle is extinguished. It is desirable
to keep the paschal candle in the baptistery with due honour so that it is lit at the
celebration of Baptism and the candles of those baptised are lit from it.

7 June

THE MOST HOLY TRINITY

*Love is the badge of the Christian, as Jesus told us: "By this all men will know
that you are my disciples, if you have love for one another". It's a contradiction
to think of Christians who hate. And the devil always seeks this: to make us
hate, because he's always a troublemaker; he doesn't know love; God is love!
We are all called to witness and proclaim the message that "God is love", that
God isn't far and insensitive to our human affairs. He is close to us, always
beside us, walking with us to share our joys and our sorrows, our hopes and
our struggles. He loves us very much and for that reason he became man,
he came into the world not to condemn it, but so the world would be saved
through Jesus...A person who loves others for the very joy of love is a reflection
of the Trinity. A family in which each person loves and helps one another is
a reflection of the Trinity. A parish in which each person loves and shares
spiritual and material effects is a reflection of the Trinity.* (Pope Francis)

Solemnity

Entrance Antiphon	Ant. ad introitum
B LEST be God the Father, and the Only Begotten Son of God, and also the Holy Spirit, for he has shown us his merciful love.	B ENEDICTUS sit Deus Pater, Unigenitusque Dei Filius, Sanctus quoque Spiritus, quia fecit nobiscum misericordiam suam.

The **Gloria in excelsis** (Glory to God in the highest) is said.

Collect

God our Father, who by sending
    into the world
the Word of truth and the Spirit
    of sanctification
made known to the human race
    your wondrous mystery,
grant us, we pray, that in professing
    the true faith,
we may acknowledge the Trinity
    of eternal glory
and adore your Unity,
    powerful in majesty.
Through our Lord Jesus Christ,
    your Son,
who lives and reigns with you
    in the unity of the Holy Spirit,
one God, for ever and ever.

Collecta

Deus Pater, qui Verbum veritatis
et Spiritum sanctificationis mittens
    in mundum,
admirabile mysterium tuum
    hominibus declarasti,
da nobis, in confessione veræ fidei,
æternæ gloriam Trinitatis agnoscere,
et Unitatem adorare
    in potentia maiestatis.
Per Dominum nostrum Iesum
    Christum Filium tuum,
qui tecum vivit et regnat
    in unitate Spiritus Sancti,
Deus, per omnia sæcula sæculorum.

FIRST READING

A reading from the book of Exodus   34:4-6,8-9

Lord, Lord, a God of tenderness and compassion.

With the two tablets of stone in his hands, Moses went up the mountain of Sinai in the early morning as the Lord had commanded him. And the Lord descended in the form of a cloud, and Moses stood with him there.

He called on the name of the Lord. The Lord passed before him and proclaimed, 'Lord, Lord, a God of tenderness and compassion, slow to anger, rich in kindness and faithfulness.' And Moses bowed down to the ground at once and worshipped. 'If I have indeed won your favour, Lord,' he said 'let my Lord come with us, I beg. True, they are a headstrong people, but forgive us our faults and our sins, and adopt us as your heritage.'

The word of the Lord.

Responsorial Psalm   Dn 3:52-56. R. v.52

You are blest, Lord God of our fathers.
R. **To you glory and praise for evermore.**

Blest your glorious holy name.
R. **To you glory and praise for evermore.**

You are blest in the temple of your glory.
R. **To you glory and praise for evermore.**

You are blest on the throne of your kingdom.
R. **To you glory and praise for evermore.**

You are blest who gaze into the depths.
R. **To you glory and praise for evermore.**

You are blest in the firmament of heaven.
R. **To you glory and praise for evermore.**

SECOND READING

A reading from the second letter of St Paul to the Corinthians   13:11-13
The grace of Jesus Christ, the love of God, and the fellowship of the Holy Spirit.

Brothers, we wish you happiness; try to grow perfect; help one another. Be united; live in peace, and the God of love and peace will be with you.

Greet one another with the holy kiss. All the saints send you greetings.

The grace of the Lord Jesus Christ, the love of God and the fellowship of the Holy Spirit be with you all.

The word of the Lord.

Gospel Acclamation   Cf. Rv 1:8

R. **Alleluia, alleluia!**
Glory be to the Father, and to the Son, and to the Holy Spirit,
the God who is, who was, and who is to come.
R. **Alleluia!**

GOSPEL

A reading from the holy Gospel according to John   3:16-18
God sent his Son so that through him the world might be saved.

Jesus said to Nicodemus:

'God loved the world so much
that he gave his only Son,
so that everyone who believes in him may not be lost

but may have eternal life.
For God sent his Son into the world
not to condemn the world,
but so that through him the world might be saved.
No one who believes in him will be condemned;
but whoever refuses to believe is condemned already,
because he has refused to believe
in the name of God's only Son.

The Gospel of the Lord.

The Creed is said.

Prayer over the Offerings

Sanctify by the invocation
    of your name,
we pray, O Lord our God,
this oblation of our service,
and by it make of us an eternal
    offering to you.
Through Christ our Lord.

Super oblata

Sanctifica, quæsumus,
    Domine Deus noster,
per tui nominis invocationem,
hæc munera nostræ servitutis,
et per ea nosmetipsos tibi perfice
    munus æternum.
Per Christum Dominum nostrum.

Preface: The Mystery of the Most
Holy Trinity.

Præfatio: De mysterio Sanctissimæ
Trinitatis.

It is truly right and just,
    our duty and our salvation,
always and everywhere
    to give you thanks,
Lord, holy Father,
    almighty and eternal God.

Vere dignum et iustum est,
    æquum et salutare,
nos tibi semper et ubique
    gratias agere:
Domine, sancte Pater,
    omnipotens æterne Deus:

For with your Only Begotten Son
    and the Holy Spirit
you are one God, one Lord:
not in the unity of a single person,
but in a Trinity of one substance.

Qui cum Unigenito Filio tuo
    et Spiritu Sancto
unus es Deus, unus es Dominus:
non in unius singularitate personæ,
sed in unius Trinitate substantiæ.

For what you have revealed to us
    of your glory
we believe equally of your Son
and of the Holy Spirit,
so that, in the confessing of the true
    and eternal Godhead,

Quod enim de tua gloria,
    revelante te, credimus,
hoc de Filio tuo,
hoc de Spiritu Sancto,
sine discretione sentimus.

you might be adored in what
   is proper to each Person,
their unity in substance,
and their equality in majesty.

Ut in confessione veræ
   sempiternæque Deitatis,
et in personis proprietas,
et in essentia unitas,
et in maiestate adoretur æqualitas.

For this is praised by Angels
   and Archangels,
Cherubim, too, and Seraphim,
who never cease to cry out each day,
as with one voice they acclaim:

Quem laudant Angeli
   atque Archangeli,
Cherubim quoque ac Seraphim,
qui non cessant clamare cotidie,
   una voce dicentes:

Holy, Holy, Holy Lord God of hosts...

Sanctus, Sanctus, Sanctus . . .

Communion Antiphon   Ga 4:6

Ant. ad communionem

Since you are children of God,
God has sent into your hearts
   the Spirit of his Son,
the Spirit who cries out:
   Abba, Father.

Quoniam autem estis filii,
misit Deus Spiritum Filii sui
   in corda vestra
clamantem: Abba, Pater.

Prayer after Communion

Post communionem

May receiving this Sacrament,
   O Lord our God,
bring us health of body and soul,
as we confess your eternal holy
   Trinity and undivided Unity.
Through Christ our Lord.

Proficiat nobis ad salutem
   corporis et animæ,
Domine Deus noster,
   huius sacramenti susceptio,
et sempiternæ sanctæ Trinitatis
eiusdemque individuæ
   Unitatis confessio.
Per Christum Dominum nostrum

14 June

THE MOST HOLY BODY AND BLOOD OF CHRIST
(CORPUS CHRISTI)

If we look around, we realize that there are so many offers of food which do not come from the Lord and which appear to be more satisfying. Some nourish themselves with money, others with success and vanity, others with power and pride. But the food that truly nourishes and satiates us is only that which the Lord gives us! The food the Lord offers us is different from other food, and perhaps it doesn't seem as flavourful to us as certain other dishes the world offers us. So we dream of other dishes, like the Hebrews in the desert, who longed for the meat and onions they ate in Egypt, but forgot that they had eaten those meals at the table of slavery. Do I dream about eating flavourful foods, but in slavery? The Father tells us: "I fed you with manna, which you did not know". Let us recover this memory. And let us learn to recognize the false bread that deceives and corrupts, because it comes from selfishness, from self-reliance and from sin.

(Pope Francis

Solemnity

Entrance Antiphon Cf. Ps 80:17	Ant. ad introitum

HE fed them with the finest wheat
and satisfied them with honey
from the rock.

CIBAVIT eos ex adipe frumenti, et de petra melle saturavit eos.

The Gloria in excelsis (Glory to God in the highest) is said.

Collect	Collecta

O God, who in this
   wonderful Sacrament
have left us a memorial
   of your Passion,
grant us, we pray,
so to revere the sacred mysteries
   of your Body and Blood
that we may always experience
   in ourselves
the fruits of your redemption.
Who live and reign
   with God the Father
in the unity of the Holy Spirit,
   one God, for ever and ever.

Deus, qui nobis sub
   sacramento mirabili
passionis tuæ memoriam reliquisti,
tribue, quæsumus,
ita nos Corporis et Sanguinis tui
   sacra mysteria venerari,
ut redemptionis tuæ fructum
   in nobis iugiter sentiamus.
Qui vivis et regnas cum Deo Patre
in unitate Spiritus Sancti,
Deus, per omnia sæcula sæculorum.

FIRST READING

A reading from the book of Deuteronomy   8:2-3,14-16

He fed you with manna which neither you nor your fathers had known.

Moses said to the people: 'Remember how the Lord your God led you for forty years in the wilderness, to humble you, to test you and know your inmost heart – whether you would keep his commandments or not. He humbled you, he made you feel hunger, he fed you with manna which neither you nor your fathers had known, to make you understand that man does not live on bread alone but that man lives on everything that comes from the mouth of the Lord.

'Do not then forget the Lord your God who brought you out of the land of Egypt, out of the house of slavery: who guided you through this vast and dreadful wilderness, a land of fiery serpents, scorpions, thirst; who in this waterless place brought you water from the hardest rock; who in this wilderness fed you with manna that your fathers had not known.'

The word of the Lord.

Responsorial Psalm   Ps 147:12-15,19-20. R. v.12

R. **O praise the Lord, Jerusalem!**
   Or: **Alleluia!**

O praise the Lord, Jerusalem!
Zion, praise your God!
He has strengthened the bars of your gates,
he has blessed the children within you. R.

He established peace on your borders,
he feeds you with finest wheat.
He sends out his word to the earth
and swiftly runs his command. R.

He makes his word known to Jacob,
to Israel his laws and decrees.
He has not dealt thus with other nations;
He has not taught them his decrees. R.

SECOND READING

A reading from the first letter of St Paul to the Corinthians   10:16-17

That there is only one loaf means that, though there are many of us, we form a single body.

The blessing-cup that we bless is a communion with the blood of Christ, and the bread that we break is a communion with the body of Christ. The fact that there is only one loaf means that, though there are many of us, we form a single body because we all have a share in this one loaf.

The word of the Lord.

SEQUENCE

The Sequence may be said or sung in full, or using the shorter form indicated by the asterisked verses.

Sing forth, O Zion, sweetly sing
The praises of thy Shepherd-King,
    In hymns and canticles divine;
Dare all thou canst, thou hast no song
Worthy his praises to prolong,
    So far surpassing powers like thine.

Lauda Sion Salvatorem
Lauda ducem et pastorem
    In hymnis et canticis.
Quantum potes, tantum aude:
Quia major omni laude,
    Nec laudare sufficis.

Today no theme of common praise
Forms the sweet burden of thy lays –
    The living, life-dispensing food –
That food which at the sacred board
Unto the brethren twelve our Lord
    His parting legacy bestowed.

Laudis thema specialis,
Panis vivus et vitalis,
    Hodie proponitur.
Quem in sacræ mensa cenæ,
Turbæ fratrum duodenæ
    Datum non ambigitur.

Then be the anthem clear and strong,
Thy fullest note, thy sweetest song,
    The very music of thy breast:
For now shines forth the day sublime
That brings remembrance of the time
    When Jesus first his table blessed.

Sit laus plena, sit sonora,
Sit iucunda, sit decora
    Mentis iubilatio.
Dies enim solemnis agitur,
In qua mensæ prima recolitur
    Huius institutio.

Within our new King's banquet-hall
They meet to keep the festival
    That closed the ancient paschal rite:
The old is by the new replaced;
The substance hath
    the shadows chased;
    And rising day dispels the night.

In hac mensa novi Regis,
Novum Pascha novæ legis,
    Phase vetus terminat.
Vetustatem novitas,
Umbram fugat veritas,
    Noctem lux eliminat.

Christ willed what He Himself
   had done
Should be renewed while time
   should run,
     in memory of His parting hour:
Thus, tutored in His school divine,
We consecrate the bread and wine;
     And lo – a Host of saving power.

Quod in cœna Christus gessit,
Faciendum hoc expressit
   In sui memoriam.
Docti sacris institutis,
Panem, vinum, in salutis
   Consecramus hostiam.

This faith to Christian men is given –
Bread is made flesh by words
   from heaven:
     Into his Blood the wine is turned:
What though it baffles
   nature's powers
Of sense and sight? This faith of ours
     Proves more than nature
     e'er discerned.

Dogma datur Christianis,
Quod in carnem transit panis,
   Et vinum in sanguinem.
Quod non capis, quod non vides,
Animosa firmat fides,
   Præter rerum ordinem.

Concealed beneath the two-fold sign
Meet symbols of the gifts divine,
   There lie the mysteries adored:
The living body is our food;
Our drink the ever precious blood;
   In each, one undivided Lord.

Sub diversis speciebus,
Signis tantum, et non rebus,
   Latent res eximiæ.
Caro cibus, sanguis potus:
Manet tamen Christus totus,
   Sub utraque specie.

Not he that eateth it divides
The sacred food, which whole abides
   Unbroken still, nor knows decay;
Be one, or be a thousand fed,
They eat alike the Living Bread
   Which, still received,
   ne'er wastes away.

A sumente non concisus,
Non confractus, non divisus:
   Integer accipitur.
Sumit unus, sumunt mille:
Quantum isti, tantum ille:
   Nec sumptus consumitur.

The good, the guilty share therein,
With sure increase of grace or sin,
   The ghostly life, or ghostly death:
Death to the guilty; to the good
Immortal life. See how one food
   Man's joy or woe accomplisheth.

Sumunt boni, sumunt mali:
Sorte tamen inæquali,
   Vitæ vel interitus.
Mors est malis, vita bonis:
Vide paris sumptionis
   Quam sit dispar exitus.

We break the Sacrament; but bold
And firm thy faith shall keep its hold;
Deem not the whole doth
　　more enfold
　　Than in the fractured part resides:
Deem not that Christ doth broken lie;
'Tis but the sign that meets the eye;
The hidden deep reality
　　In all its fulness still abides.

*Behold the bread of angels, sent
For pilgrims in their banishment,
The bread for God's true
　　children meant,
　　That may not unto dogs be given:
Oft in the olden types foreshadowed;
In Isaac on the altar bowed,
And in the ancient paschal food,
　　And in the manna sent
　　from heaven.

*Come then, good shepherd,
　　bread divine,
Still show to us Thy mercy sign;
Oh, feed us still, still keep us Thine;
So may we see Thy glories shine
　　In fields of immortality;

*O Thou, the wisest, mightiest, best,
Our present food, our future rest,
Come, make us each Thy
　　chosen guest,
Coheirs of Thine, and comrades blest
　　With saints whose dwelling
　　is with Thee.
Amen. Alleluia.

Fracto demum Sacramento,
Ne vacilles, sed memento,
Tantum esse sub fragmento,
　　Quantum toto tegitur.
Nulla rei fit scissura:
Signi tantum fit fractura:
Qua nec status nec statura
　　Signati minuitur.

*Ecce panis Angelorum,
Factus cibus viatorum:
Vere panis filiorum,
　　Non mittendus canibus.
In figuris præsignatur,
Cum Isaac immolatur:
Agnus paschæ deputatur
　　Datur manna patribus.

*Bone pastor, panis vere,
Iesu, nostri miserere:
Tu nos pasce, nos tuere:
Tu nos bona fac videre
　　In terra viventium.

*Tu, qui cuncta scis et vales:
Qui nos pascis hic mortales:
Tuos ibi commensales,
Cohæredes et sodales,
　　Fac sanctorum civium.
Amen. Alleluia.

Gospel Acclamation   Jn 6:51

R. **Alleluia, alleluia!**

I am the living bread which has come down from heaven, says the Lord.
Anyone who eats this bread will live for ever.

R. **Alleluia**

GOSPEL

A reading from the holy Gospel according to John   6:51-58

My flesh is real food and my blood is real drink.

Jesus said to the Jews:

'I am the living bread which has come down from heaven.
Anyone who eats this bread will live for ever;
and the bread that I shall give
is my flesh, for the life of the world.'

Then the Jews started arguing with one another: 'How can this man
give us his flesh to eat?' they said. Jesus replied:

'I tell you most solemnly,
if you do not eat the flesh of the Son of Man
and drink his blood,
you will not have life in you.
Anyone who does eat my flesh and drink my blood
has eternal life,
and I shall raise him up on the last day.
For my flesh is real food
and my blood is real drink.
He who eats my flesh and drinks my blood
lives in me
and I live in him.
As I, who am sent by the living Father,
myself draw life from the Father,
so whoever eats me will draw life from me.
This is the bread come down from heaven,
not like the bread our ancestors ate:
they are dead,
but anyone who eats this bread will live for ever.'

The Gospel of the Lord.

The Creed is said.

Prayer over the Offerings | Super oblata

Grant your Church, O Lord,
     we pray,
the gifts of unity and peace,
whose signs are to be seen in mystery
in the offerings we here present.
Through Christ our Lord.

Ecclesiæ tuæ, quæsumus, Domine,
unitatis et pacis propitius
     dona concede,
quæ sub oblatis muneribus
     mystice designantur.
Per Christum Dominum nostrum.

Preface of the Holy Eucharist I or II, pp.68-71.

Communion Antiphon   Jn 6:57 | Ant. ad communionem

Whoever eats my flesh
     and drinks my blood
remains in me and I in him,
     says the Lord.

Qui manducat meam carnem
     et bibit meum sanguinem,
in me manet et ego in eo,
     dicit Dominus.

Prayer after Communion | Post communionem

Grant, O Lord, we pray,
that we may delight for all eternity
in that share in your divine life,
which is foreshadowed
     in the present age
by our reception of your precious
     Body and Blood.
Who live and reign for ever and ever.

Fac nos, quæsumus, Domine,
divinitatis tuæ sempiterna
     fruitione repleri,
quam pretiosi Corporis
     et Sanguinis tui
temporalis perceptio præfigurat.
Qui vivis et regnas
     in sæcula sæculorum.

It is desirable that a procession take place after the Mass in which the Host to be carried in the procession is consecrated. However, nothing prohibits a procession from taking place even after a public and lengthy period of adoration following the Mass. If a procession takes place after Mass, when the Communion of the faithful is over, the monstrance in which the consecrated host has been placed is set on the altar. When the Prayer after Communion has been said, the Concluding Rites are omitted and the procession forms.

19 June

THE MOST SACRED HEART OF JESUS

Jesus remains faithful, he never betrays us: even when we were wrong, he always waits for us to forgive us: he is the face of the merciful Father. This love, this steadfastness of the Lord manifests the humility of his heart: Jesus did not come to conquer men like the kings and the powerful of this world, but he came to offer love with gentleness and humility. This is how he defined himself: "learn from me; for I am gentle and lowly in heart". And the significance of the feast of the Sacred Heart of Jesus, which we are celebrating today, is to discover ever more and to let ourselves be enfolded by the humble faithfulness and the gentleness of Christ's love, revelation of the Father's mercy.

(Pope Francis)

Solemnity

Entrance Antiphon Ps 32:11,19	Ant. ad introitum

THE designs of his Heart
are from age to age,
to rescue their souls from death,
and to keep them alive in famine.

COGITATIONES Cordis eius in
generatione et generationem,
ut eruat a morte animas eorum
et alat eos in fame.

The Gloria in excelsis (Glory to God in the highest) is said.

Collect	Collecta

Grant, we pray, almighty God,
that we, who glory in the Heart
   of your beloved Son
and recall the wonders of his
   love for us,
may be made worthy to receive
an overflowing measure of grace
from that fount of heavenly gifts.

Concede, quæsumus,
   omnipotens Deus,
ut qui, dilecti Filii tui
   Corde gloriantes,
eius præcipua in nos beneficia
   recolimus caritatis,
de illo donorum fonte cælesti
supereffluentem gratiam
   mereamur accipere.

Through our Lord Jesus Christ,
  your Son,
who lives and reigns with you in the
  unity of the Holy Spirit,
one God, for ever and ever.

Or:

O God, who in the Heart of your Son,
wounded by our sins,
bestow on us in mercy
the boundless treasures of your love,
grant, we pray,
that, in paying him the homage
  of our devotion
we may also offer
  worthy reparation.
Through our Lord Jesus Christ,
  your Son,
who lives and reigns with you
  in the unity of the Holy Spirit,
one God, for ever and ever.

Per Dominum nostrum Iesum
  Christum Filium tuum,
qui tecum vivit et regnat in unitate
  Spiritus Sancti, Deus,
per omnia sæcula sæculorum.

Vel:

Deus, qui nobis in Corde Filii tui,
nostris vulnerato peccatis,
infinitos dilectionis thesauros
misericorditer largiri dignaris,
concede, quæsumus,
ut, illi devotum pietatis nostræ
  præstantes obsequium,
dignæ quoque satisfactionis
  exhibeamus officium.
Per Dominum nostrum Iesum
  Christum Filium tuum,
qui tecum vivit et regnat
  in unitate Spiritus Sancti,
Deus, per omnia sæcula sæculorum.

FIRST READING

A reading from the book of Deuteronomy   7:6-11

The Lord set his heart on you and chose you.

Moses said to the people: 'You are a people consecrated to the Lord your God; it is you that the Lord our God has chosen to be his very own people out of all the peoples on the earth.

'If the Lord set his heart on you and chose you, it was not because you outnumbered other peoples: you were the least of all peoples. It was for love of you and to keep the oath he swore to your fathers that the Lord brought you out with his mighty hand and redeemed you from the house of slavery, from the power of Pharaoh king of Egypt. Know then that the Lord your God is God indeed, the faithful God who is true to his covenant and his graciousness for a thousand generations towards those who love him and keep his commandments, but who punishes in their own persons those that hate him; he makes him work out his punishment in person.

You are therefore to keep and observe the commandments and statutes and ordinances that I lay down for you today.'

The word of the Lord.

Responsorial Psalm   Ps 102:1-4,6-8,10. R. v.17

R. **The love of the Lord is everlasting**
   upon those who hold him in fear.

My soul, give thanks to the Lord,
all my being, bless his holy name.
My soul, give thanks to the Lord
and never forget all his blessings. R.

It is he who forgives all your guilt,
who heals every one of your ills,
who redeems your life from the grave,
who crowns you with love and compassion. R.

The Lord does deeds of justice,
gives judgment for all who are oppressed.
He made known his ways to Moses
and his deeds to Israel's sons. R.

The Lord is compassion and love,
slow to anger and rich in mercy.
He does not treat us according to our sins
nor repay us according to our faults. R.

SECOND READING

A reading from the first letter of St John   4:7-16

Love comes from God.

My dear people,
let us love one another
since love comes from God
and everyone who loves is begotten by God and knows God.
Anyone who fails to love can never have known God,
because God is love.
God's love for us was revealed
when God sent into the world his only Son
so that we could have life through him;
this is the love I mean:

not our love for God,
but God's love for us when he sent his Son
to be the sacrifice that takes our sins away.
My dear people,
since God has loved us so much,
we too should love one another.
No one has ever seen God;
but as long as we love one another
God will live in us
and his love will be complete in us.
We can know that we are living in him
and he is living in us
because he lets us share his Spirit.
We ourselves saw and we testify
that the Father sent his Son
as saviour of the world.
If anyone acknowledges that Jesus is the Son of God,
God lives in him, and he in God.
We ourselves have known and put our faith in
God's love towards ourselves.
God is love
and anyone who lives in love lives in God,
and God lives in him.

   The word of the Lord.

Gospel Acclamation   Mt 11:29

R. **Alleluia, alleluia!**
Shoulder my yoke and learn from me,
for I am gentle and humble in heart.
R. **Alleluia!**

GOSPEL

A reading from the holy Gospel according to Matthew   11:25-30

I am gentle and humble in heart.

Jesus exclaimed, 'I bless you, Father, Lord of heaven and of earth, for hiding these things from the learned and the clever and revealing them to mere children. Yes, Father, for that is what it pleased you to do. Everything has been entrusted to me by my Father; and no one knows the Son except the Father, just as no one knows the Father except the Son and those to whom the Son chooses to reveal him.

'Come to me, all you who labour and are overburdened, and I will give you rest. Shoulder my yoke and learn from me, for I am gentle and humble in heart, and you will find rest for your souls. Yes, my yoke is easy and my burden light.'

The Gospel of the Lord.

The Creed is said.

Prayer over the Offerings

Look, O Lord, we pray,
   on the surpassing charity
in the Heart of your beloved Son,
that what we offer may be a gift
   acceptable to you
and an expiation of our offences.
Through Christ our Lord.

Super oblata

Respice, quæsumus, Domine,
ad ineffabilem Cordis dilecti Filii
   tui caritatem,
ut quod offerimus sit tibi
   munus acceptum
et nostrorum expiatio delictorum.
Per Christum Dominum nostrum.

Preface: The boundless charity of Christ.

Præfatio: De immense caritate Christi.

It is truly right and just,
   our duty and our salvation,
always and everywhere
   to give you thanks,
Lord, holy Father,
   almighty and eternal God,
through Christ our Lord.

Vere dignum et iustum est,
   æquum et salutare,
nos tibi semper et ubique
   gratias agere:
Domine, sancte Pater,
   omnipotens æterne Deus:
per Christum Dominum nostrum:

For raised up high on the Cross,
he gave himself up for us
   with a wonderful love
and poured out blood and water
   from his pierced side,
the wellspring of the Church's
   Sacraments,
so that, won over to the open heart
   of the Saviour,
all might draw water joyfully
   from the springs of salvation.

Qui, mira caritate, exaltatus in cruce,
pro nobis tradidit semetipsum,
atque de transfixo latere sanguinem
   fudit et aquam,
ex quo manarent Ecclesiæ
   sacramenta,
ut omnes, ad Cor apertum
   Salvatoris attracti,
iugiter haurirent e fontibus salutis
   in gaudio.

And so, with all the Angels
   and Saints,
we praise you, as without end
   we acclaim:

Holy, Holy, Holy Lord God of hosts...

Et ideo, cum Sanctis
   et Angelis universis,
te collaudamus, sine fine dicentes:

Sanctus, Sanctus, Sanctus . . .

Communion Antiphon Cf. Jn 7:37-38

Ant. ad communionem

Thus says the Lord:
Let whoever is thirsty come to me
   and drink.
Streams of living water will flow
from within the one who believes
   in me.

Dicit Dominus:
Si quis sitit, veniat ad me et bibat.
Qui credit in me, flumina de ventre
   eius fluent aquæ vivæ.

Or: Jn 19:34

Vel:

One of the soldiers opened his side
   with a lance,
and at once there came forth blood
   and water.

Unus militum lancea
   latus eius aperuit,
et continuo exivit sanguis et aqua.

Prayer after Communion

Post communionem

May this sacrament of charity,
   O Lord,
make us fervent with the fire
   of holy love,
so that, drawn always to your Son,
we may learn to see him in
   our neighbour.
Through Christ our Lord.

Sacramentum caritatis, Domine,
sancta nos faciat dilectione fervere,
qua, ad Filium tuum
   semper attracti,
ipsum in fratribus
   agnoscere discamus.
Qui vivit et regnat
   in sæcula sæculorum.

21 June

TWELFTH SUNDAY IN ORDINARY TIME

Entrance Antiphon   Cf. Ps 27:8-9

THE Lord is the strength
of his people,
a saving refuge for the one
    he has anointed.
Save your people, Lord,
    and bless your heritage,
and govern them for ever.

Ant. ad introitum

DOMINUS fortitudo plebis suæ,
et protector salutarium Christi
    sui est.
Salvum fac populum
    tuum, Domine,
et benedic hereditati tuæ,
et rege eos usque in sæculum.

Collect

Grant, O Lord,
that we may always revere and love
    your holy name,
for you never deprive
    of your guidance
those you set firm
    on the foundation of your love.
Through our Lord Jesus Christ,
    your Son,
who lives and reigns with you
    in the unity of the Holy Spirit,
one God, for ever and ever.

Collecta

Sancti nominis tui, Domine,
timorem pariter et amorem fac nos
    habere perpetuum,
quia numquam tua
    gubernatione destituis,
quos in soliditate tuæ
    dilectionis instituis.
Per Dominum nostrum Iesum
    Christum Filium tuum,
qui tecum vivit et regnat
    in unitate Spiritus Sancti,
Deus, per omnia sæcula sæculorum.

FIRST READING

A reading from the prophet Jeremiah   20:10-13

He has delivered the soul of the needy from the hands of evil men.

Jeremiah said:
    I hear so many disparaging me,
    '"Terror from every side!"
    Denounce him! Let us denounce him!'
    All those who used to be my friends
    watched for my downfall,
    'Perhaps he will be seduced into error.
    Then we will master him
    and take our revenge!'

But the Lord is at my side, a mighty hero;
my opponents will stumble, mastered,
confounded by their failure;
everlasting, unforgettable disgrace will be theirs.
But you, Lord of Hosts, you who probe with justice,
who scrutinise the loins and heart,
let me see the vengeance you will take on them,
for I have committed my cause to you.
Sing to the Lord,
praise the Lord,
for he has delivered the soul of the needy
from the hands of evil men.

The word of the Lord.

Responsional Psalm   Ps 68:8-10,14,17,33-35. R. v.14

R. **In your great love, answer me, O God.**

It is for you that I suffer taunts,
that shame covers my face,
that I have become a stranger to my brothers,
an alien to my own mother's sons.
I burn with zeal for your house
and taunts against you fall on me. R.

This is my prayer to you,
my prayer for your favour.
In your great love, answer me, O God,
with your help that never fails:
Lord, answer, for your love is kind;
in your compassion, turn towards me. R.

The poor when they see it will be glad
and God-seeking hearts will revive;
for the Lord listens to the needy
and does not spurn his servants in their chains.
Let the heavens and the earth give him praise,
the sea and all its living creatures. R.

SECOND READING

A reading from the letter of St Paul to the Romans   5:12-15

The gift considerably outweighed the fall.

Sin entered the world through one man, and through sin death, and thus death has spread through the whole human race because everyone has sinned. Sin existed in the world long before the Law was given. There was no law and so no one could be accused of the sin of 'law-breaking', yet death reigned over all from Adam to Moses, even though their sin, unlike that of Adam, was not a matter of breaking a law.

Adam prefigured the One to come, but the gift itself considerably outweighed the fall. If it is certain that through one man's fall so many died, it is even more certain that divine grace, coming through the one man, Jesus Christ, came to so many as an abundant free gift.

The word of the Lord.

Gospel Acclamation   Jn 1:14,12

R. **Alleluia, alleluia!**
The Word was made flesh and lived among us;
to all who did accept him
he gave power to become children of God.
R. **Alleluia!**

Or: Jn 15:26,27

R. **Alleluia, alleluia!**
The Spirit of truth will be my witness;
and you too will be my witnesses.
R. **Alleluia!**

GOSPEL

A reading from the holy Gospel according to Matthew   10:26-33

Do not be afraid of those who kill the body.

Jesus instructed the Twelve as follows: 'Do not be afraid. For everything that is now covered will be uncovered, and everything now hidden will be made clear. What I say to you in the dark, tell in the daylight; what you hear in whispers, proclaim from the house-tops.

'Do not be afraid of those who kill the body but cannot kill the soul; fear him rather who can destroy both body and soul in hell. Can you not buy two sparrows for a penny? And yet not one falls to the ground without your Father knowing. Why, every hair on your head has been counted. So there is no need to be afraid; you are worth more than hundreds of sparrows.

'So if anyone declares himself for me in the presence of men, I will declare myself for him in the presence of my Father in heaven. But the one who disowns me in the presence of men, I will disown in the presence of my Father in heaven.'

The Gospel of the Lord.

Prayer over the Offerings
Receive, O Lord, the sacrifice
    of conciliation and praise
and grant that,
    cleansed by its action,
we may make offering of a heart
    pleasing to you.
Through Christ our Lord.

Super oblata
Suscipe, Domine,
    sacrificium placationis et laudis,
et præsta, ut,
    huius operatione mundati,
beneplacitum tibi nostræ mentis
    offeramus affectum.
Per Christum Dominum nostrum.

Preface of Sundays in Ordinary Time I-VIII, pp.60-67.

Communion Antiphon   Ps 144:15
The eyes of all look to you, Lord,
and you give them their food
    in due season.

Ant. ad communionem
Oculi omnium in te sperant,
    Domine,
et tu das illis escam in
    tempore opportuno.

Or: Jn 10:11,15
I am the Good Shepherd,
and I lay down my life for my sheep,
    says the Lord.

Vel:
Ego sum pastor bonus,
et animam meam pono pro ovibus
    meis, dicit Dominus.

Prayer after Communion
Renewed and nourished
by the Sacred Body and Precious
    Blood of your Son,
we ask of your mercy, O Lord,
that what we celebrate
    with constant devotion
may be our sure pledge
    of redemption.
Through Christ our Lord.

Post communionem
Sacri Corporis et Sanguinis pretiosi
    alimonia renovati,
quæsumus, Domine,
    clementiam tuam,
ut, quod gerimus
    devotione frequenti,
certa redemptione capiamus.
Per Christum Dominum nostrum.

24 June

THE NATIVITY OF SAINT JOHN THE BAPTIST

Today, the liturgy invites us to celebrate the Solemnity of the Birth of St John the Baptist, whose life was totally directed to Christ, as was that of Mary, Christ's Mother. John the Baptist was the forerunner, the "voice" sent to proclaim the Incarnate Word. Thus, commemorating his birth actually means celebrating Christ, the fulfilment of the promises of all the prophets, among whom the greatest was the Baptist, called to "prepare the way" for the Messiah. All the Gospels introduce the narrative of Jesus's public life with the account of his baptism by John in the River Jordan. When Jesus, after receiving baptism, emerged from the water, John saw the Spirit descending upon him in the form of a dove. It was then that he "knew" the full reality of Jesus of Nazareth and began to make him "known to Israel", pointing him out as the Son of God and Redeemer of man: "Behold, the Lamb of God, who takes away the sin of the world!"

(Pope Benedict XVI)

Solemnity

At the Vigil Mass

This Mass is used on the evening of 23 June, either before or after First Vespers (Evening Prayer I) of the Solemnity.

Entrance Antiphon Lk 1:15-14	Ant. ad introitum

HE will be great in the sight of the Lord
and will be filled
    with the Holy Spirit,
even from his mother's womb;
and many will rejoice at his birth.
	HIC erit magnus coram Domino,
	et Spiritu Sancto replebitur adhuc
	    ex utero matris suæ,
	et multi in nativitate
	    eius gaudebunt.

The Gloria in excelsis (Glory to God in the highest) is said.

Collect	Collecta

Grant, we pray, almighty God,
that your family may walk
    in the way of salvation
and, attentive to what Saint John
    the Precursor urged,
may come safely to the One
    he foretold,
our Lord Jesus Christ.
	Præsta, quæsumus,
	    omnipotens Deus,
	ut familia tua per viam
	    salutis incedat,
	et, beati Ioannis Præcursoris
	    hortamenta sectando,
	ad eum quem prædixit,
	    secura perveniat,

Who lives and reigns with you
   in the unity of the Holy Spirit,
one God, for ever and ever.

Dominum nostrum
   Iesum Christum.
Qui tecum vivit et regnat
   in unitate Spiritus Sancti,
Deus, per omnia sæcula sæculorum.

FIRST READING

A reading from the prophet Jeremiah   1:4-10

Before I formed you in the womb, I knew you.

In the days of Josiah, the word of the Lord was addressed to me, saying,

  'Before I formed you in the womb I knew you;
  before you came to birth I consecrated you;
  I have appointed you as prophet to the nations.'

I said, 'Ah, Lord, look, I do not know how to speak: I am a child!'

But the Lord replied,

  'Do not say, "I am a child."
  Go now to those to whom I send you
  and say whatever I command you.
  Do not be afraid of them,
  for I am with you to protect you –
  it is the Lord who speaks!'

Then the Lord put out his hand and touched my mouth and said to me:

  'There! I am putting my words into your mouth.
  Look, today I am setting you
  over nations and over kingdoms,
  to tear up and to knock down,
  to destroy and to overthrow,
  to build and to plant.'

  The word of the Lord.

Responsorial Psalm   Ps 70:1-6,15,17. R. v.6

R. **From my mother's womb you have been my help.**

  In you, O Lord, I take refuge;
  let me never be put to shame.
  In your justice rescue me, free me:
  pay heed to me and save me. R.

  Be a rock where I can take refuge,
  a mighty stronghold to save me;
  for you are my rock, my stronghold.
  Free me from the hand of the wicked. R.

It is you, O Lord, who are my hope,
my trust, O Lord, since my youth.
On you I have leaned from my birth,
from my mother's womb you have been my help. R.

My lips will tell of your justice
and day by day of your help.
O God, you have taught me from my youth
and I proclaim your wonders still. R.

SECOND READING

A reading from the first letter of St Peter   1:8-12

It was this salvation that the prophets were looking and searching so hard for.

You did not see Jesus Christ, yet you love him; and still without seeing
him, you are already filled with joy so glorious that it cannot be described,
because you believe; and you are sure of the end to which your faith looks
forward, that is, the salvation of your souls.

It was this salvation that the prophets were looking and searching so
hard for; their prophecies were about the grace which was to come to you.
The Spirit of Christ which was in them foretold the sufferings of Christ and
the glories that would come after them, and they tried to find out at what
time and in what circumstances all this was to be expected. It was revealed
to them that the news they brought of all the things which have now been
announced to you, by those who preached to you the Good News through
the Holy Spirit sent from heaven, was for you and not for themselves. Even
the angels long to catch a glimpse of these things.

The word of the Lord.

Gospel Acclamation   Cf. Jn 1:7; Lk 1:17

R. **Alleluia, alleluia!**
He came as a witness,
as a witness to speak for the light,
preparing for the Lord a people fit for him.
R. **Alleluia!**

GOSPEL

A reading from the holy Gospel according to Luke   1:5-17

She is to bear you a son and you must name him John.

In the days of King Herod of Judaea there lived a priest called Zechariah
who belonged to the Abijah section of the priesthood, and he had a wife,
Elizabeth by name, who was a descendant of Aaron. Both were worthy in

the sight of God, and scrupulously observed all the commandments and observances of the Lord. But they were childless: Elizabeth was barren and they were both getting on in years.

Now it was the turn of Zechariah's section to serve, and he was exercising his priestly office before God when it fell to him by lot, as the ritual custom was, to enter the Lord's sanctuary and burn incense there. And at the hour of incense the whole congregation was outside, praying.

Then there appeared to him the angel of the Lord, standing on the right of the altar of incense. The sight disturbed Zechariah and he was overcome with fear. But the angel said to him, 'Zechariah, do not be afraid, your prayer has been heard. Your wife Elizabeth is to bear you a son and you must name him John. He will be your joy and delight and many will rejoice at his birth, for he will be great in the sight of the Lord; he must drink no wine, no strong drink. Even from his mother's womb he will be filled with the Holy Spirit, and he will bring back many of the sons of Israel to the Lord their God. With the spirit and power of Elijah, he will go before him to turn the hearts of fathers towards their children and the disobedient back to the wisdom that the virtuous have, preparing for the Lord a people fit for him.'

The Gospel of the Lord.

The Creed is said.

Prayer over the Offerings	Super oblata
Look with favour, O Lord, upon the offerings made by your people on the Solemnity of Saint John the Baptist, and grant that what we celebrate in mystery we may follow with deeds of devoted service. Through Christ our Lord.	Munera populi tui, Domine, propitius intende, in beati Ioannis Baptistæ sollemnitate delata, et præsta, ut, quæ mysterio gerimus, debitæ servitutis actione sectemur. Per Christum Dominum nostrum.

Proper Preface, as in the following Mass, pp.358-359.

Communion Antiphon Lk 1:68	Ant. ad communionem
Blessed be the Lord, the God of Israel! He has visited his people and redeemed them.	Benedictus Dominus Deus Israel, quia visitavit et fecit redemptionem plebi suæ.

Prayer after Communion | Post communionem

May the marvellous prayer of Saint John the Baptist
accompany us who have eaten our fill
at this sacrificial feast, O Lord,
and, since Saint John proclaimed your Son
to be the Lamb who would take away our sins,
may he implore now for us your favour.
Through Christ our Lord.

Sacris dapibus satiatos,
beati Ioannis Baptistæ nos, Domine,
præclara comitetur oratio,
et, quem Agnum nostra ablaturum crimina nuntiavit,
ipsum Filium tuum poscat nobis fore placatum.
Qui vivit et regnat
in sæcula sæculorum.

At the Mass during the Day

Entrance Antiphon Jn 1:6-7; Lk 1:17 | Ant. ad introitum

A MAN was sent from God, whose name was John.
He came to testify to the light,
to prepare a people fit for the Lord.

F UIT homo missus a Deo, cui nomen erat Ioannes.
Hic venit, ut testimonium perhiberet de lumine,
parare Domino plebem perfectam.

The Gloria in excelsis (Glory to God in the highest) is said.

Collect | Collecta

O God, who raised up Saint John the Baptist
to make ready a nation fit for Christ the Lord,
give your people, we pray, the grace of spiritual joys
and direct the hearts of all the faithful
into the way of salvation and peace.
Through our Lord Jesus Christ, your Son,
who lives and reigns with you in the unity of the Holy Spirit,
one God, for ever and ever.

Deus, qui beatum Ioannem Baptistam suscitasti,
ut perfectam plebem Christo Domino præpararet,
da populis tuis spiritalium gratiam gaudiorum,
et omnium fidelium mentes dirige in viam salutis et pacis.
Per Dominum nostrum Iesum Christum Filium tuum,
qui tecum vivit et regnat in unitate Spiritus Sancti,
Deus, per omnia sæcula sæculorum.

FIRST READING

A reading from the prophet Isaiah   49:1-6

I will make you the light of the nations.

Islands, listen to me,
pay attention, remotest peoples.
The Lord called me before I was born,
from my mother's womb he pronounced my name.

He made my mouth a sharp sword,
and hid me in the shadow of his hand.
He made me into a sharpened arrow,
and concealed me in his quiver.

He said to me, 'You are my servant (Israel)
in whom I shall be glorified';
while I was thinking, 'I have toiled in vain,
I have exhausted myself for nothing';

and all the while my cause was with the Lord,
my reward with my God.
I was honoured in the eyes of the Lord,
my God was my strength.

And now the Lord has spoken,
he who formed me in the womb to be his servant,
to bring Jacob back to him,
to gather Israel to him:

'It is not enough for you to be my servant,
to restore the tribes of Jacob and bring back the survivors of Israel;
I will make you the light of the nations
so that my salvation may reach to the ends of the earth.'

The word of the Lord.

Responsorial Psalm   Ps 138:1-3,13-15. R. v.14

R. **I thank you for the wonder of my being.**

O Lord, you search me and you know me,
you know my resting and my rising,
you discern my purpose from afar.
You mark when I walk or lie down,
all my ways lie open to you. R.

For it was you who created my being,
knit me together in my mother's womb.

I thank you for the wonder of my being,
for the wonders of all your creation. R.

Already you knew my soul,
my body held no secret from you
when I was being fashioned in secret
and moulded in the depths of the earth. R.

SECOND READING

A reading from the Acts of the Apostles   13:22-26

Jesus, whose coming was heralded by John.

Paul said: 'God made David the king of our ancestors, of whom he
approved in these words, "I have elected David son of Jesse, a man after my
own heart, who will carry out my whole purpose." To keep his promise,
God has raised up for Israel one of David's descendants, Jesus, as Saviour,
whose coming was heralded by John when he proclaimed a baptism of
repentance for the whole people of Israel. Before John ended his career he
said, "I am not the one you imagine me to be; that one is coming after me
and I am not fit to undo his sandal."

'My brothers, sons of Abraham's race, and all you who fear God, this
message of salvation is meant for you.'

The word of the Lord.

Gospel Acclamation   Cf. Lk 1:76

R. **Alleluia, alleluia!**
As for you, little child, you shall be called
a prophet of God, the Most High.
You shall go ahead of the Lord
to prepare his ways before him.
R. **Alleluia!**

GOSPEL

A reading from the holy Gospel according to Luke   1:57-66,80

His name is John.

The time came for Elizabeth to have her child, and she gave birth to a son;
and when her neighbours and relations heard that the Lord had shown her
so great a kindness, they shared her joy.

Now on the eighth day they came to circumcise the child; they were
going to call him Zechariah after his father, but his mother spoke up. 'No,'
she said 'he is to be called John.' They said to her, 'But no one in your
family has that name', and made signs to his father to find out what he

wanted him called. The father asked for a writing-tablet and wrote, 'His name is John.' And they were all astonished. At that instant his power of speech returned and he spoke and praised God. All their neighbours were filled with awe and the whole affair was talked about throughout the hill country of Judaea. All those who heard of it treasured it in their hearts. 'What will this child turn out to be?' they wondered. And indeed the hand of the Lord was with him. Meanwhile, the child grew up and his spirit matured. And he lived out in the wilderness until the day he appeared openly to Israel.

The Gospel of the Lord.

The Creed is said.

Prayer over the Offerings

We place these offerings on
　　your altar, O Lord,
to celebrate with fitting honour
　　the nativity of him
who both foretold the coming
　　of the world's Saviour
and pointed him out
　　when he came.
Who lives and reigns
　　for ever and ever.

Super oblata

Tua, Domine, muneribus
　　altaria cumulamus,
illius nativitatem honore
　　debito celebrantes,
qui Salvatorem mundi
　　et cecinit affuturum,
et adesse monstravit.
Qui vivit et regnat
　　in sæcula sæculorum.

Preface: The mission of the Precursor

It is truly right and just,
　　our duty and our salvation,
always and everywhere
　　to give you thanks,
Lord, holy Father,
　　almighty and eternal God,
through Christ our Lord.

In his Precursor, Saint John
　　the Baptist,
we praise your great glory,
for you consecrated him
　　for a singular honour
among those born of women.

Præfatio: De missione Præcursoris

Vere dignum et iustum est,
　　æquum et salutare,
nos tibi semper et ubique
　　gratias agere:
Domine, sancte Pater,
　　omnipotens æterne Deus:
per Christum Dominum nostrum.

In cuius Præcursore beato Ioanne
tuam magnificentiam collaudamus,
quem inter natos mulierum honore
　　præcipuo consecrasti.

His birth brought great rejoicing;
even in the womb he leapt for joy
at the coming of human salvation.
He alone of all the prophets
pointed out the Lamb of redemption.

And to make holy the flowing waters,
he baptised the very author
    of Baptism
and was privileged to bear him
    supreme witness
by the shedding of his blood.

And so, with the Powers of heaven,
we worship you constantly on earth,
and before your majesty
without end we acclaim:

Holy, Holy, Holy Lord God of hosts...

Qui cum nascendo multa
    gaudia præstitisset,
et nondum editus exsultasset
    ad humanæ salutis adventum,
ipse solus omnium prophetarum
Agnum redemptionis ostendit.

Sed et sanctificandis etiam
    aquæ fluentis
ipsum baptismatis lavit auctorem,
et meruit fuso sanguine supremum
illi testimonium exhibere.

Et ideo, cum cælorum virtutibus,
in terris te iugiter prædicamus,
maiestati tuæ sine fine clamantes:

Sanctus, Sanctus, Sanctus. . .

Communion Antiphon Cf. Lk 1:78

Ant. ad communionem

Through the tender mercy
    of our God,
the Dawn from on high will visit us.

Per viscera misericordiæ Dei nostri,
visitavit nos Oriens ex alto.

Prayer after Communion

Post communionem

Having feasted at the banquet
    of the heavenly Lamb,
we pray, O Lord,
that, finding joy in the nativity
    of Saint John the Baptist,
your Church may know as
    the author of her rebirth
the Christ whose coming
    John foretold.
Who lives and reigns
    for ever and ever.

Cælestis Agni convivio refecti,
quæsumus, Domine,
    ut Ecclesia tua,
sumens de beati Ioannis Baptistæ
    generatione lætitiam,
quem ille prænuntiavit venturum,
suæ regenerationis
    cognoscat auctorem.
Qui vivit et regnat
    in sæcula sæculorum.

In England, Wales & Scotland

28 June

In Ireland

29 June

SAINTS PETER AND PAUL, APOSTLES

"Now I am sure that the Lord has sent his angel and rescued me from the hand of Herod" ... Peter realized that the Lord had freed him from fear and from chains. Yes, the Lord liberates us from every fear and from all that enslaves us, so that we can be truly free... What are we afraid of? And if we are afraid, what forms of refuge do we seek, to find security? Do we look for support from those who wield worldly power? Or do we let ourselves be deceived by the pride which seeks gratification and recognition, thinking that these will offer us security?... The witness of the Apostle Peter reminds us that our true refuge is trust in God. Trust in God banishes all fear and sets us free from every form of slavery and all worldly temptation.

(Pope Francis)

Solemnity

At the Vigil Mass

This Mass is used on the evening of 27/28 June, either before or after First Vespers (Evening Prayer I) of the Solemnity.

Entrance Antiphon	Ant. ad introitum
Peter the Apostle, and Paul the teacher of the Gentiles, these have taught us your law, O Lord.	Petrus apostolus et Paulus doctor gentium, ipsi nos docuerunt legem tuam, Domine.

The Gloria in excelsis (Glory to God in the highest) is said.

Collect	Collecta

Grant, we pray, O Lord our God,
that we may be sustained
by the intercession of the blessed
   Apostles Peter and Paul,
that, as through them you gave
   your Church
the foundations of her
   heavenly office,
so through them you may help
   her to eternal salvation.
Through our Lord Jesus Christ,
   your Son,
who lives and reigns with you
   in the unity of the Holy Spirit,
one God, for ever and ever.
	Da nobis, quæsumus, Domine
	   Deus noster,
	beatorum apostolorum Petri
	   et Pauli
	intercessionibus sublevari,
	ut, per quos Ecclesiæ tuæ
	superni muneris
	   rudimenta donasti,
	per eos subsidia perpetuæ
	   salutis impendas.
	Per Dominum nostrum Iesum
	   Christum Filium tuum,
	qui tecum vivit et regnat
	   in unitate Spiritus Sancti,
	Deus, per omnia sæcula sæculorum.

FIRST READING

A reading from the Acts of the Apostles

3:1-10

I will give you what I have: in the name of Jesus, walk!

Once, when Peter and John were going up to the Temple for the prayers at the ninth hour, it happened that there was a man being carried past. He was a cripple from birth; and they used to put him down every day near the Temple entrance called the Beautiful Gate so that he could beg from the people going in. When this man saw Peter and John on their way into the Temple he begged from them. Both Peter and John looked straight at him and said, 'Look at us.' He turned to them expectantly, hoping to get something from them, but Peter said, 'I have neither silver nor gold, but I will give you what I have: in the name of Jesus Christ the Nazarene, walk!' Peter then took him by the hand and helped him to stand up. Instantly his feet and ankles became firm, he jumped up, stood, and began to walk, and he went with them into the Temple, walking and jumping and praising God. Everyone could see him walking and praising God, and they recognised him as the man who used to sit begging at the Beautiful Gate of the Temple. They were all astonished and unable to explain what had happened to him.

The word of the Lord.

Responsorial Psalm   Ps 18:2-5. R. v.5

R. **Their word goes forth through all the earth.**

The heavens proclaim the glory of God
and the firmament shows forth the work of his hands.
Day unto day takes up the story
and night unto night makes known the message. R.

No speech, no word, no voice is heard
yet their span extends through all the earth,
their words to the utmost bounds of the world. R.

SECOND READING

A reading from the letter of St Paul to the Galatians   1:11-20

God specially chose me while I was still in my mother's womb.

The Good News I preached is not a human message that I was given by
men, it is something I learnt only through a revelation of Jesus Christ. You
must have heard of my career as a practising Jew, how merciless I was in
persecuting the Church of God, how much damage I did to it, how I stood
out among other Jews of my generation, and how enthusiastic I was for the
traditions of my ancestors.

Then God, who had specially chosen me while I was still in my mother's
womb, called me through his grace and chose to reveal his Son in me, so
that I might preach the Good News about him to the pagans. I did not
stop to discuss this with any human being, nor did I go up to Jerusalem to
see those who were already apostles before me, but I went off to Arabia at
once and later went straight back from there to Damascus. Even when after
three years I went up to Jerusalem to visit Cephas and stayed with him for
fifteen days, I did not see any of the other apostles; I only saw James, the
brother of the Lord, and I swear before God that what I have just written is
the literal truth.

The word of the Lord.

Gospel Acclamation   Jn 21:17

R. **Alleluia, alleluia!**
Lord, you know everything;
you know I love you.
R. **Alleluia!**

GOSPEL

A reading from the holy Gospel according to John   21:15-19

Feed my lambs, feed my sheep.

After Jesus had shown himself to his disciples and eaten with them, he said to Simon Peter, 'Simon son of John, do you love me more than these others do?' He answered, 'Yes Lord, you know I love you.' Jesus said to him, 'Feed my lambs.' A second time he said to him, 'Simon son of John, do you love me?' He replied, 'Yes, Lord, you know I love you.' Jesus said to him, 'Look after my sheep.' Then he said to him a third time, 'Simon son of John, do you love me?' Peter was upset that he asked him the third time, 'Do you love me?' and said, 'Lord, you know everything; you know I love you.' Jesus said to him, 'Feed my sheep.

> 'I tell you most solemnly,
> when you were young
> you put on your own belt
> and walked where you liked;
> but when you grow old
> you will stretch out your hands,
> and somebody else will put a belt round you
> and take you where you would rather not go.'

In these words he indicated the kind of death by which Peter would give glory to God. After this he said, 'Follow me.'

The Gospel of the Lord.

The Creed is said.

Prayer over the Offerings	Super oblata
We bring offerings to your altar, O Lord, as we glory in the solemn feast of the blessed Apostles Peter and Paul, so that the more we doubt our own merits, the more we may rejoice that we are to be saved by your loving kindness. Through Christ our Lord.	Munera, Domine, tuis altaribus adhibemus, de beatorum apostolorum Petri et Pauli sollemnitatibus gloriantes, ut quantum sumus de nostro merito formidantes, tantum de tua benignitate gloriemur salvandi. Per Christum Dominum nostrum.

Proper Preface, as in the following Mass, p.368.

Communion Antiphon   Cf. Jn 21:15,17

Simon, Son of John,
do you love me more than these?
Lord, you know everything;
you know that I love you.

Ant. ad communionem

Simon Ioannis, diligis me plus his?
Domine, tu omnia nosti;
tu scis, Domine, quia amo te.

Prayer after Communion

By this heavenly Sacrament,
O Lord, we pray,
strengthen your faithful,
whom you have enlightened
with the teaching of the Apostles.
Through Christ our Lord.

Post communionem

Cælestibus sacramentis,
quæsumus, Domine,
fideles tuos corrobora,
quos Apostolorum
doctrina illuminasti.
Per Christum Dominum nostrum.

A formula of Solemn Blessing, pp.144-147, may be used.

At the Mass during the Day

Entrance Antiphon

THESE are the ones who,
living in the flesh,
planted the Church with their blood;
they drank the chalice of the Lord
and became the friends of God.

Ant. ad introitum

ISTI sunt qui, viventes in carne,
plantaverunt Ecclesiam
sanguine suo:
calicem Domini biberunt,
et amici Dei facti sunt.

The Gloria in excelsis (Glory to God in the highest) is said.

Collect

O God, who on the Solemnity
of the Apostles Peter and Paul
give us the noble and holy joy
of this day,
grant, we pray, that your Church
may in all things follow the teaching
of those through whom she received
the beginnings of right religion.
Through our Lord Jesus Christ,
your Son,
who lives and reigns with you
in the unity of the Holy Spirit,
one God, for ever and ever.

Collecta

Deus, qui huius diei venerandam
sanctamque lætitiam
in apostolorum Petri et Pauli
sollemnitate tribuisti,
da Ecclesiæ tuæ eorum in omnibus
sequi præceptum,
per quos religionis sumpsit exordium.

Per Dominum nostrum Iesum
Christum Filium tuum,
qui tecum vivit et regnat
in unitate Spiritus Sancti,
Deus, per omnia sæcula sæculorum.

FIRST READING

A reading from the Acts of the Apostles   12:1-11

Now I know the Lord really did save me from Herod.

King Herod started persecuting certain members of the Church. He
beheaded James the brother of John, and when he saw that this pleased
the Jews he decided to arrest Peter as well. This was during the days of
Unleavened Bread, and he put Peter in prison, assigning four squads of
four soldiers each to guard him in turns. Herod meant to try Peter in public
after the end of Passover week. All the time Peter was under guard the
Church prayed to God for him unremittingly.

On the night before Herod was to try him, Peter was sleeping between
two soldiers, fastened with double chains, while guards kept watch at the
main entrance to the prison. Then suddenly the angel of the Lord stood
there, and the cell was filled with light. He tapped Peter on the side and
woke him. 'Get up!' he said 'Hurry!' – and the chains fell from his hands.
The angel then said, 'Put on your belt and sandals.' After he had done this,
the angel next said, 'Wrap your cloak round you and follow me.' Peter
followed him, but had no idea that what the angel did was all happening
in reality; he thought he was seeing a vision. They passed through two
guard posts one after the other, and reached the iron gate leading to the
city. This opened of its own accord; they went through it and had walked
the whole length of one street when suddenly the angel left him. It was
only then that Peter came to himself. 'Now I know it is all true,' he said.
'The Lord really did send his angel and has saved me from Herod and from
all that the Jewish people were so certain would happen to me.'

The word of the Lord.

Responsorial Psalm   Ps 33:2-9. R. v.5. Alt. R. v.8

R. **From all my terrors the Lord set me free.**
   Or: **The angel of the Lord rescues those who revere him.**

   I will bless the Lord at all times
   his praise always on my lips;
   in the Lord my soul shall make its boast.
   The humble shall hear and be glad. R.

   Glorify the Lord with me.
   Together let us praise his name.
   I sought the Lord and he answered me;
   from all my terrors he set me free. R.

Look towards him and be radiant;
let your faces not be abashed.
This poor man called; the Lord heard him
and rescued him from all his distress. R.

The angel of the Lord is encamped
around those who revere him, to rescue them.
Taste and see that the Lord is good.
He is happy who seeks refuge in him. R.

R. **From all my terrors the Lord set me free.**
  Or: **The angel of the Lord rescues those who revere him.**

SECOND READING

A reading from the second letter of St Paul to Timothy   4:6-8,17-18

All there is to come now is the crown of righteousness reserved for me.

My life is already being poured away as a libation, and the time has come for me to be gone. I have fought the good fight to the end; I have run the race to the finish; I have kept the faith; all there is to come now is the crown of righteousness reserved for me, which the Lord, the righteous judge, will give to me on that Day; and not only to me but to all those who have longed for his Appearing.

The Lord stood by me and gave me power, so that through me the whole message might be proclaimed for all the pagans to hear; and so I was rescued from the lion's mouth. The Lord will rescue me from all evil attempts on me, and bring me safely to his heavenly kingdom. To him be glory for ever and ever. Amen.

The word of the Lord.

Gospel Acclamation   Mt 16:18

R. **Alleluia, alleluia!**
You are Peter and on this rock I will build my Church.
And the gates of the underworld can never hold out against it.
R. **Alleluia!**

GOSPEL

A reading from the holy Gospel according to Matthew   16:13-19

You are Peter, and I will give you the keys of the kingdom of heaven.

When Jesus came to the region of Caesarea Philippi he put this question to his disciples, 'Who do people say the Son of Man is?' And they said, 'Some say he is John the Baptist, some Elijah, and others Jeremiah or one of the prophets.' 'But you,' he said 'who do you say I am?' Then Simon Peter spoke up, 'You are the Christ,' he said 'the Son of the living God.' Jesus replied, 'Simon son of Jonah, you are a happy man! Because it was not flesh and blood that revealed this to you but my Father in heaven. So I now say to you: You are Peter and on this rock I will build my Church. And the gates of the underworld can never hold out against it. I will give you the keys of the kingdom of heaven: whatever you bind on earth shall be considered bound in heaven; whatever you loose on earth shall be considered loosed in heaven.'

The Gospel of the Lord.

The Creed is said.

Prayer over the Offerings

May the prayer of the Apostles,
   O Lord,
accompany the sacrificial gift
that we present to your name
   for consecration,
and may their intercession make
   us devoted to you
in celebration of the sacrifice.
Through Christ our Lord.

Super oblata

Hostiam, Domine, quam nomini
   tuo exhibemus sacrandam,
apostolica prosequatur oratio,
nosque tibi reddat in sacrificio
   celebrando devotos.
Per Christum Dominum nostrum.

Preface: The twofold mission of Peter and Paul in the Church.

Præfatio: De duplici missione Petri et Pauli in Ecclesia.

It is truly right and just,
     our duty and our salvation,
always and everywhere to give
     you thanks,
Lord, holy Father,
     almighty and eternal God.

Vere dignum et iustum est,
     æquum et salutare,
nos tibi semper et ubique
     gratias agere:
Domine, sancte Pater,
     omnipotens æterne Deus.

For by your providence
the blessed Apostles Peter and Paul
     bring us joy:
Peter, foremost in confessing
     the faith,
Paul, its outstanding preacher,
Peter, who established the early
     Church from the remnant
     of Israel,
Paul, master and teacher
     of the Gentiles that you call.

Quia nos beati apostoli
     Petrus et Paulus
tua dispositione lætificant:
hic princeps fidei confitendæ,
ille intellegendæ clarus assertor;
hic reliquiis Israel instituens
     Ecclesiam primitivam,
ille magister et doctor
     gentium vocandarum.

And so, each in a different way
gathered together the one family
     of Christ;
and revered together throughout
     the world,
they share one Martyr's crown.

Sic diverso consilio unam Christi
     familiam congregantes,
par mundo venerabile,
     una corona sociavit.

And therefore, with all the Angels
     and Saints,
we praise you, as without end
     we acclaim:

Et ideo, cum Sanctis
     et Angelis universis
te collaudamus, sine fine dicentes:

Holy, Holy, Holy Lord God of hosts...

Sanctus, Sanctus, Sanctus. . .

Communion Antiphon Cf. Mt 16:16,18

Peter said to Jesus:
  You are the Christ,
  the Son of the living God.
And Jesus replied: You are Peter,
and upon this rock I will build
  my Church.

Prayer after Communion

Grant us, O Lord,
who have been renewed
  by this Sacrament,
so to live in the Church,
that, persevering in the breaking
  of the Bread
and in the teaching of the Apostles,
we may be one heart and one soul,
made steadfast in your love.
Through Christ our Lord.

Ant. ad communionem

Dixit Petrus ad Iesum:
  Tu es Christus, Filius Dei vivi.
Respondit Iesus: Tu es Petrus,
et super hanc petram ædificabo
  Ecclesiam meam.

Post communionem

Da nobis, Domine,
  hoc sacramento refectis,
ita in Ecclesia conversari,
ut, perseverantes in fractione panis
Apostolorumque doctrina,
cor unum simus et anima una,
  tua caritate firmati.
Per Christum Dominum nostrum.

A formula of Solemn Blessing, pp.144-147, may be used.

In Ireland

28 June

THIRTEENTH SUNDAY IN ORDINARY TIME

Entrance Antiphon   Ps 46:2

ALL peoples, clap your hands.
Cry to God with shouts of joy!

Ant. ad introitum

OMNES gentes,
plaudite manibus,
iubilate Deo in voce exsultationis.

Collect

O God, who through the grace
   of adoption
chose us to be children of light,
grant, we pray,
that we may not be wrapped
   in the darkness of error
but always be seen to stand
   in the bright light of truth.
Through our Lord Jesus Christ,
   your Son,
who lives and reigns with you
   in the unity of the Holy Spirit,
one God, for ever and ever.

Collecta

Deus, qui, per adoptionem gratiæ,
lucis nos esse filios voluisti,
præsta, quæsumus, ut errorum
   non involvamur tenebris,
sed in splendore veritatis semper
   maneamus conspicui.
Per Dominum nostrum Iesum
   Christum Filium tuum,
qui tecum vivit et regnat
   in unitate Spiritus Sancti,
Deus, per omnia sæcula sæculorum.

FIRST READING

A reading from the second book of the Kings   4:8-11,14-16

This is a holy man of God, let him rest there.

One day as Elisha was on his way to Shunem, a woman of rank who lived there pressed him to stay and eat there. After this he always broke his journey for a meal when he passed that way. She said to her husband, 'Look, I am sure the man who is constantly passing our way must be a holy man of God. Let us build him a small room on the roof, and put him a bed in it, and a table and chair and lamp; whenever he comes to us he can rest there.'

One day when he came, he retired to the upper room and lay down. 'What can be done for her?' he asked. Gehazi, his servant, answered, 'Well, she has no son and her husband is old.' Elisha said, 'Call her.' The servant called her and she stood at the door. 'This time next year,' Elisha said 'you will hold a son in your arms.'

The word of the Lord.

Responsorial Psalm   Ps 88:2-3,16-19. R. v.2

R. **I will sing for ever of your love, O Lord.**

I will sing for ever of your love, O Lord;
through all ages my mouth will proclaim your truth.
Of this I am sure, that your love lasts for ever,
that your truth is firmly established as the heavens. R.

Happy the people who acclaim such a king,
who walk, O Lord, in the light of your face,
who find their joy every day in your name,
who make your justice the source of their bliss. R.

For it is you, O Lord, who are the glory of their strength;
it is by your favour that our might is exalted:
for our ruler is in the keeping of the Lord;
our king in the keeping of the Holy One of Israel. R.

SECOND READING

A reading from the letter of St Paul to the Romans   6:3-4,8-11

When we were baptised we went into the tomb with Christ, so that we too might live a new life.

When we were baptised in Christ Jesus we were baptised in his death; in other words, when we were baptised we went into the tomb with him and joined him in death, so that as Christ was raised from the dead by the Father's glory, we too might live a new life.

But we believe that having died with Christ we shall return to life with him: Christ, as we know, having been raised from the dead will never die again. Death has no power over him any more. When he died, he died, once for all, to sin, so his life now is life with God; and in that way, you too must consider yourselves to be dead to sin but alive for God in Christ Jesus.

The word of the Lord.

Gospel Acclamation   Cf. Ac 16:14

R. **Alleluia, alleluia!**
Open our heart, O Lord,
to accept the words of your Son.
R. **Alleluia!**

Or: 1 P 2:9

R. **Alleluia, alleluia!**
You are a chosen race, a royal priesthood, a people set apart
to sing the praises of God
who called you out of darkness into his wonderful light.
R. **Alleluia!**

GOSPEL

A reading from the holy Gospel according to Matthew   10:37-42

Anyone who does not take his cross is not worthy of me. Anyone who welcomes you welcomes me.

Jesus instructed the Twelve as follows: 'Anyone who prefers father or mother to me is not worthy of me. Anyone who prefers son or daughter to me is not worthy of me. Anyone who does not take his cross and follow in my footsteps is not worthy of me. Anyone who finds his life will lose it; anyone who loses his life for my sake will find it.

'Anyone who welcomes you welcomes me; and those who welcome me welcome the one who sent me.

'Anyone who welcomes a prophet because he is a prophet will have a prophet's reward; and anyone who welcomes a holy man because he is a holy man will have a holy man's reward.

'If anyone gives so much as a cup of cold water to one of these little ones because he is a disciple, then I tell you solemnly, he will most certainly not lose his reward.'

The Gospel of the Lord.

Prayer over the Offerings	Super oblata
O God, who graciously accomplish the effects of your mysteries, grant, we pray, that the deeds by which we serve you may be worthy of these sacred gifts. Through Christ our Lord.	Deus, qui mysteriorum tuorum dignanter operaris effectus, præsta, quæsumus, ut sacris apta muneribus fiant nostra servitia. Per Christum Dominum nostrum.

Preface of Sundays in Ordinary Time I-VIII, pp.60-67.

Communion Antiphon Cf. Ps 102:1	Ant. ad communionem
Bless the Lord, O my soul, and all within me, his holy name.	Benedic, anima mea, Domino, et ea quæ intra me sunt nomini sancto eius.

Or: Jn 17:20-21

O Father, I pray for them,
   that they may be one in us,
that the world may believe that you
   have sent me, says the Lord.

Prayer after Communion

May this divine sacrifice
   we have offered and received
fill us with life, O Lord, we pray,
so that, bound to you
   in lasting charity,
we may bear fruit that lasts for ever.
Through Christ our Lord.

Vel:

Pater, pro eis rogo,
   ut ipsi in nobis unum sint,
ut credat mundus quia tu me
   misisti, dicit Dominus.

Post communionem

Vivificet nos, quæsumus, Domine,
divina quam obtulimus et
   sumpsimus hostia,
ut, perpetua tibi caritate coniuncti,
fructum qui semper
   maneat afferamus.
Per Christum Dominum nostrum.

---

5 July

FOURTEENTH SUNDAY IN ORDINARY TIME

Entrance Antiphon   Cf. Ps 47:10-11

YOUR merciful love, O God,
   we have received in the midst
of your temple.
Your praise, O God, like your name,
reaches the ends of the earth;
your right hand is filled
   with saving justice.

Ant. ad introitum

SUSCEPIMUS, Deus,
   misericordiam tuam
in medio templi tui.
Secundum nomen tuum, Deus,
ita et laus tua in fines terræ;
iustitia plena est dextera tua.

Collect

O God, who in the abasement
   of your Son
have raised up a fallen world,
fill your faithful with holy joy,
for on those you have rescued
   from slavery to sin
you bestow eternal gladness.
Through our Lord Jesus Christ,
   your Son,
who lives and reigns with you

Collecta

Deus, qui in Filii tui humilitate
iacentem mundum erexisti,
fidelibus tuis sanctam
   concede lætitiam,
ut, quos eripuisti
   a servitute peccati,
gaudiis facias perfrui sempiternis.
Per Dominum nostrum Iesum
   Christum Filium tuum,
qui tecum vivit et regnat

| in the unity of the Holy Spirit, | in unitate Spiritus Sancti, |
| one God, for ever and ever. | Deus, per omnia sæcula sæculorum. |

FIRST READING

A reading from the prophet Zechariah   9:9-10

See now, your king comes humbly to you.

The Lord says this:
 'Rejoice heart and soul, daughter of Zion!
 Shout with gladness, daughter of Jerusalem!
 See now, your king comes to you;
 he is victorious, he is triumphant,
 humble and riding on a donkey,
 on a colt, the foal of a donkey.
 He will banish chariots from Ephraim
 and horses from Jerusalem;
 the bow of war will be banished.
 He will proclaim peace for the nations.
 His empire shall stretch from sea to sea,
 from the River to the ends of the earth.'

 The word of the Lord.

Responsorial Psalm   Ps 144:1-2,8-11,13-14. R. v.1

R. **I will bless your name for ever,**
 O God my King.
 Or: **Alleluia!**

I will give you glory, O God my King,
I will bless your name for ever.
I will bless you day after day
and praise your name for ever. R.

The Lord is kind and full of compassion,
slow to anger, abounding in love.
How good is the Lord to all,
compassionate to all his creatures. R.

All your creatures shall thank you, O Lord,
and your friends shall repeat their blessing.
They shall speak of the glory of your reign
and declare your might, O God. R.

The Lord is faithful in all his words
and loving in all his deeds.
The Lord supports all who fall
and raises all who are bowed down. R.

SECOND READING

A reading from the letter of St Paul to the Romans   8:9,11-13
If by the Spirit you put an end to the misdeeds of the body you will live.

Your interests are not in the unspiritual, but in the spiritual, since the Spirit of God has made his home in you. In fact, unless you possessed the Spirit of Christ you would not belong to him, and if the Spirit of him who raised Jesus from the dead is living in you, then he who raised Jesus from the dead will give life to your own mortal bodies through his Spirit living in you.

So then, my brothers, there is no necessity for us to obey our unspiritual selves or to live unspiritual lives. If you do live in that way, you are doomed to die, but if by the Spirit you put an end to the misdeeds of the body you will live.

The word of the Lord.

Gospel Acclamation   Cf. Mt 11:25

R. **Alleluia, alleluia!**
Blessed are you, Father,
Lord of heaven and earth;
for revealing the mysteries of the kingdom.
to mere children.
R. **Alleluia!**

GOSPEL

A reading from the holy Gospel according to Matthew   11:25-30
I am gentle and humble in heart.

Jesus exclaimed, 'I bless you, Father, Lord of heaven and of earth, for hiding these things from the learned and the clever and revealing them to mere children. Yes, Father, for that is what it pleased you to do. Everything has been entrusted to me by my Father; and no one knows the Son except the Father, just as no one knows the Father except the Son and those to whom the Son chooses to reveal him.

'Come to me, all you who labour and are overburdened, and I will give you rest. Shoulder my yoke and learn from me, for I am gentle and humble in heart, and you will find rest for your souls. Yes, my yoke is easy and my burden light.'

The Gospel of the Lord.

Prayer over the Offerings

May this oblation dedicated
  to your name
purify us, O Lord,
and day by day bring our conduct
closer to the life of heaven.
Through Christ our Lord.

Super oblata

Oblatio nos, Domine,
  tuo nomini dicata purificet,
et de die in diem ad cælestis vitæ
  transferat actionem.
Per Christum Dominum nostrum.

Preface of Sundays in Ordinary Time I-VIII, pp.60-67.

Communion Antiphon   Ps 33:9

Taste and see that the Lord is good;
blessed the man who seeks refuge
  in him.

Ant. ad communionem

Gustate et videte, quoniam suavis
  est Dominus;
beatus vir, qui sperat in eo.

Or: Mt 11:28

Come to me, all who labour
  and are burdened,
and I will refresh you,
  says the Lord.

Vel:

Venite ad me, omnes qui laboratis
  et onerati estis,
et ego reficiam vos, dicit Dominus.

Prayer after Communion

Grant, we pray, O Lord,
that, having been replenished
  by such great gifts,
we may gain the prize of salvation
and never cease to praise you.
Through Christ our Lord.

Post communionem

Tantis, Domine, repleti muneribus,
præsta, quæsumus, ut et salutaria
  dona capiamus,
et a tua numquam laude cessemus.
Per Christum Dominum nostrum.

12 July

FIFTEENTH SUNDAY IN ORDINARY TIME

Entrance Antiphon   Cf. Ps 16:15

AS for me, in justice I shall
  behold your face;
I shall be filled with the vision
  of your glory.

Ant. ad introitum

EGO autem cum iustitia
  apparebo in conspectu tuo;
satiabor dum manifestabitur
  gloria tua.

Collect

O God, who show the light
  of your truth
to those who go astray,
so that they may return
  to the right path,
give all who for the faith they profess
are accounted Christians
the grace to reject whatever
  is contrary to the name of Christ
and to strive after all that does
  it honour.
Through our Lord Jesus Christ,
  your Son,
who lives and reigns with you
  in the unity of the Holy Spirit,
one God, for ever and ever.

Collecta

Deus, qui errantibus,
  ut in viam possint redire,
veritatis tuæ lumen ostendis,
da cunctis qui christiana
  professione censentur,
et illa respuere, quæ huic inimica
  sunt nomini,
et ea quæ sunt apta sectari.
Per Dominum nostrum Iesum
  Christum Filium tuum,
qui tecum vivit et regnat
  in unitate Spiritus Sancti,
Deus, per omnia sæcula sæculorum.

FIRST READING

A reading from the prophet Isaiah 55:10-11

The rain makes the earth give growth.

Thus says the Lord: 'As the rain and the snow come down from the heavens and do not return without watering the earth, making it yield and giving growth to provide seed for the sower and bread for the eating, so the word that goes from my mouth does not return to me empty, without carrying out my will and succeeding in what it was sent to do.'

  The word of the Lord.

Responsorial Psalm Ps 64:10-14. R. Lk 8:8

R. **Some seed fell into rich soil
  and produced its crop.**

  You care for the earth, give it water,
  you fill it with riches.
  Your river in heaven brims over
  to provide its grain. R.

  And thus you provide for the earth;
  you drench its furrows,
  you level it, soften it with showers,
  you bless its growth. R.

  You crown the year with your goodness.
  Abundance flows in your steps,
  in the pastures of the wilderness it flows. R.

The hills are girded with joy,
the meadows covered with flocks,
the valleys are decked with wheat.
They shout for joy, yes, they sing. R.

R. **Some seed fell into rich soil
and produced its crop.**

SECOND READING

A reading from the letter of St Paul to the Romans   8:18-23
The whole creation is eagerly waiting for God to reveal his sons.

I think that what we suffer in this life can never be compared to the glory,
as yet unrevealed, which is waiting for us. The whole creation is eagerly
waiting for God to reveal his sons. It was not for any fault on the part of
creation that it was made unable to attain its purpose, it was made so by
God; but creation still retains the hope of being freed, like us, from its
slavery to decadence, to enjoy the same freedom and glory as the children
of God. From the beginning till now the entire creation, as we know, has
been groaning in one great act of giving birth; and not only creation, but
all of us who possess the first-fruits of the Spirit, we too groan inwardly as
we wait for our bodies to be set free.

The word of the Lord.

Gospel Acclamation   1 S 3:9; Jn 6:68

R. **Alleluia, alleluia!**
Speak, Lord, your servant is listening:
you have the message of eternal life.
R. **Alleluia!**

Or:

R. **Alleluia, alleluia!**
The seed is the word of God, Christ the sower;
whoever finds this seed will remain for ever.
R. **Alleluia!**

GOSPEL

A reading from the holy Gospel according to Matthew   13:1-23
A sower went out to sow.

[Jesus left the house and sat by the lakeside, but such crowds gathered
round him that he got into a boat and sat there. The people all stood on
the beach, and he told them many things in parables.

He said, 'Imagine a sower going out to sow. As he sowed, some seeds fell on the edge of the path, and the birds came and ate them up. Others fell on patches of rock where they found little soil and sprang up straight away, because there was no depth of earth; but as soon as the sun came up they were scorched and, not having any roots, they withered away. Others fell among thorns, and the thorns grew up and choked them. Others fell on rich soil and produced their crop, some a hundredfold, some sixty, some thirty. Listen, anyone who has ears!']

Then the disciples went up to him and asked, 'Why do you talk to them in parables?' 'Because' he replied 'the mysteries of the kingdom of heaven are revealed to you, but they are not revealed to them. For anyone who has will be given more, and he will have more than enough; but from anyone who has not, even what he has will be taken away. The reason I talk to them in parables is that they look without seeing and listen without hearing or understanding. So in their case this prophecy of Isaiah is being fulfilled:

You will listen and listen again, but not understand,
see and see again, but not perceive.
For the heart of this nation has grown coarse,
their ears are dull of hearing, and they have shut their eyes,
for fear they should see with their eyes,
hear with their ears,
understand with their heart,
and be converted
and be healed by me.

'But happy are your eyes because they see, your ears because they hear! I tell you solemnly, many prophets and holy men longed to see what you see, and never saw it; to hear what you hear, and never heard it.

'You, therefore, are to hear the parable of the sower. When anyone hears the word of the kingdom without understanding, the evil one comes and carries off what was sown in his heart: this is the man who received the seed on the edge of the path. The one who received it on patches of rock is the man who hears the word and welcomes it at once with joy. But he has no root in him, he does not last; let some trial come, or some persecution on account of the word, and he falls away at once. The one who received the seed in thorns is the man who hears the word but the worries of this world and the lure of riches choke the word and so he produces nothing. And the one who received the seed in rich soil is the man who hears the

word and understands it; he is the one who yields a harvest and produces
now a hundredfold, now sixty, now thirty.'

| [The Gospel of the Lord.]

Shorter Form, verses 1-9. Read between [ ]

Prayer over the Offerings	Super oblata

Look upon the offerings
    of the Church, O Lord,
as she makes her prayer to you,
and grant that, when consumed
    by those who believe,
they may bring ever
    greater holiness.
Through Christ our Lord.
	Respice, Domine, munera
	    supplicantis Ecclesiæ,
	et pro credentium
	    sanctificationis incremento
	sumenda concede.
	Per Christum Dominum nostrum.

Preface of Sundays in Ordinary Time I-VIII, pp.60-67.

Communion Antiphon Cf. Ps 83:4-5	Ant. ad communionem

The sparrow finds a home,
and the swallow a nest for her young:
by your altars, O Lord of hosts,
    my King and my God.
Blessed are they who dwell
    in your house,
for ever singing your praise.
	Passer invenit sibi domum,
	et turtur nidum,
	    ubi reponat pullos suos.
	Altaria tua, Domine virtutum,
	    Rex meus, et Deus meus!
	Beati qui habitant in domo tua,
	in sæculum sæculi laudabunt te.

Or: Jn 6:57	Vel:

Whoever eats my flesh
    and drinks my blood
remains in me and I in him,
    says the Lord.
	Qui manducat meam carnem
	    et bibit meum sanguinem,
	in me manet et ego in eo,
	    dicit Dominus.

Prayer after Communion	Post communionem

Having consumed these gifts,
    we pray, O Lord,
that, by our participation
    in this mystery,
its saving effects upon us may grow.
Through Christ our Lord.
Sumptis muneribus,
	quæsumus, Domine,
	ut, cum frequentatione mysterii,
	crescat nostræ salutis effectus.
	Per Christum Dominum nostrum.

19 July

SIXTEENTH SUNDAY IN ORDINARY TIME

| Entrance Antiphon | Ps 53:6,8 | Ant. ad introitum |

S EE, I have God for my help.
The Lord sustains my soul.
I will sacrifice to you
with willing heart,
and praise your name, O Lord,
for it is good.

E CCE Deus adiuvat me,
et Dominus susceptor est
animæ meæ.
Voluntarie sacrificabo tibi,
et confitebor nomini tuo, Domine,
quoniam bonum est.

Collect

Collecta

Show favour, O Lord, to your servants
and mercifully increase the gifts
of your grace,
that, made fervent in hope,
faith and charity,
they may be ever watchful
in keeping your commands.
Through our Lord Jesus Christ,
your Son,
who lives and reigns with you
in the unity of the Holy Spirit,
one God, for ever and ever.

Propitiare, Domine, famulis tuis,
et clementer gratiæ tuæ super eos
dona multiplica,
ut, spe, fide et caritate ferventes,
semper in mandatis tuis vigili
custodia perseverent.
Per Dominum nostrum Iesum
Christum Filium tuum,
qui tecum vivit et regnat
in unitate Spiritus Sancti,
Deus, per omnia sæcula sæculorum.

FIRST READING

A reading from the book of Wisdom   12:13,16-19

After sin you will grant repentance.

There is no god, other than you, who cares for everything,
to whom you might have to prove that you never judged unjustly.
Your justice has its source in strength,
your sovereignty over all makes you lenient to all.
You show your strength when your sovereign power is questioned
and you expose the insolence of those who know it;
but, disposing of such strength, you are mild in judgement,
you govern us with great lenience,
for you have only to will, and your power is there.
By acting thus you have taught a lesson to your people
how the virtuous man must be kindly to his fellow men,
and you have given your sons the good hope
that after sin you will grant repentance.

The word of the Lord.

Responsorial Psalm   Ps 85:5-6,9-10,15-16. R. v.5

R. **O Lord, you are good and forgiving.**

O Lord, you are good and forgiving,
full of love to all who call.
Give heed, O Lord, to my prayer
and attend to the sound of my voice. R.

All the nations shall come to adore you
and glorify your name, O Lord:
for you are great and do marvellous deeds,
you who alone are God. R.

But you, God of mercy and compassion,
slow to anger, O Lord,
abounding in love and truth,
turn and take pity on me. R.

SECOND READING

A reading from the letter of St Paul to the Romans   8:26-27

The Spirit expresses our plea in a way that could never be put into words.

The Spirit comes to help us in our weakness. For when we cannot choose
words in order to pray properly, the Spirit himself expresses our plea in a
way that could never be put into words, and God who knows everything in
our hearts knows perfectly well what he means, and that the pleas of the
saints expressed by the Spirit are according to the mind of God.

The word of the Lord.

Gospel Acclamation   Cf. Ep 1:17,18

R. **Alleluia, alleluia!**
May the Father of our Lord Jesus Christ
enlighten the eyes of our mind,
so that we can see what hope his call holds for us.
R. **Alleluia!**

Or: Cf. Mt 11:25

R. **Alleluia, alleluia!**
Blessed are you, Father,
Lord of heaven and earth,
for revealing the mysteries of the kingdom
to mere children.
R. **Alleluia!**

GOSPEL

A reading from the holy Gospel according to Matthew   13:24-43

Let them both grow till the harvest.

[Jesus put another parable before the crowds: 'The kingdom of heaven may be compared to a man who sowed good seed in his field. While everybody was asleep his enemy came, sowed darnel all among the wheat, and made off. When the new wheat sprouted and ripened, the darnel appeared as well. The owner's servants went to him and said, "Sir, was it not good seed that you sowed in your field? If so, where does the darnel come from?" "Some enemy has done this" he answered. And the servants said, "Do you want us to go and weed it out?" But he said, "No, because when you weed out the darnel you might pull up the wheat with it. Let them both grow till the harvest; and at harvest time I shall say to the reapers: First collect the darnel and tie it in bundles to be burnt, then gather the wheat into my barn."']

He put another parable before them, 'The kingdom of heaven is like a mustard seed which a man took and sowed in his field. It is the smallest of all the seeds, but when it has grown it is the biggest shrub of all and becomes a tree so that the birds of the air come and shelter in its branches.'

He told them another parable, 'The kingdom of heaven is like the yeast a woman took and mixed in with three measures of flour till it was leavened all through.'

In all this Jesus spoke to the crowds in parables; indeed, he would never speak to them except in parables. This was to fulfill the prophecy:

I will speak to you in parables
and expound things hidden since the foundation of the world.

Then, leaving the crowds, he went to the house; and his disciples came to him and said, 'Explain the parable about the darnel in the field to us.' He said in reply, 'The sower of the good seed is the Son of Man. The field is the world; the good seed is the subjects of the kingdom; the darnel, the subjects of the evil one; the enemy who sowed them, the devil; the harvest is the end of the world, the reapers are the angels. Well then, just as the darnel is gathered up and burnt in the fire, so it will be at the end of time. The Son of Man will send his angels and they will gather out of his kingdom all things that provoke offences and all who do evil, and throw them into the blazing furnace, where there will be weeping and grinding of teeth. Then the virtuous will shine like the sun in the kingdom of their Father. Listen, anyone who has ears!'

[The Gospel of the Lord.]

Shorter Form, verses 24-30. Read between [ ]

Prayer over the Offerings

O God, who in the one
    perfect sacrifice
brought to completion varied
    offerings of the law,
accept, we pray, this sacrifice
    from your faithful servants
and make it holy, as you blessed
    the gifts of Abel,
so that what each has offered
    to the honour of your majesty
may benefit the salvation of all.
Through Christ our Lord.

Super oblata

Deus, qui legalium
    differentiam hostiarum
unius sacrificii perfectione sanxisti,
accipe sacrificium a devotis
    tibi famulis,
et pari benedictione,
    sicut munera Abel, sanctifica,
ut, quod singuli obtulerunt
    ad maiestatis tuæ honorem,
cunctis proficiat ad salutem.
Per Christum Dominum nostrum.

Preface of Sundays in Ordinary Time I-VIII, pp.60-67.

Communion Antiphon Ps 110:4-5

The Lord, the gracious, the merciful,
has made a memorial of his wonders;
he gives food to those who fear him.

Ant. ad communionem

Memoriam fecit mirabilium suorum
misericors et miserator Dominus;
escam dedit timentibus se.

Or: Rv 3:20

Behold, I stand at the door
    and knock, says the Lord.
If anyone hears my voice
    and opens the door to me,
I will enter his house and dine
    with him, and he with me.

Vel:

Ecce sto ad ostium et pulso,
    dicit Dominus:
si quis audierit vocem meam,
    et aperuerit mihi ianuam,
intrabo ad illum, et cenabo
    cum illo, et ipse mecum.

Prayer after Communion

Graciously be present to your people,
    we pray, O Lord,
and lead those you have imbued
    with heavenly mysteries
to pass from former ways
    to newness of life.
Through Christ our Lord.

Post communionem

Populo tuo, quæsumus, Domine,
    adesto propitius,
et, quem mysteriis
    cælestibus imbuisti,
fac ad novitatem vitæ
    de vetustate transire.
Per Christum Dominum nostrum.

26 July

SEVENTEENTH SUNDAY IN ORDINARY TIME

Entrance Antiphon Cf. Ps 67:6-7,36

GOD is in his holy place,
God who unites those
who dwell in his house;
he himself gives might and strength
to his people.

Ant. ad introitum

DEUS in loco sancto suo;
Deus qui inhabitare facit
unanimes in domo,
ipse dabit virtutem et fortitudinem
plebi suæ.

Collect

O God, protector of those
who hope in you,
without whom nothing has firm
foundation, nothing is holy,
bestow in abundance your mercy
upon us
and grant that, with you as our ruler
and guide,
we may use the good things that pass
in such a way as to hold fast even now
to those that ever endure.
Through our Lord Jesus Christ,
your Son,
who lives and reigns with you
in the unity of the Holy Spirit,
one God, for ever and ever.

Collecta

Protector in te sperantium, Deus,
sine quo nihil est validum,
nihil sanctum,
multiplica super nos
misericordiam tuam
ut, te rectore, te duce, sic bonis
transeuntibus nunc utamur,
ut iam possimus
inhærere mansuris.
Per Dominum nostrum Iesum
Christum Filium tuum,
qui tecum vivit et regnat
in unitate Spiritus Sancti,
Deus, per omnia sæcula sæculorum.

FIRST READING

A reading from the first book of the Kings   3:5,7-12

You have asked for a discerning judgement for yourself.

The Lord appeared to Solomon in a dream and said, 'Ask what you would
like me to give you.' Solomon replied, 'Lord, my God, you have made
your servant king in succession to David my father. But I am a very young
man, unskilled in leadership. Your servant finds himself in the midst of
this people of yours that you have chosen, a people so many its numbers
cannot be counted or reckoned. Give your servant a heart to understand
how to discern between good and evil, for who could govern this people of

yours that is so great?' It pleased the Lord that Solomon should have asked for this. 'Since you have asked for this' the Lord said 'and not asked for long life for yourself or riches or the lives of your enemies, but have asked for a discerning judgement for yourself, here and now I do what you ask. I give you a heart wise and shrewd as none before you has had and none will have after you.'

The word of the Lord.

Responsorial Psalm   Ps 118:57,72,76-77,127-130. R. v.97

R. **Lord how I love your law!**

My part, I have resolved, O Lord,
is to obey your word.
The law from your mouth means more to me
than silver and gold. R.

Let your love be ready to console me
by your promise to your servant.
Let your love come to me and I shall live
for your law is my delight. R.

That is why I love your commands
more than finest gold,
That is why I rule my life by your precepts:
I hate false ways. R.

Your will is wonderful indeed;
therefore I obey it.
The unfolding of your word gives light
and teaches the simple. R.

SECOND READING

A reading from the letter of St Paul to the Romans   8:28-30

God intended us to become true images of his Son.

We know that by turning everything to their good God co-operates with all those who love him, with all those that he has called according to his purpose. They are the ones he chose specially long ago and intended to become true images of his Son, so that his Son might be the eldest of many brothers. He called those he intended for this; those he called he justified, and with those he justified he shared his glory.

The word of the Lord.

Gospel Acclamation   Jn 15:15

R. **Alleluia, alleluia!**
I call you friends, says the Lord,
because I have made known to you
everything I have learnt from my Father.
R. **Alleluia!**

Or: Cf. Mt 11:25

R. **Alleluia, alleluia!**
Blessed are you, Father,
Lord of heaven and earth,
for revealing the mysteries of the kingdom
to mere children.
R. **Alleluia!**

GOSPEL

A reading from the holy Gospel according to Matthew   13:44-52

He sells everything he owns and buys the field.

[Jesus said to the crowds: 'The kingdom of heaven is like treasure hidden in a field which someone has found; he hides it again, goes off happy, sells everything he owns and buys the field.

'Again, the kingdom of heaven is like a merchant looking for fine pearls; when he finds one of great value he goes and sells everything he owns and buys it.]

'Again, the kingdom of heaven is like a dragnet cast into the sea that brings in a haul of all kinds. When it is full, the fishermen haul it ashore; then, sitting down, they collect the good ones in a basket and throw away those that are no use. This is how it will be at the end of time: the angels will appear and separate the wicked from the just to throw them into the blazing furnace where there will be weeping and grinding of teeth.

'Have you understood all this?' They said, 'Yes.' And he said to them, 'Well then, every scribe who becomes a disciple of the kingdom of heaven is like a householder who brings out from his storeroom things both new and old.'

[The Gospel of the Lord.]

Shorter Form, verses 44-46. Read between [ ]

Prayer over the Offerings

Accept, O Lord, we pray, the offerings
which we bring from the abundance of your gifts,
that through the powerful working of your grace
these most sacred mysteries may sanctify our present way of life
and lead us to eternal gladness.
Through Christ our Lord.

Super oblata

Suscipe, quæsumus, Domine, munera,
quæ tibi de tua largitate deferimus,
ut hæc sacrosancta mysteria, gratiæ tuæ operante virtute,
et præsentis vitæ nos conversatione sanctificent,
et ad gaudia sempiterna perducant.
Per Christum Dominum nostrum.

Preface of Sundays in Ordinary Time I-VIII, pp.60-67.

Communion Antiphon   Ps 102:2

Bless the Lord, O my soul,
and never forget all his benefits.

Ant. ad communionem

Benedic, anima mea, Domino,
et noli oblivisci omnes retributiones eius.

Or: Mt 5:7-8

Blessed are the merciful,
for they shall receive mercy.
Blessed are the clean of heart,
for they shall see God.

Vel:

Beati misericordes,
quoniam ipsi misericordiam consequentur.
Beati mundo corde,
quoniam ipsi Deum videbunt.

Prayer after Communion

We have consumed, O Lord,
this divine Sacrament,
the perpetual memorial of the Passion of your Son;
grant, we pray, that this gift,
which he himself gave us with love beyond all telling,
may profit us for salvation.
Through Christ our Lord.

Post communionem

Sumpsimus, Domine,
divinum sacramentum,
passionis Filii tui memoriale perpetuum;
tribue, quæsumus,
ut ad nostram salutem hoc munus proficiat,
quod ineffabili nobis caritate ipse donavit.
Qui vivit et regnat in sæcula sæculorum.

2 August

EIGHTEENTH SUNDAY IN ORDINARY TIME

Entrance Antiphon   Ps 69:2,6

O GOD, come to my assistance;
   O Lord, make haste to help me!
You are my rescuer, my help;
O Lord, do not delay.

Ant. ad introitum

DEUS, in adiutorium
   meum intende;
Domine, ad adiuvandum me festina.
Adiutor meus et liberator meus es tu;
Domine, ne moreris.

Collect

Draw near to your servants, O Lord,
and answer their prayers
   with unceasing kindness,
that, for those who glory in you
   as their Creator and guide,
you may restore what you
   have created
and keep safe what you have restored.
Through our Lord Jesus Christ,
   your Son,
who lives and reigns with you
   in the unity of the Holy Spirit,
one God, for ever and ever.

Collecta

Adesto, Domine, famulis tuis,
et perpetuam benignitatem
   largire poscentibus,
ut his, qui te auctorem et
   gubernatorem gloriantur habere,
et creata restaures,
   et restaurata conserves.
Per Dominum nostrum Iesum
   Christum Filium tuum,
qui tecum vivit et regnat
   in unitate Spiritus Sancti,
Deus, per omnia sæcula sæculorum.

FIRST READING

A reading from the prophet Isaiah   55:1-3

Come and eat.

Thus says the Lord:
   Oh, come to the water all you who are thirsty;
   though you have no money, come!
   Buy corn without money, and eat,
   and, at no cost, wine and milk.
   Why spend money on what is not bread,
   your wages on what fails to satisfy?
   Listen, listen to me and you will have good things to eat
   and rich food to enjoy.
   Pay attention, come to me;
   listen, and your soul will live.
   With you I will make an everlasting covenant
   out of the favours promised to David.
The word of the Lord.

Responsorial Psalm   Ps 144:8-9,15-18. R. v.16

R. **You open wide your hand, O Lord,**
you grant our desires.

The Lord is kind and full of compassion,
slow to anger, abounding in love.
How good is the Lord to all,
compassionate to all his creatures. R.

The eyes of all creatures look to you
and you give them their food in due time.
You open wide your hand,
grant the desires of all who live. R.

The Lord is just in all his ways
and loving in all his deeds.
He is close to all who call him,
call on him from their hearts. R.

SECOND READING

A reading from the letter of St Paul to the Romans   8:35,37-39

No created thing can ever come between us and the love of God made visible in Christ.

Nothing can come between us and the love of Christ, even if we are
troubled or worried, or being persecuted, or lacking food or clothes, or
being threatened or even attacked. These are the trials through which we
triumph, by the power of him who loved us.

For I am certain of this: neither death nor life, no angel, no prince,
nothing that exists, nothing still to come, not any power, or height or
depth, nor any created thing, can ever come between us and the love of
God made visible in Christ Jesus our Lord.

The word of the Lord.

Gospel Acclamation   Lk 19:38

R. **Alleluia, alleluia!**
Blessings on the King who comes,
in the name of the Lord!
Peace in heaven
and glory in the highest heavens!
R. **Alleluia!**

Or: Mt 4:4

R. **Alleluia, alleluia!**
Man does not live on bread alone,
but on every word that comes from the mouth of God.
R. **Alleluia!**

GOSPEL

A reading from the holy Gospel according to Matthew 14:13-21

They all ate as much as they wanted.

When Jesus received the news of John the Baptist's death he withdrew by boat to a lonely place where they could be by themselves. But the people heard of this and, leaving the towns, went after him on foot. So as he stepped ashore he saw a large crowd; and he took pity on them and healed their sick.

When evening came, the disciples went to him and said, 'This is a lonely place, and the time has slipped by; so send the people away, and they can go to the villages to buy themselves some food.' Jesus replied, 'There is no need for them to go: give them something to eat yourselves.' But they answered, 'All we have with us is five loaves and two fish.' 'Bring them here to me,' he said. He gave orders that the people were to sit down on the grass; then he took the five loaves and the two fish, raised his eyes to heaven and said the blessing. And breaking the loaves he handed them to his disciples who gave them to the crowds. They all ate as much as they wanted, and they collected the scraps remaining, twelve baskets full. Those who ate numbered about five thousand men, to say nothing of women and children.

The Gospel of the Lord.

Prayer over the Offerings	Super oblata

Graciously sanctify these gifts,
    O Lord, we pray,
and, accepting the oblation
    of this spiritual sacrifice,
make of us an eternal offering to you.
Through Christ our Lord.
	Propitius, Domine, quæsumus,
	    hæc dona sanctifica,
	et, hostiæ spiritalis
	    oblatione suscepta,
	nosmetipsos tibi perfice
	    munus æternum.
	Per Christum Dominum nostrum.

Preface of Sundays in Ordinary Time I-VIII, pp.60-67.

Communion Antiphon Ws 16:20	Ant. ad communionem

You have given us, O Lord,
    bread from heaven,
endowed with all delights
    and sweetness in every taste.
	Panem de cælo dedisti
	    nobis, Domine,
	habentem omne delectamentum,
	et omnem saporem suavitatis.

Or: Jn 6:35	Vel:

I am the bread of life, says the Lord;
whoever comes to me will not hunger
and whoever believes in me will
    not thirst.
	Ego sum panis vitæ, dicit Dominus.
	Qui venit ad me non esuriet,
	    et qui credit in me non sitiet.

Prayer after Communion

Accompany with constant
    protection, O Lord,
those you renew with these
    heavenly gifts
and, in your never-failing care
    for them,
make them worthy
    of eternal redemption.
Through Christ our Lord.

Post communionem

Quos cælesti recreas munere,
perpetuo, Domine,
    comitare præsidio,
et, quos fovere non desinis,
dignos fieri sempiterna
    redemptione concede.
Per Christum Dominum nostrum.

9 August

NINETEENTH SUNDAY IN ORDINARY TIME

Entrance Antiphon Cf. Ps 73:20,19,22,23

L OOK to your covenant, O Lord,
    and forget not the life of your
    poor ones for ever.
Arise, O God, and defend your cause,
and forget not the cries of those
    who seek you.

Ant. ad introitum

R ESPICE, Domine,
    in testamentum tuum,
et animas pauperum tuorum
    ne derelinquas in finem.
Exsurge, Domine,
    et iudica causam tuam,
et ne obliviscaris voces
    quærentium te.

Collect

Almighty ever-living God,
whom, taught by the Holy Spirit,
we dare to call our Father,
bring, we pray, to perfection
    in our hearts
the spirit of adoption as your sons
    and daughters,
that we may merit
    to enter into the inheritance
which you have promised.
Through our Lord Jesus Christ,
    your Son,
who lives and reigns with you
    in the unity of the Holy Spirit,
one God, for ever and ever.

Collecta

Omnipotens sempiterne Deus,
quem, docente Spiritu Sancto,
paterno nomine
    invocare præsumimus,
perfice in cordibus nostris spiritum
    adoptionis filiorum,
ut promissam hereditatem
    ingredi mereamur.
Per Dominum nostrum Iesum
    Christum Filium tuum,
qui tecum vivit et regnat
    in unitate Spiritus Sancti,
Deus, per omnia sæcula sæculorum.

FIRST READING

A reading from the first book of the Kings 19:9,11-13

Stand on the mountain before the Lord.

When Elijah reached Horeb, the mountain of God, he went into the cave and spent the night in it. Then he was told, 'Go out and stand on the mountain before the Lord.' Then the Lord himself went by. There came a mighty wind, so strong it tore the mountains and shattered the rocks before the Lord. But the Lord was not in the wind. After the wind came an earthquake. But the Lord was not in the earthquake. After the earthquake came a fire. But the Lord was not in the fire. And after the fire there came the sound of a gentle breeze. And when Elijah heard this, he covered his face with his cloak and went out and stood at the entrance of the cave.

The word of the Lord.

Responsorial Psalm Ps 84:9-14. R. v.8

R. **Let us see, O Lord your mercy
and give us your saving help**.

I will hear what the Lord God has to say,
a voice that speaks of peace.
His help is near for those who fear him
and his glory will dwell in our land. R.

Mercy and faithfulness have met;
justice and peace have embraced.
Faithfulness shall spring from the earth
and justice look down from heaven. R.

The Lord will make us prosper
and our earth shall yield its fruit.
Justice shall march before him
and peace shall follow his steps. R.

SECOND READING

A reading from the letter of St Paul to the Romans 9:1-5

I would willingly be condemned if it could help my brothers.

What I want to say is no pretence; I say it in union with Christ – it is the truth – my conscience in union with the Holy Spirit assures me of it too. What I want to say is this: my sorrow is so great, my mental anguish so endless, I would willingly be condemned and be cut off from Christ if it could help my brothers of Israel, my own flesh and blood. They were adopted as sons, they were given the glory and the covenants; the Law and the ritual were drawn up for them, and the promises were made to them. They are descended from the patriarchs and from their flesh and blood came Christ who is above all, God for ever blessed! Amen.

The word of the Lord.

Gospel Acclamation   Lk 19:38

R. **Alleluia, alleluia!**
Blessings on the King who comes, in the name of the Lord!
Peace in heaven and glory in the highest heavens!
R. **Alleluia**

Or: Ps 129:5

R. **Alleluia, alleluia!**
My soul is waiting for the Lord,
I count on his word.
R. **Alleluia**

GOSPEL

A reading from the holy Gospel according to Matthew   14:22-33
Tell me to come to you across the water.

Jesus made the disciples get into the boat and go on ahead to the other side while he would send the crowds away. After sending the crowds away he went up into the hills by himself to pray. When evening came, he was there alone, while the boat, by now far out on the lake, was battling with a heavy sea, for there was a headwind. In the fourth watch of the night he went towards them, walking on the lake, and when the disciples saw him walking on the lake they were terrified. 'It is a ghost' they said, and cried out in fear. But at once Jesus called out to them, saying, 'Courage! It is I! Do not be afraid.' It was Peter who answered. 'Lord,' he said 'if it is you, tell me to come to you across the water.' 'Come' said Jesus. Then Peter got out of the boat and started walking towards Jesus across the water, but as soon as he felt the force of the wind, he took fright and began to sink. 'Lord! Save me!' he cried. Jesus put out his hand at once and held him. 'Man of little faith,' he said 'why did you doubt?' And as they got into the boat the wind dropped. The men in the boat bowed down before him and said, 'Truly, you are the Son of God.'

The Gospel of the Lord.

Prayer over the Offerings

Be pleased, O Lord, to accept
   the offerings of your Church,
for in your mercy you have given
   them to be offered
and by your power
   you transform them
into the mystery of our salvation.
Through Christ our Lord.

Super oblata

Ecclesiæ tuæ, Domine, munera
   placatus assume,
quæ et misericors
   offerenda tribuisti,
et in nostræ salutis potenter efficis
   transire mysterium.
Per Christum Dominum nostrum.

Preface of Sundays in Ordinary Time I-VIII, pp.60-67.

Communion Antiphon Ps 147:12,14

O Jerusalem, glorify the Lord,
who gives you your fill
   of finest wheat.

Or: Cf. Jn 6:51

The bread that I will give,
   says the Lord,
is my flesh for the life of the world.

Ant. ad communionem

Lauda, Ierusalem, Dominum,
qui adipe frumenti satiat te.

Vel:

Panis, quem ego dedero,
caro mea est pro sæculi vita,
dicit Dominus.

Prayer after Communion

May the communion
   in your Sacrament
that we have consumed, save us,
   O Lord,
and confirm us in the light
   of your truth.
Through Christ our Lord.

Post communionem

Sacramentorum tuorum, Domine,
communio sumpta nos salvet,
et in tuæ veritatis luce confirmet.
Per Christum Dominum nostrum.

In Ireland
15 August

In England, Wales & Scotland
16 August

THE ASSUMPTION
OF THE BLESSED VIRGIN MARY

Mary's Assumption shows us our own destiny as God's adoptive children and members of the body of Christ. Like Mary our Mother, we are called to share fully in the Lord's victory over sin and death, and to reign with him in his eternal Kingdom. This is our vocation. The "great sign" presented in today's first reading invites us to contemplate Mary enthroned in glory beside her divine Son. It also invites us to acknowledge the future which even now the Risen Lord is opening before us...True freedom is found in our loving embrace of the Father's will. From Mary, full of grace, we learn that Christian freedom is more than liberation from sin. It is freedom for a new, spiritual way of seeing earthly realities. It is the freedom to love God and our brothers and sisters with a pure heart, and to live a life of joyful hope for the coming of Christ's Kingdom.

(Pope Francis)

Solemnity

At the Vigil Mass

This Mass is used on the evening of 14/15 August, either before or after First Vespers (Evening Prayer I) of the Solemnity.

Entrance Antiphon	Ant. ad introitum
GLORIOUS things are spoken of you, O Mary, who today were exalted above the choirs of Angels into eternal triumph with Christ.	GLORIOSA dicta sunt de te, Maria, quæ hodie exaltata es super choros Angelorum, et in æternum cum Christo triumphas.

The Gloria in excelsis (Glory to God in the highest) is said.

Collect	Collecta
O God, who, looking on the lowliness of the Blessed Virgin Mary, raised her to this grace, that your Only Begotten Son was born of her according to the flesh and that she was crowned this day	Deus, qui beatam Virginem Mariam, eius humilitatem respiciens, ad hanc gratiam evexisti, ut Unigenitus tuus ex ipsa secundum carnem nasceretur,

with surpassing glory,
grant through her prayers,
that, saved by the mystery
of your redemption,
we may merit to be exalted by you
on high.
Through our Lord Jesus Christ,
your Son,
who lives and reigns with you
in the unity of the Holy Spirit,
one God, for ever and ever.

et hodierna die superexcellenti
gloria coronasti,
eius nobis precibus concede,
ut, redemptionis tuæ
mysterio salvati,
a te exaltari mereamur.
Per Dominum nostrum Iesum
Christum Filium tuum,
qui tecum vivit et regnat
in unitate Spiritus Sancti,
Deus, per omnia sæcula sæculorum.

FIRST READING

A reading from the first book of Chronicles 15:3-4,15-16; 16:1-2

They brought in the ark of God and set it inside the tent which David had pitched for it.

David gathered all Israel together in Jerusalem to bring the ark of God up to the place he had prepared for it. David called together the sons of Aaron and the sons of Levi. And the Levites carried the ark of God with the shafts on their shoulders, as Moses had ordered in accordance with the word of the Lord.

David then told the heads of the Levites to assign duties for their kinsmen as cantors, with their various instruments of music, harps and lyres and cymbals, to play joyful tunes. They brought the ark of God in and put it inside the tent that David had pitched for it; and they offered holocausts before God, and communion sacrifices. And when David had finished offering holocausts and communion sacrifices, he blessed the people in the name of the Lord.

The word of the Lord.

Responsorial Psalm Ps 131:6-7,9-10,13-14. R. v.8

R. **Go up, Lord, to the place of your rest,**
you and the ark of your strength.

At Ephrata we heard of the ark;
we found it in the plains of Yearim.
'Let us go to the place of his dwelling;
let us go to kneel at his footstool.' R.

Your priests shall be clothed with holiness:
your faithful shall ring out their joy.

For the sake of David your servant
do not reject your anointed. R.

For the Lord has chosen Zion;
he has desired it for his dwelling:
'This is my resting-place for ever,
here have I chosen to live.' R.

R. **Go up, Lord, to the place of your rest,
you and the ark of your strength.**

SECOND READING

A reading from the first letter of St Paul to the Corinthians   15:54-57
He gave us victory through our Lord Jesus Christ.

When this perishable nature has put on imperishability, and when this
mortal nature has put on immortality, then the words of scripture will
come true: Death is swallowed up in victory. Death, where is your victory?
Death, where is your sting? Now the sting of death is sin, and sin gets its
power from the Law. So let us thank God for giving us the victory through
our Lord Jesus Christ.

The word of the Lord.

Gospel Acclamation   Lk 11:28
R. **Alleluia, alleluia!**
Happy are those
who hear the word of God,
and keep it.
R. **Alleluia!**

GOSPEL

A reading from the holy Gospel according to Luke   11:27-28
Happy the womb that bore you!

As Jesus was speaking, a woman in the crowd raised her voice and said,
'Happy the womb that bore you and the breasts you sucked!' But he
replied, 'Still happier those who hear the word of God and keep it!'

The Gospel of the Lord.

The Creed is said.

Prayer over the Offerings

Receive, we pray, O Lord,
the sacrifice of conciliation
    and praise,
which we celebrate on
    the Assumption of the holy
    Mother of God,
that it may lead us to your pardon
and confirm us in perpetual
    thanksgiving.
Through Christ our Lord.

Super oblata

Suscipe, quæsumus, Domine,
sacrificium placationis et laudis,
quod in sanctæ Dei Genetricis
    Assumptione celebramus,
ut ad veniam nos
    obtinendam perducat,
et in perpetua gratiarum
    constituat actione.
Per Christum Dominum nostrum.

Proper Preface, as in the following Mass, p.403.

Communion Antiphon Cf. Lk 11:27

Blessed is the womb
    of the Virgin Mary,
which bore the Son
    of the eternal Father.

Ant. ad communionem

Beata viscera Mariæ Virginis,
quæ portaverunt æterni
    Patris Filium.

Prayer after Communion

Having partaken of this
    heavenly table,
we beseech your mercy,
    Lord our God,
that we, who honour
    the Assumption of the Mother
    of God,
may be freed from every threat
    of harm.
Through Christ our Lord.

Post communionem

Mensæ cælestis participes effecti,
imploramus clementiam tuam,
    Domine Deus noster,
ut, qui Assumptionem Dei
    Genetricis colimus,
a cunctis malis
    imminentibus liberemur.
Per Christum Dominum nostrum.

A formula of Solemn Blessing, pp.144-145, may be used.

At the Mass during the Day

Entrance Antiphon   Cf. Rv 12:1

A GREAT sign appeared
    in heaven:
a woman clothed with the sun,
    and the moon beneath her feet,
and on her head a crown
    of twelve stars.

Ant. ad introitum

S IGNUM magnum apparuit
    in cælo:
mulier amicta sole, et luna sub
    pedibus eius,
et in capite eius corona
    stellarum duodecim.

Or:

Let us all rejoice in the Lord,
as we celebrate the feast day
    in honour of the Virgin Mary,
at whose Assumption
    the Angels rejoice
and praise the Son of God.

Vel:

Gaudeamus omnes in Domino,
diem festum celebrantes sub
    honore Mariæ Virginis,
de cuius Assumptione
    gaudent Angeli,
et collaudant Filium Dei.

The Gloria in excelsis (Glory to God in the highest) is said.

Collect

Almighty ever-living God,
who assumed the Immaculate Virgin
    Mary, the Mother of your Son,
body and soul into heavenly glory,
grant, we pray,
that, always attentive to the things
    that are above,
we may merit to be sharers
    of her glory.
Through our Lord Jesus Christ,
    your Son,
who lives and reigns with you
    in the unity of the Holy Spirit,
one God, for ever and ever.

Collecta

Omnipotens sempiterne Deus,
qui immaculatam Virginem
    Mariam, Filii tui Genetricem,
corpore et anima ad cælestem
    gloriam assumpsisti,
concede, quæsumus, ut,
    ad superna semper intenti,
ipsius gloriæ mereamur
    esse consortes.
Per Dominum nostrum Iesum
    Christum Filium tuum,
qui tecum vivit et regnat
in unitate Spiritus Sancti,
Deus, per omnia sæcula sæculorum.

FIRST READING

A reading from the book of the Apocalypse   11:19; 12:1-6,10

A woman adorned with the sun standing on the moon.

The sanctuary of God in heaven opened, and the ark of the covenant could be seen inside it.

Now a great sign appeared in heaven: a woman, adorned with the sun, standing on the moon, and with the twelve stars on her head for a crown. She was pregnant, and in labour, crying aloud in the pangs of childbirth. Then a second sign appeared in the sky, a huge red dragon which had seven heads and ten horns, and each of the seven heads crowned with a coronet. Its tail dragged a third of the stars from the sky and dropped them to the earth, and the dragon stopped in front of the woman as she was having the child, so that he could eat it as soon as it was born from its mother. The woman brought a male child into the world, the son who was to rule all nations with an iron sceptre, and the child was taken straight up to God and to his throne, while the woman escaped into the desert, where God had made a place of safety ready. Then I heard a voice shout from heaven, 'Victory and power and empire for ever have been won by our God, and all authority for his Christ.'

The word of the Lord.

Responsorial Psalm   Ps 44:10-12,16. R. v.10

R. **On your right stands the queen,**
   in garments of gold.

The daughters of kings are among your loved ones.
On your right stands the queen in gold of Ophir.
Listen, O daughter, give ear to my words:
forget your own people and your father's house. R.

So will the king desire your beauty:
He is your lord, pay homage to him.
They are escorted amid gladness and joy;
they pass within the palace of the king. R.

SECOND READING

A reading from the first letter of St Paul to the Corinthians   15:20-26

Christ as the first-fruits and then, those who belong to him.

Christ has been raised from the dead, the first-fruits of all who have fallen asleep. Death came through one man and in the same way the resurrection of the dead has come through one man. Just as all men die in Adam, so all men will be brought to life in Christ; but all of them in their proper order: Christ as the first-fruits and then, after the coming of Christ, those who belong to him. After that will come the end, when he hands over the kingdom to God the Father, having done away with every sovereignty, authority and power. For he must be king until he has put all his enemies under his feet and the last of the enemies to be destroyed is death, for everything is to be put under his feet.

The word of the Lord.

Gospel Acclamation

R. **Alleluia, alleluia!**
Mary has been taken up into heaven;
all the choirs of angels are rejoicing.
R. **Alleluia!**

GOSPEL

A reading from the holy Gospel according to Luke   1:39-56

The Almighty has done great things for me, he has exalted up the lowly.

Mary set out and went as quickly as she could to a town in the hill country of Judah. She went into Zechariah's house and greeted Elizabeth. Now as soon as Elizabeth heard Mary's greeting, the child leapt in her womb and Elizabeth was filled with the Holy Spirit. She gave a loud cry and said, 'Of all women you are the most blessed, and blessed is the fruit of your womb. Why should I be honoured with a visit from the mother of my Lord? For the moment your greeting reached my ears, the child in my womb leapt for joy. Yes, blessed is she who believed that the promise made her by the Lord would be fulfilled.'

And Mary said:

> 'My soul proclaims the greatness of the Lord
> and my spirit exults in God my saviour;
> because he has looked upon his lowly handmaid.
> Yes, from this day forward all generations will call me blessed,
> for the Almighty has done great things for me.
> Holy is his name,
> and his mercy reaches from age to age for those who fear him.
> He has shown the power of his arm,
> he has routed the proud of heart.
> He has pulled down princes from their thrones and exalted the lowly.
> The hungry he has filled with good things, the rich sent empty away.
> He has come to the help of Israel his servant, mindful of his mercy
> – according to the promise he made to our ancestors –
> of his mercy to Abraham and to his descendants for ever.'

Mary stayed with Elizabeth about three months and then went back home.

The Gospel of the Lord.

The Creed is said.

Prayer over the Offerings

May this oblation, our tribute
    of homage,
rise up to you, O Lord,
and, through the intercession
    of the most Blessed Virgin Mary,
whom you assumed into heaven,
may our hearts,
    aflame with the fire of love,
constantly long for you.
Through Christ our Lord.

Super oblata

Ascendat ad te, Domine, nostræ
    devotionis oblatio,
et, beatissima Virgine Maria
in cælum assumpta intercedente,
corda nostra, caritatis igne succensa,
ad te iugiter aspirent.
Per Christum Dominum nostrum.

Preface: The Glory of Mary
assumed into heaven.

Præfatio: De Gloria
Mariæ Assumptæ.

It is truly right and just, our duty
    and our salvation,
always and everywhere to give
    you thanks,
Lord, holy Father, almighty
    and eternal God,
through Christ our Lord.

Vere dignum et iustum est,
    æquum et salutare,
nos tibi semper et ubique
    gratias agere:
Domine, sancte Pater,
    omnipotens æterne Deus:
per Christum Dominum nostrum.

For today the Virgin Mother of God
was assumed into heaven
as the beginning and image
of your Church's coming
    to perfection
and a sign of sure hope and comfort
    to your pilgrim people;
rightly you would not allow her
to see the corruption of the tomb,
since from her own body she
    marvellously brought forth
your incarnate Son,
    the Author of all life.

Quoniam hodie Virgo Deipara
    in cælos assumpta est,
Ecclesiæ tuæ consummandæ
    initium et imago,
ac populo peregrinanti certæ spei
    et solacii documentum;
corruptionem enim sepulcri
eam videre merito noluisti,
quæ Filium tuum,
    vitæ omnis auctorem,
ineffabiliter de se
    genuit incarnatum.

And so, in company with the choirs
    of Angels,
we praise you, and with joy
    we proclaim:

Holy, Holy, Holy Lord God of hosts...

Et ideo, choris angelicis sociati,
te laudamus, in gaudio confitentes:
Sanctus, Sanctus, Sanctus. . .

Communion Antiphon Lk 1:48-49

All generations will call me blessed,
for he who is mighty has done
    great things for me.

Ant. ad communionem

Beatam me dicent
    omnes generationes,
quia fecit mihi magna
    qui potens est.

Prayer after Communion

Having received the Sacrament
    of salvation,
we ask you to grant, O Lord,
that, through the intercession
    of the Blessed Virgin Mary,
whom you assumed into heaven,
we may be brought to the glory
    of the resurrection.
Through Christ our Lord.

Post communionem

Sumptis, Domine,
    salutaribus sacramentis,
da, quæsumus,
ut, intercessione beatæ Mariæ
    Virginis in cælum assumptæ,
ad resurrectionis
    gloriam perducamur.
Per Christum Dominum nostrum.

A formula of Solemn Blessing, p.144-145, may be used.

In Ireland

16 August

TWENTIETH SUNDAY IN ORDINARY TIME

Entrance Antiphon   Ps 83:10-11

TURN your eyes, O God,
    our shield;
and look on the face
    of your anointed one;
one day within your courts
is better than a thousand elsewhere.

Ant. ad introitum

PROTECTOR noster,
    aspice, Deus,
et respice in faciem Christi tui,
quia melior est dies una in atriis
    tuis super millia.

Collect

O God, who have prepared
    for those who love you
good things which no eye can see,
fill our hearts, we pray,
    with the warmth of your love,
so that, loving you in all things
    and above all things,
we may attain your promises,
which surpass every human desire.
Through our Lord Jesus Christ,
    your Son,
who lives and reigns with you
    in the unity of the Holy Spirit,
one God, for ever and ever.

Collecta

Deus, qui diligentibus te bona
    invisibilia præparasti,
infunde cordibus nostris
    tui amoris affectum,
ut, te in omnibus et super
    omnia diligentes,
promissiones tuas, quæ omne
    desiderium superant,
consequamur.
Per Dominum nostrum Iesum
    Christum Filium tuum,
qui tecum vivit et regnat
    in unitate Spiritus Sancti,
Deus, per omnia sæcula sæculorum.

FIRST READING

A reading from the prophet Isaiah   56:1,6-7

I will bring foreigners to my holy mountain.

Thus says the Lord: Have a care for justice, act with integrity, for soon my salvation will come and my integrity be manifest.

   Foreigners who have attached themselves to the Lord to serve him and to love his name and be his servants – all who observe the sabbath, not profaning it, and cling to my covenant – these I will bring to my holy mountain. I will make them joyful in my house of prayer. Their holocausts and their sacrifices will be accepted on my altar, for my house will be called a house of prayer for all the peoples.

   The word of the Lord.

Responsorial Psalm   Ps 66:2-3,5-6,8. R. v.4

R. **Let the peoples praise you, O God;
    let all the peoples praise you.**

   O God, be gracious and bless us
   and let your face shed its light upon us.
   So will your ways be known upon earth
   and all nations learn your saving help. R.

   Let the nations be glad and exult
   for you rule the world with justice.
   With fairness you rule the peoples,
   you guide the nations on earth. R.

Let the peoples praise you, O God;
let all the peoples praise you.
May God still give us his blessing
till the ends of the earth revere him. R.

R. **Let the peoples praise you, O God;**
let all the peoples praise you.

SECOND READING

A reading from the letter of St Paul to the Romans   11:13-15,29-32
With Israel, God never takes back his gifts or revokes his choice.

Let me tell you pagans this: I have been sent to the pagans as their apostle,
and I am proud of being sent, but the purpose of it is to make my own
people envious of you, and in this way save some of them. Since their
rejection meant the reconciliation of the world, do you know what their
admission will mean? Nothing less than a resurrection from the dead!
God never takes back his gifts or revokes his choice.

Just as you changed from being disobedient to God, and now enjoy
mercy because of their disobedience, so those who are disobedient now
– and only because of the mercy shown to you – will also enjoy mercy
eventually. God has imprisoned all men in their own disobedience only to
show mercy to all mankind.

The word of the Lord.

Gospel Acclamation   Cf. Jn 10:27
R. **Alleluia, alleluia!**
The sheep that belong to me listen to my voice,
says the Lord,
I know them and they follow me.
R. **Alleluia!**

Or: Cf. Mt 4:23
R. **Alleluia, alleluia!**
Jesus proclaimed the Good News of the kingdom,
and cured all kinds of sicknesses among the people.
R. **Alleluia!**

GOSPEL

A reading from the holy Gospel according to Matthew   15:21-28
Woman, you have great faith.

Jesus left Gennesaret and withdrew to the region of Tyre and Sidon. Then
out came a Canaanite woman from that district and started shouting, 'Sir,
Son of David, take pity on me. My daughter is tormented by a devil.' But

he answered her not a word. And his disciples went and pleaded with him. 'Give her what she wants,' they said 'because she is shouting after us.' He said in reply, 'I was sent only to the lost sheep of the House of Israel.' But the woman had come up and was kneeling at his feet. 'Lord,' she said 'help me.' He replied, 'It is not fair to take the children's food and throw it to the house-dogs.' She retorted, 'Ah yes, sir; but even house-dogs can eat the scraps that fall from their master's table.' Then Jesus answered her, 'Woman, you have great faith. Let your wish be granted.' And from that moment her daughter was well again.

The Gospel of the Lord.

Prayer over the Offerings	Super oblata
Receive our oblation, O Lord, by which is brought about a glorious exchange, that, by offering what you have given, we may merit to receive your very self. Through Christ our Lord.	Suscipe, Domine, munera nostra, quibus exercentur commercia gloriosa, ut, offerentes quæ dedisti, teipsum mereamur accipere. Per Christum Dominum nostrum.

Preface of Sundays in Ordinary Time I-VIII, pp.60-67.

Communion Antiphon Ps 129:7	Ant. ad communionem
With the Lord there is mercy; in him is plentiful redemption.	Apud Dominum misericordia, et copiosa apud eum redemptio.

Or: Jn 6:51-52	Vel:
I am the living bread that came down from heaven, says the Lord. Whoever eats of this bread will live for ever.	Ego sum panis vivus, qui de cælo descendi, dicit Dominus: si quis manducaverit ex hoc pane, vivet in æternum.

Prayer after Communion	Post communionem
Made partakers of Christ through these Sacraments, we humbly implore your mercy, Lord, that, conformed to his image on earth, we may merit also to be his coheirs in heaven. Who lives and reigns for ever and ever.	Per hæc sacramenta, Domine, Christi participes effecti, clementiam tuam humiliter imploramus, ut, eius imaginis conformes in terris, et eius consortes in cælis fieri mereamur. Qui vivit et regnat in sæcula sæculorum.

23 August

TWENTY-FIRST SUNDAY IN ORDINARY TIME

Entrance Antiphon   Cf. Ps 85:1-3

TURN your ear, O Lord,
and answer me;
save the servant who trusts in you,
my God.
Have mercy on me, O Lord,
for I cry to you all the day long.

Ant. ad introitum

INCLINA, Domine, aurem tuam
ad me, et exaudi me.
Salvum fac servum tuum,
Deus meus, sperantem in te.
Miserere mihi, Domine,
quoniam ad te clamavi tota die.

Collect

O God, who cause the minds
of the faithful
to unite in a single purpose,
grant your people to love
what you command
and to desire what you promise,
that, amid the uncertainties
of this world,
our hearts may be fixed on that place
where true gladness is found.
Through our Lord Jesus Christ,
your Son,
who lives and reigns with you
in the unity of the Holy Spirit,
one God, for ever and ever.

Collecta

Deus, qui fidelium mentes unius
efficis voluntatis,
da populis tuis id amare
quod præcipis,
id desiderare quod promittis,
ut, inter mundanas varietates,
ibi nostra fixa sint corda,
ubi vera sunt gaudia.
Per Dominum nostrum Iesum
Christum Filium tuum,
qui tecum vivit et regnat
in unitate Spiritus Sancti,
Deus, per omnia sæcula sæculorum.

FIRST READING

A reading from the prophet Isaiah   22:19-23

I place the key of the House of David upon his shoulder.

Thus says the Lord of hosts to Shebna, the master of the palace:
I dismiss you from your office,
I remove you from your post,
and the same day I call on my servant
Eliakim son of Hilkiah.
I invest him with your robe,
gird him with your sash,
entrust him with your authority,
and he shall be a father

to the inhabitants of Jerusalem
and to the House of Judah.
I place the key of the House of David
on his shoulder;
should he open, no one shall close,
should he close, no one shall open.
I drive him like a peg
into a firm place;
he will become a throne of glory
for his father's house.

The word of the Lord.

Responsorial Psalm   Ps 137:1-3,6,8. R. v.8

R. **Your love, O Lord, is eternal,
discard not the work of your hands.**

I thank you, Lord, with all my heart,
you have heard the words of my mouth.
Before the angels I will bless you.
I will adore before your holy temple. R.

I thank you for your faithfulness and love
which excel all we ever knew of you.
On the day I called, you answered;
you increased the strength of my soul. R.

The Lord is high yet he looks on the lowly
and the haughty he knows from afar.
Your love, O Lord, is eternal,
discard not the work of your hands. R.

SECOND READING

A reading from the letter of St Paul to the Romans   11:33-36

All that exists comes from him; all is by him and from him.

How rich are the depths of God – how deep his wisdom and knowledge –
and how impossible to penetrate his motives or understand his methods!
Who could ever know the mind of the Lord? Who could ever be his
counsellor? Who could ever give him anything or lend him anything? All
that exists comes from him; all is by him and for him. To him be glory for
ever! Amen.

The word of the Lord.

Gospel Acclamation   2 Co 5:19

R. **Alleluia, alleluia!**
God in Christ was reconciling the world to himself,
and he has entrusted to us the news that they are reconciled.
R. **Alleluia!**

Or: Mt 16:18

R. **Alleluia, alleluia!**
You are Peter,
and on this rock I will build my Church.
And the gates of the underworld can never hold out against it.
R. **Alleluia!**

GOSPEL

A reading from the holy Gospel according to Matthew   16:13-20

You are Peter, and I will give you the keys of the kingdom of heaven.

When Jesus came to the region of Caesarea Philippi he put this question
to his disciples, 'Who do people say the Son of Man is?' And they said,
'Some say he is John the Baptist, some Elijah, and others Jeremiah or one
of the prophets.' 'But you,' he said, 'who do you say I am?' Then Simon
Peter spoke up, 'You are the Christ,' he said 'the Son of the living God.'
Jesus replied, 'Simon son of Jonah, you are a happy man! Because it was
not flesh and blood that revealed this to you but my Father in heaven. So
I now say to you: You are Peter and on this rock I will build my Church.
And the gates of the underworld can never hold out against it. I will give
you the keys of the kingdom of heaven: whatever you bind on earth shall
be considered bound in heaven; whatever you loose on earth shall be
considered loosed in heaven.' Then he gave the disciples strict orders not
to tell anyone that he was the Christ.

The Gospel of the Lord.

Prayer over the Offerings	Super oblata
O Lord, who gained for yourself a people by adoption through the one sacrifice offered once for all, bestow graciously on us, we pray, the gifts of unity and peace in your Church. Through Christ our Lord.	Qui una semel hostia, Domine, adoptionis tibi populum acquisisti, unitatis et pacis in Ecclesia tua propitius nobis dona concedas. Per Christum Dominum nostrum.

Preface of Sundays in Ordinary Time I-VIII, pp.60-67.

Communion Antiphon Cf. Ps 103:13-15 | Ant. ad communionem

The earth is replete with the fruits
   of your work, O Lord;
you bring forth bread from the earth
and wine to cheer the heart.

De fructu operum tuorum,
   Domine, satiabitur terra,
ut educas panem de terra,
   et vinum lætificet cor hominis.

Or: Cf. Jn 6:54 | Vel:

Whoever eats my flesh
   and drinks my blood
has eternal life, says the Lord,
and I will raise him up
   on the last day.

Qui manducat meam carnem
   et bibit meum sanguinem,
habet vitam æternam,
   dicit Dominus;
et ego resuscitabo eum
   in novissimo die.

Prayer after Communion | Post communionem

Complete within us, O Lord,
   we pray,
the healing work of your mercy
and graciously perfect
   and sustain us,
so that in all things we may
   please you.
Through Christ our Lord.

Plenum, quæsumus, Domine,
in nobis remedium tuæ
   miserationis operare
ac tales nos esse perfice propitius
   et sic foveri,
ut tibi in omnibus
   placere valeamus.
Per Christum Dominum nostrum.

30 August

TWENTY-SECOND SUNDAY IN ORDINARY TIME

Entrance Antiphon   Cf. Ps 85:3,5 | Ant. ad introitum

HAVE mercy on me, O Lord,
for I cry to you all the day long.
O Lord, you are good and forgiving,
full of mercy to all who call to you.

MISERERE mihi, Domine,
quoniam ad te clamavi
   tota die:
quia tu, Domine, suavis ac mitis es,
et copiosus in misericordia
   omnibus invocantibus te.

Collect

God of might, giver of every
    good gift,
put into our hearts the love
    of your name,
so that, by deepening our sense
    of reverence,
you may nurture in us what is good
and, by your watchful care,
keep safe what you have nurtured.
Through our Lord Jesus Christ,
    your Son,
who lives and reigns with you
    in the unity of the Holy Spirit,
one God, for ever and ever.

Collecta

Deus virtutum, cuius est totum
    quod est optimum,
insere pectoribus nostris tui
    nominis amorem,
et præsta, ut in nobis,
religionis augmento,
    quæ sunt bona nutrias,
ac, vigilanti studio,
    quæ sunt nutrita custodias.
Per Dominum nostrum Iesum
    Christum Filium tuum,
qui tecum vivit et regnat
    in unitate Spiritus Sancti,
Deus, per omnia sæcula sæculorum.

FIRST READING

A reading from the prophet Jeremiah   20:7-9

The word of the Lord has meant insult for me.

You have seduced me, Lord, and I have let myself be seduced;
you have overpowered me: you were the stronger.
I am a daily laughing-stock,
everybody's butt.
Each time I speak the word, I have to howl
and proclaim: 'Violence and ruin!'
The word of the Lord has meant for me
insult, derision, all day long.
I used to say, 'I will not think about him,
I will not speak in his name anymore.'
Then there seemed to be a fire burning in my heart,
imprisoned in my bones.
The effort to restrain it wearied me,
I could not bear it.

    The word of the Lord.

Responsorial Psalm   Ps 62:2-6,8-9. R. v.2

R. **For you my soul is thirsting, O Lord my God.**

O God, you are my God, for you I long;
for you my soul is thirsting.
My body pines for you
like a dry, weary land without water. R.

So I gaze on you in the sanctuary
to see your strength and your glory.
For your love is better than life,
my lips will speak your praise. R.

So I will bless you all my life,
in your name I will lift up my hands.
My soul shall be filled as with a banquet,
my mouth shall praise you with joy. R.

For you have been my help;
in the shadow of your wings I rejoice.
My soul clings to you;
your right hand holds me fast. R.

SECOND READING

A reading from the letter of St Paul to the Romans   12:1-2

Offer your bodies as a living sacrifice.

Think of God's mercy, my brothers, and worship him, I beg you, in a way
that is worthy of thinking beings, by offering your living bodies as a holy
sacrifice, truly pleasing to God. Do not model yourselves on the behaviour
of the world around you, but let your behaviour change, modelled by your
new mind. This is the only way to discover the will of God and know what
is good, what it is that God wants, what is the perfect thing to do.

   The word of the Lord.

Gospel Acclamation   Cf. Ep 1:17-18

R. **Alleluia, alleluia!**
May the Father of our Lord Jesus Christ
enlighten the eyes of our mind,
so that we can see
what hope his call holds for us.
R. **Alleluia!**

GOSPEL

A reading from the holy Gospel according Matthew   16:21-27

If anyone wants to be a follower of mine, let him renounce himself.

Jesus began to make it clear to his disciples that he was destined to go to Jerusalem and suffer grievously at the hands of the elders and chief priests and scribes, to be put to death and to be raised up on the third day. Then, taking him aside, Peter started to remonstrate with him. 'Heaven preserve you, Lord,' he said. 'This must not happen to you.' But he turned and said to Peter, 'Get behind me, Satan! You are an obstacle in my path, because the way you think is not God's way but man's.'

Then Jesus said to his disciples, 'If anyone wants to be a follower of mine, let him renounce himself and take up his cross and follow me. For anyone who wants to save his life will lose it; but anyone who loses his life for my sake will find it. What, then, will a man gain if he wins the whole world and ruins his life? Or what has a man to offer in exchange for his life?

'For the Son of Man is going to come in the glory of his Father with his angels, and, when he does, he will reward each one according to his behaviour.'

The Gospel of the Lord.

Prayer over the Offerings	Super oblata
May this sacred offering, O Lord, confer on us always the blessing of salvation, that what it celebrates in mystery it may accomplish in power. Through Christ our Lord.	Benedictionem nobis, Domine, conferat salutarem sacra semper oblatio, ut, quod agit mysterio, virtute perficiat. Per Christum Dominum nostrum.

Preface of Sundays in Ordinary Time I-VIII, pp.60-67.

Communion Antiphon Ps 30:20	Ant. ad communionem
How great is the goodness, Lord, that you keep for those who fear you.	Quam magna multitudo dulcedinis tuæ, Domine, quam abscondisti timentibus te.
Or: Mt 5:9-10	Vel:
Blessed are the peacemakers, for they shall be called children of God. Blessed are they who are persecuted for the sake of righteousness, for theirs is the Kingdom of Heaven.	Beati pacifici, quoniam filii Dei vocabuntur. Beati qui persecutionem patiuntur propter iustitiam, quoniam ipsorum est regnum cælorum.

Prayer after Communion

Renewed by this bread
   from the heavenly table,
we beseech you, Lord,
that, being the food of charity,
it may confirm our hearts
and stir us to serve you
   in our neighbour.
Through Christ our Lord.

Post communionem

Pane mensæ cælestis refecti, te,
   Domine, deprecamur,
ut hoc nutrimentum caritatis corda
   nostra confirmet,
quatenus ad tibi ministrandum
   in fratribus excitemur.
Per Christum Dominum nostrum.

6 September

TWENTY-THIRD SUNDAY IN ORDINARY TIME

Entrance Antiphon Ps 118:137,124

YOU are just, O Lord,
   and your judgement is right;
treat your servant in accord
   with your merciful love.

Ant. ad introitum

IUSTUS es, Domine,
   et rectum iudicium tuum;
fac cum servo tuo secundum
   misericordiam tuam.

Collect

O God, by whom we are redeemed
   and receive adoption,
look graciously upon your beloved
   sons and daughters,
that those who believe in Christ
may receive true freedom
and an everlasting inheritance.
Through our Lord Jesus Christ,
   your Son,
who lives and reigns with you
   in the unity of the Holy Spirit,
one God, for ever and ever.

Collecta

Deus, per quem nobis
et redemptio venit
   et præstatur adoptio,
filios dilectionis tuæ
   benignus intende,
ut in Christo credentibus
et vera tribuatur libertas,
   et hereditas æterna.
Per Dominum nostrum Iesum
   Christum Filium tuum,
qui tecum vivit et regnat
   in unitate Spiritus Sancti,
Deus, per omnia sæcula sæculorum.

FIRST READING

A reading from the prophet Ezekiel   33:7-9

If you do not speak to the wicked man, I will hold you responsible for his death.

The word of the Lord was addressed to me as follows, 'Son of man, I have appointed you as sentry to the House of Israel. When you hear a word from my mouth, warn them in my name. If I say to a wicked man:

Wicked wretch, you are to die, and you do not speak to warn the wicked man to renounce his ways, then he shall die for his sin, but I will hold you responsible for his death. If, however, you do warn a wicked man to renounce his ways and repent, and he does not repent, then he shall die for his sin but you yourself will have saved your life.'

The word of the Lord.

Responsorial Psalm   Ps 94:1-2,6-9. R. v.8

R. **O that today you would listen to his voice!**
   Harden not your hearts.

Come, ring out our joy to the Lord;
hail the rock who saves us.
Let us come before him, giving thanks,
with songs let us hail the Lord. R.

Come in; let us bow and bend low;
let us kneel before the God who made us
for he is our God and we
the people who belong to his pasture,
the flock that is led by his hand. R.

O that today you would listen to his voice!
'Harden not your hearts as at Meribah,
as on that day at Massah in the desert
when your fathers put me to the test;
when they tried me, though they saw my work.' R.

SECOND READING

A reading from the letter of St Paul to the Romans   13:8-10
Love is the answer to every one of the commandments.

Avoid getting into debt, except the debt of mutual love. If you love your fellow men you have carried out your obligations. All the commandments: You shall not commit adultery, you shall not kill, you shall not steal, you shall not covet, and so on, are summed up in this single command: You must love your neighbour as yourself. Love is the one thing that cannot hurt your neighbour; that is why it is the answer to every one of the commandments.

The word of the Lord.

Gospel Acclamation   Jn 17:17

R. **Alleluia, alleluia!**
Your word is truth, O Lord,
consecrate us in the truth.
R. **Alleluia!**

Or: 2 Co 5:19

R. **Alleluia, alleluia!**
God in Christ was reconciling the world to himself,
and he has entrusted to us the news that they are reconciled.
R. **Alleluia!**

GOSPEL

A reading from the holy Gospel according to Matthew   18:15-20

If he listens to you, you have won back your brother.

Jesus said to his disciples: 'If your brother does something wrong, go and
have it out with him alone, between your two selves. If he listens to you,
you have won back your brother. If he does not listen, take one or two
others along with you: the evidence of two or three witnesses is required
to sustain any charge. But if he refuses to listen to these, report it to the
community; and if he refuses to listen to the community, treat him like a
pagan or a tax collector.

'I tell you solemnly, whatever you bind on earth shall be considered
bound in heaven; whatever you loose on earth shall be considered loosed
in heaven.

'I tell you solemnly once again, if two of you on earth agree to ask
anything at all, it will be granted to you by my Father in heaven. For where
two or three meet in my name, I shall be there with them.'

   The Gospel of the Lord.

Prayer over the Offerings	Super oblata
O God, who give us the gift	Deus, auctor sinceræ
of true prayer and of peace,	devotionis et pacis,
graciously grant that,	da, quæsumus,
through this offering,	ut et maiestatem tuam
we may do fitting homage to your	convenienter hoc
divine majesty	munere veneremur,
and, by partaking	et sacri participatione mysterii
of the sacred mystery,	fideliter sensibus uniamur.
we may be faithfully united	Per Christum Dominum nostrum.
in mind and heart.	
Through Christ our Lord.	

Preface of Sundays in Ordinary Time I-VIII, pp.60-67.

Communion Antiphon Cf. Ps 41:2-3

Like the deer that yearns
   for running streams,
so my soul is yearning for you,
   my God;
my soul is thirsting for God,
   the living God.

Or: Jn 8:12

I am the light of the world,
   says the Lord;
whoever follows me will not walk
   in darkness,
but will have the light of life.

Prayer after Communion

Grant that your faithful, O Lord,
whom you nourish and endow
   with life
through the food of your Word
   and heavenly Sacrament,
may so benefit from your beloved
   Son's great gifts
that we may merit an eternal share
   in his life.
Who lives and reigns
   for ever and ever.

Ant. ad communionem

Quemadmodum desiderat cervus
   ad fontes aquarum,
ita desiderat anima mea
   ad te, Deus:
sitivit anima mea ad Deum
   fortem vivum.

Vel:

Ego sum lux mundi,
   dicit Dominus:
qui sequitur me non ambulat
   in tenebris,
sed habebit lumen vitæ.

Post communionem

Da fidelibus tuis, Domine,
quos et verbi tui et cælestis
   sacramenti pabulo
nutris et vivificas,
ita dilecti Filii tui tantis
   muneribus proficere,
ut eius vitæ semper consortes
   effici mereamur.
Qui vivit et regnat
   in sæcula sæculorum.

13 September

TWENTY-FOURTH SUNDAY IN ORDINARY TIME

Entrance Antiphon   Cf. Sir 36:18

GIVE peace, O Lord,
to those who wait for you,
that your prophets be found true.
Hear the prayers of your servant,
and of your people Israel.

Ant. ad introitum

DA pacem, Domine,
sustinentibus te,
ut prophetæ tui fideles inveniantur;
exaudi preces servi tui,
et plebis tuæ Israel.

Collect

Look upon us, O God,
Creator and ruler of all things,
and, that we may feel the working
    of your mercy,
grant that we may serve you
    with all our heart.
Through our Lord Jesus Christ,
    your Son,
who lives and reigns with you
    in the unity of the Holy Spirit,
one God, for ever and ever.

Collecta

Respice nos, rerum omnium Deus
    creator et rector,
et, ut tuæ propitiationis
    sentiamus effectum,
toto nos tribue tibi corde servire.
Per Dominum nostrum Iesum
    Christum Filium tuum,
qui tecum vivit et regnat
    in unitate Spiritus Sancti,
Deus, per omnia sæcula sæculorum.

FIRST READING

A reading from the book of Ecclesiasticus   27:30-28:7

Forgive your neighbour the hurt he does you, and when you pray, your sins will be forgiven.

Resentment and anger, these are foul things,
and both are found with the sinner.
He who exacts vengeance will experience the vengeance of the Lord,
who keeps strict account of sin.
Forgive your neighbour the hurt he does you,
and when you pray, your sins will be forgiven.
If a man nurses anger against another,
can he then demand compassion from the Lord?
Showing no pity for a man like himself,
can he then plead for his own sins?
Mere creature of flesh, he cherishes resentment;
who will forgive him his sins?
Remember the last things, and stop hating,
remember dissolution and death, and live by the commandments.
Remember the commandments, and do not bear your neighbour ill-will;
remember the covenant of the Most High, and overlook the offence.
    The word of the Lord.

Responsorial Psalm   Ps 102:1-4,9-12. R. v.8

R. **The Lord is compassion and love,**
   slow to anger and rich in mercy.

My soul, give the thanks to the Lord,
all my being, bless his holy name.
My soul, give thanks to the Lord
and never forget all his blessings. R.

It is he who forgives all your guilt,
who heals every one of your ills,
who redeems your life from the grave,
who crowns you with love and compassion. R.

His wrath will come to an end;
he will not be angry for ever.
He does not treat us according to our sins
nor repay us according to our faults. R.

For as the heavens are high above the earth
so strong is his love for those who fear him.
As far as the east is from the west
so far does he remove our sins. R.

SECOND READING

A reading from the letter of St Paul to the Romans   14:7-9

Alive or dead we belong to the Lord.

The life and death of each of us has its influence on others; if we live, we live for the Lord; and if we die, we die for the Lord, so that alive or dead we belong to the Lord. This explains why Christ both died and came to life, it was so that he might be Lord both of the dead and of the living.

   The word of the Lord.

Gospel Acclamation   1 S 3:9; Jn 6:68

R. **Alleluia, alleluia!**
Speak, Lord, your servant is listening:
you have the message of eternal life.
R. **Alleluia!**

Or: Jn 13:34

R. **Alleluia, alleluia!**
I give you a new commandment:
love one another, just as I have loved you,
says the Lord.
R. **Alleluia!**

GOSPEL

A reading from the holy Gospel according to Matthew   18:21-35

I do not tell you to forgive seven times, but seventy-seven times.

Peter went up to Jesus and said, 'Lord, how often must I forgive my brother if he wrongs me? As often as seven times?' Jesus answered, 'Not seven, I tell you, but seventy-seven times.

'And so the kingdom of heaven may be compared to a king who decided to settle his accounts with his servants. When the reckoning began, they brought him a man who owed ten thousand talents; but he had no means of paying, so his master gave orders that he should be sold, together with his wife and children and all his possessions, to meet the debt. At this, the servant threw himself down at his master's feet. "Give me time," he said "and I will pay the whole sum." And the servant's master felt so sorry for him that he let him go and cancelled the debt. Now as this servant went out, he happened to meet a fellow servant who owed him one hundred denarii; and he seized him by the throat and began to throttle him. "Pay what you owe me," he said. His fellow servant fell at his feet and implored him, saying, "Give me time and I will pay you." But the other would not agree; on the contrary, he had him thrown into prison till he should pay the debt. His fellow servants were deeply distressed when they saw what had happened, and they went to their master and reported the whole affair to him. Then the master sent for him. "You wicked servant," he said "I cancelled all that debt of yours when you appealed to me. Were you not bound, then, to have pity on your fellow servant just as I had pity on you?" And in his anger the master handed him over to the torturers till he should pay all his debt. And that is how my heavenly Father will deal with you unless you each forgive your brother from your heart.'

The Gospel of the Lord.

Prayer over the Offerings	Super oblata
Look with favour on our supplications, O Lord, and in your kindness accept these, your servants' offerings, that what each has offered to the honour of your name may serve the salvation of all. Through Christ our Lord.	Propitiare, Domine, supplicationibus nostris, et has oblationes famulorum tuorum benignus assume, ut, quod singuli ad honorem tui nominis obtulerunt, cunctis proficiat ad salutem. Per Christum Dominum nostrum.

Preface of Sundays in Ordinary Time I-VIII, pp.60-67.

Communion Antiphon Cf. Ps 35:8
How precious is your mercy, O God!
The children of men seek shelter
   in the shadow of your wings.

Or: Cf. 1 Co 10:16
The chalice of blessing that we bless
is a communion in the Blood
   of Christ;
and the bread that we break
is a sharing in the Body of the Lord.

Prayer after Communion
May the working of this heavenly
   gift, O Lord, we pray,
take possession of our minds
   and bodies,
so that its effects,
   and not our own desires,
may always prevail in us.
Through Christ our Lord.

Ant. ad communionem
Quam pretiosa
   est misericordia tua, Deus!
Filii hominum sub umbra alarum
   tuarum confugient.

Vel:
Calix benedictionis,
   cui benedicimus,
communicatio Sanguinis Christi est;
et panis, quem frangimus,
participatio Corporis Domini est.

Post communionem
Mentes nostras et corpora possideat,
quæsumus, Domine,
   doni cælestis operatio,
ut non noster sensus in nobis,
sed eius præveniat semper effectus.
Per Christum Dominum nostrum.

---

20 September

TWENTY-FIFTH SUNDAY IN ORDINARY TIME

Entrance Antiphon
I AM the salvation of the people,
   says the Lord.
Should they cry to me in any distress,
I will hear them, and I will be their
   Lord for ever.

Ant. ad introitum
SALUS populi ego sum,
   dicit Dominus.
De quacumque tribulatione
   clamaverint ad me,
exaudiam eos, et ero illorum
   Dominus in perpetuum.

Collect
O God, who founded all the
   commands of your sacred Law
upon love of you
   and of our neighbour,
grant that, by keeping your precepts,
we may merit to attain eternal life.

Collecta
Deus, qui sacræ legis omnia constituta
in tua et proximi dilectione posuisti,
da nobis, ut,
   tua præcepta servantes,
ad vitam mereamur
   pervenire perpetuam.

Through our Lord Jesus Christ,
    your Son,
who lives and reigns with you
    in the unity of the Holy Spirit,
one God, for ever and ever.
	Per Dominum nostrum Iesum
	    Christum Filium tuum,
	qui tecum vivit et regnat
	    in unitate Spiritus Sancti,
	Deus, per omnia sæcula sæculorum.

FIRST READING

A reading from the prophet Isaiah   55:6-9

My thoughts are not your thoughts.

Seek the Lord while he is still to be found,
call to him while he is still near.
Let the wicked man abandon his way,
the evil man his thoughts.
Let him turn back to the Lord who will take pity on him,
to our God who is rich in forgiving;
for my thoughts are not your thoughts,
my ways not your ways – it is the Lord who speaks.
Yes, the heavens are as high above earth
as my ways are above your ways,
my thoughts above your thoughts.

    The word of the Lord.

Responsorial Psalm   Ps 144:2-3,8-9,17-18. R. v.18

R. **The Lord is close to all who call him.**

    I will bless you day after day
    and praise your name for ever.
    The Lord is great, highly to be praised,
    his greatness cannot be measured. R.

    The Lord is kind and full of compassion,
    slow to anger, abounding in love.
    How good is the Lord to all,
    compassionate to all his creatures. R.

    The Lord is just in all his ways
    and loving in all his deeds.
    He is close to all who call him,
    who call on him from their hearts. R.

SECOND READING

A reading from the letter of St Paul to the Philippians   1:20-24,27

Life to me is Christ

Christ will be glorified in my body, whether by my life or by my death. Life
to me, of course, is Christ, but then death would bring me something more;

but then again, if living in this body means doing work which is having good results – I do not know what I should choose. I am caught in this dilemma: I want to be gone and be with Christ, which would be very much the better, but for me to stay alive in this body is a more urgent need for your sake.

Avoid anything in your everyday lives that would be unworthy of the gospel of Christ.

The word of the Lord.

Gospel Acclamation   Lk 19:38

R. **Alleluia, alleluia!**
Blessings on the King who comes,
in the name of the Lord!
Peace in heaven
and glory in the highest heavens!
R. **Alleluia!**

Or: Cf. Ac 16:14

R. **Alleluia, alleluia!**
Open our hearts, O Lord,
to accept the words of your Son.
R. **Alleluia!**

GOSPEL

A reading from the holy Gospel according to Matthew   20:1-16

Why be envious because I am generous?

Jesus told this parable to his disciples: 'The kingdom of heaven is like a landowner going out at daybreak to hire workers for his vineyard. He made an agreement with the workers for one denarius a day, and sent them to his vineyard. Going out at about the third hour he saw others standing idle in the market place and said to them, "You go to my vineyard too and I will give you a fair wage." So they went. At about the sixth hour and again at about the ninth hour, he went out and did the same. Then at about the eleventh hour he went out and found more men standing round, and he said to them, "Why have you been standing here idle all day?" "Because no one has hired us" they answered. He said to them, "You go into my vineyard too." In the evening, the owner of the vineyard said to his bailiff, "Call the workers and pay them their wages, starting with the last arrivals and ending with the first." So those who were hired at about the eleventh hour came forward and received one denarius each. When the first came, they expected to get more, but they too received one denarius each. They took it, but grumbled at the landowner. "The men who came last" they said "have done only one hour, and you have treated them the same as us, though we have done a heavy day's work in all the heat." He answered one of them and said, "My friend, I am not being unjust to you; did we not agree on one denarius? Take your earnings and go. I choose to pay the last-comer as much as I pay you. Have I no right to do what I like with my own? Why be envious because I am generous?" Thus the last will be first, and the first, last.'

The Gospel of the Lord.

Prayer over the Offerings	Super oblata
Receive with favour, O Lord, we pray, the offerings of your people, that what they profess with devotion and faith may be theirs through these heavenly mysteries. Through Christ our Lord.	Munera, quæsumus, Domine, tuæ plebis propitiatus assume, ut, quæ fidei pietate profitentur, sacramentis cælestibus apprehendant. Per Christum Dominum nostrum.

Preface of Sundays in Ordinary Time I-VIII, pp.60-67.

Communion Antiphon Ps 118:4-5	Ant. ad communionem
You have laid down your precepts to be carefully kept; may my ways be firm in keeping your statutes.	Tu mandasti mandata tua custodiri nimis; utinam dirigantur viæ meæ ad custodiendas iustificationes tuas.

Or: Jn 10:14	Vel:
I am the Good Shepherd, says the Lord; I know my sheep, and mine know me.	Ego sum pastor bonus, dicit Dominus; et cognosco oves meas, et cognoscunt me meæ.

Prayer after Communion	Post communionem
Graciously raise up, O Lord, those you renew with this Sacrament, that we may come to possess your redemption both in mystery and in the manner of our life. Through Christ our Lord.	Quos tuis, Domine, reficis sacramentis, continuis attolle benignus auxiliis, ut redemptionis effectum et mysteriis capiamus et moribus. Per Christum Dominum nostrum.

27 September

TWENTY-SIXTH SUNDAY IN ORDINARY TIME

Entrance Antiphon Dn 3:31,29,30,43,42

ALL that you have done to us,
O Lord,
 you have done with true judgement,
for we have sinned against you
and not obeyed
    your commandments.
But give glory to your name
and deal with us according
    to the bounty of your mercy.

Ant. ad introitum

OMNIA, quæ fecisti nobis,
Domine,
in vero iudicio fecisti, quia
    peccavimus tibi,
et mandatis tuis non obœdivimus;
sed da gloriam nomini tuo,
et fac nobiscum secundum
    multitudinem misericordiæ tuæ.

Collect

O God, who manifest
    your almighty power
above all by pardoning
    and showing mercy,
bestow, we pray, your grace
    abundantly upon us
and make those hastening to attain
    your promises
heirs to the treasures of heaven.
Through our Lord Jesus Christ,
    your Son,
who lives and reigns with you
    in the unity of the Holy Spirit,
one God, for ever and ever.

Collecta

Deus, qui omnipotentiam tuam
parcendo maxime
    et miserando manifestas,
multiplica super nos gratiam tuam,
ut, ad tua promissa currentes,
cælestium bonorum facias
    esse consortes.
Per Dominum nostrum Iesum
    Christum Filium tuum,
qui tecum vivit et regnat
    in unitate Spiritus Sancti,
Deus, per omnia sæcula sæculorum.

FIRST READING

A reading from the prophet Ezekiel   18:25-28

When the sinner renounces sin, he shall certainly live.

The word of the Lord was addressed to me as follows: 'You object, "What the Lord does is unjust." Listen, you House of Israel: is what I do unjust? Is it not what you do that is unjust? When the upright man renounces his integrity to commit sin and dies because of this, he dies because of the evil that he himself has committed. When the sinner renounces sin to become law-abiding and honest, he deserves to live. He has chosen to renounce all his previous sins; he shall certainly live; he shall not die.'

The word of the Lord.

Responsial Psalm   Ps 24:4-9. R. v.6

R. **Remember your mercy, Lord.**

> Lord, make me know your ways.
> Lord, teach me your paths.
> Make me walk in truth, and teach me:
> for you are God my saviour. R.

> Remember your mercy, Lord,
> and the love you have shown from of old.
> Do not remember the sins of my youth.
> In your love remember me,
> because of your goodness, O Lord. R.

> The Lord is good and upright.
> He shows the path to those who stray,
> he guides the humble in the right path;
> he teaches his way to the poor. R.

SECOND READING

A reading from the letter of St Paul to the Philippians   2:1-11

In your minds you must be the same as Christ Jesus.

[If our life in Christ means anything to you, if love can persuade at all, or the Spirit that we have in common, or any tenderness and sympathy, then be united in your convictions and united in your love, with a common purpose and a common mind. That is the one thing which would make me completely happy. There must be no competition among you, no conceit; but everybody is to be self-effacing. Always consider the other person to be better than your self, so that nobody thinks of his own interests first but everybody thinks of other people's interests instead. In your minds you must be the same as Christ Jesus:]

> His state was divine,
> yet he did not cling
> to his equality with God
> but emptied himself
> to assume the condition of a slave,
> and became as men are;

and being as all men are,
he was humbler yet,
even to accepting death,
death on a cross.
But God raised him high
and gave him the name
which is above all other names
so that all beings
in the heavens, on earth and in the underworld,
should bend the knee at the name of Jesus
and that every tongue should acclaim
Jesus Christ as Lord,
to the glory of God the Father.

[The word of the Lord.]

Shorter Form, verses 1-5. Read between [ ]

Gospel Acclamation   Jn 14:23
R. **Alleluia, alleluia!**
If anyone loves me he will keep my word.
and my Father will love him,
and we shall come to him.
R. **Alleluia!**

Or: Jn 10:27

R. **Alleluia, alleluia!**
The sheep that belong to me listen to my voice,
says the Lord,
I know them and they follow me.
R. **Alleluia!**

GOSPEL

A reading from the holy Gospel according to Matthew   21:28-32

He thought better of it and went. Tax collectors and prostitutes are making their way into the kingdom of God before you.

Jesus said to the chief priests and the elders of the people, 'What is your opinion? A man had two sons. He went and said to the first, "My boy, you go and work in the vineyard today." He answered, "I will not go", but afterwards thought better of it and went. The man then went and said the same thing to the second who answered, "Certainly, sir", but did not go. Which of the two did the father's will?' 'The first' they said. Jesus said to them, 'I tell you solemnly, tax collectors and prostitutes are making their way into the kingdom of God before you. For John came to you, a pattern of true righteousness, but you did not believe him, and yet the tax collectors and prostitutes did. Even after seeing that, you refused to think better of it and believe in him.'

The Gospel of the Lord.

Prayer over the Offerings

Grant us, O merciful God,
that this our offering may find
    acceptance with you
and that through it the wellspring
    of all blessing
may be laid open before us.
Through Christ our Lord.

Preface of Sundays in Ordinary Time I-VIII, pp.60-67.

Super oblata

Concede nobis, misericors Deus,
ut hæc nostra oblatio tibi
    sit accepta,
et per eam nobis fons omnis
    benedictionis aperiatur.
Per Christum Dominum nostrum.

Communion Antiphon Cf. Ps 118:49-50

Remember your word to your servant,
    O Lord,
by which you have given me hope.
This is my comfort when I am
    brought low.

Or: 1 Jn 3:16

By this we came to know
    the love of God:
that Christ laid down his life for us;
so we ought to lay down our lives
    for one another.

Ant. ad communionem

Memento verbi tui
    servo tuo, Domine,
in quo mihi spem dedisti;
hæc me consolata est
    in humilitate mea.

Vel:

In hoc cognovimus caritatem Dei:
quoniam ille animam suam
    pro nobis posuit;
et nos debemus pro fratribus
    animas ponere.

Prayer after Communion

May this heavenly mystery, O Lord,
restore us in mind and body,
that we may be coheirs in glory
    with Christ,
to whose suffering we are united
whenever we proclaim his Death.
Who lives and reigns
    for ever and ever.

Post communionem

Sit nobis, Domine,
    reparatio mentis et corporis
cæleste mysterium, ut simus eius
    in gloria coheredes,
cui, mortem ipsius
    annuntiando, compatimur.
Qui vivit et regnat
    in sæcula sæculorum.

4 October

TWENTY-SEVENTH SUNDAY IN ORDINARY TIME

Entrance Antiphon   Cf. Est 4:17

WITHIN your will, O Lord,
all things are established,
and there is none that can resist
    your will.
For you have made all things,
    the heaven and the earth,
and all that is held within the circle
    of heaven;
you are the Lord of all.

Collect

Almighty ever-living God,
who in the abundance
    of your kindness
surpass the merits and the desires
    of those who entreat you,
pour out your mercy upon us
to pardon what conscience dreads
and to give what prayer does
    not dare to ask.
Through our Lord Jesus Christ,
    your Son,
who lives and reigns with you
    in the unity of the Holy Spirit,
one God, for ever and ever.

Ant. ad introitum

IN voluntate tua, Domine,
universa sunt posita,
et non est qui possit resistere
    voluntati tuæ.
Tu enim fecisti omnia,
    cælum et terram,
et universa quæ cæli
    ambitu continentur;
Dominus universorum tu es.

Collecta

Omnipotens sempiterne Deus,
    qui abundantia pietatis tuæ
et merita supplicum excedis et vota,
effunde super nos
    misericordiam tuam,
ut dimittas quæ conscientia metuit,
et adicias quod oratio non præsumit.
Per Dominum nostrum Iesum
    Christum Filium tuum,
qui tecum vivit et regnat
    in unitate Spiritus Sancti,
Deus, per omnia sæcula sæculorum.

FIRST READING

A reading from the prophet Isaiah   5:1-7
The vineyard of the Lord of hosts is the House of Israel.

Let me sing to my friend
the song of his love for his vineyard.
My friend had a vineyard
on a fertile hillside.
He dug the soil, cleared it of stones,
and planted choice vines in it.

In the middle he built a tower,
he dug a press there too.
He expected it to yield grapes,
but sour grapes were all that it gave.

And now, inhabitants of Jerusalem
and men of Judah,
I ask you to judge
between my vineyard and me.
What could I have done for my vineyard
that I have not done?
I expected it to yield grapes.
Why did it yield sour grapes instead?

Very well, I will tell you
what I am going to do to my vineyard:
I will take away its hedge for it to be grazed on,
and knock down its wall for it to be trampled on.
I will lay it waste, unpruned, undug;
overgrown by the briar and the thorn.
I will command the clouds
to rain no rain on it.
Yes, the vineyard of the Lord of hosts
is the House of Israel,
and the men of Judah
that chosen plant.
He expected justice, but found bloodshed,
integrity, but only a cry of distress.

The word of the Lord.

Responsorial Psalm   Ps 79:9,12-16,19-20. R. Is 5:7

R. **The vineyard of the Lord is the House of Israel.**

You brought a vine out of Egypt;
to plant it you drove out the nations.
It stretched out its branches to the sea,
to the Great River it stretched out its shoots. R.

Then why have you broken down its walls?
It is plucked by all who pass by.
It is ravaged by the boar of the forest,
devoured by the beasts of the field. R.

God of hosts, turn again, we implore,
look down from heaven and see.
Visit this vine and protect it,
the vine your right hand has planted. R.

And we shall never forsake you again:
give us life that we may call upon your name.
God of hosts, bring us back;
let your face shine on us and we shall be saved. R.

R. **The vineyard of the Lord is the House of Israel.**

SECOND READING

A reading from the letter of St Paul to the Philippians   4:6-9
The God of peace will be with you.

There is no need to worry; but if there is anything you need, pray for it, asking God for it with prayer and thanksgiving, and that peace of God, which is so much greater than we can understand, will guard your hearts and your thoughts, in Christ Jesus. Finally, brothers, fill your minds with everything that is true, everything that is noble, everything that is good and pure, everything that we love and honour, and everything that can be thought virtuous or worthy of praise. Keep doing all the things that you learnt from me and have been taught by me and have heard or seen that I do. Then the God of peace will be with you.

The word of the Lord.

Gospel Acclamation   Jn 15:15

R. **Alleluia, alleluia!**
I call you friends, says the Lord,
because I have made known to you
everything I have learnt from my Father.
R. **Alleluia!**

Or: Cf. Jn 15:16

R. **Alleluia, alleluia!**
I chose you from the world
to go out and bear fruit,
fruit that will last,
says the Lord.
R. **Alleluia!**

GOSPEL

A reading from the holy Gospel according to Matthew   21:33-43

He will lease the vineyard to other tenants.

Jesus said to the chief priests and the elders of the people, 'Listen to another parable. There was a man, a landowner, who planted a vineyard; he fenced it round, dug a winepress in it and built a tower; then he leased it to tenants and went abroad. When vintage time drew near he sent his servants to the tenants to collect his produce. But the tenants seized his servants, thrashed one, killed another and stoned a third. Next he sent some more servants, this time a larger number, and they dealt with them in the same way. Finally he sent his son to them. "They will respect my son" he said. But when the tenants saw the son, they said to each other, "This is the heir. Come on, let us kill him and take over his inheritance." So they seized him and threw him out of the vineyard and killed him. Now when the owner of the vineyard comes, what will he do to those tenants?' They answered, 'He will bring those wretches to a wretched end and lease the vineyard to other tenants who will deliver the produce to him when the season arrives.' Jesus said to them, 'Have you never read in the scriptures:

It was the stone rejected by the builders
that became the keystone.
This was the Lord's doing
and it is wonderful to see?

'I tell you, then, that the kingdom of God will be taken from you and given to a people who will produce its fruit.'

The Gospel of the Lord.

Prayer over the Offerings	Super oblata

Accept, O Lord, we pray,
the sacrifices instituted
   by your commands
and, through the sacred mysteries,
which we celebrate
   with dutiful service,
graciously complete
   the sanctifying work
by which you are pleased
   to redeem us.
Through Christ our Lord.
	Suscipe, quæsumus, Domine,
	sacrificia tuis instituta præceptis,
	et sacris mysteriis,
	quæ debitæ servitutis
	   celebramus officio,
	sanctificationem tuæ nobis
	   redemptionis dignanter adimple.
	Per Christum Dominum nostrum.

Preface of Sundays in Ordinary Time I-VIII, pp.60-67.

Communion Antiphon   Lm 3:25

The Lord is good to those
   who hope in him,
to the soul that seeks him.

Or: Cf. 1 Co 10:17

Though many, we are one bread,
   one body,
for we all partake of the one Bread
   and one Chalice.

Prayer after Communion

Grant us, almighty God,
that we may be refreshed
   and nourished
by the Sacrament which
   we have received,
so as to be transformed
   into what we consume.
Through Christ our Lord.

Ant. ad communionem

Bonus est Dominus
   sperantibus in eum,
animæ quærenti illum.

Vel:

Unus panis et unum corpus
   multi sumus,
omnes qui de uno pane et de uno
   calice participamus.

Post communionem

Concede nobis, omnipotens Deus,
ut de perceptis sacramentis
   inebriemur atque pascamur,
quatenus in id quod
   sumimus transeamus.
Per Christum Dominum nostrum.

11 October

TWENTY-EIGHTH SUNDAY IN ORDINARY TIME

Entrance Antiphon   Ps 129:3-4

I F you, O Lord,
  should mark iniquities,
Lord, who could stand?
But with you is found forgiveness,
O God of Israel.

Collect

May your grace, O Lord, we pray,
at all times go before us
   and follow after
and make us always determined
to carry out good works.
Through our Lord Jesus Christ,
   your Son,
who lives and reigns with you
   in the unity of the Holy Spirit,
one God, for ever and ever.

Ant. ad introitum

S I iniquitates observaveris,
  Domine,
Domine, quis sustinebit?
Quia apud te propitiatio est,
   Deus Israel.

Collecta

Tua nos, quæsumus,
   Domine, gratia
semper et præveniat et sequatur,
ac bonis operibus iugiter præstet
   esse intentos.
Per Dominum nostrum Iesum
   Christum Filium tuum,
qui tecum vivit et regnat
   in unitate Spiritus Sancti,
Deus, per omnia sæcula sæculorum.

FIRST READING

A reading from the prophet Isaiah   25:6-10

The Lord will prepare a banquet, and will wipe away tears from every cheek.

On this mountain,
the Lord of hosts will prepare for all people
a banquet of rich food, a banquet of fine wines,
of food rich and juicy, of fine strained wines.
On this mountain he will remove
the mourning veil covering all peoples,
and the shroud enwrapping all nations,
he will destroy Death for ever.
The Lord will wipe away
the tears from every cheek;
he will take away his people's shame
everywhere on earth,
for the Lord has said so.
That day, it will be said: See, this is our God
in whom we hoped for salvation;
the Lord is the one in whom we hoped.
We exult and we rejoice
that he has saved us;
for the hand of the Lord
rests on this mountain.

The word of the Lord.

Responsorial Psalm   Ps 22. R. v.6

R. **In the Lord's own house shall I dwell
for ever and ever.**

The Lord is my shepherd;
there is nothing I shall want.
Fresh and green are the pastures
where he gives me repose.
Near restful waters he leads me,
to revive my drooping spirit. R.

He guides me along the right path;
he is true to his name.
If I should walk in the valley of darkness
no evil would I fear.
You are there with your crook and your staff;
with these you give me comfort. R.

You have prepared a banquet for me
in the sight of my foes.
My head you have anointed with oil;
my cup is overflowing. R.

Surely goodness and kindness shall follow me
all the days of my life.
In the Lord's own house shall I dwell
for ever and ever. R.

R. **In the Lord's own house shall I dwell
for ever and ever.**

SECOND READING

A reading from the letter of St Paul to the Philippians   4:12-14,19-20
There is nothing I cannot master with the help of the One who gives me strength.

I know how to be poor and I know how to be rich too. I have been through my initiation and now I am ready for anything anywhere: full stomach or empty stomach, poverty or plenty. There is nothing I cannot master with the help of the One who gives me strength. All the same, it was good of you to share with me in my hardships. In return my God will fulfil all your needs, in Christ Jesus, as lavishly as only God can. Glory to God, our Father, for ever and ever. Amen.

The word of the Lord.

Gospel Acclamation   Jn 1:12,14

R. **Alleluia, alleluia!**
The Word has made flesh and lived among us;
to all who did accept him
he gave power to become children of God.
R. **Alleluia!**

Or: Cf. Ep 1:17-18

R. **Alleluia, alleluia!**
May the Father of our Lord Jesus Christ
enlighten the eyes of our mind,
so that we can see what hope his call holds for us.
R. **Alleluia!**

GOSPEL

A reading from holy Gospel according to Matthew   22:1-14
Invite everyone you can find to the wedding.

[Jesus said to the chief priests and elders of the people: 'The kingdom of heaven may be compared to a king who gave a feast for his son's wedding.

He sent his servants to call those who had been invited, but they would not come. Next he sent some more servants. "Tell those who have been invited" he said "that I have my banquet all prepared, my oxen and fattened cattle have been slaughtered, everything is ready. Come to the wedding." But they were not interested: one went off to his farm, another to his business, and the rest seized his servants, maltreated them and killed them. The king was furious. He despatched his troops, destroyed those murderers and burnt their town. Then he said to his servants, "The wedding is ready; but as those who were invited proved to be unworthy, go to the crossroads in the town and invite everyone you can find to the wedding." So these servants went out on to the roads and collected together everyone they could find, bad and good alike; and the wedding hall was filled with guests.]When the king came in to look at the guests he noticed one man who was not wearing a wedding garment, and said to him, "How did you get in here, my friend, without a wedding garment?" And the man was silent. Then the king said to the attendants, "Bind him hand and foot and throw him out into the dark, where there will be weeping and grinding of teeth." For many are called, but few are chosen.'

| [The Gospel of the Lord.]

Shorter Form, verses 1-10. Read between [ ]

Prayer over the Offerings	Super oblata
Accept, O Lord,	Suscipe, Domine,
the prayers of your faithful	fidelium preces cum
with the sacrificial offerings,	oblationibus hostiarum,
that, through these acts	ut, per hæc piæ devotionis officia,
of devotedness,	ad cælestem gloriam transeamus.
we may pass over to the glory	Per Christum Dominum nostrum.
of heaven.	
Through Christ our Lord.	

Preface of Sundays in Ordinary Time I-VIII, pp.60-67.

Communion Antiphon Cf. Ps 33:11	Ant. ad communionem
The rich suffer want and go hungry,	Divites eguerunt et esurierunt;
but those who seek the Lord lack	quærentes autem Dominum non
no blessing.	minuentur omni bono.

Or: 1 Jn 3:2	Vel:
When the Lord appears,	Cum apparuerit Dominus,
we shall be like him,	similes ei erimus,
for we shall see him as he is.	quoniam videbimus eum sicuti est.

Prayer after Communion

We entreat your majesty most
    humbly, O Lord,
that, as you feed us
    with the nourishment
which comes from the most holy
    Body and Blood of your Son,
so you may make us sharers
    of his divine nature.
Who lives and reigns
    for ever and ever.

Post communionem

Maiestatem tuam, Domine,
    suppliciter deprecamur,
ut, sicut nos Corporis
    et Sanguinis sacrosancti
pascis alimento,
ita divinæ naturæ facias
    esse consortes.
Per Christum Dominum nostrum.

18 October

TWENTY-NINTH SUNDAY IN ORDINARY TIME

Entrance Antiphon   Cf. Ps 16:6.8

To you I call; for you will surely
    heed me, O God;
turn your ear to me; hear my words.
Guard me as the apple of your eye;
in the shadow of your wings
    protect me.

Ant. ad introitum

Ego clamavi,
    quoniam exaudisti me, Deus;
inclina aurem tuam,
    et exaudi verba mea.
Custodi me, Domine,
    ut pupillam oculi;
sub umbra alarum tuarum
    protege me.

Collect

Almighty ever-living God,
grant that we may always conform
    our will to yours
and serve your majesty in sincerity
    of heart.
Through our Lord Jesus Christ,
    your Son,
who lives and reigns with you
    in the unity of the Holy Spirit,
one God, for ever and ever.

Collecta

Omnipotens sempiterne Deus,
fac nos tibi semper et devotam
    gerere voluntatem,
et maiestati tuæ sincero
    corde servire.
Per Dominum nostrum Iesum
    Christum Filium tuum,
qui tecum vivit et regnat
    in unitate Spiritus Sancti,
Deus, per omnia sæcula sæculorum.

FIRST READING

A reading from the prophet Isaiah   45:1.4-6

I have taken Cyrus by his right hand to subdue nations before him.

Thus says the Lord to his anointed, to Cyrus,
whom he has taken by his right hand
to subdue nations before him
and strip the loins of kings,
to force gateways before him
that their gates be closed no more:

It is for the sake of my servant Jacob,
of Israel my chosen one,
that I have called you by your name,
conferring a title though you do not know me.
I am the Lord, unrivalled;
there is no other God besides me.
Though you do not know me, I arm you
that men may know from the rising to the setting of the sun
that, apart from me, all is nothing.

The word of the Lord.

Responsorial Psalm   Ps 95:1,3-5,7-10. R. v.7

R. **Give the Lord glory and power.**

O sing a new song to the Lord,
sing to the Lord all the earth.
Tell among the nations his glory
and his wonders among all the peoples. R.

The Lord is great and worthy of praise,
to be feared above all gods;
the gods of the heathens are naught.
It was the Lord who made the heavens. R.

Give the Lord, you families of peoples,
give the Lord glory and power,
give the Lord the glory of his name.
Bring an offering and enter his courts. R.

Worship the Lord in his temple.
O earth, tremble before him.
Proclaim to the nations: 'God is king.'
He will judge the peoples in fairness. R.

SECOND READING

A reading from the first letter of St Paul to the Thessalonians   1:1-5

We constantly remember your faith, your love and your hope.

From Paul, Silvanus and Timothy, to the Church in Thessalonika which is in God the Father and the Lord Jesus Christ; wishing you grace and peace from God the Father and the Lord Jesus Christ.

We always mention you in our prayers and thank God for you all, and constantly remember before God our Father how you have shown your faith in action, worked for love and persevered through hope, in our Lord Jesus Christ.

We know, brothers, that God loves you and that you have been chosen, because when we brought the Good News to you, it came to you not only as words, but as power and as the Holy Spirit and as utter conviction.

The word of the Lord.

Gospel Acclamation   Jn 17:17

R. **Alleluia, alleluia!**
Your word is truth, O Lord,
consecrate us in the truth.
R. **Alleluia!**

Or: Ph 2:15-16

R. **Alleluia, alleluia!**
You will shine on the world like bright stars
because you are offering it the word of life.
R. **Alleluia!**

GOSPEL

A reading from the holy Gospel according to Matthew   22:15-21

Give back to Caesar what belongs to Caesar – and to God what belongs to God.

The Pharisees went away to work out between them how to trap Jesus in what he said. And they sent their disciples to him, together with the Herodians, to say, 'Master, we know that you are an honest man and teach the way of God in an honest way, and that you are not afraid of anyone, because a man's rank means nothing to you. Tell us your opinion, then. Is it permissible to pay taxes to Caesar or not?' But Jesus was aware of their malice and replied, 'You hypocrites! Why do you set this trap for me? Let me see the money you pay the tax with.' They handed him a denarius, and he said, 'Whose head is this? Whose name?' 'Caesar's' they replied. He then said to them, 'Very well, give back to Caesar what belongs to Caesar – and to God what belongs to God.'

The Gospel of the Lord.

Prayer over the Offerings	Super oblata

Grant us, Lord, we pray,
a sincere respect for your gifts,
that, through the purifying action
    of your grace,
we may be cleansed by the very
    mysteries we serve.
Through Christ our Lord.
	Tribue nos, Domine, quæsumus,
	donis tuis libera mente servire,
	ut, tua purificante nos gratia,
	iisdem quibus famulamur
	    mysteriis emundemur.
	Per Christum Dominum nostrum.

Preface of Sundays in Ordinary Time I-VIII, pp.60-67.

Communion Antiphon Cf. Ps 32:18-19	Ant. ad communionem

Behold, the eyes of the Lord
are on those who fear him,
who hope in his merciful love,
to rescue their souls from death,
to keep them alive in famine.
	Ecce oculi Domini super
	    timentes eum,
	et in eis qui sperant super
	    misericordia eius;
	ut eruat a morte animas eorum,
	    et alat eos in fame.

Or: Mk 10:45	Vel:
The Son of Man has come to give his life as a ransom for many.	Filius hominis venit, ut daret animam suam redemptionem pro multis.

Prayer after Communion	Post communionem

Grant, O Lord, we pray,
that, benefiting from participation
    in heavenly things,
we may be helped by what you give
    in this present age
and prepared for the gifts
    that are eternal.
Through Christ our Lord.
	Fac nos, quæsumus, Domine,
	cælestium rerum
	    frequentatione proficere,
	ut et temporalibus
	    beneficiis adiuvemur,
	et erudiamur æternis.
	Per Christum Dominum nostrum.

25 October

THIRTIETH SUNDAY IN ORDINARY TIME

Entrance Antiphon   Cf. Ps 104:3-4

LET the hearts that seek
the Lord rejoice;
turn to the Lord and his strength;
constantly seek his face.

Ant. ad introitum

LÆTETUR cor
quærentium Dominum.
Quærite Dominum et confirmamini,
quærite faciem eius semper.

Collect

Almighty ever-living God,
increase our faith, hope and charity,
and make us love
   what you command,
so that we may merit
   what you promise.
Through our Lord Jesus Christ,
   your Son,
who lives and reigns with you
   in the unity of the Holy Spirit,
one God, for ever and ever.

Collecta

Omnipotens sempiterne Deus,
da nobis fidei,
   spei et caritatis augmentum,
et, ut mereamur assequi
   quod promittis,
fac nos amare quod præcipis.
Per Dominum nostrum Iesum
   Christum Filium tuum,
qui tecum vivit et regnat
   in unitate Spiritus Sancti,
Deus, per omnia sæcula sæculorum.

FIRST READING

A reading from the book of Exodus   22:20-26

If you are harsh with the widow, the orphan, my anger will flare against you.

The Lord said to Moses, 'Tell the sons of Israel this, "You must not molest
the stranger or oppress him, for you lived as strangers in the land of Egypt.
You must not be harsh with the widow, or with the orphan; if you are
harsh with them, they will surely cry out to me, and be sure I shall hear
their cry; my anger will flare and I shall kill you with the sword, your own
wives will be widows, your own children orphans.

   "If you lend money to any of my people, to any poor man among you,
you must not play the usurer with him: you must not demand interest
from him.

   "If you take another's cloak as a pledge, you must give it back to him before
sunset. It is all the covering he has; it is the cloak he wraps his body in; what
else would he sleep in? If he cries to me, I will listen, for I am full of pity."'

   The word of the Lord.

Responsorial Psalm   Ps 17:2-4,47,51. R. v.2

R. **I love you, Lord, my strength.**

I love you, Lord, my strength,
my rock, my fortress, my saviour.
My God is the rock where I take refuge;
my shield, my mighty help, my stronghold.
The Lord is worthy of all praise:
when I call I am saved from my foes. R.

Long life to the Lord, my rock!
Praised be the God who saves me.
He has given great victories to his king
and shown his love for his anointed. R.

SECOND READING

A reading from the first letter of St Paul to the Thessalonians   1:5-10

You broke with idolatry and became servants of God; you are now waiting for his Son.

You observed the sort of life we lived when we were with you, which was
for your instruction, and you were led to become imitators of us, and
of the Lord; and it was with the joy of the Holy Spirit that you took to
the gospel, in spite of the great opposition all round you. This has made
you the great example to all believers in Macedonia and Achaia since it
was from you that the word of the Lord started to spread – and not only
throughout Macedonia and Achaia, for the news of your faith in God has
spread everywhere. We do not need to tell other people about it: other
people tell us how we started the work among you, how you broke with
idolatry when you were converted to God and became servants of the real,
living God; and how you are now waiting for Jesus, his Son, whom he
raised from the dead, to come from heaven to save us from the retribution
which is coming.

The word of the Lord.

Gospel Acclamation   Cf. Ac 16:14

R. **Alleluia, alleluia!**
Open our heart, O Lord,
to accept the words of your Son.
R. **Alleluia!**

Or: Jn 14:23

R. **Alleluia, alleluia!**
If anyone loves me he will keep my word,
and my Father will love him,
and we shall come to him.
R. **Alleluia!**

GOSPEL

A reading from the holy Gospel according to Matthew   22:34-40

You must love the Lord your God and your neighbour as yourself.

When the Pharisees heard that Jesus had silenced the Sadducees they got
together and, to disconcert him, one of them put a question, 'Master,
which is the greatest commandment of the Law?' Jesus said, 'You must
love the Lord your God with all your heart, with all your soul, and with all
your mind. This is the greatest and the first commandment. The second
resembles it: you must love your neighbour as yourself. On these two commandments hang the whole Law, and the Prophets also.'

The Gospel of the Lord.

Prayer over the Offerings	Super oblata
Look, we pray, O Lord, on the offerings we make to your majesty, that whatever is done by us in your service may be directed above all to your glory. Through Christ our Lord.	Respice, quæsumus, Domine, munera quæ tuæ offerimus maiestati, ut, quod nostro servitio geritur, ad tuam gloriam potius dirigatur. Per Christum Dominum nostrum.

Preface of Sundays in Ordinary Time I-VIII, pp.60-67.

Communion Antiphon Cf. Ps 19:6	Ant. ad communionem
We will ring out our joy at your saving help and exult in the name of our God.	Lætabimur in salutari tuo, et in nomine Dei nostri magnificabimur.
Or: Ep 5:2	Vel:
Christ loved us and gave himself up for us, as a fragrant offering to God.	Christus dilexit nos, et tradidit semetipsum pro nobis, oblationem Deo in odorem suavitatis.

Prayer after Communion	Post communionem
May your Sacraments, O Lord, we pray, perfect in us what lies within them, that what we now celebrate in signs we may one day possess in truth. Through Christ our Lord.	Perficiant in nobis, Domine, quæsumus, tua sacramenta quod continent, ut, quæ nunc specie gerimus, rerum veritate capiamus. Per Christum Dominum nostrum.

1 November

ALL SAINTS

What does it means to bear the seal of God in one's very life and person? The Apostle John again tells us: it means that in Jesus Christ we have truly become children of God. Are we conscious of this great gift? We are all children of God! Do we remember that in Baptism we received the "seal" of our Heavenly Father, and that we became his children? To put it simply: we bear God's surname, our surname is God, because we are the children of God. Here lies the root of the vocation to holiness! The saints whom we remember today are those who lived in the grace of their Baptism, those who kept the "seal" intact, behaving as children of God, seeking to emulate Jesus; and now they have reached the goal, because they finally "see God as he is".

(Pope Francis)

Solemnity

Entrance Antiphon	Ant. ad introitum
L ET us all rejoice in the Lord, as we celebrate the feast day in honour of all the Saints, at whose festival the Angels rejoice and praise the Son of God.	G AUDEAMUS omnes in Domino, diem festum celebrantes sub honore Sanctorum omnium, de quorum sollemnitate gaudent Angeli, et collaudant Filium Dei.

The Gloria in excelsis (Glory to God in the highest) is said.

Collect	Collecta
Almighty ever-living God,	Omnipotens sempiterne Deus,
by whose gift we venerate in one celebration	qui nos omnium Sanctorum tuorum merita
the merits of all the Saints,	sub una tribuisti celebritate
bestow on us, we pray,	venerari, quæsumus,
through the prayers of so many intercessors,	ut desideratam nobis tuæ propitiationis abundantiam,
an abundance of the reconciliation with you	multiplicatis intercessoribus, largiaris.
for which we earnestly long.	
Through our Lord Jesus Christ, your Son,	Per Dominum nostrum Iesum Christum Filium tuum,
who lives and reigns with you in the unity of the Holy Spirit,	qui tecum vivit et regnat in unitate Spiritus Sancti,
one God, for ever and ever.	Deus, per omnia sæcula sæculorum.

FIRST READING

A reading from the book of the Apocalypse   7:2-4,9-14

I saw a huge number, impossible to count, of people from every nation, race, tribe and language.

I, John, saw another angel rising where the sun rises, carrying the seal of the living God; he called in a powerful voice to the four angels whose duty was to devastate land and sea, 'Wait before you do any damage on land or at sea or to the trees, until we have put the seal on the foreheads of the servants of our God.' Then I heard how many were sealed: a hundred and forty-four thousand, out of all the tribes of Israel.

After that I saw a huge number, impossible to count, of people from every nation, race, tribe and language; they were standing in front of the throne and in front of the Lamb, dressed in white robes and holding palms in their hands. They shouted aloud, 'Victory to our God, who sits on the throne, and to the Lamb!' And all the angels who were standing in a circle round the throne, surrounding the elders and the four animals, prostrated themselves before the throne, and touched the ground with their foreheads, worshipping God with these words: 'Amen. Praise and glory and wisdom and thanksgiving and honour and power and strength to our God for ever and ever. Amen.'

One of the elders then spoke, and asked me, 'Do you know who these people are, dressed in white robes, and where they have come from?' I answered him, 'You can tell me, my Lord.' Then he said, 'These are the people who have been through the great persecution, and they have washed their robes white again in the blood of the Lamb.'

The word of the Lord.

Responsial Psalm   Ps 23:1-6. R. Cf. v.6

R. **Such are the men who seek your face, O Lord.**

The Lord's is the earth and its fullness,
the world and all its peoples.
It is he who set it on the seas;
on the waters he made it firm. R.

Who shall climb the mountain of the Lord?
Who shall stand in his holy place?
The man with clean hands and pure heart,
who desires not worthless things. R.

He shall receive blessings from the Lord
and reward from the God who saves him.
Such are the men who seek him,
seek the face of the God of Jacob. R.

SECOND READING

A reading from the first letter of St John   3:1-3

We shall see God as he really is.

Think of the love that the Father has lavished on us,
by letting us be called God's children;
and that is what we are.
Because the world refused to acknowledge him,
therefore it does not acknowledge us.
My dear people, we are already the children of God
but what we are to be in the future has not yet been revealed,
all we know is, that when it is revealed
we shall be like him
because we shall see him as he really is.
Surely everyone who entertains this hope
must purify himself, must try to be as pure as Christ.

The word of the Lord.

Gospel Acclamation   Mt 11:28

R. **Alleluia, alleluia!**
Come to me, all of you who labour
    and are overburdened,
and I will give you rest, says the Lord.
R. **Alleluia!**

GOSPEL

A reading from the holy Gospel according to Matthew   5:1-12

Rejoice and be glad, for your reward will be great in heaven.

Seeing the crowds, Jesus went up the hill. There he sat down and was joined by his disciples. Then he began to speak. This is what he taught them:

    'How happy are the poor in spirit;
    theirs is the kingdom of heaven.
    Happy the gentle:
    they shall have the earth for their heritage.
    Happy those who mourn:
    they shall be comforted.
    Happy those who hunger and thirst for what is right:
    they shall be satisfied.
    Happy the merciful:
    they shall have mercy shown them.
    Happy the pure in heart:
    they shall see God.
    Happy the peacemakers:
    they shall be called sons of God.
    Happy those who are persecuted in the cause of right:
    theirs is the kingdom of heaven.

'Happy are you when people abuse you and persecute you and speak all kinds of calumny against you on my account. Rejoice and be glad, for your reward will be great in heaven.'

    The Gospel of the Lord.

The Creed is said.

Prayer over the Offerings

May these offerings we bring
    in honour of all the Saints
be pleasing to you, O Lord,
and grant that, just as we believe
    the Saints
to be already assured of immortality,
so we may experience their concern
    for our salvation.
Through Christ our Lord.

Preface: The glory of Jerusalem,
our mother.

It is truly right and just,
    our duty and our salvation,
always and everywhere
    to give you thanks,
Lord, holy Father,
    almighty and eternal God.

For today by your gift we celebrate
    our mother,
the festival of your city,
the heavenly Jerusalem,
    where the great array
    of our brothers and sisters
already gives you eternal praise.

Towards her, we eagerly hasten
    as pilgrims advancing by faith,
rejoicing in the glory bestowed
    upon those exalted members
    of the Church
through whom you give us,
    in our frailty, both strength
    and good example.

And so, we glorify you with the
    multitude of Saints and Angels,
as with one voice of praise
    we acclaim:

Holy, Holy, Holy Lord God of hosts...

Super oblata

Grata tibi sint, Domine, munera,
quæ pro cunctorum offerimus
    honore Sanctorum,
et concede,
ut, quos iam credimus de sua
    immortalitate securos,
sentiamus de nostra salute sollicitos.
Per Christum Dominum nostrum.

Præfatio: De gloria matris
nostræ Ierusalem

Vere dignum et iustum est,
    æquum et salutare,
nos tibi semper et ubique
    gratias agere:
Domine, sancte Pater,
    omnipotens æterne Deus:

Nobis enim hodie civitatem tuam
    quæ mater nostra est,

tribuis celebrare,
cælestique Ierusalem,
ubi iam te in æternum fratrum
    nostrorum corona collaudat.

Ad quam peregrini,
    per fidem accedentes,
alacriter festinamus,
    congaudentes de Ecclesiæ
sublimium glorificatione
    membrorum,
qua simul fragilitati nostræ
    adiumenta et exempla concedis.

Et ideo, cum ipsorum
    Angelorumque frequentia,
una te magnificamus,
    laudis voce clamantes:

Sanctus, Sanctus, Sanctus. . .

Communion Antiphon Mt 5:8-10

Blessed are the clean of heart,
for they shall see God.
Blessed are the peacemakers,
for they shall be called
children of God.
Blessed are they who are persecuted
for the sake of righteousness,
for theirs is the Kingdom of Heaven.

Ant. ad communionem

Beati mundo corde, quoniam ipsi
Deum videbunt;
beati pacifici, quoniam filii
Dei vocabuntur;
beati qui persecutionem patiuntur
propter iustitiam,
quoniam ipsorum
est regnum cælorum.

Prayer after Communion

As we adore you, O God, who alone
are holy
and wonderful in all your Saints,
we implore your grace,
so that, coming to perfect holiness
in the fullness of your love,
we may pass from this pilgrim table
to the banquet
of our heavenly homeland.
Through Christ our Lord.

Post communionem

Mirabilem te, Deus,
et unum Sanctum in omnibus
Sanctis tuis adorantes,
tuam gratiam imploramus,
qua, sanctificationem
in tui amoris plenitudine
consummantes,
ex hac mensa peregrinantium
ad cælestis patriæ
convivium transeamus.
Per Christum Dominum nostrum.

A formula of Solemn Blessing, pp.146-149, may be used.

2 November

THE COMMEMORATION
OF ALL THE FAITHFUL DEPARTED
(ALL SOULS' DAY)

Yesterday and today, many have been visiting cemeteries, which, as the word itself implies, is the "place of rest", as we wait for the final awakening. It is lovely to think that it will be Jesus himself to awaken us. Jesus himself revealed that the death of the body is like a sleep from which he awakens us. With this faith we pause — even spiritually — at the graves of our loved ones, of those who loved us and did us good. But today we are called to remember everyone, even those who no one remembers. We remember the victims of war and violence; the many "little ones" of the world, crushed by hunger and poverty; we remember the anonymous who rest in the communal ossuary. We remember our brothers and sisters killed because they were Christian; and those who sacrificed their lives to serve others. We especially entrust to the Lord those who have left us during the past year. Remembering the dead, caring for their graves and prayers of suffrage, are the testimony of confident hope, rooted in the certainty that death does not have the last word on human existence, for man is destined to a life without limits, which has its roots and its fulfilment in God.

(Pope Francis)

The Masses that follow may be used at the discretion of the celebrant.

1

Entrance Antiphon Cf. 1 Th 4:14; 1 Co 15:22	Ant. ad introitum
Just as Jesus died and has risen again, so through Jesus God will bring with him those who have fallen asleep; and as in Adam all die, so also in Christ will all be brought to life.	Sicut Iesus mortuus est et resurrexit, ita et Deus eos qui dormierunt per Iesum adducet cum eo. Et sicut in Adam omnes moriuntur, ita et in Christo omnes vivificabuntur.

The **Gloria in excelsis** (Glory to God in the highest) is omitted.

Collect	Collecta
Listen kindly to our prayers, O Lord, and, as our faith in your Son, raised from the dead, is deepened, so may our hope of resurrection for your departed servants also find new strength. Through our Lord Jesus Christ, your Son, who lives and reigns with you in the unity of the Holy Spirit, one God, for ever and ever.	Preces nostras, quæsumus, Domine, benignus exaudi, ut, dum attollitur nostra fides in Filio tuo a mortuis suscitato, in famulorum tuorum præstolanda resurrectione spes quoque nostra firmetur. Per Dominum nostrum Iesum Christum Filium tuum, qui tecum vivit et regnat in unitate Spiritus Sancti, Deus, per omnia sæcula sæculorum.

Readings, pp.455-457.

Prayer over the Offerings

Look favourably on our offerings,
O Lord,
so that your departed servants
may be taken up into glory
with your Son,
in whose great mystery of love
we are all united.
Who lives and reigns
for ever and ever.

Preface for the Dead, pp.74-79.

Super oblata

Nostris, Domine,
propitiare muneribus,
ut famuli tui defuncti assumantur
in gloriam cum Filio tuo,
cuius magno pietatis
iungimur sacramento.
Qui vivit et regnat
in sæcula sæculorum.

Communion Antiphon Cf. Jn 11:25-26

I am the Resurrection and the Life,
says the Lord.
Whoever believes in me, even
though he dies, will live,
and everyone who lives and believes
in me will not die for ever.

Ant. ad communionem

Ego sum resurrectio et vita, dicit
Dominus.
Qui credit in me, etiam si mortuus
fuerit, vivet;
et omnis, qui vivit et credit in me,
non morietur in æternum.

Prayer after Communion

Grant we pray, O Lord, that your
departed servants,
for whom we have celebrated this
paschal Sacrament,
may pass over to a dwelling place of
light and peace.
Through Christ our Lord.

Post communionem

Præsta, quæsumus, Domine,
ut famuli tui defuncti
in mansionem lucis transeant
et pacis,
pro quibus paschale celebravimus
sacramentum.
Per Christum Dominum nostrum.

A formula of Solemn Blessing, pp.148-151, may be used.

2

Entrance Antiphon Cf. 4 Esdr 2:34-35

Eternal rest grant unto them, O Lord,
and let perpetual light shine
upon them.

Ant. ad introitum

Requiem æternam dona eis, Domine,
et lux perpetua luceat eis.

Collect

O God, glory of the faithful and
    life of the just,
by the Death and Resurrection
    of whose Son
we have been redeemed,
look mercifully on your departed
    servants,
that, just as they professed the
    mystery of our resurrection,
so they may merit to receive the
    joys of eternal happiness.
Through our Lord Jesus Christ,
    your Son,
who lives and reigns with you
    in the unity of the Holy Spirit,
one God, for ever and ever.

Readings, pp.455-457.

Collecta

Deus, gloria fidelium
    et vita iustorum,
cuius Filii morte et resurrectione
    redempti sumus,
propitiare famulis tuis defunctis,
ut, qui resurrectionis nostræ
    mysterium agnoverunt,
æternæ beatitudinis gaudia
    percipere mereantur.
Per Dominum nostrum Iesum
    Christum Filium tuum,
qui tecum vivit et regnat
    in unitate Spiritus Sancti,
Deus, per omnia sæcula sæculorum.

Prayer over the Offerings

Almighty and merciful God,
by means of these
    sacrificial offerings
wash away, we pray,
    in the Blood of Christ,
the sins of your departed servants,
for you purify unceasingly by your
    merciful forgiveness
those you once cleansed in the
    waters of Baptism.
Through Christ our Lord.

Preface for the Dead, pp.74-79.

Super oblata

Omnipotens et misericors Deus,
his sacrificiis ablue, quæsumus,
    famulos tuos defunctos
a peccatis eorum
    in sanguine Christi,
ut, quos mundasti
    aqua baptismatis,
indesinenter purifices
    indulgentia pietatis.
Per Christum Dominum nostrum.

Communion Antiphon Cf. 4 Esdr 2:35,34

Let perpetual light shine upon
    them, O Lord,
with your Saints for ever,
    for you are merciful.

Ant. ad communionem

Lux æterna luceat eis, Domine,
cum Sanctis tuis in æternum,
    quia pius es.

Prayer after Communion

Having received the Sacrament of
    your Only Begotten Son,
who was sacrificed for us
    and rose in glory,
we humbly implore you, O Lord,
for your departed servants,
that, cleansed by
    the paschal mysteries,
they may glory in the gift of the
    resurrection to come.
Through Christ our Lord.

A formula of Solemn Blessing, pp.148-151, may be used.

Post communionem

Sumpto sacramento Unigeniti tui,
qui pro nobis immolatus
    resurrexit in gloria,
te, Domine, suppliciter exoramus
    pro famulis tuis defunctis,
ut, paschalibus mysteriis mundati,
futuræ resurrectionis
    munere glorientur.
Per Christum Dominum nostrum.

3

Entrance Antiphon   Cf. Rm 8:11

God, who raised Jesus from the dead,
will give life also to your
    mortal bodies,
through his Spirit that dwells in you.

Ant. ad introitum

Deus, qui suscitavit Iesum a mortuis,
vivificabit et mortalia corpora nostra,
propter inhabitantem Spiritum
    eius in nobis.

Collect

O God, who willed that your Only
    Begotten Son,
having conquered death,
should pass over into the realm
    of heaven,
grant, we pray,
    to your departed servants
that, with the mortality
    of this life overcome,
they may gaze eternally on you,
their Creator and Redeemer.
Through our Lord Jesus Christ,
    your Son,
who lives and reigns with you in
    the unity of the Holy Spirit,
one God, for ever and ever.

Readings, pp.455-457.

Collecta

Deus, qui Unigenitum tuum,
    devicta morte,
ad cælestia transire fecisti,
concede famulis tuis defunctis,
ut, huius vitæ mortalitate devicta,
te conditorem et redemptorem
possint perpetuo contemplari.

Per Dominum nostrum Iesum
    Christum Filium tuum,
qui tecum vivit et regnat
    in unitate Spiritus Sancti,
Deus, per omnia sæcula sæculorum.

Prayer over the Offerings

Receive, Lord, in your kindness,
the sacrificial offering we make
for all your servants who sleep
    in Christ,
that, set free from the bonds
    of death
by this singular sacrifice,
they may merit eternal life.
Through Christ our Lord.

Preface for the Dead, pp.74-79.

Super oblata

Pro omnibus famulis tuis in Christo
    dormientibus
hostiam, Domine, suscipe
    benignus oblatam,
ut, per hoc sacrificium singulare
    vinculis mortis exuti,
vitam mereantur æternam.
Per Christum Dominum nostrum.

Communion Antiphon Cf. Ph 3:20-21

We await a saviour,
    the Lord Jesus Christ,
who will change our mortal bodies,
to conform with his glorified body.

Ant. ad communionem

Salvatorem exspectamus
    Dominum Iesum Christum,
qui reformabit corpus
    humilitatis nostræ,
configuratum corpori claritatis suæ.

Prayer after Communion

Through these sacrificial gifts
which we have received, O Lord,
bestow on your departed servants
    your great mercy
and, to those you have endowed
    with the grace of Baptism,
grant also the fullness of
    eternal joy.
Through Christ our Lord.

A formula of Solemn Blessing, pp.148-151, may be used.

Post communionem

Multiplica, Domine,
    his sacrificiis susceptis,
super famulos tuos defunctos
    misericordiam tuam,
et, quibus donasti
    baptismi gratiam,
da eis æternorum
    plenitudinem gaudiorum.
Per Christum Dominum nostrum.

FIRST READING

The readings below may be used for all the Masses of 2 November. Alternative readings may be taken from the Masses of the Dead.

A reading from the prophet Isaiah 25:6-9
The Lord will destroy Death for ever.

On this mountain,
the Lord of hosts will prepare for all peoples
a banquet of rich food.

On this mountain he will remove
the mourning veil covering all peoples,
and the shroud enwrapping all nations,
he will destroy Death for ever.
The Lord will wipe away
the tears from every cheek;
he will take away his people's shame
everywhere on earth,
for the Lord has said so.
That day, it will be said: See, this is our God
in whom we hoped for salvation;
the Lord is the one in whom we hoped.
We exult and we rejoice
that he has saved us.

   The word of the Lord.

Responsorial Psalm　　　　　Ps 26:1,4,7-9,13-14. R. v.1. Alt. R. v.13

R. **The Lord is my light and my help.**

  Or: **I am sure I shall see the Lord's goodness**
  in the land of the living.

The Lord is my light and my help;
whom shall I fear?
The Lord is the stronghold of my life;
before whom shall I shrink? R.

There is one thing I ask of the Lord,
for this I long,
to live in the house of the Lord,
all the days of my life,
to savour the sweetness of the Lord,
to behold his temple. R.

O Lord, hear my voice when I call;
have mercy and answer.
It is your face, O Lord, that I seek;
hide not your face. R.

I am sure I shall see the Lord's goodness
in the land of the living.
Hope in him, hold firm and take heart.
Hope in the Lord! R.

SECOND READING

A reading from the letter of St Paul to the Romans 5:5-11

Having died to make us righteous, is it likely that he would now fail to save us from God's anger?

Hope is not deceptive, because the love of God has been poured into our hearts by the Holy Spirit which has been given us. We were still helpless when at his appointed moment Christ died for sinful men. It is not easy to die even for a good man – though of course for someone really worthy, a man might be prepared to die – but what proves that God loves us is that Christ died for us while we were still sinners. Having died to make us righteous, is it likely that he would now fail to save us from God's anger? When we were reconciled to God by the death of his Son, we were still enemies; now that we have been reconciled, surely we may count on being saved by the life of his Son? Not merely because we have been reconciled but because we are filled with joyful trust in God, through our Lord Jesus Christ, through whom we have already gained our reconciliation.

The word of the Lord.

Gospel Acclamation Jn 6:39

R. **Alleluia, alleluia!**
It is my Father's will, says the Lord,
that I should lose nothing
of all that he has given to me,
and that I should raise it up on the last day.
R. **Alleluia!**

GOSPEL

A reading from the holy Gospel according to Matthew 11:25-30

You have hidden these things from the learned and have revealed them to mere children.

Jesus exclaimed, 'I bless you, Father, Lord of heaven and of earth, for hiding these things from the learned and the clever and revealing them to mere children. Yes, Father, for that is what it pleased you to do. Everything has been entrusted to me by my Father; and no one knows the Son except the Father, just as no one knows the Father except the Son and those to whom the Son chooses to reveal him.

'Come to me, all you who labour and are over burdened, and I will give you rest. Shoulder my yoke and learn from me, for I am gentle and humble in heart, and you will find rest for your souls. Yes, my yoke is easy and my burden light.'

The Gospel of the Lord.

8 November

THIRTY-SECOND SUNDAY IN ORDINARY TIME

Entrance Antiphon   Cf. Ps 87:3

L ET my prayer come
    into your presence.
Incline your ear to my cry for help,
    O Lord.

Ant. ad introitum

I NTRET oratio mea
    in conspectu tuo;
inclina aurem tuam ad
    precem meam, Domine.

Collect

Almighty and merciful God,
graciously keep from us all adversity,
so that, unhindered in mind
    and body alike,
we may pursue in freedom of heart
the things that are yours.
Through our Lord Jesus Christ,
    your Son,
who lives and reigns with you
    in the unity of the Holy Spirit,
one God, for ever and ever.

Collecta

Omnipotens et misericors Deus,
universa nobis adversantia
    propitiatus exclude,
ut, mente et corpore pariter expediti,
quæ tua sunt liberis
    mentibus exsequamur.
Per Dominum nostrum Iesum
    Christum Filium tuum,
qui tecum vivit et regnat
    in unitate Spiritus Sancti,
Deus, per omnia sæcula sæculorum.

FIRST READING

A reading from the book of Wisdom   6:12-16

Wisdom is found by those who look for her.

Wisdom is bright, and does not grow dim.
By those who love her she is readily seen,
and found by those who look for her.
Quick to anticipate those who desire her, she makes herself known to them.
Watch for her early and you will have no trouble;
you will find her sitting at your gates.
Even to think about her is understanding fully grown;
be on the alert for her and anxiety will quickly leave you.
She herself walks about looking for those who are worthy of her
and graciously shows herself to them as they go,
in every thought of theirs coming to meet them.

    The word of the Lord.

Responsional Psalm   Ps 62:2-8. R. v.2

R. **For you my soul is thirsting, O God, my God.**

O God, you are my God, for you I long;
for you my soul is thirsting.
My body pines for you
like a dry, weary land without water. R.

So I gaze on you in the sanctuary
to see your strength and your glory.
For your love is better than life,
my lips will speak your praise. R.

So I will bless you all my life,
in your name I will lift up my hands.
My soul shall be filled as with a banquet,
my mouth shall praise you with joy. R.

On my bed I remember you.
On you I muse through the night
for you have been my help;
in the shadow of your wings I rejoice. R.

SECOND READING

A reading from the first letter of St Paul to the Thessalonians   4:13-18
God will bring with him those who have died in Jesus.

[We want you to be quite certain, brothers, about those who have died, to
make sure that you do not grieve about them, like the other people who
have no hope. We believe that Jesus died and rose again, and that it will be
the same for those who have died in Jesus: God will bring them with him.]
We can tell you this from the Lord's own teaching, that any of us who are
left alive until the Lord's coming will not have any advantage over those
who have died. At the trumpet of God, the voice of the archangel will call
out the command and the Lord himself will come down from heaven;
those who have died in Christ will be the first to rise, and then those of us
who are still alive will be taken up in the clouds, together with them, to
meet the Lord in the air. So we shall stay with the Lord for ever. With such
thoughts as these you should comfort one another.

[The word of the Lord.]

Shorter Form, verses 13-14. Read between [ ]

Gospel Acclamation   Mt 24:42,44

R. **Alleluia, alleluia!**
Stay awake and stand ready,
because you do not know the hour
when the Son of Man is coming.
R. **Alleluia!**

GOSPEL

A reading from the holy Gospel according to Matthew   25:1-13

The bridegroom is here! Go out and meet him.

Jesus told this parable to his disciples: 'The kingdom of heaven will be like this: Ten bridesmaids took their lamps and went to meet the bridegroom. Five of them were foolish and five were sensible: the foolish ones did take their lamps, but they brought no oil, whereas the sensible ones took flasks of oil as well as their lamps. The bridegroom was late, and they all grew drowsy and fell asleep. But at midnight there was a cry, "The bridegroom is here! Go out and meet him." At this, all those bridesmaids woke up and trimmed their lamps, and the foolish ones said to the sensible ones, "Give us some of your oil: our lamps are going out." But they replied, "There may not be enough for us and for you; you had better go to those who sell it and buy some for yourselves." They had gone off to buy it when the bridegroom arrived. Those who were ready went in with him to the wedding hall and the door was closed. The other bridesmaids arrived later. "Lord, Lord," they said "open the door for us." But he replied, "I tell you solemnly, I do not know you." So stay awake, because you do not know either the day or the hour.'

The Gospel of the Lord.

Prayer over the Offerings	Super oblata
Look with favour, we pray, O Lord, upon the sacrificial gifts offered here, that, celebrating in mystery the Passion of your Son, we may honour it with loving devotion. Through Christ our Lord.	Sacrificiis præsentibus, Domine, quæsumus, intende placatus, ut, quod passionis Filii tui mysterio gerimus, pio consequamur affectu. Per Christum Dominum nostrum.

Preface of Sundays in Ordinary Time I-VIII, pp.60-67.

Communion Antiphon Cf. Ps 22:1-2

The Lord is my shepherd;
    there is nothing I shall want.
Fresh and green are the pastures
    where he gives me repose,
near restful waters he leads me.

Or: Cf. Lk 24:35

The disciples recognised the Lord
    Jesus in the breaking of bread.

Prayer after Communion

Nourished by this sacred gift,
    O Lord,
we give you thanks and beseech
    your mercy,
that, by the pouring forth
    of your Spirit,
the grace of integrity may endure
in those your heavenly power
    has entered.
Through Christ our Lord.

Ant. ad communionem

Dominus regit me,
    et nihil mihi deerit;
in loco pascuæ ibi me collocavit,
super aquam refectionis
    educavit me.

Vel:

Cognoverunt discipuli Dominum
    Iesum in fractione panis.

Post communionem

Gratias tibi, Domine, referimus
    sacro munere vegetati,
tuam clementiam implorantes,
ut, per infusionem Spiritus tui,
in quibus cælestis virtus introivit,
sinceritatis gratia perseveret.
Per Christum Dominum nostrum.

15 November

THIRTY-THIRD SUNDAY IN ORDINARY TIME

Entrance Antiphon Jr 29:11,12,14

THE Lord said: I think thoughts
of peace and not of affliction.
You will call upon me,
    and I will answer you,
and I will lead back your captives
    from every place.

Ant. ad introitum

DICIT Dominus:
Ego cogito cogitationes pacis
    et non afflictionis;
invocabitis me, et ego exaudiam vos,
et reducam captivitatem vestram
    de cunctis locis.

Collect

Grant us, we pray, O Lord our God,
the constant gladness of being
    devoted to you,
for it is full and lasting happiness
to serve with constancy
the author of all that is good.
Through our Lord Jesus Christ,
    your Son,
who lives and reigns with you
    in the unity of the Holy Spirit,
one God, for ever and ever.

Collecta

Da nobis, quæsumus,
    Domine Deus noster,
in tua semper devotione gaudere,
quia perpetua est et plena felicitas,
si bonorum omnium iugiter
    serviamus auctori.
Per Dominum nostrum Iesum
    Christum Filium tuum,
qui tecum vivit et regnat
    in unitate Spiritus Sancti,
Deus, per omnia sæcula sæculorum.

FIRST READING

A reading from the book of Proverbs   31:10-13,19-20,30-31

A perfect wife - who can find her?

A perfect wife – who can find her?
She is far beyond the price of pearls.
Her husband's heart has confidence in her,
from her he will derive no little profit.
Advantage and not hurt she brings him
all the days of her life.
She is always busy with wool and with flax,
she does her work with eager hands.
She sets her hands to the distaff,
her fingers grasp the spindle.
She holds out her hands to the poor,
she opens her arms to the needy.
Charm is deceitful, and beauty empty;
the woman who is wise is the one to praise.
Give her a share in what her hands have worked for,
and let her works tell her praises at the city gates.

    The word of the Lord.

Responsorial Psalm   Ps 127:1-5. R. v.1

R. **O blessed are those who fear the Lord.**

O blessed are those who fear the Lord
and walk in his ways!
By the labour of your hands you shall eat.
You will be happy and prosper. R.

Your wife like a fruitful vine
in the heart of your house;
your children like shoots of the olive,
around your table. R.

Indeed thus shall be blessed
the man who fears the Lord.
May the Lord bless you from Zion
in a happy Jerusalem
all the days of your life. R.

SECOND READING

A reading from the first letter of St Paul to the Thessalonians   5:1-6

Let not the Day of the Lord overtake you like a thief.

You will not be expecting us to write anything to you, brothers, about 'times and seasons', since you know very well that the Day of the Lord is going to come like a thief in the night. It is when people are saying, 'How quiet and peaceful it is' that the worst suddenly happens, as suddenly as labour pains come on a pregnant woman; and there will be no way for anybody to evade it.

But it is not as if you live in the dark, my brothers, for that Day to overtake you like a thief. No, you are all sons of light and sons of the day: we do not belong to the night or to darkness, so we should not go on sleeping, as everyone else does, but stay wide awake and sober.

The word of the Lord.

Gospel Acclamation   Rv 2:10
R. **Alleluia, alleluia!**
Even if you have to die, says the Lord,
keep faithful, and I will give you
the crown of life.
R. **Alleluia!**
Or: Jn 15:4,5

R. **Alleluia, alleluia!**
Make your home in me, as I make mine in you,
says the Lord.
Whoever remains in me bears fruit in plenty.
R. **Alleluia!**

GOSPEL

A reading from the holy Gospel according to Matthew   25:14-30
You have been faithful in small things; come and join in your master's happiness.

[Jesus spoke this parable to his disciples: 'The kingdom of heaven is like a man on his way abroad who summoned his servants and entrusted his property to them. To one he gave five talents, to another two, to a third one; each in proportion to his ability. Then he set out.] The man who had received the five talents promptly went and traded with them and made five more. The man who had received two made two more in the same way. But the man who had received one went off and dug a hole in the ground and hid his master's money. [Now a long time after, the master of those servants came back and went through his accounts with them. The man who had received the five talents came forward bringing five more. "Sir," he said "you entrusted me with five talents; here are five more that I have made."] His master said to him, "Well done, good and faithful servant; you have shown you can be faithful in small things, I will trust you with greater; come and join in your master's happiness." Next the man with the two talents came forward. "Sir," he said "you entrusted me with two talents; here are two more that I have made." His master said to him, "Well done, good and faithful servant; you have shown you can be faithful in small things, I will trust you with greater; come and join in your master's happiness." Last came forward the man who had the one talent. "Sir," said he "I had heard you were a hard man, reaping where you have not sown and gathering where you have not scattered; so I was afraid, and I went off and hid your talent in the ground. Here it is; it was yours, you have it back." But his master answered him, "You wicked and lazy servant! So you knew that I reap where I have not sown and gather where I have not scattered? Well then, you should have deposited my money with the bankers, and on my return I would have recovered my capital with interest. So now, take the talent from him and give it to the man who has the five talents. For to everyone who has will be given more, and he will have more than enough; but from the man who has not, even what he has will be taken away. As for this good-for-nothing servant, throw him out into the dark, where there will be weeping and grinding of teeth.'"

| [The Gospel of the Lord.]

Shorter Form, verses 14-15, 19-20. Read between [ ]

Prayer over the Offerings

Grant, O Lord, we pray,
that what we offer in the sight
   of your majesty
may obtain for us the grace
   of being devoted to you
and gain us the prize
   of everlasting happiness.
Through Christ our Lord.

Super oblata

Concede, quæsumus, Domine,
ut oculis tuæ maiestatis
   munus oblatum
et gratiam nobis
   devotionis obtineat,
et effectum beatæ
   perennitatis acquirat.
Per Christum Dominum nostrum.

Preface of Sundays in Ordinary Time I-VIII, pp.60-67.

Communion Antiphon   Ps 72:28

To be near God is my happiness,
to place my hope in God the Lord.
Or: Mk 11:23-24
Amen, I say to you:
   Whatever you ask in prayer,
believe that you will receive,
and it shall be given to you,
   says the Lord.

Ant. ad communionem

Mihi autem adhærere Deo bonum est,
ponere in Domino Deo spem meam.
Vel:
Amen dico vobis,
   quidquid orantes petitis,
credite quia accipietis, et fiet vobis,
   dicit Dominus.

Prayer after Communion

We have partaken of the gifts
   of this sacred mystery,
humbly imploring, O Lord,
that what your Son commanded
   us to do
in memory of him
may bring us growth in charity.
Through Christ our Lord.

Post communionem

Sumpsimus, Domine,
   sacri dona mysterii,
humiliter deprecantes,
ut, quæ in sui commemorationem
nos Filius tuus facere præcepit,
in nostræ proficiant
   caritatis augmentum.
Per Christum Dominum nostrum.

22 November

OUR LORD JESUS CHRIST, KING OF THE UNIVERSE

Solemnity

Entrance Antiphon Rv 5:12; 1:6	Ant. ad introitum
HOW worthy is the Lamb who was slain, to receive power and divinity, and wisdom and strength and honour. To him belong glory and power for ever and ever.	DIGNUS est Agnus, qui occisus est, accipere virtutem et divinitatem et sapientiam et fortitudinem et honorem. Ipsi gloria et imperium in sæcula sæculorum.

The Gloria in excelsis (Glory to God in the highest) is said.

Collect	Collecta
Almighty ever-living God, whose will is to restore all things in your beloved Son, the King of the universe, grant, we pray, that the whole creation, set free from slavery, may render your majesty service and ceaselessly proclaim your praise. Through our Lord Jesus Christ, your Son, who lives and reigns with you in the unity of the Holy Spirit, one God, for ever and ever.	Omnipotens sempiterne Deus, qui in dilecto Filio tuo, universorum Rege, omnia instaurare voluisti, concede propitius, ut tota creatura, a servitute liberata, tuæ maiestati deserviat ac te sine fine collaudet. Per Dominum nostrum Iesum Christum Filium tuum, qui tecum vivit et regnat in unitate Spiritus Sancti, Deus, per omnia sæcula sæculorum.

FIRST READING

A reading from the prophet Ezekiel   34:11-12,15-17

As for you, my sheep, I will judge between sheep and sheep.

The Lord says this: I am going to look after my flock myself and keep all of
it in view. As a shepherd keeps all his flock in view when he stands up in
the middle of his scattered sheep, so shall I keep my sheep in view. I shall
rescue them from wherever they have been scattered during the mist and
darkness. I myself will pasture my sheep, I myself will show them where to
rest – it is the Lord who speaks. I shall look for the lost one, bring back the
stray, bandage the wounded and make the weak strong. I shall watch over
the fat and healthy. I shall be a true shepherd to them.

As for you, my sheep, the Lord says this: I will judge between sheep and
sheep, between rams and he-goats.

The word of the Lord.

Responsorial Psalm   cf. Ps 22:1-3,5-6. R. v.1

R. **The Lord is my shepherd;**
   there is nothing I shall want.

The Lord is my shepherd;
there is nothing I shall want.
Fresh and green are the pastures
where he gives me repose. R.

Near restful waters he leads me,
to revive my drooping spirit.
He guides me along the right path;
he is true to his name. R.

You have prepared a banquet for me
in the sight of my foes.
My head you have anointed with oil;
my cup is overflowing. R.

Surely goodness and kindness shall follow
me all the days of my life.
In the Lord's own house shall I dwell
for ever and ever. R.

SECOND READING

A reading from the first letter of St Paul to the Corinthians   15:20-26,28

He will hand over the kingdom to God the Father; so that God may be all in all.

Christ has been raised from the dead, the first-fruits of all who have fallen asleep. Death came through one man and in the same way the resurrection of the dead has come through one man. Just as all men die in Adam, so all men will be brought to life in Christ; but all of them in their proper order: Christ as the first-fruits and then, after the coming of Christ, those who belong to him. After that will come the end, when he hands over the kingdom to God the Father, having done away with every sovereignty, authority and power. For he must be king until he has put all his enemies under his feet and the last of the enemies to be destroyed is death. And when everything is subjected to him, then the Son himself will be subject in his turn to the One who subjected all things to him, so that God may be all in all.

The word of the Lord.

Gospel Acclamation   Mk 11:10

R. **Alleluia, alleluia!**
Blessings on him who comes in the name of the Lord!
Blessings on the coming kingdom of our father David!
R. **Alleluia!**

GOSPEL

A reading from the holy Gospel according to Matthew   25:31-46

He will take his seat on his throne of glory, and he will separate men one from another.

Jesus said to his disciples: 'When the Son of Man comes in his glory, escorted by all the angels, then he will take his seat on his throne of glory. All the nations will be assembled before him and he will separate men one from another as the shepherd separates sheep from goats. He will place the sheep on his right hand and the goats on his left. Then the King will say to those on his right hand, "Come, you whom my Father has blessed, take for your heritage the kingdom prepared for you since the foundation of the world. For I was hungry and you gave me food; I was thirsty and you gave me drink; I was a stranger and you made me welcome; naked and you clothed me, sick and you visited me, in prison and you came to see me." Then the virtuous will say to him in reply, "Lord, when did we see you hungry and feed you; or thirsty and give you drink? When did we see you a stranger and make you welcome; naked and clothe you; sick or in prison and go to see you?" And the King will answer, "I tell you solemnly, in so far as you did this to one of the least of these brothers of mine, you did it to me." Next he will say to those on his left hand, "Go away from me, with your curse upon you, to the eternal fire prepared for the devil and his angels. For I was hungry and you never gave me food; I was thirsty and you never gave me anything to drink; I was a stranger and you never made me welcome, naked and you never clothed me, sick and in prison and you never visited me." Then it will be their turn to ask, "Lord, when did we see you hungry or thirsty, a stranger or naked, sick or in prison, and did not come to your help?" Then he will answer, "I tell you solemnly, in so far as you neglected to do this to one of the least of these, you neglected to do it to me." And they will go away to eternal punishment, and the virtuous to eternal life.'

The Gospel of the Lord.

The Creed is said.

Prayer over the Offerings

As we offer you, O Lord,
    the sacrifice
by which the human race
    is reconciled to you,
we humbly pray
that your Son himself may bestow
    on all nations
the gifts of unity and peace.
Through Christ our Lord.

Super oblata

Hostiam tibi, Domine,
humanæ reconciliationis
    offerentes, suppliciter deprecamur,
ut ipse Filius tuus cunctis gentibus
unitatis et pacis dona concedat.
Qui vivit et regnat
    in sæcula sæculorum.

Preface: Christ, King of the Universe.

It is truly right and just,
    our duty and our salvation,
always and everywhere
    to give you thanks,
Lord, holy Father,
    almighty and eternal God.

For you anointed your Only
    Begotten Son,
our Lord Jesus Christ,
    with the oil of gladness
as eternal Priest and King
    of all creation,

Præfatio: De Christo universorum Rege.

Vere dignum et iustum est,
    æquum et salutare,
nos tibi semper
    et ubique gratias agere:
Domine, sancte Pater,
    omnipotens æterne Deus:

Qui Unigenitum Filium tuum,
Dominum nostrum
    Iesum Christum,
Sacerdotem æternum
    et universorum Regem,
oleo exsultationis unxisti:

so that, by offering himself
    on the altar of the Cross
as a spotless sacrifice
    to bring us peace,
he might accomplish the mysteries
    of human redemption
and, making all created things
    subject to his rule,
he might present to the immensity
    of your majesty
an eternal and universal kingdom,
a kingdom of truth and life,
a kingdom of holiness and grace,
a kingdom of justice, love and peace.

And so, with Angels and Archangels,
with Thrones and Dominions,
and with all the hosts and Powers
    of heaven,
we sing the hymn of your glory,
as without end we acclaim:

Holy, Holy, Holy Lord God of hosts...

ut, seipsum in ara crucis
hostiam immaculatam
    et pacificam offerens,
redemptionis humanæ
    sacramenta perageret:
et, suo subiectis imperio
    omnibus creaturis,
æternum et universale regnum
immensæ tuæ traderet maiestati:
regnum veritatis et vitæ;
regnum sanctitatis et gratiæ;
regnum iustitiæ,
    amoris et pacis.

Et ideo cum Angelis et Archangelis,
cum Thronis et Dominationibus,
cumque omni
    militia cælestis exercitus,
hymnum gloriæ tuæ canimus,
sine fine dicentes:

Sanctus, Sanctus, Sanctus . . .

Communion Antiphon Ps 28:10-11

The Lord sits as King for ever.
The Lord will bless his people
    with peace.

Ant. ad communionem

Sedebit Dominus Rex in æternum;
Dominus benedicet populo suo
    in pace.

Prayer after Communion

Having received the food
    of immortality,
we ask, O Lord,
that, glorying in obedience
to the commands of Christ,
    the King of the universe,
we may live with him eternally
    in his heavenly Kingdom.
Who lives and reigns
    for ever and ever.

Post communionem

Immortalitatis alimoniam consecuti,
quæsumus, Domine,
ut, qui Christi Regis universorum
gloriamur obœdire mandatis,
cum ipso in cælesti regno sine fine
    vivere valeamus.
Qui vivit et regnat
    in sæcula sæculorum.

RITE OF EUCHARISTIC EXPOSITION AND BENEDICTION

The service of Benediction developed during the Middle Ages during the Corpus Christi processions in which the Blessed Sacrament was held up for veneration. The service was subsequently used at other times throughout the year as an opportunity to give thanks for the Mass and adore Christ present under the form of bread.

Today, the Church encourages this rite to be celebrated in the context of a longer period of reading, prayer and reflection.

Exposition

First of all, the minister exposes the Blessed Sacrament while a hymn is sung, during which he incenses the Sacrament. The following or another hymn may be chosen.

O saving Victim, opening wide,	O salutaris hostia,
The gate of heav'n to man below	Quæ cæli pandis ostium;
Our foes press on from every side;	Bella premunt hostilia,
Thine aid supply,	Da robur, fer auxilium.
thy strength bestow.	
To thy great name be endless praise,	Uni Trinoque Domino
Immortal Godhead, One in Three;	Sit sempiterna gloria,
O grant us endless length of days	Qui vitam sine termino
In our true native land with thee.	Nobis donet in patria.
Amen.	Amen.

Adoration

A time for silent prayer, readings from Scripture, litanies or other prayers and hymns may be used. On some occasions, the Prayer of the Church might be said or sung.

Of the Glorious Body Telling	Pange Lingua
Of the glorious Body telling,	Pange lingua gloriosi
O my tongue, its mysteries sing,	Corporis mysterium,
And the Blood, all price excelling,	Sanguinisque pretiosi,
Which the world's eternal King,	Quem in mundi pretium
In a noble womb once dwelling	Fructus ventris generosi,
Shed for the world's ransoming.	Rex effudit gentium.

Given for us, for us descending,
Of a Virgin to proceed,
Man with man in
   converse blending,
Scattered he the Gospel seed,
Till his sojourn drew to ending,
Which he closed in wondrous deed.

Nobis datus, nobis natus
Ex intacta Virgine,
Et in mundo conversatus,
Sparso verbi semine,
Sui moras incolatus
Miro clausit ordine.

At the last great Supper lying
Circled by his brethren's band,
Meekly with the law complying,
First he finished its command
Then, immortal Food supplying,
Gave himself with his own hand.

In supremae nocte cœnæ
Recumbens cum fratribus,
Observata lege plene
Cibis in legalibus,
Cibum turbæ duodenæ
Se dat suis manibus

Word made Flesh,
   by word he maketh
Very bread his Flesh to be;
Man in wine Christ's Blood
   partaketh,
And if senses fail to see,
Faith alone the true heart waketh
To behold the mystery.

Verbum caro, panem verum
Verbo carnem efficit,
Fitque sanguis Christi merum,
Et, si sensus deficit,
Ad firmandum cor sincerum
Sola fides sufficit.

Sweet Sacrament Divine

Sweet Sacrament divine,
Hid in thine earthly home;
Lo! round thy lowly shrine,
With suppliant hearts we come;
Jesus, to thee our voice we raise
In songs of love and heartfelt praise
Sweet Sacrament divine. (repeat)

Sweet Sacrament of rest,
Ark from the ocean's roar,
Within thy shelter blest
Soon may we reach the shore;
Save us, for still the tempest raves,
Save, lest we sink beneath the waves:
Sweet Sacrament of rest. (repeat)

Sweet Sacrament of peace,
Dear home of every heart,
Where restless yearnings cease,
And sorrows all depart.
There in thine ear, all trustfully,
We tell our tale of misery,
Sweet Sacrament of peace. (repeat)

Sweet Sacrament divine,
Earth's light and jubilee,
In thy far depths doth shine
The Godhead's majesty;
Sweet light, so shine on us, we pray
That earthly joys may fade away:
Sweet Sacrament divine. (repeat)

(Francis Stanfield)

Benediction

Towards the end of the exposition, the priest or deacon goes to the altar, genuflects and kneels. Then this hymn or a suitable alternative is sung, during which the minister incenses the sacrament.

Therefore we, before him bending	Tantum ergo Sacramentum
This great Sacrament revere	Veneremur cernui,
Types and shadows have	Et antiquum documentum
their ending	Novo cedat ritui;
for the newer rite is here	Præstet fides supplementum
Faith, our outward sense befriending	Sensuum defectui.
Makes the inward vision clear.	
Glory let us give, and blessing	Genitori, Genitoque
To the Father and the Son	Laus et iubilatio.
Honour, might, and praise addressing	Salus, honor, virtus quoque
While eternal ages run	Sit et benedictio;
Ever too his love confessing	Procedenti ab utroque
Who, from both, with both is one.	Compar sit laudatio.
Amen.	Amen.

The minister then says the following prayer (or a suitable alternative)

Let us pray.	Oremus.
Lord Jesus Christ,	Deus, qui nobis sub
you gave us the eucharist	sacramento mirabili
as the memorial of your suffering	passionis tuæ memoriam reliquisti:
and death.	tribue, quæsumus,
May our worship of this sacrament	ita nos Corporis et Sanguinis
of your body and blood	tui sacra mysteria venerari,
help us to experience the salvation	ut redemptionis tuæ
you won for us	fructum in nobis
and the peace of the kingdom	iugiter sentiamus.
where you live with the Father	Qui vivis et regnas
and the Holy Spirit,	in sæcula sæculorum.
one God, for ever and ever.	R. Amen.
R. Amen.	

The Priest or Deacon now puts on the humeral veil and blesses the congregation with the Blessed Sacrament.

The Divine Praises formerly said at this point may more properly be included within the period of adoration.

The Divine Praises

Blessed be God.
Blessed be his holy Name.
Blessed be Jesus Christ, true God and true Man.
Blessed be the name of Jesus.
Blessed be his most Sacred Heart.
Blessed be his most Precious Blood.
Blessed be Jesus in the most holy Sacrament of the Altar.
Blessed be the Holy Spirit, the Paraclete.
Blessed be the great Mother of God, Mary, most holy.
Blessed be her holy and Immaculate Conception.
Blessed be her glorious Assumption.
Blessed be the name of Mary, Virgin and Mother.
Blessed be St Joseph, her spouse most chaste.
Blessed be God in his Angels and in his Saints.

Reposition

Immediately after the Blessed Sacrament is reposed in the tabernacle, the following may be sung:

Ant. Let us adore for ever the most holy Sacrament.

Ps. O praise the Lord,
   all you nations
Acclaim him, all you peoples
For his mercy is confirmed upon us
and the truth of the Lord
   remains for ever.

Glory be to the Father,
   and to the Son
and to the Holy Spirit
As it was in the beginning, is now
and ever shall be,
   world without end. Amen.

Ant. Let us adore for ever the most holy Sacrament.

Ant. Adoremus in æternum sanctissimum Sacramentum.

Ps. Laudate Dominum,
   omnes gentes;
laudate eum omnes populi.
Quoniam confirmata est super
   nos misericordia eius;
et veritas Domini manet
   in æternum.

Gloria Patri, et Filio,
   et Spiritui Sancto.
Sicut erat in principio,
   et nunc, et semper,
et in sæcula sæculorum. Amen.

Ant. Adoremus in æternum sanctissimum Sacramentum.

An alternative acclamation:

O Sacrament most holy,
   O Sacrament divine!
All praise, and all thanksgiving,
Be every moment thine!